A CULTURAL HISTORY OF HAIR

VOLUME 2

A Cultural History of Hair
General Editor: Geraldine Biddle-Perry

Volume 1
A Cultural History of Hair in Antiquity
Edited by Mary Harlow

Volume 2
A Cultural History of Hair in the Middle Ages
Edited by Roberta Milliken

Volume 3
A Cultural History of Hair in the Renaissance
Edited by Edith Snook

Volume 4
A Cultural History of Hair in the Age of Enlightenment
Edited by Margaret K. Powell and Joseph Roach

Volume 5
A Cultural History of Hair in the Age of Empire
Edited by Sarah Heaton

Volume 6
A Cultural History of Hair in the Modern Age
Edited by Geraldine Biddle-Perry

A CULTURAL HISTORY OF HAIR

IN THE MIDDLE AGES

VOLUME 2

Edited by Roberta Milliken

BLOOMSBURY ACADEMIC
LONDON • NEW YORK • OXFORD • NEW DELHI • SYDNEY

BLOOMSBURY ACADEMIC
Bloomsbury Publishing Plc, 50 Bedford Square, London, WC1B 3DP, UK
Bloomsbury Publishing Inc, 1359 Broadway, New York, NY 10018, USA
Bloomsbury Publishing Ireland, 29 Earlsfort Terrace, Dublin 2, D02 AY28, Ireland

BLOOMSBURY, BLOOMSBURY ACADEMIC and the Diana logo are trademarks of Bloomsbury Publishing Plc

First published in Great Britain 2021
Paperback edition published 2022
Reprinted 2025

Copyright © Bloomsbury Publishing, 2022

Roberta Milliken has asserted her right under the Copyright, Designs and Patents Act, 1988, to be identified as Editor of this work.

Series design: Raven Design
Cover image: Bataille, Nicolas. Apocalypse d'Angers, 1373–1387. A series of tapestries woven for Louis I., Duke of Anjou. The Great Whore of Babylon © Erich Lessing / Art Resource NY

All rights reserved. No part of this publication may be: i) reproduced or transmitted in any form, electronic or mechanical, including photocopying, recording or by means of any information storage or retrieval system without prior permission in writing from the publishers; or ii) used or reproduced in any way for the training, development or operation of artificial intelligence (AI) technologies, including generative AI technologies. The rights holders expressly reserve this publication from the text and data mining exception as per Article 4(3) of the Digital Single Market Directive (EU) 2019/790.

Bloomsbury Publishing Plc does not have any control over, or responsibility for, any third-party websites referred to or in this book. All internet addresses given in this book were correct at the time of going to press. The author and publisher regret any inconvenience caused if addresses have changed or sites have ceased to exist, but can accept no responsibility for any such changes.

A catalogue record for this book is available from the British Library.

A catalog record for this book is available from the Library of Congress.

ISBN:	HB:	978-1-4742-3203-6
	HB set:	978-1-4742-3212-8
	PB:	978-1-3502-8548-4
	PB set:	978-1-3502-8751-8
	ePDF:	978-1-3501-0303-0
	eBook:	978-1-3501-0304-7

Typeset by Integra Software Services Pvt. Ltd.
Printed and bound in Great Britain

For product safety related questions contact productsafety@bloomsbury.com.

To find out more about our authors and books visit www.bloomsbury.com and sign up for our newsletters.

CONTENTS

LIST OF FIGURES vi
GENERAL EDITOR'S PREFACE xiii

INTRODUCTION 1
Roberta Milliken

1 Religion and Ritualized Belief, 800–1500 19
  Alexa Sand

2 Self and Society 37
  Hanna Hopwood Griffiths

3 Fashion and Adornment 53
  Laura Michele Diener

4 Production and Practice 71
  Laura Michele Diener

5 Health and Hygiene: Hair in the Medical Traditions 91
  Fernando Salmón and Montserrat Cabré

6 Gender and Sexuality 107
  Martha Easton

7 Race and Ethnicity: Hair and Medieval Ethnic Identities 123
  Kim M. Phillips

8 Hair and Social Class 137
  John Block Friedman

9 Cultural Representations: Head and Body Hair in Medieval Art 153
  Penny Howell Jolly

NOTES 172
BIBLIOGRAPHY 207
CONTRIBUTORS 227
INDEX 230

LIST OF FIGURES

INTRODUCTION

I.1 Wildman carrying off woman, detail (1300–1340). British Library, Royal 10 E IV, fol. 72v. © The British Library Board — 7

I.2 Forced tonsure of a man (1360–1375). British Library, Royal 6 E VI, fol. 313. © The British Library Board — 8

I.3 Knights Templar before Jerusalem. On the battlements are three Saracen warriors (ca. fourteenth century). Bibliothèque Nationale, Paris. Photo: HIP/Art Resource, NY — 9

I.4 St. Eugenia (ca. twelfth century). Basilica St. Madeleine, Vézelay. Photo: Roberta Milliken — 11

I.5 Novice's haircut and veiling, Miniatura del s.XIV, perteneciente al "DECRETO Di GRAZIANO" donde se representa a un "GRUPO DE MONJAS VISTIENDO A UNA NIÑA." Photo: Album/Art Resource, NY — 12

I.6 The Perfumer's Shop, detail (1430–1450). British Library, Cotton Tiberius A. VII, fol. 93. © The British Library Board — 13

I.7 Calendar page for October, detail (1410–1430). Paris, France, Bedford Hours, MS 18850, fol. 10v. © The British Library Board — 14

I.8 Pregnant woman being beaten and shorn, detail (ca. 1300). Heidelberg University Library, Heidelberger Sachsenspiegel, Cod. Pal. germ. 164, fol. 12v. Courtesy of Heidelberg University Library — 15

I.9 Edward on his throne, Harold leaving on horse for Normandy, Bayeux Tapestry, section 2B (eleventh century). Musée de la Tapisserie. © Ministère de la Culture/Médiathèque du Patrimoine, Dist.RMN-Grand Palais/Art Resource. Photo: Jean Gourbeix/Simon Guillot — 16

CHAPTER ONE

1.1 *Samson and Delilah,* Vézelay, Benedictine Abbey Church of Sainte-Marie-Madeleine, nave capital (Salet number 87, 1120–1132). © Jane Vadnal — 22

1.2 *Absalom's Death,* detail, Eadwine Psalter, Canterbury (ca. 1160). Cambridge, Trinity College, R. 17. 1, fol. 8r. Courtesy of the Masters and Fellows of Trinity College Cambridge — 23

LIST OF FIGURES

1.3 Mary Magdalene, from a sculptural group depicting the resurrection of Lazarus for the Church of Saint-Lazare (ca. 1130). Autun, Musée Rolin. Photo: Foto Marburg/Art Resource, NY 25

1.4 *The Penitent Magdalene*, fresco, Eglise Saint-Érige, Auron (Alpes-Maritimes) (1451). Photo: MHR93_0912012_E (c) Monuments historiques, 2004. Reproduction subject to authorization by the rights holder—Briez, Serge. © DRac Paca, CRMH, 1989, Jean Marx 26

1.5 Jean Pucelle, *Saint Agnes*, detail, winter portion, Belleville Breviary, Paris (1323–1326). Paris, Bibliothèque Nationale, MS lat. 10483, fol. 135v. Photo: BnF 28

1.6 *Saint Stephen of Muret and Hugh of Lacerta*, champlevé enamel plaque from the main altar of the abbey of Grandmont, Limoges (ca. 1189–1190). Paris, Musée nationale du Moyen Age—Thermes de Cluny. Photo: Jean-Gilles Berizzi. © RMN-Grand Palais/Art Resource, NY 31

1.7 Attributed to the Master of the Codex of Saint George, *Tonsuring an Ordinand*, Stefaneschi Pontifical, Avignon (1320–1330). Paris, BnF ms. lat. 15619, fol. 2r. Photo: BnF 34

CHAPTER TWO

2.1 Pulling hair, an insult or injury for which compensation was due in Cyfraith Hywel Dda, detail. Peniarth MS 28, fol. 15v. Courtesy of Llyfrgell Genedlaethol Cymru/The National Library of Wales 41

2.2 Alexander the Great and his wife, detail, an example of the complex plaits of the period in Brwydrau Alecsander Fawr. Peniarth MS 481D, fol. 61v. Courtesy of Llyfrgell Genedlaethol Cymru/The National Library of Wales 44

2.3 Llio's Stone in Penllyn, Wales. Courtesy of Tudur Dylan Jones 46

2.4 Mermaid with comb and mirror. Oxford, Bodleian Library, MS Douce 62, fol. 51r 47

2.5 The Bedford Master, *The Annunciation* (ca. 1440–1450). Paris. Courtesy of the Getty's Open Content Program 49

2.6 The elaborate hairstyles of the fifteenth century in Brwydrau Alecsander Fawr, detail. Peniarth MS 481D, fol. 66v. Courtesy of Llyfrgell Genedlaethol Cymru/The National Library of Wales 51

CHAPTER THREE

3.1 A Lady attended by her maid, from the Luttrell Psalter (ca. 1325–1335). Add. 42130, fol. 63. © The British Library Board 55

3.2 King Canute and Queen Aelfgifu (Emma) presenting a cross upon the altar of New Minster, *Liber Vitae* (ca. 1031). MS Stowe 944, fol. 6. © The British Library Board 57

3.3	Detail of a miniature of Christine de Pisan, presenting her manuscript to Queen Isabeau of France, Paris (ca. 1410–1414). Harley 4431, fol. 3. © The British Library Board	64
3.4	Jan van Eyck, *Portrait of Margaret van Eyck*, painting (1439). Groeningemuseum, Bruges, Belgium. Photo: The Archive at Art Resource, NY	65
3.5	Piero della Francesco, *Portrait of Battista Sforza, Duchess of Urbino* (ca. 1465). Uffizi, Florence, Italy. Photo: Scala/Art Resource, NY	68

CHAPTER FOUR

4.1	Bone double-sided composite comb with matching carrying case, Saxon-Norman (tenth to eleventh century). Museum of London	73
4.2	Comb, Lovers in a garden (ca. 1320). Ivory. Paris, France. © Victoria and Albert Museum, London	74
4.3	Hans Memling, *Bathsheba bathing* (1485). Mixed Media on oak. Staatsgalerie, Stuttgart, Germany. Photo: bpk Bildagentur/Art Resource, NY	76
4.4	Copper pins with stone (probably red jasper) heads. Museum of London	80
4.5	Matthew Daniel, plaited hairpiece with silk, drawing (mid-fourteenth century). Museum of London	81
4.6	Jan van Eyck, Eve, with the slaying of Abel. Wing from the Ghent Altarpiece. Cathedral of St. Bavo, Ghent, Belgium. Photo: Scala/Art Resource, NY	83
4.7	Rogier van der Weyden, *Portrait of a Lady*, painting (ca. 1460). Courtesy National Gallery of Art, Washington	85
4.8	Miniature of the abbess of the White Nuns cutting the hair of a novice, from *Lancelot du Lac* (ca. 1316). MS Add. 10293, fol. 261. © The British Library Board	86
4.9	Anselm of Canterbury, a monk receiving the tonsure, from *Similitudines* (Likenesses) (first half of the thirteenth century). MS Cotton Cleopatra, C. XI fol. 27v. © The British Library Board	87
4.10	Matthew Daniel, fifteenth-century men's razor, drawing from Richard Corson's *Fashions in Hair: The First Five Thousand Years*	88

CHAPTER FIVE

5.1	Diagram of the four elements and the regional winds. John of Ardene, *Medical treatises* (fifteenth century). London, British Library, Sloane 795, fol. 20r. © The British Library Board	92
5.2	Old King James I of Aragon (left) and younger King Alfonso of Castile (right) before the representatives of the aljama of Murcia. *Cantigas de Santa María* (Castile, ca. 1280–1284). El Escorial, Madrid, San Lorenzo del Escorial, T I 1, Cantiga 169, fol. 226v, 3–4. © Patrimonio Nacional	96

LIST OF FIGURES

5.3 Representation of Sorrow (*Tristece*) with grey hair, detail from Guillaume de Lorris and Jean de Meun, *Roman de la Rose* (Paris, ca. 1320–1340). London, British Library, Royal 19 b XIII, fol. 7r, detail. © The British Library Board   99

5.4 Adam and Eve nude in the garden of delights. He has curly hair and wears no beard, while she has wavy hair. Eve's hair is ostensibly longer, as female hair was supposed to be. Ibn Butlan, *Tacuinum sanitatis* (fragments, Bavaria, first half of the fifteenth century). Granada, Biblioteca Real, Universidad de Granada, Códice C- 67, fol. 99r. Courtesy of the Royal Library of the University of Granada   100

5.5 A male patient showing his diseased scalp to a physician, detail from the French version of Mattheus Platearius, *Circa instans* (Amiens, first quarter of the fourteenth century). London, British Library, Sloane 1977, fol. 50v, detail. © The British Library Board   102

5.6 A woman removing lice with a brush from the scalp of a kneeling man holding a bowl, detail from *Hortus sanitatis* (Mainz: Jacob Meydenbach, 1491), unnumbered. London, Wellcome Library, EPB 5.e.12   102

5.7 Liturgical comb (ca. 1200–1210). Ivory. Canterbury, England. New York, The Metropolitan Museum of Art, Accession number 1988.279. Courtesy of The Metropolitan Museum of Art. www.metmuseum.org   103

5.8 Queen Semiramis in her room, attended by two courtesans and combing herself while receiving a messenger, detail from the French version of Giovanni Boccaccio *De claris mulieribus* (Paris, ca. 1410). London, British Library, Royal 20 C V, fol. 5ra. © The British Library Board   105

CHAPTER SIX

6.1 *The Bishop of Assisi Giving a Palm to Saint Clare*, Germany (ca. 1360). The Cloisters Collection, 1984.343, www.metmuseum.org   107

6.2 *Enthroned Virgin and Child*, France (1150–1200). The Cloisters Collection, 67.153, www.metmuseum.org   110

6.3 Jean Bourdichon, *Bathsheba Bathing* (1498–1499). Tours, France. The J. Paul Getty Museum, Los Angeles, Ms. 79, recto   112

6.4 Jean Bondel and Nicolas Bataille, *The Great Whore of Babylon* (Rev. 17:3–6) in the *Apocalypse d'Angers* (1373–1387), a series of tapestries woven for Louis I, Duke of Anjou. Angers, Musée des Tapisseries. Photo: Erich Lessing/Art Resource, NY   113

6.5 Paul Herman and Jean de Limbourg, *Saint Catherine tended by angels*, from *The Belles Heures* of John, Duke of Berry, France (1405–1408/9). New York, The Cloisters Collection, 1954, MS. 54.1.1, fol. 17v. www.metmuseum.org   114

6.6 Reliquary bust of a companion of Saint Ursula, Germany (sixteenth century, ca. 1520–30). Oak, polychromed and gilt on plaster ground; glass opening for relic. Gift of J. P. Morgan, 1917 (17.190.728). Photo © The Metropolitan Museum of Art. Image source: Art Resource, NY   115

6.7 Figural tribune (left side) on pulpit in the Church of San Pietro, Gropina, Loro Ciuffernna, Arezzo, Italy (twelfth century). Photo: Syrio. Public domain 116

6.8 *Woman with a Skull,* Cathedral of Santiago de Compostela, Puerta de las Platerías, left tympanum, Spain, early twelfth century. Photo: Scala/Art Resource, NY 116

6.9 *Saint Mary of Egypt, Prayer Book of Charles the Bold* Rouen, France (1480–1490). The J. Paul Getty Museum, Los Angeles, Ms. 37, fol. 153v 118

6.10 Master E. S., playing card with wild woman with unicorn, Germany (fifteenth century). Engraving: second state. Harris Brisbane Dick Fund, 1922 (22.83.16). Photo © The Metropolitan Museum of Art. Image source: Art Resource, NY 118

6.11 Vulva figure depicted as a pilgrim, Arnemuiden, the Netherlands (1425–1475). Van Beuningen Family Collection, Langbroek, the Netherlands 119

6.12 *Maximilian and Mary of Burgundy in front of the Virgin,* miniature from the *Hours of Mary of Burgundy,* manuscript, France (fifteenth century). Österreichische Nationalbibliothek. © DeA Picture Library/Art Resource, NY 120

CHAPTER SEVEN

7.1 Two Connacht men sitting in a curragh holding paddles. Late-thirteenth-century manuscript of *Topographia Hibernica* by Giraldus Cambrensis (Gerald of Wales) (ca. 1147–ca. 1220). Laud Misc. 720 fol. 226v. Photo: Bodleian Libraries, University of Oxford/The Art Archive at Art Resource/Art Resource, NY 127

7.2 *The Martyrdom of Simon of Trent,* 1493 (1849). A nineteenth-century version of a fifteenth-century manuscript illustration in *Liber chronicarum* (the Nuremberg Chronicle) by Hartmann Schedel. Cabinet des Estampes, Bibliothèque Royale, Brussels, Belgium. Photo: HIP/Art Resource, NY 130

7.3 Benozzo de Lesse Gozzoli (ca. 1420–1497). The Arab philosopher Averroës, from *The Triumph of Saint Thomas Aquinas,* detail. Musée de Louvre, Paris. Photo: Gianni Dagli Orti/The Art Archive at Art Resource, NY 131

7.4 Capital (c. 1230). Limestone. Apulia, Italy. Overall: 35.9 × 33 × 33 cm. Base: Diam. 19.7 cm. Hole for Pin Mount: Diam. 1.4 × 5.5 cm. Gift of James Hazen Hyde, 1955 (55.66). The Metropolitan Museum of Art. Image © The Metropolitan Museum of Art. Image source: Art Resource, NY 132

7.5 Master of Egerton (fl. 1405–1420). Banquet of the Great Khan. From Marco Polo (1254–1324), *Livre des merveilles* (Paris, 1410?–1412?). Français 2810 fol. 39r. Bibliothèque Nationale de France (BnF). © BnF, Dist. RMN- Grand Palais/Art Resource, NY 134

LIST OF FIGURES

7.6 Ambrogio Lorenzetti (fl. ca. 1311–1348). Head of a Tartar. Detail from the *Martyrdom of the Franciscans* at Tana. S. Francesco. Photo: Scala/Art Resource, NY 135

7.7 Master BXG (1466–1490), *The Savage Family*. Engraving. Collection Rothschild. 288LR. Photo: Tony Querrac. Musée de Louvre, Paris. © BnF, Dist. RMN-Grand Palais/Art Resource, NY 136

CHAPTER EIGHT

8.1 Master of the Mainz Mocking, *Mocking of Christ* (ca. 1390). Upper right-hand wing of the Idar-Oberstein Altar-Triptych, "Crag-Church" or Felsenkirche, Idar-Oberstein, Germany. Photo: John Block Friedman 139

8.2 Master E. S., *Love Garden with Bald Fool* (1460). Cleveland Museum of Art 1993.161. Courtesy of the Cleveland Museum of Art 140

8.3 The Poet Neidhart besieged by peasants (1315). Codex Manesse, Heidelberg Universitätsbibliothek MS Cod. Pal. Germ. 848, LXIII, fol. 273r. Courtesy of Heidelberg University Library 142

8.4 Ambras Heldenbuch, Hans Ried and others, Helmbrecht with long hair (1517). MS A, Vienna, Österreichische Nationalbibliothek MS Cod. S.N., 2663, fol. 225. Courtesy of the Austrian National Library 143

8.5 Jean Fouquet, Agnès Sorel as the Virgin (1420–1450). *Melun Diptych,* right leaf. Antwerp, Musée Royal des Beaux-Arts. Courtesy of the Musée des Beaux-Arts 146

8.6 Apotropaic carving from the Porta Tosa, Milan (ca. 1185). Milan, Castello Sforzesco Museum of Ancient Art, number 528. Photo: Penny Howell Jolly 150

8.7 Anonymous, *Bridal Portrait* (1470). Oil on panel. South German. Cleveland Museum of Art 1932.179. Courtesy of the Cleveland Museum of Art 150

CHAPTER NINE

9.1 *Charlemagne*, detail (ninth century). Paris, Louvre. Photo: Erich Lessing/Art Resource, NY 154

9.2 Fra Angelico, *Crucifixion,* detail, (ca. 1420–1423). New York, The Metropolitan Museum of Art, Maitland F. Griggs Collection, Bequest of Maitland F. Griggs, 1943 (43.98.5). Photo © The Metropolitan Museum of Art 157

9.3 Lukas Moser, Tiefenbronn Altarpiece, detail (1432). Tiefenbronn, St. Maria-Magdalena. Photo: Erich Lessing/Art Resource, NY 158

9.4 Ambrogio Lorenzetti, *Effects of Good Government in the City of Siena* (1338–1342). Siena, Palazzo Pubblico. Photo: Scala/Art Resource, NY 159

9.5   Jan van Eyck, *Madonna and Child*, ca. 1436. Frankfurt, Städeliches Kunstinstitut. Photo: Foto Marburg/Art Resource, NY   160

9.6   *Temptation and Fall*, Morgan Crusader Bible, detail of fol. 1v, MS M. 638 (Paris, France, ca. 1244–1254). The Pierpont Morgan Library, New York. Purchased by J. P. Morgan (1867–1943) in 1916. Photo: The Pierpont Morgan Library, New York   161

9.7   Fra Filippo Lippi, *Portrait of a Woman and Man* (ca. 1440). New York, The Metropolitan Museum of Art, Marquand Collection. Gift of Henry G. Marquand, 1889 (89.15.19). Photo © The Metropolitan Museum of Art   162

9.8   Jean de Liège, *Bust of Marie de France* (1381). New York, The Metropolitan Museum of Art, Gift of George Blumenthal, 1941 (41.100.132). Photo © The Metropolitan Museum of Art   164

9.9   Workshop of Robert Campin, Merode Triptych, detail of the donors (ca. 1427–1432). New York, The Metropolitan Museum of Art, The Cloisters Collection, 1956 (56.7). Photo © The Metropolitan Museum of Art   165

9.10 Magdalene Master, *St. Mary Magdalene* (late thirteenth century). Florence, Accademia. Photo: Scala/Art Resource, NY   167

9.11 *Psalm 53*, Bible, Garrett 28, detail of fol. 224r, English (1270–1280). Manuscripts Division, Department of Rare Books and Special Collections, Princeton University Library, Princeton. Photo credit: Princeton University Library   169

9.12 Bari Throne, detail (1098). Bari, Basilica of San Nicola. Photo: Scala /Art Resource, NY   170

GENERAL EDITOR'S PREFACE

A Cultural History of Hair offers an unparalleled examination of the most malleable part of the human body. This fascinating set explores hair's intrinsic relationship to the construction and organization of diverse social bodies and strategies of identification throughout history. The six illustrated volumes, edited by leading specialists in the field, evidence the significance of human hair on the head and face and its styling, dressing, and management across the following historical periods: antiquity, the Middle Ages, the Renaissance, the Age of Enlightenment, the Age of Empire, and the Modern Age.

Using an innovative range of historical and theoretical sources, each volume is organized around the same key themes: religion and ritualized belief, self and societal identification, fashion and adornment, production and practice, health and hygiene, gender and sexuality, race and ethnicity, class and social status, representation. The aim is to offer readers a comprehensive account of human hair-related beliefs and practices in any given period and through time. It is not an encyclopedia. *A Cultural History of Hair* is an interdisciplinary collection of complex ideas and debates brought together in the work of an international range of scholars.

Geraldine Biddle-Perry

Introduction

ROBERTA MILLIKEN

This is a book about hair—which means that it is also a book about history, about culture, and about language as well as symbolism. At first glance, thinking so specifically about hair might give one pause. Is something that is so common significant enough to warrant careful consideration? The topic can seem rather frivolous. Hair is after all something that we all see and care for regularly, something that might initially seem to have more to do with trivial practices than a topic for academic inquiry. However, the attention that we give to hair, the many ways we use hair to signify meaning, and the diverse ways that we also regard it, speak to its significance and reveal it to be a potent signifier, one that is woven into the fabric of not only our history but our culture. So though it is common, far from disqualifying it from careful study, this in fact recommends it, as such aspects of culture are often the richest and most illuminating. This is something that appears to be true throughout history and thus inspires both this volume and this series on the topic.

But meaning(s) can be elusive when studying social symbols as complicated and as rich as hair—especially when we are looking at them in a time like the Middle Ages, a time that seems quite distant from our own. If hair is a language, the next obvious question to ask is what does it communicate? Is there a common grammar even if it is the most basic sort? Is there a general consensus with regard to meaning? Delving into the perceptions of hair as revealed in visual arts, literature, and other historical artifacts during this very rich time period helps us to answer such questions. At the same time, it provides us an opportunity to refine our understanding of the people of the time as well as our enduring connections to them.

THE MIDDLE AGES

Contexts, of course, matter a great deal. Before discussing hair as a topic in the Middle Ages, it seems worthwhile to mention some general aspects of this expansive time span in order to clarify the general framework within which these studies operate, to dispel popular misconceptions associated with the Middle Ages and to highlight certain important general cultural features. First, there is no agreement among scholars about when precisely the period begins and when it ends. Some set the demarcations as early as 300 and as late as 1500, presumably leaving room for more generous transitional periods, whereas the publisher of this series has chosen a more conservative approach by limiting the medieval period to 800–1450. What this conveys is not the whimsicality of these distinctions as much as the idea that these time periods are themselves imposed and constructed. Though artificial and rather flexible, such boundaries are thoughtfully set for two reasons: (1) to help us organize the past and (2) because there are perceived identifiable and unifying trends to these spans of time that differentiate them from others in history's continuum. However practical and useful these distinctions may be, scholars also caution that they can give us a less than accurate sense of history in that the traditional demarcations of eras tend to focus attention on that which changes instead of the great and inevitable continuity of ideas, beliefs, and culture from one era to the next.[1] That history is a continuum is often then obfuscated, yet it is essential to acknowledge. In other words, though we often look for differences to set the demarcations of historical periods, the persistence of ideas, customs, beliefs, and practices is always a strong current that makes such boundaries porous at best.

This means that the reader of this series will no doubt notice, too, the messiness of the continuum, as there is no primary or "master" narrative behind it. Social change and anything triggering it are rarely orderly or all-inclusive. This suggests that though many ideas are often recycled from place to place, from generation to generation, from century to century, many other "new" or different ideas can also be noted. Sometimes the fresh view takes root, inspiring more widespread change; sometimes the view will coexist side by side with an older, competing view; sometimes an older view will be revised to take a newer shape; and sometimes an idea thought long dead will suddenly be revived. In this description of history's fluctuations we see that imprecision is inherent within dates that mark the beginning or end of most changes, let alone those that inspire the labeling of an era as rich and complicated as Europe in the Middle Ages. To exemplify this, we might note that what is often called the Italian Renaissance is commonly thought to begin in the fourteenth century, a time that typically is considered to fall within the scope of the Middle Ages. Even so, to suddenly exclude Italy after 1299 from the discussion of medieval history because of this label would seem to offer a distorted and false view of the past. At the same time, it would be equally problematic not to include references to fourteenth-century Italian thinkers and artists in a volume dedicated to exploring the Renaissance. This is to say, then, that readers should not be surprised to note some overlap of ideas from one volume to another in this series.

In considering the many centuries that comprise the Middle Ages, it is safe to say that the period has long suffered from an abundance of misunderstandings. Foremost among them is the popular perception of it as an unusually brutal, ignorant, and strife-filled time of general ugliness and suffering. This impression was created in the early modern period by intellectuals who seem to have considered the interval after the decline of Rome and before their own as regressive, a kind of lapse or an eclipse of the brightly ordered and superior artistry, intellect, and culture of antiquity.[2] This view certainly privileged the "new" ways of the Renaissance thinkers, but it did so at the expense of the in-between years or the Middle Ages which were additionally pejoratively labeled the Dark Ages.[3] This designation effectively encapsulated the views of the period as backward, distinctly unenlightened, coarse, and grim. So pervasive and strong were these views that, by extension, even the term "medieval" was associated with crude or primitive practices and/or thinking.[4] These pervasive labels and understandings proved exceptionally durable, and the Middle Ages came to represent a time of general barbarity in all things from language to artistry, from politics to religion, from education to laws, and so on.

Those who study the Middle Ages have long strived to dispel such limited and distorted views and rescue the age from the depths of its flat and darkly shadowed past. They are quick to point out how the terminology associated with the time period is grossly misleading and in so doing discuss the vibrant era as one of great change and accomplishment. While there were, of course, many challenges and upheavals as well as times of suffering that could be noted over the course of these centuries, there does not seem to be any more violence and misery in the Middle Ages than in any other time. To, therefore, focus on its negative aspects in fact gives a skewed view, one that seems to deliberately ignore the many wonderful innovations, beauties, and creative accomplishments that can also readily be noted through the many centuries that make up this period of history.

To list all of the noteworthy accomplishments of the timespan of 800 to 1450 would transform this introduction into a book itself. However, some of the important cultural highlights would include the growth and institutionalization of Christianity throughout Europe. The imposing authority and stature of the church is seen in the great political sway it held both locally and nationally. The time span housed what has been called the golden age of monasticism where the industrious religious copied manuscripts and lavishly adorned them with intricate details and colorful illustrations. The landscape was peppered with sturdy Romanesque churches, and later, the spires of Gothic cathedrals reached to the heavens. The impressive architecture of these edifices was rivaled only by the artistry that filled their interiors: their cavernous naves were often decorated with sculptures and meticulously painted with colorful representations of holy figures and lessons; their columns were embellished with carvings; and their stained glass windows glowed like jewels in the light. The growth of monastic systems as well as the church's dedication to learning led to the formation of great libraries. These holdings grew when the writings from ancient Greeks and Romans as well as Muslims were rediscovered during the Crusades, leading eventually to the birth of universities.

Though this was the time of castles, land-based wealth, and feudal politics and manorialism, it was also over this span that we can chart the shift to the monetary system and the rise of cities and towns. These changes opened up new possibilities for a great many people and introduced the concept of social mobility. During these centuries, too, the understandings of kingship evolved, understandings marked by the consolidation of power that unified lands and people as well as shaped them into the kinds of nations that we recognize today. New governmental systems were consequently designed to manage territories, wealth, and people. Though it was additionally the time in which people withstood the onslaught of the terrible and mystifying Black Plague that decimated great numbers of the population and spawned fierce anxiety, it was also the time in which the literary arts flourished: from the marvelous poetry of the Anglo-Saxons to the courtly romances; from the ever popular fabliaux to the ambitious churchly dramas of the cycle plays; and from the holy mystical visions to the learned translations.

Unfortunately, even given all of these many accomplishments, the inaccurate and misleading shadow the humanists cast all those many centuries ago often still persists, darkening the way the Middle Ages are remembered and leading to other misapprehensions. It is not uncommon for the period to act as a historical sponge of sorts that anachronistically absorbs particularly terrible and gruesome events that in fact date from later times in our distant past. For instance, the witch persecutions that swept Europe, Galileo's trial for heresy, and widespread slavery are routinely—though wrongly—thought to have happened during the Middle Ages.[5] The contrasts that created the titles and boundaries of eras seem to fuel such misidentifications, for if an event is particularly violent, grisly, and/or distasteful, reason would seem to dictate that it could not belong to a period thought to be as generally luminous as the Renaissance. It seems more fitting for it to belong to the time that is perceived to be, and named accordingly, the Dark Ages. This is a testament to the strength of such perceptions and at the same time the privilege of constructing labels and naming rights. Therefore, it is good to be mindful of such power.

THE IMPORTANCE OF APPEARANCES

Another aspect of the Middle Ages that bears mentioning involves the importance of appearances. Of course, appearances play an enormous role in any time period; however, in the Middle Ages, the way one looked was a fundamental tenet of social order. Being able to quickly identify the class and status of people was believed a very important if not essential component in maintaining general peace and harmony. This kind of basic recognition was thought paramount for properly navigating everyday life and the rules of both etiquette and conduct. After all what would happen if a nun were thought an ordinary fishwife or a priest weren't known by sight? How could order be maintained if a peasant were able to wear a certain kind of hairstyle and coat and thereby be mistaken for a wealthy merchant, or if a prostitute were thought to be a lady? Such thoughts threatened and worried those in positions of power—especially in times marked by economic or political upheavals. Sumptuary legislation was thought to be one solution to the problem, and thus it routinely enjoyed popularity throughout the Middle Ages. This legislation was originally designed to control the flaunting of food, drink, and household goods—but it most importantly came to focus on dress, and though sumptuary laws were in theory to apply to everyone, the main concern was prohibiting the lower classes from imitating the nobility.[6] This meant certain jewels, fabrics, furs, metals, and other decorative elements were illegal for those of the lower classes to wear whether they could afford them or not. Such legislation was regularly enacted throughout the Middle Ages—though inevitably its enforcement proved challenging and its effectiveness was doubtful.[7]

Other kinds of visual signs were used to mark those who fell outside the perceived boundaries of "mainstream" society, people such as heretics, prostitutes, criminals, beggars, and Jews. The Christian church certainly participated in perpetuating the traditions that linked appearances with social order. In dutifully following the legacies of the Church Fathers, medieval theologians over and over again stress the fundamental lesson of Deuteronomy 22:5 of how, in dress, it is important to distinguish between men and women. Additionally, the learned churchmen teach that those in the religious ranks should look different than those who are not; they are also attentive to the advice set by the church fathers that admonished ordinary people—particularly women—to avoid lavish dress and adornments. Hair and the attention paid to it are things that also find their way into such discussions rather regularly. In medieval commentaries we hear many echoes, for instance, of Tertullian's treatise on *The Apparel of Women,* where the learned churchman in the midst of advising ordinary women how to dress, inquires,

> What profit, again, do you derive for your salvation from all the labor spent in arranging your hair? Why can you not leave your hair alone, instead of at one time tying it up, at another letting it hang loose, now cultivating it, now thinning it out? Some women prefer to tie it up in little curls, while others let it fall down wild and disheveled—a hardly commendable kind of simplicity. Besides, some of you affix to your heads I know not what monstrosities of sewn and woven wigs …[8]

The listing of offensive and vain practices continues until the respected leader finally concludes by exhorting women to stop lavishing such attention on their hair and to cover it instead, as God commands, with a veil. Of course, it is the concern the revered churchman has for others that primarily fuels this directive, but behind it is an undeniable exasperation. Tertullian clearly thinks that the attention women pay to their hair is silly. And lest we think such views are limited to women alone, we can detect the same kind of exasperation later in the same treatise when Tertullian chastises men who also manipulate their hair to enhance their appearances. According to him, their faults include "cutting the beard a bit too sharply ... shaving around the mouth, arranging and dyeing the hair, darkening the first signs of gray hair, disguising the down on the whole body with some female ointments ... then always taking occasion to look in a mirror."[9]

Over and over again in treatises designed to give advice to good Christians—whether rich or poor—Church Fathers exhort followers to eschew all forms of worldly display that reveal vanity and pride. The authorities duly warn that outward signs of worldliness jeopardize the heavenly rewards of men and women in the afterlife: the time, thought, work, and expense devoted to such extravagances would be better spent on other more godly pursuits. At worst, to dress in any way that was not simple and functional, then, was deemed dangerous; at best, it was foolish. Such medieval understandings provide an important context for studying the roles hair played during this period in that they underscore the importance of appearances while revealing their direct connections to social identities.

HISTORY AND CULTURAL HISTORY

If the misconceptions about the Middle Ages remind us that perceptions matter, that rather than being a simple straightforward repository of truth and facts that history itself is an active story about the past that is written by people who are shaped by their own society and, thus, have their own biases, views, and beliefs, historiography itself reminds us that our understandings of history fluctuate. Traditional approaches to medieval history tended to be narrowly focused on wars and other political and economic struggles, with those who led or were most directly involved with these occurrences garnering the most attention. However, the "new" history, uncomfortable with the limited view of the past created by traditional approaches and fueled perhaps by Marxist ideas, expanded inquiry to involve class, economics, and authority. By the 1970s the scope broadened even further as the desire to provide more inclusive views of the past led to the consideration of the ordinary, those minorities who were commonly excluded from extensive study—for instance women, homosexuals, heretics, and Muslims.[10] The quest to discover information pertaining to such populations expanded the kinds of resources historians considered and encouraged more interdisciplinary conversations. This turn and all that went with it was not something that was entirely foreign to medievalists, and they often were at the forefront of such innovative approaches to studying the past.[11]

Other currents of thought overlapped and expanded historical inquiry. The cultural history movement took inspiration from anthropologists and focused attention on the expressive meanings inherent in cultural artifacts or those values, perceptions, products, conventions, and procedures that are both passed on and used to form a social identity.[12] As Peter Burke explains, "The word 'cultural' distinguishes it from intellectual history, suggesting an emphasis on mentalities, assumptions or feelings rather than ideas or systems of thought."[13] Instead of shying away from the symbolic representations created by people in a specific time and place found, for instance, in the visual arts and literary expressions, cultural historians embrace these aspects and fold them into the study of practices in everyday life.[14] The process naturally invites interdisciplinary inquiry at the same time that it also diffuses elite distinctions such as "high art" in order to be more inclusive. The shift in perspective on history is designed to reveal a more profound view of the past, one that aspires to present an authentic historical view that does not neglect the past's imagination. At the heart of this kind of inquiry is a fresh acknowledgment of the complexity of providing any accurate sense of history or, put another way, an acknowledgment of the untidy nature of both personal identity and group identities—both large and small— that inform any historical understandings. Cultural history, then, deliberately reminds us to guard against trivializing any aspect of culture, for each component can offer interesting information about the past and, therefore, is worthy of study.

HAIR STUDIES

This brings the discussion back to hair. Scholars have long recognized the value of studying hair. Why and how it was used in a variety of cultural rituals piqued the interest of social scientists in the twentieth century who diligently explored the general significance of hair in very expansive ways and in turn offered their responses to them. By focusing primarily on magical and religious practices and marriage and fertility customs, these early scholars acknowledged the complicated and potent symbolism of hair, but at the same time sought to identify some universal underlying basis for that symbolism. In other words, they attempted to reveal the basic building blocks for the symbol that could be used in its interpretation regardless of when or where it was found.

One of the first such scholars was Sir James Frazer who explored hair—especially that of the head—as an extension of the person to whom it belonged.[15] As such, the anthropologist catalogued the ways in which hair can be viewed as having deep enduring connections to strength, reason, and virility, and how these connections can explain many customs designed to protect hair—whether it is still attached to the head or not—as well as the numerous magical uses (i.e. to cause injuries and natural disturbances) and religious rites of purification that make use of it. Another scholar, Charles Berg, approaching the topic from a psychoanalytical perspective, maintained that behaviors regarding hair have not changed much over time from antiquity to the present and that these behaviors are so prevalent as to be ordinary.[16] However, his examinations of hair practices lead him to conclude that in all there is a deep, though unconscious correlation between sexual potency and hair. Rituals and practices among both men and women underscore the connection between hair and genitals so that hair displays can be equated with exhibitionism and fecundity, and the removal of hair with castration. According to Berg, the length, thickness, and curliness of hair further amplify strength and sexual virility, while the thinness or lack of hair suggests frigidity or impotence.

Two other earlier scholars bear mentioning here: E.R. Leach and C.R. Hallpike. Leach generally agreed with Berg's findings.[17] Though Leach did acknowledge the sexual significance of hair, he also voiced his reservation about focusing exclusively on such unconscious meanings of hair and using them as general explanations of all symbolism involving hair, as he found them too restrictive and simplistic for so complicated a symbol. A more refined understanding of hair, according to Leach, includes expanding Berg's points pertaining to the unconscious interrelatedness of hair and sexual potency to include the conscious symbolism involving hair that is present in many rites and rituals as well. Similarly, Leach thinks it important to recognize that there are both public and

FIGURE I.1 Wildman carrying off woman, detail (1300–1340). British Library, Royal 10 E IV, fol. 72v. © The British Library Board.

private symbols because even though the differences between them are often subtle, they are, nonetheless, important for the sake of clarity. Hallpike, however, resisted the strict correlation between hair and sexuality advocated by Berg and Leach.[18] In doing so, he advocated a different way of interpreting the ritual uses of hair, one that suggests that hair length is related to social control. Long hair, according to Hallpike, is related to animality and is indicative of being outside of society. The image of the hairy Wildman in Figure I.1 who is carrying off a woman against her will would seem to support Hallpike's argument that the more hirsute have less to do with mainstream society and are also less cooperative with it. According to Hallpike, the cutting of hair, in contrast, can then represent reentering a society and abiding the discipline associated with it. This transformation can be communicated through many practices, one of which can be seen in Figure I.2 which depicts the forced tonsure of a man.

The 1970s mark a shift in the ways in which scholars viewed the symbolism of hair in that it is then that scholars appear less comfortable with any universal interpretations of hair. Instead there seems to be more of an acceptance of hair as a complex and rich symbol that is, therefore, multivalent.[19] The importance of context(s) in discerning the various meanings of such symbolism is stressed by these scholars who also then start to recognize the evolution of meanings over time and the differences among cultures with regard to the symbol. Raymond Firth, for example, calls for an even more expansive interpretation of hair to better accommodate the complexity of the roles he sees it play in society.[20] According to Firth, the context of such behaviors needs to always be considered, for both public and private meanings do change over time and from culture to culture. In fact, because of this, previous scholarly views offered by Leach, Berg, and Hallpike need to be amended: the cutting of hair can be understood to signify sexual loss or submission to social control, but it could just as well indicate a personal sacrifice or loss, one that reveals an individual's personality traits and/or beliefs.

This kind of more flexible interpretation of hair is also advocated by P. Hershman and Anthony Synnott. Hershman argues against any universal understanding of hair.[21] He posits that it is more useful to view hair as a "structuring device" that allows for the expression of many meanings.[22] Consequently, hair can be used as a sexual symbol, but

FIGURE I.2 Forced tonsure of a man (1360–1375). British Library, Royal 6 E VI, fol. 313. © The British Library Board.

that does not mean that it cannot be used to represent nonsexual ideas as well. Studying the many meanings of hair in this way reveals that at times there are tensions between religious/ritual contexts and other cultural contexts. For Hershman, this seems particularly relevant when gender differences are also considered. Because hair is so idiosyncratic and malleable, Anthony Synnott, in turn, views it as an especially potent symbol of both individual and group identities due to the many kinds of hair (i.e. body, face, and head) as well as its many lengths, styles, and colors.[23] In order to better understand the significance of so rich and complex a symbol, Synnott theorized that the meanings of hair have their roots in three general yet basic "opposing" principles: those of opposing sexes have opposing hair; those of opposing ideologies have opposing hair, an illustration of which can be seen in Figure I.3; and body hair is opposite to head hair. It is in the interplay of these principles, suggests Synnott, that hair becomes a way to represent major social divisions in and between cultures.

More recent scholarship on hair is much indebted to these earlier scholars. In characterizing it, one can note the continuance and refinement of many important principles. First and perhaps foremost, is that we still view hair as a subtle and deceptively complicated cultural symbol, one that plays an integral role in establishing identity—both personal and social. Moreover, it is fairly common for hair to be associated to

FIGURE I.3 Knights Templar before Jerusalem. On the battlements are three Saracen warriors (ca. fourteenth century). Bibliothèque Nationale, Paris. Photo: HIP/Art Resource, NY.

varying degrees with sexuality and sexual potency. Related to this is that long hair seems a particular marker of women while facial hair marks men, and hair length is often related to social belonging and/or control. However, though contemporary scholars might generally accept these notions, it is also important to note that they do so while simultaneously understanding that there is a flexibility and fluidity behind all of these principles that prevent them from ever forming anything as grand or as rigid as a comprehensive grammar of hair. In fact, it is rare for any recent scholarship to advocate any specific universal interpretation of hair as a symbol. Instead there seems a more general embracing of the multivalent nature of the symbol that in turn leads to more focused studies of it within particular contexts. The scopes of more contemporary studies thus tend to be limited to specific time periods, places, and/or groups while the lenses of the academics are likewise aimed at a certain kind of hair—whether it be the presence or absence of it; the length or style of it; its location on the head, face, or body; or the roles it plays in rituals. Many such studies are interested in the expressive quality of hair, how it is used as a marker of class, sex, gender, race, age, and nationality. Related issues of beauty, belonging, power, and shame are also often attached to hair, further complicating the messages and revealing the emotional content or expressiveness of such a rich signifier. It is to get at such nuanced sophisticated topics that contemporary scholars often make use of more blended, interdisciplinary approaches.

Certainly this flexibility of approaches can be seen in the work of medieval scholars who study hair, as many consider the ideas expressed by the social scientists as they engage some of these recent critical approaches in formulating their own opinions on the meaning(s) of the rich cultural symbol. Not many are comfortable using the broad time span of the Middle Ages as a way to frame their more generalized studies of hair, but there are some scholarly writings that explore the variety of meanings communicated by it among the various groups who populate the era. Perhaps one of the most influential and wide-reaching is the article "The Symbolic Meanings of Hair in the Middle Ages" by Robert Bartlett.[24] As the title suggests, Bartlett explores the variety of meanings hair has during this specific time period in western Europe, all of which demonstrate that such meanings are both highly contextual and often ambiguous. Simon Coates offers another comparable study of hair and how it communicated various ages, ethnicities, and statuses throughout the period.[25]

There are many more medievalists who restrict the scope of their inquiries further. Quite a few, for instance, focus their studies of hair on a particular nation during a defined time. Not surprisingly, the Merovingian kings whose distinctive tresses led to their being identified as the "long-haired kings" are a popular topic. Why the rulers grew their hair long, how they wore it, and what it signified are questions engaged by scholars such as Averil Cameron, Maximilian Diesenberger, Paul Edward Dutton, Erik Goosmann, Jean Hoyou, and Peter H. Johnsson.[26] Conrad Leyser similarly focuses on this time period though he expands his discussion to explore the politics behind the short hair required in Caesarius of Arles' *Rule for Virgins*.[27] Carl Phelpstead and William Sayers concentrate on hair within the particular nations of Iceland and Ireland, respectively, while H. Platelle and Pauline Stafford examine eleventh- and twelfth-century hairstyles.[28] Still other medievalists, focus on the significance of hair among other groups of people. Ilse Friesen, for example, specifically studies "hairy" holy women, while my own, earlier work concentrates on women as a group.[29]

Other medieval scholars limit the scope of their studies to concentrate on particular kinds of hair. For instance, Laura Clark, Giles Constable, and Zehava Jacoby focus on beards, while Penny Howell Jolly studies pubic hair and Margaret Sleeman examines hair tokens.[30] Robert Mills, Edward James, and Daniel McCarthy's work explores specific kinds of haircuts or styles like the tonsure.[31] The role hair plays in the identities or representations of a certain holy person such as a particular saint or biblical figure has occupied the attention of other medieval scholars, namely Paul Belcher, Susan Wade, Lewis Wallace, and Karen Winstead.[32]

In 2003, a conference was held at the University of Provence that was dedicated to exploring the role hair plays in medieval literature and art. The proceedings from this gathering—twenty-seven to be exact—were gathered by Chantal Connochie-Bourgne.[33] Topics explored by this group of scholars include the role hair plays in certain romances, *chansons de geste,* fabliaux, elegies, and other forms of poetry as well as the role it plays in the artistic expression of modesty, grief, beauty, and femininity. Of course, perhaps it goes without saying that the medieval era is usually featured in many encyclopedic discussions charting the history of hairstyles, mustaches, and beards.[34] Histories of fashion also may make reference to hairstyles and hair accessories.[35] Finally, many other scholars have written about topics that are very closely related to hair. For instance, Diane Wolfthal's article on the comb or Elizabeth Kuhns, Désirée Koslin, and Margaret Scott's respective work on medieval fashion including headdresses and veiling practices could also be included here.[36] Given the prominence of the church, those scholars, such as Mary Rose D'Angelo, J. Duncan Derret, and Gabriela Signori, who focus on biblical exegesis and the works of influential church teachings that involve hair could also be of value.[37]

FIGURE I.4 St. Eugenia (ca. twelfth century). Basilica St. Madeleine, Vézelay. Photo: Roberta Milliken.

THE CONTRIBUTIONS OF THIS VOLUME

The present volume brings together numerous other fine historians and literary scholars who certainly need to be added to the catalogue of studies of hair in the Middle Ages. The book is structured so that hair can be considered from a variety of culturally rich angles. In the following chapters each of the nine distinguished authors discusses a particular aspect or theme involving hair. The art historian Alexa Sand begins the study in Chapter One by considering the variety of roles hair plays in religion and ritualized belief. Opening with a discussion of foundational and exemplary biblical characters in whose stories hair imagery helps to impart moral lessons, Sand moves on to consider the iconography of certain saints who are comparably distinguished by hair. The notable part hair plays identifying churchmen and women is also discussed, including tonsuring practices for men and certain transgressive holy women such as Saint Eugenia who is featured revealing her breasts to prove that she is in fact a woman in Figure I.4; shaving customs; veiling traditions, an example of which is depicted in Figure I.5; and other rites associated with hair cutting and combing.

Chapter Two is constructed around the theme of Self and Society. Hanna Hopwood Griffiths considers how and what hair contributes to the identity of medieval people, the role it plays not just in marking groups but a member's place within that group. Drawing from literary texts and legal documents, Hopwood explores how hair is used in different ways by men and women in legal codes, social mores, and ritualistic rites of passage to enforce acceptable behaviors and instill order as well as at times reveal a sense of self—all of which underscore its social significance.

In Chapter Three historian Laura Michele Diener discusses the fashionable trends of men's and women's hairstyles over the span of the Middle Ages. From braids to false

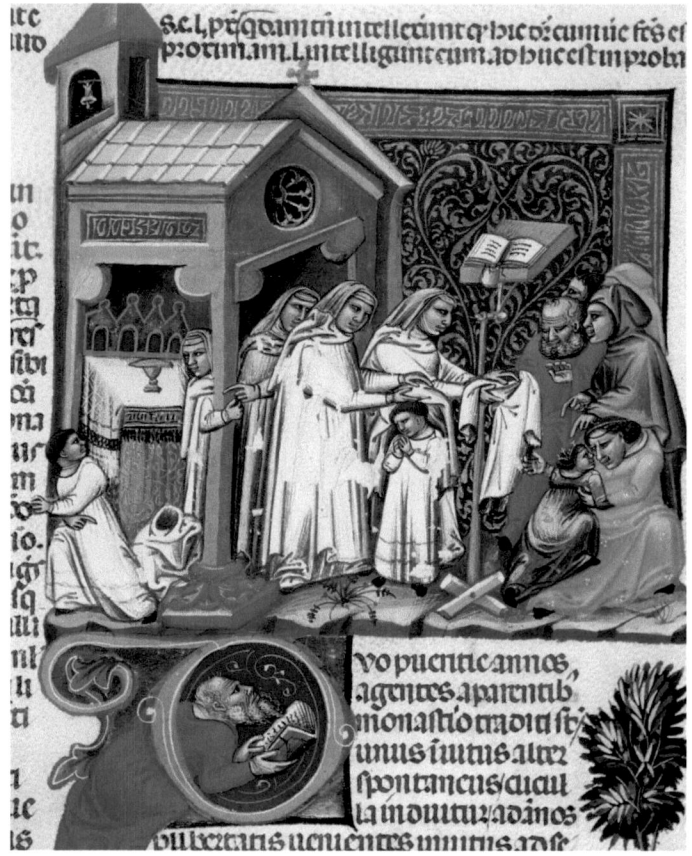

FIGURE I.5 Novice's haircut and veiling, Miniatura del s.XIV, perteneciente al "DECRETO Di GRAZIANO" donde se representa a un "GRUPO DE MONJAS VISTIENDO A UNA NIÑA." Photo: Album/Art Resource, NY.

hairpieces, from dyeing practice to the plucking of foreheads, and from covering the head to decorating tresses with jeweled hairpins, Diener gives an overview of the kinds of hairstyles women adopted to conform to understandings of beauty and fashion. Men and their hairstyles along with whether they sported beards and/or mustaches are also included in the discussion. Diener continues this historical exploration in Chapter Four, as she considers the means medieval people used to care for and control their hair—whether it be on the head, the face, or the body. Tools such as razors, combs, and hairpins are discussed as are the beginnings of the professional trades that catered to hair care. An image of such a burgeoning trade is featured in Figure I.6. Various jars of products designed to perfume or care for hair are shelved behind the saleswoman while other grooming implements including combs, mirrors, and razors are displayed for sale on the table in front of her.

The role hair plays in understandings of health and hygiene is the topic of Chapter Five, as Fernando Salmón and Montserrat Cabré explore how hair was understood according to the predominant medieval scientific understandings of the body known as humoralism. Using medical and historical texts, Salmón and Cabré discuss how hair was

FIGURE I.6 The Perfumer's Shop, detail (1430–1450). British Library, Cotton Tiberius A. VII, fol. 93. © The British Library Board.

thought to function both as a defense and an adornment, as well as a natural marker of sexual difference. Additionally, they review how hair was used as a diagnostic tool of sorts whereby the many features of a person's hair (color, texture, thickness, etc.) could reveal his/her health or temperament. The medical lore that recommended both general hair-care practices and remedies for certain afflictions is also discussed in this chapter.

In Chapter Six, art historian Martha Easton studies the role hair plays in the performance of gender. Beginning with the basic social convention that men have short hair and that women have long hair, Easton delves deeper into these social expectations to explore the complex and often thorny ways hair refines and contributes to medieval cultural understandings of femininity and masculinity. Virtue is attached to how women wear their hair, so how and if it is displayed often communicates what kind of women are being represented—especially if the hair is blonde, as such tresses are a potent indicator of beauty that is connected to eroticism. If long hair is expected of women, then cutting a woman's hair would be a powerful signifier of change or punishment. The former is illustrated in Figure I.7 with a lovely woman cutting off her hair to represent the seasonal change to autumn when "the earth takes off its ornaments," and the latter is exemplified in Figure I.8 where a pregnant woman is receiving the "hide and hair" punishment presumably for a sexual transgression, meaning she is beaten by one man while another cuts off her hair. That long hair is expected of women is also a reason why shorter hair is expected of men. Easton goes on to discuss how virility is often associated with men's hair whether it be head, facial, or pubic. However, issues

FIGURE I.7 Calendar page for October, detail (1410–1430). Paris, France, Bedford Hours, MS 18850, fol. 10v. © The British Library Board.

involving class, status, age, and religious affiliations affect the sporting of beards and mustaches as well.

The uses of hair in the depictions of race and ethnicity are the topics engaged by historian Kim M. Phillips in Chapter Seven. After exploring what ethnicity means and how it influences understandings of identity in the Middle Ages, Phillips examines how hair—particularly head and facial hair—is one of several attributes that is consistently used to help to distinguish difference or those who belong to a group from those who do not belong. This Other group is often, but not always, depicted with longer, shaggier hair and at times distinctive head coverings. Such an example can again be seen in Figure I.3 where clean-shaven crusaders confront the long-bearded, turban-wearing Saracens.

In Chapter Eight, John Block Friedman explores the ways hair contributes to the recognition of different social positions and classes predominantly in the literature of the times. The discussion revolves primarily around two main patterns of behaviors related to class distinction—especially in the later Middle Ages: men grow their hair longer to indicate a rise in social class, and women, while still sporting long tresses on their heads, generally reduce the hair on their foreheads, temples, and pudenda to indicate their comparable rise in social class.

The final chapter, Chapter Nine, is devoted to cultural representations of head and body hair. Considering hair as a rich and complicated signifier or "text" of sorts, Penny Howell Jolly offers a comprehensive overview of how it was used both figuratively and literally to communicate an impressive amount of ideas and sentiments. Drawing principally from artistic examples, Jolly explores the variety of meanings behind baldness,

INTRODUCTION   15

FIGURE I.8 Pregnant woman being beaten and shorn, detail (ca. 1300). Heidelberg University Library, Heidelberger Sachsenspiegel, Cod. Pal. germ. 164, fol. 12v. Courtesy of Heidelberg University Library.

pubic hair, beards of various lengths as well as the texture, color, and arrangement of hair, while showing hair's connection to ideals ranging from beauty to virginity; wisdom to lust; and youth to holiness. Moreover, the use of hair to express highly charged emotions reveals it to be a complicated, powerful, and flexible vehicle by which one is able to better understand the subtleties of important cultural issues such as gender, class, nationality, religion, sexuality, and Otherness.

CONCLUSION

The goal of the multifaceted approach to hair inherent in cultural studies and adopted by this volume is to offer a more comprehensive and, therefore, novel consideration of hair in the Middle Ages. The reader will no doubt notice areas of overlap between the discussions; these are inevitable when a topic is examined from such a variety of perspectives. However, the hope is that far from detracting from the various examinations, the interdisciplinarity that girds these moments will help provide a deeper, more complete and nuanced understanding of the specific issues involving hair. For instance, the depiction of the wise old bearded Edward the Confessor, the shaggier mustached English forces, and the clean-shaven short-haired Normans in the legendary needlework of the Bayeux Tapestry is of interest to art, literary, and history scholars and can be related to topics of several chapters, including self and society; race and ethnicity; class and social status; and general cultural representations (See Figure I.9).

FIGURE I.9 Edward on his throne, Harold leaving on horse for Normandy, Bayeux Tapestry, section 2B (eleventh century). Musée de la Tapisserie. © Ministère de la Culture/Médiathèque du Patrimoine, Dist.RMN-Grand Palais/Art Resource. Photo: Jean Gourbeix/Simon Guillot.

Considering the contrasting hair practices of these warring people from all of these perspectives helps to better situate them in the medieval imagination as well as adding further dimensionality to the discussion of particular topics themselves.

Additionally, though each author in the volume explores the subject of hair from a different angle and from his/her discipline, it is worth repeating that common to all is the acknowledgment that hair is a rich though often subtle signifier of identity or perhaps more accurately, identities. Hairiness as a trait in the depiction of a Wildman can then represent a wildness aligned with a bestial savagery that might also prompt concern or fear, while the hairiness of a hermit might signal a more benign difference associated with worldly renunciation and piety. Because hair is a multivalent cultural symbol, the contexts of each of these hairy men would help to communicate these diverse meanings. It would, however, be overly simplistic to say that the careful consideration of context always reveals a primary meaning that erases or cancels out other possibly different or competing meanings. Diverse interpretations of hair can coexist, and the fascinatingly complex dissonance among the variety of symbolic interpretations in medieval culture is often capable of creating fresh meanings itself. Returning to the example of hairiness, then, instead of saying that hairiness can denote a dangerous bestial wildness *or* a more comforting ascetic wildness, it is probably more accurate to say that hairiness denotes a dangerous bestial wildness *and* a more comforting ascetic wildness. The acknowledgment of the various meanings better portrays the richness and depth of the symbol that helps to reveal its pliancy as well. How much more, for instance, do we appreciate or understand the thrilling differentness of a pious man whose appearance also announces his profound asceticism because of our understanding of the Wildman (and vice versa)?

The knowledge of both kinds of hirsute wildness transforms the hermit into another sort of larger-than-life figure who communicates a fresh sense of awe that is tinged with fear and Otherness.

Such interplay of meanings sparks the imagination and speaks to a cultural sophistication that is important to acknowledge here. It is a testament to the richness of hair as a signifier as much as it also helps to display the special vibrancy of the people and the period in which they lived. The hope is that in focusing so specifically on a topic as rich as hair, and in more fully recognizing the challenging and complicated nature of how and what hair communicates, the reader can indeed get a refined sense of the medieval mindset.

CHAPTER ONE

Religion and Ritualized Belief, 800–1500

ALEXA SAND

The Bible, wellspring of meanings for medieval thinkers of every stripe, provides multiple and conflicting messages about hair. Furthermore, each generation of interpreters focused on different aspects of scriptural trichology, often glossing its moral or allegorical sense through the lens of their own cultural vision. But exegetes were not the only ones engaged with hair in a religious sense. From the institution of tonsuring practices in the fifth century to the heated denunciation of excesses of hair bleaching and styling in fifteenth-century Italy, hair played an important role in the Middle Ages, as it does today, in establishing social roles and communicating ritual status. And medieval hairstyles and head coverings conveyed religious meaning and participated in the formation of identities and interpersonal as well as political relationships.[1]

As a mutable extension of the body, hair often exercised a synecdotal function for medieval people. Control, exposure, and manipulation of hair could be interpreted as expressive or indicative of a variety of spiritual and moral states of being. For Christians, the scriptural foundation for understanding the signification of hair was broad; in particular, both Paul and Peter give specific and quite literal prescriptions on the appropriate approaches to hair for both men and women. Paul, in 1 Corinthians 11:13–15, interprets a woman's (implicitly long) hair as a divine index of her need to be covered: "You yourselves judge: doth it become a woman, to pray unto God uncovered? Doth not even nature itself teach you, that a man indeed, if he nourish his hair, it is a shame unto him? But if a woman nourish her hair, it is a glory to her; for her hair is given to her for a covering."[2] Both apostles, meanwhile, caution that women should not indulge in elaborate braids or ornaments for their hair, instead dressing it modestly and soberly (1 Timothy 2:9, and 1 Peter 3:3); in both cases, the occasion for the comment is in the proscription of women's preaching and the assertion of a wife's subjugation to her husband. Subsequent Christian theologians would extend this gendered moral understanding of hair—for example, Clement of Alexandria, who in the third book of his treatise, *The Instructor*, includes a long and detailed set of guidelines for both male and female hair, explicitly linking extravagant hairstyles, hair colors, and hair ornaments to pagan moral turpitude.[3] Other Church Fathers, particularly Tertullian and Jerome, advocate veiling for women on a biblical basis; accordingly, medieval women of all classes concerned themselves with head coverings that combined deference to the idea of the covered woman expressed by Paul with a keen sense of fashion and group identity.

Old Testament narratives and legal strictures also informed medieval religious and ritual perceptions and performances of hair. For Jews, Talmudic scholarship and Mishnah provided a guide to untangling the many and sometimes contradictory statements found in the Torah, particularly in regard to the maintenance and grooming of male facial hair. Furthermore, Christian practices provided a kind of antitype for many Jewish theologians, who cautioned Jews against engaging in such idolatrous habits as tonsure and long hair for men.[4] Meanwhile, Christians fixed upon certain Old Testament figures as typologically significant, and added to the mix hagiographic legends and a host of other (predominantly female) saints whose hair, as a figure for the body, expressed the action of Grace in the world. Muslims, Jews, and Christians looked askance at the woman whose long hair went uncovered and unbound, and at the man whose excessive attention to the cultivation of long locks aligned him suspiciously with such lustful and lust-inspiring females. Thus, the basic elements of medieval religious and ritual approaches to hair can be discerned in the biblical texts that provide the foundation for so much of medieval culture: a concern with the differentiation of gender, anxiety about sexuality and sensuality, and a strong current of misogyny.

Visual artists, theologians, poets, and ordinary people participated in shaping the perception and manipulation of human hair in a number of ways. In what follows, four distinct categories of intervention in the religious and ritual senses of hair are investigated. First, engagement with the scriptural sources of medieval moral and allegorical understandings of hair emerges as an important theme in the depiction of such pivotal biblical personages as Samson, Absalom, Eve, and Mary Magdalene. Secondly, the iconography and semiotics of hair as it relates to the saints can be seen to draw on these traditions of biblical representation. The third arena of engagement has to do with the representation and maintenance of particular coiffures associated with religious status. Finally, the liturgical dimension of hair leaves its trace in the implements of ritual grooming that survive in great numbers and in the much rarer depictions of these objects at work, through which we can begin to come at the somewhat elusive question of how hair figured in the formal and ritual practice of the Mass.

BIBLICAL PRECEDENTS

From the Psalmist's complaint that "They are multiplied above the hairs of my head, who hate me without cause" (Psalm 69:4) to Paul's previously cited pronouncements on coiffure and morality in his letters, the Christian Bible provided thousands of possible hair-related topoi. However, relatively few of these became standard features of literature, art, and ritual. Indeed, it was not really until the medieval period that artists and writers began to pay close attention to the expressive and iconographic potential of hair. And when they did, their attention mostly directed itself to a limited number of figures, overlooking some of the most vivid hair-related incidents of the Bible. For example, the dramatic scene from Ezekiel 5:1, where the Lord commands the prophet to use a sword to shave off his beard and hair, to divide it in three parts, and to weigh it upon a scale, was never developed as a visual motif and languished in the margins of medieval literature, of interest primarily to rabbis and to Christian homilists engaged in creating anti-Jewish propaganda.[5] For the most part, hair-imagery focused on only a few figures, including Samson, Absalom, Eve, and Mary Magdalene. Each of these seems to embody, through his or her hair, the same concerns already identified as central to medieval religious views of hair based in biblical precedent: Samson's hair is linked to his masculine authority while Absalom's to his effeminate vanity, Eve's to her female weakness and immodesty, and the Magdalene's to her status as a woman at once fallen and redeemed. Again, broad concerns about gender distinction, sex, and the sensual dimensions of embodied experience lie at the heart of medieval interest in the hair of these biblical characters.

The biblical figure most likely to come to mind in relation to hair is of course Samson, the Nazirite, whose special religious status includes a prohibition on the cutting of his hair (Judges 13–16). Samson's story, like those of other Old Testament heroes, was necessarily allegorized by early Christian and medieval exegetes; as a human type for Christ he is almost perfect, between his divine strength, his humbling at the hands of evil people, and the return of his potency resulting in his death/triumph. Isidore of Seville, in particular, remained an important patristic source on the Christological implications of Samson throughout the Middle Ages.[6] Erik Goosmann has put forward an interesting proposal that Samson, rather than David or Solomon, was also the first biblical prototype for kingship in the medieval Latin West.[7] The most extensive and often-cited medieval treatment of Samson is the twelfth-century abbot Gottfried of Admont's sermon for Palm Sunday that adds to patristic understanding of the Christological significance of Samson specifically in terms of his hair—"the seven locks" cut by Delilah become in his view the seven gifts of the Holy Spirit that imbue Christ with all virtue.[8] The subtlety of Gottfried's reading balances the earthier moralizing view of Chaucer's Monk, who concludes his retelling of Samson's story by saying, "This old and simple tale is meant to warn all husbands from confiding to their wives anything that they'd rather not have known, if it means danger to their limbs or lives."[9]

From late antiquity and well into the Middle Ages, artistic representations of Samson, understood as a precursor and type for Christ, emphasized not his hair but his heroic actions; in the catacombs of Via Latina, in Rome, in the fourth century, Samson appears dressed and coiffed like a respectable Roman, with a short haircut and a beard.[10] Later, medieval artists tended to at least give Samson long hair; the Byzantine illuminator of the Homilies of Gregory Nazianzus shows the hero wearing his dark hair long until Delilah's seduction (Paris, BnF ms. grec 510, fol. 347v). This narrative sequence relies on the detail of hair length for its literal sense.[11] Romanesque and Gothic sculptors frequently included episodes from the life of Samson in narrative capitals, such as a Provençal capital now at Harvard (1922.132). Not only do Samson's locks receive detailed carving, with sinuous, incised lines marking out the coarse, interwoven strands of hair in the scenes of wrestling the lion and carrying off the gates of Gaza that adorn two sides of the block, but, in the cutting scene, it takes three men and an axe to sever the Rapunzel-like braid that Delilah lifts off the nape of the sleeping hero. The same episodes feature on a contemporary capital at Vézelay (Figure 1.1). This central episode taps into two of the prevalent medieval interpretations of the story in Christian biblical exegesis. On the moral level, the scene can be understood in terms of the opposition of Samson's male spirituality, strength, and reason with Delilah's female fleshliness, susceptibility to lust, and deceitfulness. This theme of Samson's victimhood also plays a central role in the literature of gender conduct and ethics.

Samson is not the only long-haired male in the Old Testament whose tresses figured prominently in the exegetical canon. Hair plays a decisive part in the story of Absalom, the favored but rebellious son of David, whose surpassing beauty is described in 2 Samuel 14:25–6, where the weight of his hair seems to be the measure of its excellence. But it is this same bounty of hair that spells Absalom's doom when it gets caught in the

FIGURE 1.1 *Samson and Delilah*, Vézelay, Benedictine Abbey Church of Sainte-Marie-Madeleine, nave capital (Salet number 87, 1120–1132). © Jane Vadnal.

branches of an oak as he passes under on his mule, and it holds him there until Joab and his men come to slay him (2 Samuel 18:9–15). The opposition of David and Absalom was a type for the opposition of Christ and Judas, and the similarities between Absalom's death, hanging by his hair from a tree, and Judas's, hanging by a rope, were too close to be resisted by medieval writers and artists.[12] Thus, the suspended Absalom figures dramatically in one of the capitals from the nave at Vézelay; on the left side of the capital, he dangles, seemingly unconscious, from the leafy canopy as Joab drives a sword into his neck, while on the face of the capital his riderless mule dashes away. Here, Absalom's long hair streams upward from his head, gathered in Joab's fist. The gesture of pulling the hair taut underscores the thrust of Joab's sword and draws attention to the fatal agency of Absalom's luxurious tresses.[13]

In the Eadwine Psalter (Cambridge, Trinity College ms. R. 17.1, fol. 8r) C.R. Dodwell noted that the illuminator added to the source illustration the figure of Absalom hanging by his hair from an oak tree on the far right side of the composition (Figure 1.2).[14] A rubricated titulus, inside the confines of the picture's frame, gives the subtitle to Psalm 3, "a Psalm of David when he fled from the face of his son Absalom." In Augustine's exposition to this Psalm, this subtitle is glossed with the explicit linkage of David–Christ and Absalom–Judas:

> By his undutiful son be here meant that undutiful disciple who betrayed Him. From whose face although it may be understood historically that He fled, when on his departure He withdrew with the rest to the mountain; yet in a spiritual sense, when the Son of God, that is the Power and Wisdom of God, abandoned the mind of Judas; when the Devil wholly occupied him.[15]

No mention is made of Absalom's hair, nor the parallel between his fate and that of Judas's, both hanging from trees in a grotesque parody of the Crucifixion. However, this

FIGURE 1.2 *Absalom's Death*, detail, Eadwine Psalter, Canterbury (ca. 1160). Cambridge, Trinity College, R. 17. 1, fol. 8r. Courtesy of the Masters and Fellows of Trinity College Cambridge.

dormant motif is explored by the visual artist, who attends closely to the entanglement of locks and tree limbs.

A moral reading of Absalom's hair is implicit in Paul's condemnation in 1 Corinthians 11:14, "Doth not even nature itself teach you, that a man indeed, if he nourish his hair, it is a shame unto him?" Excessive attention to coiffure in a man associates him with the typically effeminate vice of vanity, closely linked to lust in medieval moral philosophy; the effete aristocrat, as opposed to the manly laborer, troubles the waters of orthodox Christian masculinity as established by Paul. As early as the ninth century, Alcuin speculated that the cataclysm of the Viking attack on Lindisfarne might have something to do with the Anglo-Saxon penchant for imitating the outlandish hairstyles of the Northmen: "Look at your trimming of the beard and hair, in which you have wished to resemble the pagans," he admonished his countrymen.[16] As Madeline Caviness has noted, reforming churchmen of the eleventh century such as Ivo of Chartres and Orderic Vitalis linked long hair on men directly to Paul's censure, condemning it as both effeminate and sexually provocative, while after the Norman Conquest of England William of Malmesbury attributed the defeat of the Anglo-Saxons at Hastings at least in part to their womanish long hair.[17]

The effeminacy of masculine long hair, as it came to be understood in the later Middle Ages, was perceived as negative, since to be female or feminine was to be in virtually every respect less laudable than to be male or masculine. Although prevailing social practices across Europe kept most women from cutting their hair short, and indeed Paul commended long hair on women as an appropriate "veiling" for their sinful heads in the presence of God (1 Corinthians 11:15), long, loose, and uncovered hair on a woman signified vice, particularly sexual misconduct. Veils, coifs, and restrained hair conversely signified feminine virtues such as modesty, chastity, and subservience. In Jewish tradition, a bared female head was understood from Mishnaic time onward as a form of nakedness, entirely inappropriate in all but the most intimate of contexts. Various medieval commentators iterated the importance of restraining the hair, and in kabbalistic thought, uncovered hair was understood to emit energy that could attract demons.[18] Diane Wolfthal cites long, unconstrained hair as one of the salient iconographic tropes of sexual availability or vulnerability. Both seductresses and rape victims signal their status through loose, tousled locks; she cites the uncovering and unbinding of the hair of the Levite's wife in the scenes of her rape and murder in the Morgan Old Testament Picture Bible (New York, Pierpont

Morgan Library ms. M.638, fol. 16r), and Potiphar's wife, drawing attention to her unconstrained hair while feigning that Joseph has raped her, in the Queen Mary Psalter (London, British Library, MS Royal 2. B. VII, fol. 16). Indeed, she points out, disheveled hair was one legal proof that a rape had occurred in some law codes.[19]

It should come as no surprise, then, that when understood as a seductress whose own seduction by the Serpent led to the Fall, Eve, wears her hair long and loose. As Roberta Milliken notes, depictions of the nude Eve or her allegorical sister, Luxuria, inevitably feature long, sensual hair, often entangled with and sometimes indistinguishable from the serpents that appear alongside these femmes fatales.[20] Whereas Carolingian, Anglo-Saxon, and Ottonian visual depictions of Genesis, for example the great Touronian Bibles, the Caedmon Genesis manuscript, and Bishop Bernward's bronze doors for Saint Michael's Church at Hildesheim, show both Adam and Eve as long-haired, perhaps reflecting a conception of the "natural" state of the human body, later medieval visualizations of the first couple come to focus increasingly on Eve's long hair as a signifier of her iniquity.

At the collegiate church of Saint-Lazare in Autun, Eve strikes a seductively horizontal posture on the famous door-lintel of about 1130. Sinuous lines define the entire composition: the trees that frame Eve's body snake upwards on trunks patterned with scale-like chevrons or pearls, underscoring the curvilinear pose and curvaceous form of Eve's body. Her hair, meanwhile, falls in finely textured strands from a center part, tracing the outer line of her face and rippling back over her shoulder and upper arm like a solid, textile cloak, obeying no law of gravity. Hair, tree trunks, body, all are unified in a muscular, writhing network of finely carved lines and patterns that makes of Eve at once a serpent, a seductress, and the woman seduced.

The moral reading of Eve's hair, like Absalom's, is predominantly negative, and that negativity is entangled with medieval constructions of femininity and the sins typically associated with the feminine (lust, vanity). However, long hair, even when uncovered and unbound, does not necessarily or always symbolize vice. As the example of Samson suggests, long hair can also articulate positive spiritual meanings; as a spiritual sign, abundant hair may make manifest the action of the Holy Spirit in the world, as in Gottfried's sermon mentioned above. A final quasi-biblical example, that of Mary Magdalene, reinforces this point. Insofar as "the Magdalene" is a biblical figure, she is mentioned multiple times in the Gospels, where she is identified as a woman from whom Jesus has cast demons, as an attendant at the Crucifixion, as one (or the only) woman who discovers the empty tomb, and as the first to see the risen Christ.[21] However, in the Middle Ages, Mary of Magdala's identity merged with those of Mary of Bethany, sister of Martha and Lazarus, identified by John as the woman who anoints Christ's feet with spikenard and dries them with her hair.[22] Other hagiographic elements would be added to the mix, but it is the blending of Mary the apostle with Mary the "great sinner" who penitentially humbles herself at the feet of Christ that will define the iconography of the Magdalene in later medieval art, literature, and theology. Her hair stands out as her defining characteristic. As a female who has something to atone for, Christian exegetes almost universally assumed that her sin was of a sexual nature (she is either described as a former prostitute or as a rich woman whose lifestyle had once included much *luxuria*, or lust). That she is mentioned as using her hair (necessarily loose and long for the purpose) to wipe the feet of Christ represents a theologically appealing reversal of the usual deployment of such an immodest mane for the seduction of men. As Katherine Ludwig Jansen remarks, "It is significant that at the moment of her conversion it was her hair—the symbol of her sexual sin—that became the emblem of her penitence."[23]

FIGURE 1.3 Mary Magdalene, from a sculptural group depicting the resurrection of Lazarus for the Church of Saint-Lazare (ca. 1130). Autun, Musée Rolin. Photo: Foto Marburg/Art Resource, NY.

In one of those rare, but fortunate, twists of archaeological conservation, a half-life-size standing figure of the Magdalene survives from Autun, and resides in the same museum as the more famous Eve lintel (Figure 1.3). This figure, part of an ensemble that depicted the Raising of Lazarus, gives us the classic, Romanesque vision of the Magdalene. Dressed in a narrow, heavily pleated robe with wide sleeves that fall back to reveal ruched undersleeves, she is wimpled, veiled, and coiffed in more layers of round-folded fabric. Only a very little bit of her hair is visible as it falls across her upper temples from beneath her turban. Where it passes under the veil, however, its rippling texture gets picked up by the small, tight pleats of that cloth, which fall down over her shoulders and back in spreading folds, almost like the cloak of hair worn by Eve. Eve's nudity and her uncovered hair, along with their negative associations here are at once formally recalled and negated by the ponderous and constricting drapery of the Magdalene.

Later medieval artists would not content themselves with this hyperbolically chaste vision of the Magdalene. Picking up on the exegetical and apocryphal tradition that understood her as a reformed prostitute, the visual rhetoric of Luxuria's long hair came into play more forcefully in Gothic representations of the biblical saint. In Giotto's *Lamentation of Christ* in the Arena Chapel at Padua (ca. 1308), Mary Magdalene sits on the ground, holding the feet of the corpse in her lap in a bitter echo of her anointing of the living feet. Her hair, unlike that of nearly every other woman in the scene, is neither covered nor restrained in braids, but falls loose at the nape and forward over her chest, painted in so naturalistic and free a fashion as to capture its slightly frizzy texture.

From this point on, Italian artists tended to depict the Magdalene with her long, usually blonde, tresses uncovered or only partially covered and loose. This more glamorous depiction of the Magdalene proposes her as an antitype to Eve and yet at the same time as a foil for the virginal Mary. She embodies both sensuality and its renunciation, her hair in particular signaling her role as a woman of the flesh even as it underscores her humility and devotion to Christ. The potential for the Magdalene's hair to convey this dual message—carnality and conversion—comes to fruition in works of the fifteenth century. In the apse of the Italian-influenced fresco cycle of the life of the Magdalene at Saint-Érige in the Maritime Alps (Figure 1.4), she stands in a meadow, facing outward, her hands joined in prayer, wearing a remarkable cloak of her own blonde hair. It falls in waves of cream, bright yellow, and deep ocher, covering her body completely and leaving bare only her face, hands, and the tips of her toes. This is the apocryphal scene of the Magdalene's elevation, which occurred during her thirty years of desert penitence, as described in Jacobus de Voragine's *Golden Legend*: "Every day at the seven canonical hours she was carried aloft by angels and with her bodily ears heard the glorious chants of the Celestial hosts."[24] The thirteenth-century account does not mention a cloak of hair, nor the condition necessitating it, to wit the Magdalene's nakedness. However, this detail is found in the ninth-century *Vita eremitica* (Life Eremitical), the earliest known hagiographic text for the Magdalene and one that circulated widely in the Latin West.[25]

The sexually provocative nature of the hermit-Magdalene's hair-clothed nudity comes through strongly in Gregor Erhart's *Magdalene* (ca. 1515; Paris, Louvre, RF 1338). Carved in the round from limewood, gessoed, and polychromed, this lifelike and life-size figure (1.77 m tall) wears a long, gilded mane that falls past her buttocks and swings across one shoulder to cover her pudenda, though not her breast. The contrast of the ropy, dark-gold hair with its reflective gilding and the smooth, ivory flesh of her body, along with the pink blush in her cheeks, nipples, and lips, her slightly upturned mouth, and the serpentine torsion of her midsection all add up to a highly eroticized vision

FIGURE 1.4 *The Penitent Magdalene*, fresco, Eglise Saint-Érige, Auron (Alpes-Maritimes) (1451). Photo: MHR93_0912012_E (c) Monuments historiques, 2004. Reproduction subject to authorization by the rights holder—Briez, Serge. © DRac Paca, CRMH, 1989, Jean Marx.

of the saint. The hermit's nakedness and the penitential hair shirts worn by many of the Dominican friars for whom she was sculpted both enter into the play of desire and renunciation embodied by the so-called *beata peccatrix* (blessed sinner).

HAGIOGRAPHIC IMAGERY AND RELICS

With the Magdalene already we begin to move from the realm of biblical types and antitypes toward the exemplary world of the saints. Hair figures prominently in the hagiographic literature of the Middle Ages, and hair made the ideal substance for relic collectors due to its natural abundance, though a surprisingly small number of reliquaries have survived that contain or are said to have once contained hair. Relics—bodily remains along with items closely associated with the bodies of saints and holy people—were the fuel that drove medieval Christianity. To approach (and if one was lucky to touch) a relic, usually encased in an elaborate container that both concealed and celebrated the object, was to enter into a communication with the sacred person that benefited the devotee in specific ways. Reliquaries took an immense variety of forms, from ornamented boxes to literal representations of the body parts or objects they contained, to sculptures in the round depicting the holy person whose traces were enclosed within, to miniature architectural forms. Hair, as a bodily relic of mutable form, was not associated with any particular type of reliquary. However, the majority of hair relics seem to be associated with the Virgin Mary; an 1884 article in the *Revue de l'art chrétien* lists dozens of archival or literary documents from the later Middle Ages that mention reliquaries venerated as containers of hairs from the Virgin's head.[26] A particularly spectacular example of a medieval hair relic comes in the form of the so-called Amulet of Charlemagne, a large sapphire pendant said to have originally enclosed a relic of the Virgin Mary in the form of her hair, although later fragments of the True Cross were substituted.[27]

Numerous saints' lives contain episodes in which long hair, hair cutting, or atypical hair growth drive the narrative forward or demonstrate divine intervention in the life of the holy person. Saint Agnes seems the Magdalene's closest relation, for her legend recounts that when she was stripped naked in the brothel to which she had been condemned, her hair grew so fast that it covered her nudity in an instant.[28] Like the Magdalene, by the fourteenth century she is occasionally depicted wearing only the luxurious cloak of her own hair; a miniature by Jean Pucelle in the winter portion of the Belleville Breviary of 1323–1326 (Figure 1.5) depicts Agnes receiving a tunic from an angel, her nudity temporarily but completely obscured by her floor-length blonde tresses. Pucelle makes the most of the titillating counterpoise of threatened rape and divinely ordained innocence. The opened flap of the tent-bordello waiting to engulf Agnes mirrors the drape of the tunic held by the angel in such a way to seem to contain a body in the act of falling backwards, perhaps in ravishment. Agnes, meanwhile, stands or kneels perfectly upright, perfectly enclosed in the tumble of her own hair, as closed up and impenetrable as the tent and the tunic seem to be open and vulnerable.

If Agnes's hair-related iconography somewhat resembles that of the Magdalene and plays with similar themes of sexual sin and saintly continence, the imagery of a number of other female saints engages transgressive hair growth as a sign of the rejection of femininity and its carnal nature. Some of these saints are not easily characterized in their use of hair as a gender-bending prop, since like Agnes their transgressive hair is a matter of miraculous growth rather than self-directed manipulation. Perhaps the most spectacular of these is Saint Wilgefortis (aka Liberata or Uncumber) who first appears in

FIGURE 1.5 Jean Pucelle, *Saint Agnes*, detail, winter portion, Belleville Breviary, Paris (1323–1326). Paris, Bibliothèque Nationale, MS lat. 10483, fol. 135v. Photo: BnF.

hagiographic accounts of the fourteenth century.[29] Forced by her pagan father to marry, Wilgefortis grows a miraculous beard that disqualifies her as a sexual partner, and so her father crucifies her. Wilgefortis assumes a masculine appearance, though because hers involves facial hair growth it is less a disguise than a divine transformation. Other female saints grew or faked beards to pass as men, but neither early Christian Galla of Rome nor fourteenth-century Paula of Avila are habitually depicted with their full complement of facial hair, as is Wilgefortis. For her, it is the salient, defining feature of her sanctity. Unlike the abundant tresses of Agnes or Mary Magdalene, it negates, rather than draws attention to, her erotic potential.

Wilgefortis's beard iterates the bearded face of Christ, an iconographic type that emerged in Rome, around the year 400, when the youthful, clean-shaven Apollonian Christ of the earliest Christian art was joined by the long-haired and bearded figure modeled on representations of Roman and Hellenistic father deities, as Thomas Mathews has demonstrated.[30] Apocrypha concerned with the physical appearance and physiognomy of Christ cannot be securely dated before the iconoclastic period, when (sometimes violent) conflict broke out in the Byzantine Empire over the issue of whether sacred images violated the biblical proscription on idols or were in fact legitimate means of communicating with God. One example of post-iconoclastic interest in the appearance of

Christ is the so-called Lentulus Letter, famous for its detailed Latin description of Christ ultimately based on a Byzantine icon-painters' manual, and is dated to the thirteenth century.³¹ The letter describes "hair the color of an unripe hazelnut, smooth almost to his ears, but below his ears curling and rather darker and more shining, hanging over his shoulders, and with a parting in the middle" along with "a full beard the color of his hair, not long, but divided in two at the chin."³²

This "true description" seems a text generated by images, rather than an image-generating text; the account of Christ's hair and beard validate an already-existing iconographic tradition. The smooth-cheeked Christ continued as a motif into the Carolingian period in the West; see, for example, the solemn, blond youth with only the slightest peach-fuzz at his chin in the Godescalc Evangelistary, dated 781–783 (Paris, BnF ms. n.a.lat. 1203, fol. 3r). But in the Byzantine sphere, the authority of the self-generated representation, or *acheiropoeton* known as the Mandylion, a "true image" of the face of Christ enshrined the bearded type in the iconographic imagination of Christianity. Originally associated with the Christian city of Edessa, in Syria, the Mandylion migrated to Constantinople in the tenth century and became one of the chief relics of the post-iconoclastic imperial chapel. Although the relic-image itself was lost, perhaps at the time of the Latin sack of Constantinople in 1204, the numerous copies it generated attest to its iconography.³³ The somber, frontal face of Christ in the Mandylion-type image may have begun as a Christian appropriation of and challenge to the iconography of the pagan gods, but by the thirteenth century in the Latin West, it participated in an entirely new visual economy. It associated with Rome's own relic-image of Christ, the Veronica (another miraculously generated and miracle-generating image of the face of Christ, housed in the Lateran) which began to be elevated in ritual status in the late twelfth century and had become, by 1300, one of the leading pilgrimage attractions in a city packed with pilgrimage attractions. Copied into manuscripts, disseminated in the form of inexpensive pilgrims' tokens, adapted by panel-painters such as Jan van Eyck into an image of the Man of Sorrows, the bearded visage would inspire its own indulgenced Office and define the representation of Christ for centuries to come.

For the Byzantines, who embraced the Mandylion-type image, the hair and beard were necessary elements of the image's iconicity. For the medieval Latin West, the element of authority and antiquity certainly pertained, but the eager devotees of the thirteenth through fifteenth centuries saw something else in this sun-darkened, sober mien. In an era of crusading, or memories of crusading, the resemblance between the bearded Christ and the idealized image of the knight who has taken the Cross could have been powerful. Although his chain-mail hood covers most of his chin, the tomb-figure, or giant, of William Marshal, first Earl of Pembroke at the Temple Church in London shows a close-trimmed mustache. A neatly barbered, short beard seems to have been fashionable among the crusaders, and distinguished them from long-bearded easterners. Additionally, beards became a point of friction between the eastern and western clergy during the Crusades; Giles Constable reports that even before the first Latin armies arrived in Constantinople, the Greek patriarchate had denounced the Roman clergy for shaving, while later sources attest to the Latins mocking the long beards of the Greeks.³⁴

The bearded image of Jesus, dominant in both East and West from 800 to 1500, keeps good company with the bearded faces of numerous male saints. As Sara Lipton has demonstrated, medieval iconography inherited the beard as a signifier of wisdom from late classical traditions of representing philosophers and magicians as bearded.³⁵

Old Testament prophets, such as those depicted on the jambs of the pilgrims' portal at the Abbey Church of Saint-Pierre, Moissac, wear luxuriant, long beards and mustaches, rendered in tapering, wavy hanks patterned with fine, regular striations. Likewise, on the jambs of the left side of the central north portal at Chartres, Old Testament patriarchs Melchizedek, Abraham, Moses, Samuel, and David sport full beards and mustaches indicative of their seniority and wisdom. But long beards, like long hair on men, generated a great deal of dissent among medieval writers. Some cited Ezekiel's shaving of his beard at the command of God (Ezekiel 5:1) as a precedent, while others referred to Clement of Alexandria's dictum that the beard was the mark of manhood and that to shave was to desecrate God's sign.[36] Thus it is not surprising that most of the saints for whom a long beard is an identifying attribute, such as Peter, Paul, Nicholas, Benedict, and Jerome (just to name a few) are either New Testament or early Christian figures; their beards situate them historically as belonging to a period closer to the time of Christ and the prophets who foretold of his coming. Hermit saints, too, may grow long beards as a sign of their choice to live outside the conventions of civilized society.

Church law in the Latin West began to insist on regular shaving by monks and clerics as early as the ninth century, but artists clearly understood that a living person's facial hair and the symbolic facial hair of a pictorial representation did not have the same juridical status. Whether or not male saints, especially revered abbots or other doctors of the church, were depicted bearded seems to have more to do with context than an interest in mimesis. For example, in the autograph manuscript of the monk Donzio's *Vita Mathildis* (Life of Matilda), illuminated around 1114 (Vatican, Cod. Vat. Lat. 4922, fol. 49r), the recently deceased Hugh of Cluny appears, probably with a certain degree of eye-witness accuracy, his hair covered by a pointed hood, his face clean-shaven. Likewise, a century and a quarter later, the Benedictine Matthew Paris depicts himself in prostrate prayer before the Virgin and Child, his monastic hood thrown back to reveal his tonsure, his chin bare except for a few stray whiskers (Royal 14 C VII, fol. 6).

However, Hugh's and Matthew's beardlessness is rare in the art of the twelfth and thirteenth century where monastic or clerical saints even of recent vintage were concerned. For example, the Grandmontine saint Stephen of Muret wears a short, curling beard with mustache and full sideburns on a Limoges enamel plaque from the altar of the abbey of Grandmont (Figure 1.6); meanwhile, his companion, the crusader Hugh of Lacerta, wears a longer, blond beard, perhaps indicative of his role as a pilgrim. And while lay saints sometimes appeared as bearded figures, they were quite as likely not to. Notably, the beards that distinguish medieval male saints of both the monastic and the nonmonastic type tend to be short. This probably also reflects social practices and legal rhetoric that characterized untamed facial hair as indicative of outsider status—for example, Jews (despite the fact that most Jews in Europe prior to the fifteenth century tended to adopt the barbering practices customary to the country in which they lived), Muslims, and outlaws.

Bearded male saints could be so for numerous reasons, including fidelity to living memories of what the recently deceased holy person had indeed looked like, but the weight of the evidence suggests that beards (or the lack thereof) went beyond the literal level of meaning. After all, when Giotto chose to eliminate the beard from his representation of Francis in his Life of Francis cycle in the Bardi Chapel at Santa Croce in Florence, in 1325–1328, he set a visual precedent in direct contradiction to the hagiographic and earlier pictorial tradition, but one which, nevertheless, endured until the Counter-Reformation. What for a twelfth- or thirteenth-century audience might have

FIGURE 1.6 *Saint Stephen of Muret and Hugh of Lacerta*, champlevé enamel plaque from the main altar of the abbey of Grandmont, Limoges (ca. 1189–1190). Paris, Musée nationale du Moyen Age—Thermes de Cluny. Photo: Jean-Gilles Berizzi. © RMN-Grand Palais/Art Resource, NY.

been an indicator of masculine maturity and authority perhaps became in the fourteenth century a disturbing indicator of clerical or monastic unruliness.

HOLY BARBERING AND HOLY GROOMING

The shaving and tonsuring of clerics and monks was a visible sign of differences between the eastern and western churches. Differing interpretations of biblical decrees involving male hair led to widely different practices over time and across space. In addition to the East/West argument over bearded clerics, debates and divergent practices developed around tonsuring; in essence, tonsure was the selective shaving of part or all of the head as a visible sign of self-sacrifice and the renunciation of worldly desires appropriate to the monastic or in some cases clerical profession. Everyone agreed that Acts 18:18, in which Paul, having taken a vow, cuts off his hair, gave the scriptural precedent for the practice. Another apostolic model was Peter, who, according to *The Golden Legend*, suffered a humiliating head-shaving at the hands of the pagans of Antioch, a "badge of shame" borne as a "mark of honor" by clerics ever since, symbolic of "a clean, unpretentious life" in which there is "nothing between the cleric and God."[37] On almost every other point regarding the tonsure disagreement broke out. Did this mean shaving the whole head, as some of the eastern churches believed? Did it mean shaving the front part of the head, as the early Celtic monastic tradition maintained? Or, did it mean shaving only the crown of the head, in allusion to the "crown" of Saint Peter, as the Roman church asserted? As we have already seen, hair could be associated with the sins of lust and vanity, and these were precisely the attachments to the physical body and to sexual desire that the religious were expected to eschew. Because the shaving of the head could also be punitive or curative (especially in regard to insanity), the monk's tonsure marked him as outside secular society, humble, and in some senses emasculated. However, only in the twelfth century did tonsure become a strictly enforced, consistent rule in the Latin church, functioning, in the words of Robert Mills, "First and foremost ... as a badge of male social position ... above all else, clerical status."[38]

Depictions of tonsured clerics abound in western medieval art—the distinctive Roman tonsure marks out the monastic or clerical personage or saint from the laity. In the Carolingian Metz Sacramentary of Charles the Bald, the scene of the emperor's coronation depicts him flanked by a pair of bishops. Both bishops wear the Roman tonsure, a fact highlighted by their gold haloes (Paris, BnF, ms. lat. 1141, fol. 2). In this example, the clerical tonsure helps to establish the social and liturgical roles of various actors in the depicted ritual. Also from the reign of Charles the Bald (a moniker much debated by historians), comes the amusingly alliterative Latin poem by the cleric Hucbald in praise of bald men: "Bless now the bald with bright ballads, oh bards!" he exults, comparing the balding head to a natural tonsure or crown, a visible indication of a man's suitability to the role of ecclesiastical leader or even king.[39]

The practice of tonsure, in the sense of the ritual cutting or shaving of the hair though probably not in terms of the Roman clerical tonsure, also pertained for women taking monastic vows, though perhaps only from the thirteenth century.[40] Probably the most famous example of female tonsure is that of Saint Clare of Assisi. Joan Mueller notes that for a woman to publicly receive tonsure and to put on the garb of a penitent, as Clare did, was one way for her to sidestep familial expectations that she would marry.[41] In a few altarpieces, the episode of Clare's tonsure is shown—as Roberta Milliken points out, the anonymous painter of the thirteenth-century Tavola (Altarpiece) of Saint Clare devotes two out of only eight scenes of Clare's life to hair cutting, first depicting Clare's tonsure and then that of her younger sister, Agnes.[42] Yet artists rarely depicted Clare or any other female monastic saint with a bare head—the veil instead served as the visual sign of female monasticism. Because of the association of female hair with sin, it would seem fitting for nuns to shave their heads or at least crop their hair short, and/or to cover it completely; as Paul (1 Corinthians 11:5–10) instructs, "every woman praying or prophesying with her head not covered, disgraceth her head: for it is all one as if she were shaven. For if a woman be not covered, let her be shorn. But if it be a shame to a woman to be shorn or made bald, let her cover her head," and further along, "therefore ought the woman to have a power over her head" (meaning a veil or covering). The female monastic practice of "taking the veil," probably rooted in ancient Roman rituals associated with marriage and widowhood, is already present in the earliest monastic rules for women, such as that of Caesarius of Arles, from the sixth century, and later medieval depictions of nuns in literature, art, and legal codes all stress the veil as the attribute by which a nun is recognized.[43]

The Cistercian monk Aelred of Rievaulx, writing to an acquaintance of a recent scandal at the nunnery of Watton, tells of a wayward girl, given to the church as a child, now grown to a woman, who carries on a sexual affair with one of the monks charged with the spiritual care of the nuns. Before she is beaten by the senior nuns and locked up in chains, however, Aelred says, "They tore the veil from her head," an act that not only precedes more violent physical abuse but also signals her loss of status as a consecrated bride of God.[44]

When a woman adopted the Roman tonsure, thus arrogating to herself the rights and privileges of the male clergy rather than taking on the properly submissive and chastity-announcing veil of the nun, she transgressed. The story of Saint Eugenia, who disguised herself as a man, became a monk, and then an abbot, is one of the few hagiographic accounts earlier than Clare's that features a woman with a tonsure.[45] Another capital from Vézelay depicts Eugenia tonsured, but ripping open her monastic habit to expose her breasts in the context of defending herself against a false accusation of attempted seduction of one of her monastery's female patrons (Figure I.4). The phenomenon of saintly transvestism, and its more venal and worldly counterpart, runs as a theme through medieval literature, expressive of anxieties about the legibility of bodies and the usurpation of male power by women. John Anson's 1974 study of the hagiographic tradition of female saints who cross-dressed in order to pursue a life of monastic discipline includes the story of Eugenia, along with those of Thecla, who briefly disguised herself as a man in order to travel more safely as a wandering hermit, and Marina, whose father disguised her as a boy when he himself entered a monastery, so as not to be divided from his only child.[46] These women's success in masquerading as men was at least in part successful due to their adoption of male hairstyles; Thecla cuts her long hair short, and Eugenia and Marina both sport the tonsure. However, when the woman's motives were not pure, and she was not a saint, such ruses could be subject to severe and sometimes divine retribution. Jane Tibbetts Schulenburg discusses a woman named Gunda who cut her hair and pretended to be a man in order to test whether the relics of Saint Calais, patron of the abbey of Anisole, would enforce a centuries-old prohibition on women entering the church; they did, and Gunda paid sorely for her transgression with bodily torment and monkish reprobation. Schulenburg goes on to demonstrate that legal codes, too, condemned female-to-male transvestism as disruptive of the order of God's creation, and that despite a few saintly exceptions to the contrary, women who cut their hair to pass themselves off as men were understood as unnatural and depraved.[47] Even Joan of Arc, later revered as a holy heroine, was sent to the stake partly on the basis of her cross-dressing, which included wearing her hair in the fashionable male bowl-cut.[48]

Ironically, though willfully cutting one's hair or shaving one's beard could signify either monastic humility or feminine resistance to the patriarchal order of medieval society, cutting or shaving off the hair of the head could also be a penance imposed on both men and women guilty of crimes or sins. For instance, an Icelandic penitential of the twelfth century mandates that men who have committed incest with relatives of the first or second degree will fast for forty days and then shave their hair.[49] Convicted prostitutes and women found guilty of bawdy behavior could have their heads shaved, according to medieval English law; Ruth Mazo Karras cites the *Liber albus* (The White Book), the first urban common law code, written in the early fifteenth century, in which hair cutting or shaving was just the first step of public humiliation for these women.[50] That both of these humiliating punishments relate to sexual crimes is no coincidence.

FIGURE 1.7 Attributed to the Master of the Codex of Saint George, *Tonsuring an Ordinand*, Stefaneschi Pontifical, Avignon (1320–1330). Paris, BnF ms. lat. 15619, fol. 2r. Photo: BnF.

The ritual of male tonsure, as Robert Mills suggests, may have to some degree signaled the cleric's renunciation of sexual potency, but above all it made physical and visible his spiritual transformation.[51] Depictions and descriptions of the ritual of tonsure are tantalizingly rare, probably because these were simply assumed to be part of the clerical life and not worthy of comment.[52] However, one place the ritual is frequently represented is in pontificals, both as a text and as part of the liturgical script for ordination, as well as in illuminated initials depicting the tonsure as the index image for the whole liturgy. Several late-thirteenth- and fourteenth-century Roman pontificals from Italy and Avignon depict the tonsuring of clerics by the Bishop of Rome himself in the usual spot at the initial of the opening prayer to the sacrament of ordination, *Oremus dilectissimi fratres* (Let Us Pray Dear Brothers); the Master of Saint George depicts the pope using a straight razor to bare the scalp of an ordinand (Figure 1.7), though other artists put a pair of shears in his hands.

Medieval methods of shaving the scalp to achieve tonsure for ordination probably did not differ that radically from modern approaches; if there were specially consecrated scissors or razors for the purpose, they are neither mentioned nor preserved. Frequent references are made in popular history books to the use of "tonsure plates," but it is not only hard to imagine how such an object would be employed if it covered exactly the part of the head that the ordaining priest was meant to shave; it is also unlikely that such objects were ever produced in significant numbers. In fact, almost every source that asserts the use of the tonsure plate refers to a single object now in the British Museum (1916,1106.1). Said to have belonged to the Cathedral of Saint Paul, London, it is cut from a larger copper bowl or basin and engraved with a rampant lion and dates to the twelfth or thirteenth century. Attached to it since at least the sixteenth century is a parchment scrap with an inscription in a fifteenth-century black letter hand, indicating,

"This is the measure and shape of the crown ... used by many venerable fathers, bishops, deacons, and the chapter." However, since pontificals do not depict the use of such an object, and such plates are not mentioned in the liturgies themselves, one suspects that this object was either misconstrued by its fifteenth-century annotator or represents an eccentric custom particular to Saint Paul's.

In contrast, liturgical combs survive in large numbers. Used to purify what hair remained on the head of the ordained priest as he prepared for the Eucharist, these fine-toothed, often double-sided combs, carved from ivory or in the later centuries from boxwood, ensured that stray hairs, or worse, nits or vermin, would not fall on the Host and sully it. They also helped tidy the hair of the cleric after he had donned the liturgical vestments, perhaps in the process disarranging his coiffure. These were personal objects, which is to say, the comb traveled with the priest rather than residing on the altar, but they were still closely linked to the liturgy in the sense that without them, the ritual purification of the clerical body could not be complete. The fact that Saint Cuthbert was buried with his ivory comb at the end of the seventh century ties this object of personal and devotional grooming closely to the body it once worked upon, as its current status as a relic attests. But the combs were not just practical and personal. William Durandus, in his *Rationale divinorum officiorum* (Rationale for the Divine Offices) wrote that the combing of the priest's hair prior to the service symbolizes the removal of worldly and superfluous thoughts.[53]

Like Cuthbert's comb, many medieval liturgical combs that survive do so because of their association with saintly figures; one particularly elegant example with a delicate carving of the Crucifixion, the so-called Heribert Comb (Cologne, Shnütgen-Museum, Inv. Nr. B-100), from late ninth-century Metz might indeed have belonged at some point to the Ottonian Archbishop Heribert, founder of the monastery of Deutz, where it was preserved among his relics. Alternatively, the combs could attach themselves to a saint by way of hagiographic iconography, as in an English example from around 1200 that features scenes of Henry II and Thomas Becket, an apt subject, given the connection between bishops' heads and bishops' combs. On one side of the comb, the murder of Becket includes the detail of a soldier striking a blow to the bishop's neatly coiffed head (Figure 5.7). Such combs, at once liturgical aids, personal grooming objects, and even at times, relics of the men who used them, illustrate the continuity between bodies, gestures, religion, and ritual in the medieval context. Hair in its symbolic and physical aspects alike, as one of the body's most mutable and manipulable features, could not but be open to wide and variable readings within the religious and ritual context.

CHAPTER TWO

Self and Society

HANNA HOPWOOD GRIFFITHS

The language of the self would be stripped of one of its richest resources without hair: and like language, or the faculty of laughter, or the use of tools, the dressing of hair in itself constitutes a mark of the human.[1]
— Marina Warner

Marina Warner's point about the expressive quality of hair speaks to the role hair plays in establishing identities, whether of a social or more personal nature. In the Middle Ages hair is certainly a vibrant signifier, though it is often difficult to separate notions of selfhood from those of social identities because the linking of the two is pervasive. One reason for this might be that a basic tenant of medieval social order and stability involved appearances: it was necessary to be able to look at a person and quickly discern what role he or she played in society as well as the individual's background and standing. Such identification was thought an important way to stave off chaos and danger. These social expectations that dictated how people should look were quite potent, as they were often rooted in a variety of traditions related to gender, class, standings, nationalities, and religious beliefs. Hair plays a formidable role in communicating these identities. Exploring how and what hair expresses about identities reveals it to be a distinctive feature in marking not only memberships in groups, but also the places of individual members within those groups. In this chapter, we will explore the role hair plays in determining the self and the individual's relationship with the wider society by looking at its interpretation in the literature, laws, and iconography of the period.

MALE HAIR AND IDENTITY

Ieuan of the Red-Grey-hair son of Bedo of the Grey-hair son of Gruffudd son of Black-haired Maredudd was a man defined not only by the color of his hair but by that of his father and great-grandfather too.[2] It was this bodily part that was also used to distinguish between his father and his father's brother, as the names Bedo of the Grey-hair and Bedo of the White-hair testify. In a poem by the Siôn Ceri (fl. ca. 1520–ca. 1540) composed at the very beginning of the sixteenth century to this Ieuan, the praiseworthy virtues associated with men during the medieval period are extolled through references to their hair and the hair of their forefathers. The poet closely associates the manliness, leadership, and bravery on the battlefield of the subject with the color of his hair and those of his male relatives:

Maredudd before was a large bodied man,
They went back [i.e. their pedigree went back] to Adda.
A man with a large retinue from the courts
A wild, brave lion, he was grey-haired
Black-haired Maredudd had a great pride
In his lineage, he's growing
Clear black hair, his complexion grey and rosy-cheeked
White and red, you have the same zest
You were a stag, with waxy-hair
(A stag) with a gold tint to its skin and to its hair.[3]

Here we find that the gold tones of Ieuan the Red's hair is in keeping with the society's belief that this was the color of nobility and thus the status of the subject is elevated.[4] In medieval Wales this color was also a symbol for the brave soldier. Furthermore, we discover that if this golden-colored hair was also of fine texture then higher praise would follow and the individual's place within his society would be raised.

Naturally, not all powerful and wealthy men had golden tones in their hair like the aforementioned Ieuan, and thus we find the poets and authors finding ways of associating the ideal masculine virtues of the period with all hair colors. For example, another Welsh poet, Guto'r Glyn, sang in the fifteenth century of how black is a symbol for youth while praising his patron Henry of the Black hair ("*Harri Ddu*"). Here again we note how the color of his hair is inextricably linked to his identity. Guto dedicates a whole poem to the color of his patron's hair, and given that the poet was paid by Harri to sing about him, the idea that he requested a poem about his hair or that the poet decided this was a worthy cause for praise demonstrates how important its role was within society. The poem, known today as "In praise of the black hair of Henry Griffith of Newcourt" and consisting of fifty-six lines, focuses on Harry's virtues as a leader and patron and associates them with his hair color. He is praised among other things for his hospitality and generosity along with his honesty, strength, and bravery:

Greetings, one with a hand like Ifor Hael,
on account of this, to noble Black Harry!
The son of Gruffudd who drives steeds and arms
is my ebony-hued stag.[5]

The poet finds ways of associating all of these ideal qualities with the color black, which according to the poet is the best color for any man's hair. Guto'r Glyn compares the hair's color with other dark, fine things such as velvet, ebony, and silk. The poet even goes as far as to draw a comparison with Jesus, noting how both men share the same hair color, thus further elevating its status.[6]

We find that the colors of the hair of male figures associated with the virtues of the day throughout the medieval tales of the *Mabinogion* where the characters are constantly referred to by their head or facial hair, again demonstrating its importance as a marker of identity. Gwri Gwallt Euryn (Gwri of the Golden Hair) in the *Pedeir Keinc*, for example, is given his name precisely because of his yellow hair.[7] Cynwrig Frychgoch's (Cynwrig the Freckly-Red head) name in *Breudwyt Ronabwy* is inextricably linked with his red hair and freckles, and another hair-related feature, this time the beard, is attached to Rinnon Ri Baruawc (Rinnon Stiff Beard) in *Culhwch and Olwen*.[8] As with the Welsh noblemen, these are all characters (whom we assume to be fictional) whose hair, beard, and hair color are attributed to them in their very name. The same can be found in Irish literature, as William Sayers notes:

> A list could be drawn up from the genealogical, topographical and other lore of the names of individuals that incorporate a reference to hair or beard, e.g., Fiacha Foltsnáithech "thread-hair," Tuirenn Beggrean "short-beard" and Tuathal Máelgarb "rough shorn," Domhnall Dúalbhuidhe "of the yellow locks" or Cathal Caircheach "the tufted" or "hairy."[9]

But hair, and hair alone, is also frequently used to describe and denote nameless characters; indeed, sometimes it is the only thing we learn about them. An example of this can been seen in *Historia Peredur vab Efrawc* (The Story of Peredur son of Efrawc): "And on the shore of the lake there was a grey-haired man sitting on a cushion of brocaded silk and wearing a garment of brocaded silk, and young lads fishing in a small boat on the lake."[10] Throughout the tale, we do not learn of this man's name, he is only referred to as "gwr gwynllwyt" (the white-grey-haired man) and due to the use of the compound adjective "white-grey," we understand that the man is old. The fact that hair alone is used, without any reference to any other physical characteristics, demonstrates its significance as a signifier of cultural codes and meanings, both as a marker of society's unwritten language and as a bodily part loaded with meaning, inextricably linked to the individual. The fact that the color of the hair is often used as a surname for the Welsh noblemen demonstrates how it was an integral part of defining the "self."

If hair was used consciously by the society in Wales in order to distinguish and rank male individuals, we find that in the wider medieval community it was also, perhaps subconsciously, the marker of a shared relationship between groups of people. It has often been remarked how one of the most important functions of hair styling in medieval society was that it was used to differentiate between ethnic tribes. For example, the Germanic Suevi's knotted hair was described by Tacitus as the "mark of that people" (*insigne gentis*), and it has been widely discussed how hair was the marker of distinction between the short-haired and clean-shaven Normans and the longer-haired, bearded Anglo Saxons.[11] Robert Bartlett notes how this bodily part played a particularly important role in areas where different populations "lived side by side" and draws attention to the situation in Ireland in the twelfth and thirteenth centuries where different hairstyles distinguished "the king's loyal subjects" from "the wild Irish."[12] He notes how some of the English adopted the Irish hairstyles, so much so that in 1297 laws were passed that condemned:

> the degenerate English of modern times who wear Irish clothes, have their heads half shaved and grow their hair long at the back, calling this *culan* [a word derived from *cul*, the back of the head], making themselves like the Irish in clothing and appearance.[13]

The reason behind this legislation was that Englishmen who grew their hair in the same style as Irishmen were being mistaken for the Irish and were subsequently being killed as Irishmen (for let us not forget that the killing of an Englishman and the killing of an Irishman led to different punishments).[14] On the other hand, when an Irishman was permitted the status to live under English law, his hair was used as a visible marker of this change.[15] This use of hair as a symbolic marker of status and social belonging is used in Irish literature too. In the old Irish epic *Táin bó Cúailnge* (The Cattle Raid of Cooley), for example, when the forces of Cormac Conn Longas advance in three troops, they are described and differentiated by their hair. The first is described as "fortíi berrtha foraib" (shorn hair); the second as "moṅga tara cenna síar" (long hair hanging down behind), and the third as "berrtha slechtai co guaille" (hair trimmed to shoulder-length).[16]

Martha Easton in her chapter "Gender and Sexuality" (Chapter Six) discusses how numerous societies shared the belief that long hair for the male figures equaled nobility, ferocity, and virility and draws upon the example of the Merovingians who were defined by their hair and widely referred to as "the long haired kings."[17] On the other hand, cropped or shaved hair was often associated with servants and peasants. Returning to medieval Ireland, for example, we find that those following a saint would use the word "mael" (cropped one) before the saint's personal name in order to demonstrate their faithfulness.[18] Whatever the style, length, or color, we find that the way in which hair was dressed signified identity and place within society.

MEN'S BODILY HAIR AND THE BEARD

Not only did the medieval society load the hair of the head with cultural meanings but it also placed a great emphasis on men's bodily hair. Again the law books can aid us in demonstrating its significance. The thirteenth-century law book the *Sachsenspiegel*, for example, explains how having pubic hair and hair under the arms as well as sporting the most visible hairy feature, the beard, would be a clear indicator that a boy has become of age.[19] Similarly, the Welsh medieval laws (also dating from the middle decades of the thirteenth century) interpret this hairy feature as a symbol for maturity, stating that when a man's facial hair grows, it is possible to make him a magistrate on account of the growth of his beard. Once more we find society associating virtuous masculine qualities specifically with hair: "For it is then that he will have a beard and that his discretion will be steady, and that it will be fair for him to judge everybody in general, both the old persons and the young ones."[20] Being beardless, therefore, would attract mockery and we find the social effects of not possessing facial hair when Cú Chulainn in the medieval Irish epic is said to be unfit to be called a warrior due to his lack of facial hair.[21] Cú Chulainn thus paints his face with berry juice and places grass onto it in order to make the Connachtmen think that he has a beard.[22]

Not only were the beard and bodily hair a sign of adulthood and sagacity, they were a potent symbol of a man's virility. Turning to the laws, again we see that wishing a blemish on the beard of one's husband is listed among the three offenses a wife could commit that would allow her husband to beat her. Society equated casting aspersions on her husband's beard to satirizing his sexual abilities and manhood: "These are the three for which he is entitled to beat her: for giving away a thing which she is not entitled to give; and for her being found with a man under deception; and for wishing a blemish on his beard."[23] Furthermore, the interjections found in the literature when the characters express shame or shock are also telling of society's high regard for the beard. In the second branch of the *Mabinogi*, for example, Heilyn expresses, "Meuyl ar uy maryf i" ("Shame upon my beard") and Peredur in his tale also states, "Meuyl ar varyf vym porthawr" ("Shame on my porter's beard").[24]

Anglo-Saxon society also placed a great amount of significance on the beard as a symbol of a man's honor and pride. This symbolic feature of the body here again is portrayed as the visual carrier of the society's morals and virtues as we learn that grabbing or holding the beard was understood as a testament of honesty. Dating from sometime between the thirteenth and the fifteenth centuries, the *Chronicle of Evesham Abbey* relates the tale

FIGURE 2.1 Pulling hair, an insult or injury for which compensation was due in Cyfraith Hywel Dda, detail. Peniarth MS 28, fol. 15v. Courtesy of Llyfrgell Genedlaethol Cymru/The National Library of Wales.

of a peasant who grabbed his beard while swearing a false oath. This in turn caused his beard to fall off:

> The countryman was an elderly man, who had a very long beard. He stood up, laid his cloak down on the ground, and grasped his beard with his hand, saying, "I swear by this beard of mine, I will remove the saint, because it is my land, and I will possess it by right of inheritance." ... Scarcely had these words been uttered, when, see! he [sic] pulled out his own beard so that it fell to the ground as if it belonged there, and had not grown naturally.[25]

If grabbing one's own beard was a pledge of sincerity, we find that grabbing another man's beard or hair was extremely offensive (Figure 2.1). One of Aethelberht's laws, for example, notes that "for seizing a man by the hair, 50 sceattas shall be paid as compensation."[26] Cutting or pulling another man's hair was also seen as a serious insult. The *Hywel Dda* laws explain the details of the punishments for a hair-related offense: "The value of hair uprooted, a penny for every finger which grasps it to pull it out, and two pence for the thumb."[27] In Alfred's laws, the compensation for the cutting of the hair is higher than compensation for damage to other parts of the body such as wounds an inch long on the skull or the loss of the little finger. Cutting a man's beard was worth twice the compensation given to the cutting of hair. It seemed that the social effects of being seen without a beard were worse than receiving life-threatening injuries.[28] Furthermore, we find the importance society placed on this body part by turning once again to the poems commissioned by the gentry. There, poems to facial hair formed their own unique corpus as a subgenre within the formal medieval Welsh praise poetry. This group consist of five poems, four in which the poets themselves sing of their own beards and one where a patron's beard is being praised. The poem to Owain ap Maredudd's beard by the late fourteenth-century poet Gruffudd Llwyd recalls a popular medieval tale where society's attitudes toward beards are expressed. The twelfth-century tale involving King Arthur, the giant Rhita, and beards found in *Historia regum Britanniae* and *Brut Dingestow*, explains how the giant Rhita sent a message to Arthur requesting him to shave his beard and send it to him, which would acknowledge that Arthur is willing to accept the giant's supremacy.[29] We learn that Rhita's aim is to make a cloak from his collection of the beards of rulers that he has killed or emasculated by shaving their faces.[30] Given the important symbolic nature of the beard, the medieval audience would understand that if Arthur were to become clean-shaven and send his hair to the giant, he would have lost his own manliness and power and added to the giant's virility.[31]

CUTTING AND SHAVING MEN'S HAIR

If shaving someone's head or beard without their permission was a punishable or humiliating offense, we find that numerous societies across Europe gave the cutting of hair the opposite symbolism in that it was seen as a rite of passage for men, where a special relationship was developed between the person whose hair was being cut and the person chosen to cut it. The Franks, for example, considered the role of the senior figure cutting the boy's hair similar to that of the adoptive father or guardian.[32] In the ninth-century *Historia Brittonum* this hair-cutting ritual is used both as a signifier of acceptance and as an opportunity to shame. Here, Guorthegirn has fathered a son of his own daughter, and the boy is placed in the care of St Germanus:

> "I [Germanus] will be a father to thee, and I will not let thee go until there be given to me a razor with scissors and a comb, and it is permitted to thee to give these to thy carnal father." And thus it was done. And the child obeyed Germanus, and went to his grandfather—that is his carnal father—Guorthegirn, and the boy said to him, "Thou art my father, shear my head and comb my hair." And he was ashamed and remained silent, and would not reply to the child, but rose up, and was very angry.[33]

The same social idea is to be found in another Arthurian legend, in the already-mentioned tale of *Culhwch and Olwen*. In order to be successful in the quest for the love of his life, Olwen, Culhwch's father advises him to go to Arthur's court and ask for a haircut as his gift. Arthur receives Culhwch and agrees to the request. The significance of the ritual is emphasized through the tools that Arthur uses, namely a gold comb and a scissors with silver handles: "Arthur took a golden comb, and shears with loops of silver, and combed his hair, and asked who he was. Arthur said, 'My heart warms towards you. I know you are of my blood.'"[34] Furthermore, in order for Culhwch and Olwen to marry, her father (Ysbaddaden the Chief Giant) demands that Culhwch complete forty progressively more challenging tasks, culminating in the shaving of Ysbaddaden's beard. So powerful was this part of the body that the removal of this highly symbolic feature would be the equivalent of killing him, leaving Culhwch free to marry Olwen.

Thus far we have been able to piece together parts of the picture that demonstrate how men created an image of the self through the value and importance placed on hair within the societies of the Middle Ages. Though varying styles (short, shaven, bearded) were used as signposts to demonstrate different values within ethnic groups or societies, there was a shared understanding of hair's importance, and it was used as a signifier of meanings. Not only did it play a part in the individual identities of the male figures, but it was equally important as a visible emblem of the social group, religion, or ethnic tribe that they belonged to, as well as being a marker of status. Hair was inscribed with meaning and so conscious decisions were made by those men on the style of their hair, thus showing where, and to whom, they belonged. Furthermore, the fact that hair color or style was at times attached to their very names in some areas makes it possible to argue that they were able to identify the "self" through the rules created by society.

WOMEN'S HAIR AND IDENTITY

The story of the relationship between hair, self, and society for the women of the Middle Ages is both similar and different. In the predominantly androcentric societies of the time, it was particularly important for a woman to follow the social codes and traditions of her culture, as the conventions involving hair were inextricably linked to a woman's identity. Long, free-flowing hair was the symbolic marker of maidenhood and virginity and, therefore, a woman's sexual availability. Thus, it could be seen as a marker of youth. However, because of its sexual connotations, visible long hair could simultaneously also distinguish the temptress or other "fallen" women. Throughout the Middle Ages, such unruly women typically tend to be portrayed with visibly long hair. With this we find one of the dualities in the symbolic code bestowed on women's hair: on the one hand, this style was a marker of virginity and innocence, but on the other, it was the bodily part most frequently associated with women who were believed not to control their sexual drives and instincts. These understandings are perhaps the reason nuns and married women (and thus sexually unavailable women) wore their hair bound and out of sight and tamed, for their controlled locks functioned as an indicator of their good and faithful nature. In short, how women dressed and displayed their hair was an efficient, visible way of demonstrating how they interacted with society's value system, how they either conformed to or disobeyed this system. Changing their hairstyle thus could demonstrate shifts in social status.

One of the most significant changes for women was the transformation from maiden to wife as a result of marriage. This transition was marked by the symbolic role of the veil and through the covering of hair, the part of the body that signaled a woman's virginity and sexual availability. Molly Myerowitz Levine in her work on the history of the marriage rituals of the Jews, Greeks, and Romans explains how the covering of hair is inextricably linked to the change in a woman's status: "Roman marriage ceremonies also seem to privilege head covering. Indeed, the Latin word *numbere* 'to marry' literally means 'to veil oneself,' and according to the *Oxford Latin Dictionary* (s.v. *nubo*) is probably cognate with *nubes* (cloud). For a woman to become married (*nubere*) is for her ritually to cover/cloud her head."[35] The married woman thus wore her hair bound and covered to signify visually her marital status.

Another remarkable change for women happened on the other end of marriage when a woman's husband died, and she then went from married woman to widow. Bartlett, for example, states that the letting down of hair "was a form of mourning exclusively the preserve of wives and widows" and goes on to explain that when married women let their hair down, they expressed a suspension of the normal social code, and this transgression he finds deliberate.[36] Not only did the letting down of the hair signify that they were "unloosing bonds, both physically and metaphorically," but it also demonstrated how they were behaving inappropriately, since "long flowing hair was a sign of maidenhood."[37] For an example of a widow as described by Bartlett above, we are able to turn to the medieval tale *Owein*. Here a woman in mourning finds herself in great distress after the loss of her husband. Her fingers are described as almost falling off, and her torn clothes show signs of extreme grief, and in line with Bartlett's analysis, the grieving woman wears her hair loose:

> And following that crowd he could see a lady, her yellow hair let down over her shoulders and covered with the blood of many wounds, and she was wearing a dress of yellow brocaded silk, which was torn, and boots of speckled leather on her feet. And it was surprising that the tips of her fingers were not worn away, so violently did she wring her hands together.[38]

Widowhood also tended to mark a woman's transition from being fertile to passing childbearing age and into old age. As her hair symbolized her fertility, this usually meant that she was more covered, as Margaret Scott explains:

> A widow's clothing, like that of a nun, was meant to indicate that its wearer was in effect dead to the world, with the shrouding of the head and neck in veils, and the dull (but not necessarily black) colouring of the rest of the clothing.[39]

How a woman dressed her hair thus played an essential role in establishing and communicating her social status. Beauty also played a significant role in the formation of

FIGURE 2.2 Alexander the Great and his wife, detail, an example of the complex plaits of the period in Brwydrau Alecsander Fawr. Peniarth MS 481D, fol. 61v. Courtesy of Llyfrgell Genedlaethol Cymru/The National Library of Wales.

a woman's identity and social status, as the beautiful woman was celebrated as a source of inspiration, longing, and reverence in medieval culture. Consequently, the beautiful woman enjoyed a place of privilege, and the part of the body that was most typically associated with her beauty was her long—preferably blonde—hair. An indication of how society valued women for their beauty, and how their beauty was measured by the loveliness of their hair, is an idea regularly expressed in medieval literature across Europe. Christine de Pisan, for example, in the early fifteenth-century conduct book *The Treasure of the City of the Ladies* draws attention to this when she states, "There is nothing in the world lovelier on a woman's head than beautiful blond hair."[40] Special attention is drawn, for example, to Emelye's long blonde hair in Geoffrey Chaucer's *The Knight's Tale* which stands out in the description of her beauty: "Her yellow hair was braided in a tress / Behind her back, a yard long, I guess."[41] Olwen's blonde tresses are praised too in *Culhwch and Olwen* where she is presented as the image of beauty (Figure 2.2): "She was sent for. And she comes—with a robe of flame-red silk about her, and a torque of red gold about the maiden's neck, with precious pearls and red jewels. Yellower was her hair than the flowers of the broom."[42]

In these examples and others, we find that when praising a woman's beauty poets and authors alike often followed a pattern that gave primacy to her hair in that they opened their descriptions with it and then worked their way down the body. We know, for example, that Matthew of Vendôme in his twelfth-century guidebook for writers championed this technique as the favored way to go about praising the beauty of a desired woman.[43] In Wales the importance of this part of the body is amplified even more as it becomes the sole focus of poems numerous enough to form another subgenre of their own. Having lavished so much attention on the first part, the hair, did the poets opt to allow the hair to become representative of the perfection and beauty of the whole body? Hair, after all, offers many possibilities to demonstrate innovation and creativity, and it is significant that no poems to any other singular part of the female body have survived. These poems are categorized as "Love Poems" or *Canu Serch* and are set apart from the more formal "Praise Poetry" (*Canu Mawl*) where money was exchanged for the poetry. It is also noteworthy in the "love" genre we find exuberant praising of hair combined with the poet's expression of his sexual desire toward the subject of the poem who is often unnamed. The most famous poem of this kind is by Dafydd Nanmor to a named Llio, where the poet revels in the red-gold color of her tresses as well as the length and texture of the hair. In this poem we find the tension between praising the long hair as a symbol of a woman's beauty (and thus her sexuality) while also attempting to tell us that Llio's hair is in line with the society's beliefs about how a "respectable" woman should keep her hair as he describes how it is placed within and covered by a *moled* (hood). Drawing inspiration from the surrounding natural landscape, he explains that the hood hides hair of the same color as the stone in Llŷn (Figure 2.3), known locally to this day as Llio's Stone (*Maen Llio*). The context of this particular image is as relevant today as it was six hundred years ago; the geographical characteristic has remained unchanged and the stone still stands glistening in yellow hues. The gold hidden in the crevices of the stone is just as the hair hidden under a headdress, or the strands of gold needlework glistening in it. The stone's shape could also be interpreted as that of a headdress.[44]

Interestingly, unlike the male patrons who requested poems of praise to their beards or whose poets decided to praise the colors of their hair within the formal praise poetry in exchange for money, we find that when it came to praising women within the formal poetry, the poets stay away from any mention of the hair on their heads, focusing instead

FIGURE 2.3 Llio's Stone in Penllyn, Wales. Courtesy of Tudur Dylan Jones.

on their other virtues such as their ability to host feasts and converse properly as well as their virginity, purity, and devoutness. In terms of their subjects' beauty, their pale complexions are typically noted while the only hair mentioned is that of their delicately arched eyebrows. We must consider that not mentioning the head hair is a deliberate omission, perhaps due in part to its sexual significance.

Sexual appetite, idleness, and vanity were all associated with the image of women paying attention to their long, long, blonde, beautiful hair. When Geoffrey de la Tour Landry gives advice to his daughters in *The Book of the Knight of La Tour Landry*, eager to express the dangers of idleness, lust, and vanity, he too gives hair some prominence. He relates the story of a woman who made the other parishioners of the church wait for her while she finished combing her long locks. They curse her in anger until suddenly the devil appears in her hand mirror, and instead of seeing the reflection of her beautiful tresses, she is confronted with the devil's backside. This association of hair, lust, and vanity warned women to be careful of such practices, as they could jeopardize not only their social standing but their fate in the afterlife.[45]

The many mermaid tales of the period also testify to this idea.[46] Not only are the long, flowing tresses of mermaids a consistent feature of these lust-filled, feminine creatures and a cause for concern and caution, but their very dwelling place, the sea, evokes similar feelings of uncertainty and danger, as Meri Lao explains:

> Water has a dual action. It can be a blessing as it slakes the thirst of man [sic], irrigates the earth, and becomes a source of life and abundance, the primordial soup; it represents purification, regeneration, and perpetuity. However, it can also be destructive, causing inundation, shipwreck, drowning and annihilation.[47]

SELF AND SOCIETY

Brunetto Latini's thirteenth-century *The Book of the Treasure* compares mermaids to prostitutes and explains that they "remain in the water because lust was made of moisture."[48] If we remember how women were believed to be cold and moist beings and thus in a consistent state of need, associating them with this kind of temptress who lived in the water would be a convenient way to emphasize further the problematic nature not only of mermaids but women's general potential for it as well.[49] *Mari-morgan*, the Breton mermaid, and the mermaids of the Isle of Man, *Ben-Varrey*, are characteristic of the kind of mermaid that tempts sailors to the bottom of the ocean with their beauty. Significantly, the seduction repeatedly takes place when the men see the mermaids combing their long hair while gazing into a mirror, and it is telling that numerous medieval church carvings and illustrations (Figure 2.4) depict a mermaid holding these objects, serving not only as a warning against the fate of falling into temptation but also as a reinforcement of the ideas associated with the many images of Lust where the same tools were used.[50]

By extension, the comb and mirror, the same tools used to convey messages about idleness and vanity, were also symbolic gestures of love and a man's desire for the beauty of a woman (Figure 4.2). Women were taught that being desired by a man was the key to her worthiness, as the early thirteenth-century German didactic poem where a mother relates advices to her daughter testifies: "If men often think of you and desire you, then you are worthy."[51] We find that women again faced a difficult code to decipher: they were supposed to be admired and valued by men on account of their beautiful, long hair, but there was also a tension between making well-groomed hair a symbol of beauty and making the grooming itself a symbol of vanity, idleness, and other vices.

FIGURE 2.4 Mermaid with comb and mirror. Oxford, Bodleian Library, MS Douce 62, fol. 51r.

CUTTING OR SHAVING WOMEN'S HAIR

A further indication of how hair was associated with a woman's sexuality is in its use in many of the punishments for adultery and other sexual offenses. Given the importance placed on a woman's locks, it is easy to see how losing the tresses would dramatically change a woman's status. With a single snip of the scissors, a woman's life could be transformed from being held in esteem to falling to the bottom of the social pyramid on account of social humiliations. Shulamith Shahar gives an example from the laws of London where the hair of women who had committed adultery was shaved before they were "forced to walk through the streets of the city led by a band of musicians to the other side of London where they were incarcerated in another gaol."[52] Similarly, throughout the Middle Ages, the prostitute who violated the rules of her trade would also risk having her locks cut off.[53] Not only was she cast out of society but she was also marked as one who had transgressed for as long as it would take for her locks to regrow. As Roberta Milliken notes,

> Considering how essential a woman's long hair was to her identity as a woman, having a shorn head during these times would be nothing short of traumatic ... Moreover, by having shorn locks, she is forced to "wear" her punishment for quite some time. The punishment transforms her visibly into an oddity that, in turn, would lead to further social marginalization. This attests again to how socially serious her transgressions were considered.[54]

Geoffrey de la Tour Landry, already alluded to, also associates hair with punishment as he recalls a tale where a holy hermit shares his visions of the fate of his nephew's vain wives after their deaths. His third wife, who had paid too much attention to her hair, is made to suffer by being punished by the devil as he, "held her by the tresses of the hair of her head."[55] Roberta Milliken in her Introduction to this volume demonstrated yet another example of how hair is used to mark women's sexual transgressions and how cutting the hair was a punishment for sexual "crimes" by drawing upon an image from the *Sachsenspiegel* of a pregnant woman who has been found guilty of illicit sexual liaison and is thus receiving the "hide and hair" punishment, which meant being beaten with rods while having her hair cut off (Figure I.8). In striking contrast then to the significance given to a boy's first haircut and the symbolic relationship established during that ritual, a secular girl or woman would generally avoid cutting her hair, as doing so might compromise both her beauty and her status.

On the other hand, as Martha Easton demonstrates in her chapter on "Gender and Sexuality" when discussing Saint Clare, cutting or shaving the hair was to some extent something women could control and thus demonstrate an element of the "self." For a woman to purposefully shave her own hair would be a clear indicator that she has eschewed the typical social rules pertaining specifically to her as a woman. This manipulation of hair in the assertion of self-agency is a common theme in numerous saints' lives. According to these holy biographies, one method young saints employed to follow their desired religious vocations instead of becoming wives or lovers was to cut or shave their own hair so that they would be undesirable and unattractive to their would-be suitors. Raymond of Cupa in his fourteenth-century *Life of Saint Catherine of Siena* provides one of many examples that relates a story of a local priest advising the saint to cut off her long, blonde hair if she wishes to remain a virgin and become a nun. She in turn "cut[s] her hair off to the roots, hating it as the cause of her grievous sin."[56] Religious women would also often cut their hair in order to mark their transition to a holy life. Indeed, this tradition was probably behind both the priest's advice to Catherine as well as her willingness to follow it. In removing their long locks, initiates to holy orders were demonstrating their abandonment of all worldly cares and ties—namely those of wife and mother. The different appearance of the religious woman in the form of both her cropped hair and her veiled habit marked her transformation to this special status.

When turning to the visual depiction of such holy models of the period, however, we find that we do not often see youthful female saints portrayed as women with shorn locks, neither do we always find them with their hair covered. What we are presented with time and again is the image of the holy woman with the very same hair as that of the worldly, beautiful woman, that is, long, blonde, and uncovered locks (Figure 2.5). We have already learned from Martha Easton's chapter of the tension that existed between blonde hair signaling goodness and virtue and blonde hair as a symbol of beauty and feminine attractiveness and the sexual connotations that symbolism carried. It is thus interesting that the "best of the virgins," the Virgin Mary, is often portrayed with her long, blonde tresses partially visible or fully on display.[57] Roberta Milliken noticed that those moments in which she is most often portrayed in this way are the assumption, the nativity, and in portraits of the mother and child. Displaying Mary's hair at these key moments signals and reinforces its connection to virginity and fertility.[58] It seems that the medieval audience was able to separate the image of the Virgin Mary's hair from the potential negative connotations associated with long, blonde hair and that this was due to the constant emphasis that the

FIGURE 2.5 The Bedford Master, *The Annunciation* (ca. 1440–1450). Paris. Courtesy of the Getty's Open Content Program.

Virgin Mary was different. As Marine Warner explained she was "alone of all her sex."[59] Though it seemed imperative that the Virgin Mary was portrayed as the most beautiful woman in the world, we must also remember that it was during the Middle Ages that the idea of Mary being so uniquely pure as to not have the stain of original sin is formulated.[60] Her virginal status then was as preeminent as her beauty. She was praised for being faultless and "pregnant without disease" and for her "chaste blood."[61]

WOMEN'S HEAD COVERINGS

The ordinary medieval woman could not expect to achieve this state of being able to fuse the boundaries and mixing the messages that hair carried. Thus, as already mentioned, covering the hair became the expected staple of the married, faithful, sexually unavailable, and sexually contained woman. Throughout the Middle Ages, head coverings became a piece of clothing of utmost importance; they hid a woman's hair and thus protected her social identity and status. Not only did the headdress signal her adherence to prescribed cultural mores but it also served to mark her status and her wealth and, therefore, her place within society. Sumptuary legislation, those laws established to regulate luxury and dress, might have been formulated to protect the noble ranks, but it also helped to codify the different classes. The *Welsh Law of Women*, for example, states what type of headdress each woman within the society's ranks should wear. According to the legislation, there are three classes of women: the wife of the king, the wife of the nobleman, and the wife of a peasant. According to the text, a noble woman is allowed to give without the permission of her husband "Her mantel and her shift and her headkerchief and her food and her drink and the store of her larder, and can lend all of her equipment."[62] However, the wife of a villain could not "Give away anything save her headcloth, nor lend anything save her sieve, and that only so that her call from the dunghill to bring it back can be heard."[63] The headcloth was similar to a bonnet that would signify a woman who was working. It was a practical piece of clothing, used to keep hair away from the face while the headkerchief of the noblewoman was a piece of clothing made of fine material, reserved for the elite. Turning to the iconography of the country, we find that stained glass windows and tombstones often depict the noblewomen in this kind of plain headdress. The fact that it remains undecorated is a symbol of their humility at the same time as its material signified their wealth. Prostitutes were thus banned from wearing this symbolic piece of clothing; they did not belong to the higher echelons of society, and it was unacceptable for such women to act as though they deserved to be perceived as having the "good" qualities attached to it. For example,

> In Arles in the later years of the twelfth century, any respectful woman who saw a prostitute wearing a veil could, and in theory was obliged to, rip it off ... In Dijon as late as the middle of the fifteenth century, taking off a woman's headdress was equivalent to accusing her of prostitution or debauchery.[64]

Although the use of head coverings or headdresses can be viewed as an attempt by society to control women, the opportunity to accessorize and embellish them was also present, and as Laura Diener discusses in the next chapter, women who had the financial means to do so took advantage of this. Thus it could be argued that such a woman was able to use the covering of her hair to demonstrate a hint of personality, an element of the self. The fourteenth and fifteenth centuries saw a great increase in

SELF AND SOCIETY 51

the range of headdresses as they became a fashion staple, a decorative symbol of status that signified wealth. Women attached precious jewels, pearls, and gemstones to their headdresses, and fine needlework was used as decoration, all of which would draw attention to this highly symbolic piece of clothing (Figure 2.6). The fifteenth century saw the rise of the kind of headdress known as the hennin, where a cylinder-shaped cone was placed far back on the head with a translucent veil placed over it. It was during this period, too, that noble women plucked their hair to ensure a wide and plain forehead and thus hardly any hair at all was visible (see Figures 3.4, 4.7, 6.12, and 8.5).

Yet even the woman with her fashionable headdress intact and hardly any hair at all visible, did not escape such censure. There was a fine line between what was acceptable and what would once again draw criticism. We find that for churchmen and other moralists, the time and attention women gave to such adornment were akin to those vain, idle, and dangerous practices to which women were commonly thought to be most susceptible. In the thirteenth century, for example, Étienne de Bourbon commented that "Women who decorate their hair show themselves venal: these are the signs of lightness and whoredom."[65] As fashionable practices grew, what followed was a deep feeling of worry especially among church officials who saw the decorated headdress in the same light as hair itself. Head coverings came to further represent the tension of demonstrating wealth, a noble upbringing and beauty on the one hand, and virginity, modesty, and humility on the other. There was no easy way for the medieval woman to navigate all of the rules placed upon her by her society, for the risks of social demotion seem inherent in any of the manipulations of conventions.

FIGURE 2.6 The elaborate hairstyles of the fifteenth century in Brwydrau Alecsander Fawr, detail. Peniarth MS 481D, fol. 66v. Courtesy of Llyfgell Genedlaethol Cymru/The National Library of Wales.

CONCLUSION

To what degree was it thus possible to distinguish the "self" from the "society" when it came to the dressing of hair? Were both elements inextricably linked? Throughout this chapter we have found that though gender distinctions played a large role in answering these questions, both men and women were faced with the same pervasive elements in their culture that defined who or what they could be. Class, age, social rituals, religious dogma, and traditional understandings of the roles of men and women all helped to steer people to fundamental understandings of how they were to act and what their capabilities were. Appearances played a large role in communicating these identities, and in this we see hair playing a formidable role. We have seen how hairstyles and beards helped men to demonstrate their identity in terms of their political allegiances, religious beliefs, and status within the social pyramid. Communities even legislated certain aspects of hair-care practices in order to strengthen and perpetuate traditions. We have also noted what the communities of the Middle Ages taught women about paying attention to their hair by restraining, adorning, displaying, and covering it so that it too would communicate their role and rank in the stratified cultures, though because they were women we note that their very basic social identities tended to revolve much more around their relationship to men as maidens, wives, and widows. It was by and large only the exceptional woman who would escape these roles and hence crop her long hair to become a nun. Publicly cutting a woman's hair, shaving her head, and exposing her tresses as a means of punishing women also helped to strengthen these views of women. However, in recognizing the variety of ways society helped to shape people's perceptions of others and potentially themselves, it is also important to acknowledge how difficult it is for anyone, let alone a person in medieval Europe, to disassociate "self" and "society." How did medieval men and women think of individuality? Was it something important to them? The growing opportunities afforded by fashion for self-expression through the manipulation of one's appearance—especially one's hair—as well as the persistent challenges to the existing cultural mores would seem to suggest that the medieval population was indeed interested in developing more authentic expressions of self. It is fascinating to see how resourcefully medieval people made use of their hair, what Marina Warner rightly calls one of the "richest resources" in "the language of the self."[66]

CHAPTER THREE

Fashion and Adornment

LAURA MICHELE DIENER

Every medieval person dressed themselves in clothing appropriate for their status, gender, and religion.[1] While doing so, they took into consideration the weather, the environment, and the events of the upcoming day. Was it a holiday or a work day? Were they going to hunt, farm, or go to church? Additionally, of course, everyone was constrained by the availability of items in their village, city, or country, not to mention their own finances and resources. The more wealth and leisure time available, the more people could enhance their dress with adornments designed for aesthetic pleasure rather than practical necessity. But regardless of whether someone was rich or poor, a peasant or an archbishop, they had to participate in the act of getting dressed. As sociologist Joanne Entwistle puts it, "the individual and very personal act of getting dressed is an act of preparing the body for the social world, making it appropriate, acceptable, indeed respectable and possibly even desirable also."[2] The same principles apply to headdresses, hair accessories, and hair arranging. Every medieval person needed to "dress" his or her hair, that is, in Entwistle's language, to make it appropriate, acceptable, respectable, and possibly desirable according to a variety of determinants. On the other hand, not all medieval people were able to or indeed wanted to adorn their hair. Only men and women with wealth could afford to invest in decorative hairpieces or spend their time braiding, curling, and barbering their hair. Some of the more elaborate styles required the help of a servant or a professional to achieve, which also required money or status to obtain. The type of adornment anyone would choose for his or her hair varied according to cultural determinations of beauty, and medieval Europeans existed in a milieu of multiple cultures. How an Arab woman in Spain adorned her hair might differ considerably from the beauty practices of a Norwegian woman. And monastic men and women, for instance, eschewed adornment of any kind.

Fashion is a form of both dress and adornment, but one that requires constant change. In the twelfth century, before medieval people spoke of fashion, they spoke admiringly of novelty.[3] For something to be in fashion, something else must be out of fashion, and thus fashion can only exist in an economically diverse environment where multiple consumer goods are available. While some scholars argue that fashion is directly tied to modernity and industrialization, others agree that it is possible to trace changing silhouettes of hair and dress among the nobility, wealthy merchants, and professionals by the later Middle Ages.[4] For the purposes of this chapter, I am defining fashion both as the styles of hair arrangement that medieval people adopted and as the concept of a changing visual ideal for hair sought after by the wealthy.

Between the twelfth and the fourteenth centuries, historians can detect the multiple social and cultural factors converging to create situations that fostered change and excess in personal dress. The Crusades brought an influx of exotic dyes, fabrics, and styles into northern Europe; the rise of cities provided centers for acquiring products and services that could enhance visual appearance; and a more diversified economy led to greater numbers of people possessing expendable income. Costume historian James Laver dates the concept of fashion to the fourteenth century, as new forms and shapes abounded in male and female dress.[5] Daniel Delis Hill agrees, tying the origins of fashion to the rise of an urban middle class of merchants and craftspeople, who possessed the money to imitate the clothing of the nobility. The nobility, in turn, attempted to maintain their elite status visually, and the various groups began an unstoppable cycle of imitation and distinction. Ecclesiastical and secular authorities participated in this cycle by preaching against consumption and enacting legislation to regulate luxury, known as sumptuary laws.[6]

Of course, fashion exists for all sorts of material objects in addition to dress, including furniture, buildings, and decorations. In this chapter, however, I will focus on the way it played out in the arrangement of hair and the associated veils, ribbons, hats, and other accessories. But I will also consider the wider concepts of dress and adornment, as even before concepts of changing fashion existed, people still needed to contain and clean their hair in ways that were considered practical, attractive, and in keeping with social and religious precepts.

This discussion considers dress, fashion, and adornment for both male and female hair and acknowledges that the extent to which women and men could alter their hair depended on gender restrictions. Women, regardless of social status, wore their hair long throughout the entire medieval period. Only women taking monastic vows would cut their hair. When fashions for women changed, they involved different ways to shape the long hair, as opposed to cutting it to different lengths. Depending on region, social status, religious affiliation, time period, and even personal preference, men could wear their hair and their beards long or short, shave their faces, their necks, and their mustaches, although their hair never dipped too far below their shoulders, indicating that certain cultural rules existed that prohibited men from looking too feminine. When male hairstyles grew longer, clergymen certainly complained.

For women, standards of modesty also acted as a determinant in hairstyles. Beginning in the early days of Christianity, Paul had sternly advised women to cover their hair. Early Church Fathers such as Tertullian and Jerome cautioned women about the sexual potency of their hair, warning them to keep it hidden from the gaze of men.[7] During the Middle Ages, women usually wore some form of headdress, although it varied from a full covering to a mere symbol. Covered hair also signaled marital status. Particularly in literature, long loose hair was usually the prerogative of maidens. Since hair could signify sexuality as well as youth, married women needed to contain their hair for all men but their husband. Uncovered hair could indicate availability for unmarried virgins, although sermons and conduct books warned girls of the perils of being too available. Female bodies were contested areas, sites of potential holiness, but also temptations to lust. In many ways, female hair was no different. It could be the shining crown of a perpetual virgin or the net that ensnared men into sin.

The sources used in this discussion include literary and artistic images, and thus they are heavily skewed on behalf of the wealthy. Not only were they the ones with the income and the leisure time to experiment with hair accessories and styling techniques, but they

FASHION AND ADORNMENT 55

also commissioned artwork and feature in the majority of medieval images. Peasants are occasionally portrayed in manuscript illuminations and paintings, but never as the patrons, so it is difficult to know if they are idealized or stock images or realistic depictions.

The illuminated manuscript illustrations, tomb effigies, portrait paintings, and other sources represent how those in power wished themselves and their family members to be remembered. The artistic depictions we have are, therefore, often idealized images as opposed to snapshots of everyday reality. Much of the artwork was commissioned by patrons who of course wanted to see themselves portrayed at their absolute best. We don't have the luxury of seeing photos of people as they wore their hair every day. We also only have access to the finished product, for the most part, as opposed to the steps involved in constructing a particular hairstyle. One notable exception is the image of a young woman braiding her hair in the Luttrell Psalter. Her maid helps her coil a braid into a metal caul, revealing the kind of preparation necessary for the popular fourteenth-century silhouette discussed later in the section on "The Fourteenth Century" (Figure 3.1).

As we examine the sources for medieval hair, we witness a continual interplay between cultural standards of gender, ideals of beauty, conceptions of modesty, and a desire for innovation and extravagance.

FIGURE 3.1 A Lady attended by her maid, from the Luttrell Psalter (ca. 1325–1335). Add. 42130, fol. 63. © The British Library Board.

THE EARLY MIDDLE AGES

For the ninth, tenth, and eleventh centuries, we have far less variety of sources than we have for later centuries. There are illuminated manuscripts, certainly, although the images tend to lack contemporary details when it comes to dress and hair. Biblical scenes, for example, can be based on ancient Roman models. In terms of portraiture, manuscripts almost also exclusively show royalty. Written descriptions of physical beauty focus on inner virtues and how they reflect modesty and good character. They are rarely specific in terms of ideal colors and styles and again may refer to ancient and biblical writings more than actual styling processes.[8] For example, when Alcuin cautions Charlemagne's daughter Gisela (ca. 792) to avoid "twisted plaits of hair," is he referring to a Carolingian hairstyle or to St. Paul's first epistle to Timothy, critiquing the braided hair of women?[9]

It is particularly difficult to write about styles of hair for women during this period, as we simply don't see very much of it. Manuscript images show that women, nuns and laywomen alike, wore their hair almost completely covered with veils. These veils derived from a multitude of traditions. Middle Eastern women had worn veils for millennia, and Roman women took up the practice via Hellenistic culture. Admonitions in early Christian writing (as well as Muslim writings later) connected veiling to female chastity.[10] Pre-conversion Germanic women had also worn veils, so in early medieval Europe, the veil, with centuries of symbolism as well as tradition behind it, was a standard hair accessory for women of all classes and phases of life. There is no indication in art that unmarried women wore their hair loose or were distinguished from married women.[11]

Veils were based on large rectangular shapes that would come directly off the warp-weighted looms, so that no material would be wasted. The Anglo-Saxons employed several words for their female headdresses, including *wimpel*, *haed*, *hod*, and *cuffie*, and there were a variety of ways to pin and drape the elaborate folds around the head and shoulders.[12] The head coverings could be woven of simple linen or wool, the major fibers of the early Middle Ages, but aristocratic and royal women certainly had access to silk imported through Mediterranean trade.[13] In the Bible of San Paolo, the Carolingian King Charles the Bald's queen wears a beautifully patterned silk veil long enough to drape over her arm in the manner of a shawl.[14] Head coverings could also be richly colored. The Virgin Mary wears a draped red veil in the Anglo-Saxon New Minster Charter (966–984),[15] and in the Carolingian panegyric poem *Karolus Magnus et Leo Papa* (written ca. 799–800), Charlemagne's sister Gisela wears "a veil of purple thread."[16] Such dyes, including kermes for reddish hues made from insects, and Tyrian purple made from shellfish, also came to northern Europe via Mediterranean trade routes.[17] The quality of material may have been the best marker to distinguish a nun from a secular woman, as both regularly wore veils. Since early medieval nuns were invariably royal and aristocratic in origin, the donning of an undyed woolen veil could have been the greatest visual demarcation of religious status.

The arrangement of hair under the veil, however, may have been quite elaborate, as evidenced by the number of bone and metal hairpins found in graves and mentioned in written sources.[18] In the *Vita Hathumodae* by Agius, Hathumoda "burned with disdain towards the clothing adorned with gold, the female headgear, head bands, hair pins ... which many other women either had or wanted."[19] The pins could hold hair in place or even add texture. Braided and curly hair may have been considered especially elegant and desirable. In the tenth-century Old English poem *Judith*, the heroine adorns herself in order to entice the evil Holofernes, and her beautification includes her *wundenlocc* (hair wound round) perhaps braided or curled.[20] A word for curling-pin exists in Old English,[21]

FASHION AND ADORNMENT

and the seventh-century scholar Aldhelm criticizes both women and men for curling the hair at their temples.[22]

The quantity of recovered early medieval pins could also hold in place embroidered bands or ribbons.[23] In the poem *Karolus Magnus et Leo Papa*, Charlemagne's daughter Rotrud wears a purple *vitta* in her hair, a word which possibly translates to a headband. In the eleventh-century *Liber Vitae* manuscript from the New Minster (ca. 1020–1030), the Anglo-Saxon Queen Emma wears a band wound around her forehead, pinned or tied under her veil and hanging almost to her knees (Figure 3.2).[24] The artist's slashes and circles indicate decorative elements, possibly woven patterning or embroidery or both.[25] The size of a headband lends itself particularly to tablet weaving, which produced long narrow strips in intricately woven patterns. Anglo-Saxon women were especially

FIGURE 3.2 King Canute and Queen Aelfgifu (Emma) presenting a cross upon the altar of New Minster, *Liber Vitae* (ca. 1031). MS Stowe 944, fol. 6. © The British Library Board.

skilled at embroidery and utilized the finest of materials, including silk thread, gold wire, and jewels. Several Anglo-Saxon wills mention these headbands, called *bends* or *baends*, embroidered in gold. Aelfgifu gave to her brother's wife Aethelflaed "the headband [*baendes*] which I have lent her." In her will, Wynflaed "grants to Ceolthryth whichever she prefers of her black tunics and her best holy veil and her best headband; and to Aethelflaed the White her ... gown and cap and headband [*bindan*]."[26]

Scandinavian women may not have covered their hair as completely as Anglo-Saxon and Carolingian women. The Icelandic family sagas were written no earlier than the thirteenth century but were meant to describe events of the Viking Age (800–1100). The beautiful and desirable Hallgerd in *Njal's Saga* wears her hair long and uncovered, and "hanging down on both sides of her waist and she had tucked it into her belt."[27] Vikings of both genders may have worn caps of silk, wool, and linen based on archaeological finds at York, London, and Dublin. One of the York caps had been dyed with madder, a plant whose root would produce colors from pink to orange to red, and another had been dyed purple from lichens.[28]

Men didn't have the same requirements for modesty as women. Early medieval manuscript images show men wearing their heads uncovered, although they would certainly want cowls and hoods for warmth. In 790, Alcuin of York, freezing in northern Britain, requested that a student bring him goat-hair hoods of black and red.[29] Facial hair varied according to geography and time. Roman traditions dictated shorter hair and clean-shaven faces, and urban Roman men had enjoyed regular access to barbers. While such barber shops wouldn't emerge again in Europe until the eleventh century, men possessed razors, shears, and tweezers for regular hair grooming, and tweezers are among the most common toilet items in pre-Christian burials.[30] Mustaches were popular for much of the early medieval period. They appear in depictions of Germanic men, for example, on the late-seventh-century helmet in the Sutton Hoo ship burial. Depictions of later Anglo-Saxon kings in manuscripts, such as Canute in the *Liber Vitae* from Winchester (ca. 1020–1030) and King Edgar in the New Minster Charter (966–984) also show them wearing mustaches, as well as short square beards with their hair clipped slightly to their ears.[31] The Carolingian King Charles the Bald appears in both the San Paolo Bible and the *Codex Aureus of St. Emmeram* as short-haired with a long mustache.[32]

One of the best sources for male attire for the eleventh century, the Bayeux Tapestry, gives us a sense of roughly contemporary male hairstyles from both sides of the English Channel. Once again, we see several of the Anglo-Saxon men, including Harold Godwinson, with long mustaches. The Anglo-Saxon King Edward, however, wears a long beard as an indicator of his age (Figure I.9). It is difficult to know if elderly men actually wore long beards or if the embroiderers used this style as a visual cue to contrast him with the younger men. The Norman Duke William is clean-shaven with his hair in a short bowl-cut with bangs. Gale Owen-Crocker suggests this style may be a lingering tradition from older Frankish military rituals where men shaved the backs of their necks after a defeat in battle.[33]

Mustaches, beards, and short hairstyles were the realm of secular men. The tonsure distinguished clerical men from their secular counterparts as well as from each other. Continental clerics wore the Roman tonsure (shaving most of the head except for a short ring all the way around). In Britain, some wore the Roman tonsure while monks trained in the Irish tradition shaved the top of their heads and let the bottom layer of hair hang long according to the Celtic tradition. The Synod of Whitby in 664 ruled in favor of the Roman tonsure, which henceforth held sway over the majority of Anglo-Saxon monks, although some still adhered stubbornly to the Celtic tonsure.[34] Monks rarely wore facial hair. Early medieval manuscripts typically depict monks as clean-shaven, and clerical regulations required shaving, such as the Council of Aachen (816), which mandated that monks shave every fifteen days.[35] The tonsure as well as the hairless face provided visual cues of spiritual authority and worldly detachment.

THE TWELFTH AND THIRTEENTH CENTURIES

Muslims and Jews had always lived among European Christians, particularly in Spain and Italy, and, beginning in the late eleventh century, political developments brought increased contact between the cultures. Christian Crusaders encountered full-body depilatories, public baths, and a host of new dyes and materials in the Middle East. Demand for beauty and health treatments to match the new fashions led to compilations and translations of medical texts available in northern Europe, such as the *Trotula* (twelfth century) and the *Book of Women's Love* (thirteenth century). The Romances of the twelfth and thirteenth centuries as well as these medical texts allow us to understand not only how people wore their hair but how they wanted their hair to look, that is, the ideal standards for beautiful hair. The heroes and heroines of the romances almost always possess ivory skin, shining eyes, and flowing blonde hair.[36] Chrétien de Troyes is alleged to have written such a tale of love featuring a woman whose hair is so lovely that it is used in naming her: Iseult the Blonde. The heroine of his *Eric and Enide*, however, possessed hair even more beautiful as the narrator makes clear, "the shining golden hair of the blonde Iseult was nothing in comparison to this maiden's hair."[37] Medical texts instructed women how to achieve this ideal beauty, recommending recipes to dye hair blonde and to render it soft, shiny, thick, flowing, and sweet-smelling. Although they mention veils, these works spend most of their time on hair texture and color rather than specific accessories or arrangements.

For information on adornment, we can turn to the variety of visual evidence, for example, the stone carvings on the elaborate cathedrals of the twelfth century. Combined with tomb effigies and manuscript illuminations, we begin to see actual hair emerging from beneath veils, worn in two lengthy braids. The newly visible hair and the interest in hair dye may have influenced each other—why spend three days dying your hair golden (as the *Trotula* recommends), not to mention buying expensive ingredients, only to cover it up entirely under a veil?[38] Artistic and cultural factors may have come into play as well. Margaret Scott connects the elongated style of women's hair with the Gothic styles of the buildings themselves beginning around 1140 with St. Denis.[39] The silks available from the Middle East were lighter and more diaphanous so that veils revealed hair even as they covered it, prompting new hair arrangements. The loosening and lengthening of women's hairstyles appears to begin in France and arrives in England after the Norman Conquest. The early medieval veil, now known as a *couvre-chef*, was worn loose with the hair center-parted and worn in two even braids on both sides of the face. The stone carvings of the Queen of Sheba from the portal of Notre-Dame de Corbeil and an ancestress of Christ from the royal portal at Chartres Cathedral both display the braids emerging from under *couvre-chefs*. The Queen of Sheba wears her braids *en galonne*, a form of braiding that divides the hair into two sections and uses a ribbon for the third.[40]

Braiding *en galonne* was one form of illusion employed to keep the newly visible hair at the ideal length and thickness. Various strategies were used to keep the braids hanging to the knees. The Bride of Cana, figured on the cloister of

Notre-Dame-en-Vaux at Chalons-sur-Marne, wears her two plaits in a silk tube bound with ribbon, and metal cylinders could do the same trick.[41] Another way to achieve the requisite long locks involved filling out braids with false hairpieces of silk and wool (Figure 4.5).

In addition to the *couvre-chef*, other different headdresses emerged at the end of the twelfth century and remained popular throughout the thirteenth century. Books of Hours, popular from the mid-thirteenth century, as well as colorfully illustrated psalters, provide an ideal source of information for hairstyles, as they frequently included detailed images of patrons as well as decorated margins and initials. The tomb effigy of Eleanor of Aquitaine (d. 1204) from Fontevrault Abbey shows her wearing a barbette, a linen band that wrapped around the head and chin, with a wimple of linen or silk overtop, held in place by a crown. The barbette was a ubiquitous item during the thirteenth century. Most women would not wear Eleanor's accompanying crown, of course, but could adopt a fillet, a stiffened crown-like band that encircled the head. Both the barbette and the fillet were held in place by pins, as was another wimple that could drape over the chin and up to the ears. Eleanor's hair is barely visible beneath her wimple, but by the latter half of the century, women began partially displaying their braided hair as well as their necks. By the later thirteenth century, the barbette had narrowed (and eventually disappeared entirely), and the fillet had also narrowed to a circlet. The wimple itself became shorter, revealing hair coiled up on the sides, a style illustrated by a fashionably dressed lady holding on to her hunting dogs in the English Alphonso Psalter (ca. 1281–1284).[42] To create the requisite fullness of the coils, women could use hairpieces. In 1273, the Dominican friar Gilles d' Orleans preached against women who wore false hair, as it could have come from women who were in Hell or Purgatory.[43] The contemporary allegorical dream poem, *Le Roman de la Rose*, speaks of possibilities for a woman to augment her natural hair with dyed hairpieces:

> She should have the hair of some dead woman brought to her, or pads of light-coloured silk, and stuff it all into false hairpieces. She should wear such horns above her ears that no stag or goat or unicorn could surpass them, not though his head were to burst with the effort, and if they need color she should dye them with many different plant-extracts, for fruit, wood, leaves, bark and roots have powerful medicinal properties.[44]

Like Christian women before the twelfth century, literary and artistic evidence indicates that Arab women throughout the Middle Ages wore their hair entirely covered with veils. The veils could include not only hair coverings but also a variety of face coverings, tucked, folded, and pinned into each other. The scanty archaeological evidence derives mainly from dryer climates like Egypt, but a medieval image from Granada Cathedral depicts Moorish women wearing a *haik*, a long piece of material wrapped around the head and body.[45] At the same time works such as the *Trotula* and the *Book of Women's Love* demonstrate that Arab and Jewish women were practicing hair removal and dyeing their hair blonde or black. The outside world, particularly a public male world outside of the woman's immediate circle, would rarely have witnessed the effects of these cosmetic techniques.

Styles for men during the twelfth century also emphasized the long and the loose. Young men at Norman courts began growing out their hair and wearing it loose around their shoulders. Norman chroniclers, Eadmer of Canterbury (writing in 1094), William of Malmesbury (writing between 1118–1125, revising in the 1130s) and Orderic Vitalis (writing between 1109 and the 1140s) all complain about the young men and their long hair.⁴⁶ For example, Orderic laments the time when "effeminate men had dominion throughout the world," when "they parted their hair in the middle, they let it grow long, as women do, and carefully tended it."⁴⁷ Illustrations of young men hawking from the Citeaux manuscript of the *Moralia in Job* (ca. 1111–1115) and the Shaftesbury Psalter (ca. 1135) depict this long loose hair.⁴⁸ The latter hawker appears to even wear fringed bangs. Orderic Vitalis described young men shaving their foreheads, with long curls at the back of their heads, attributing the newfound style to Robert Curthose, who had brought the style back from Sicily after the First Crusade.⁴⁹

Short beards go in and out of style. Henry II, who died in 1189, wears a neatly trimmed short beard on his tomb, and various stone sculptures on cathedrals show an assortment of beards as well as clean-shaven faces. Mustaches are worn occasionally but only in conjunction with beards.⁵⁰ Around 1217, a new form of helmet, closed all the way around with slits for seeing and breathing, made beards impractical for noblemen who would participate in battle.⁵¹ As they had in previous centuries, flowing unkempt beards and hair in artwork could act as symbols of age, wisdom, or barbarity. They could also identify individuals as Jewish, Muslim, Ethiopian, or simply Other.⁵² In his *Topography of Ireland*, Gerald of Wales refers to the uncouth beards of the Irish, and the illustrations to the earliest manuscript include images of their untidy beards (Figure 7.1).⁵³

During the twelfth century, the hood emerged as the universal form of headgear for men. Monks and peasants had always worn hoods, but men of all classes adopted the hood or chaperon for warmth and traveling, and eventually even court dress. In the illumination of Jean to Joinville presenting his *Vie de Saint Louis* to the king, we see several versions of the hood worn by courtiers. They are colorful and come to a wide point at the crown.⁵⁴ The points are also visible on the hoods of the mourners on the tomb of King Louis (d. 1260) at St. Denis. Hoods attached to outer garments became a recognizable aspect of professional clothing worn by physicians, lawyers, teachers, and university teachers and students. Images of physicians from anatomy books and medical texts reveal a ubiquitous hood worn tightly around the head, sometimes padded, and tied under the chin.⁵⁵ Of course, soldiers going into battle would exchange their hood for protective headgear, which involved multiple layers, including a padded coif, a chain-mail hood, and a full helmet with slits for seeing and breathing.⁵⁶

For Jewish men, headgear in addition to beards also acted as demarcations of difference. Jews had long been required to wear special badges or patches, sometimes in the shape of the communion wafer or the tablets of the Ten Commandments. During the Fourth Lateran Council, Innocent III called for greater differentiation between Christians and non-Christians.⁵⁷ In 1267, a synod in Breslau, Germany ordered Jewish men to wear a *pileus cornutus* (horned hat).⁵⁸ As the hat bore no resemblance to contemporary fashions, it not only visually identified the wearer as a non-Christian but also subjected them to ridicule. Jewish men all over Europe would wear special hats or various types for the next several centuries (Figure 7.2). Venetian Jews, for example, wore yellow caps (*baretta* or *capello*).⁵⁹ Christian governments were not unique in their desire to separate minorities. In 1198, the Almohad amir of Spain and North Africa required Jewish subjects to wear not only specifically blue-colored garments but also "headgear of a grotesque shape," rather than the standard Muslim turban.⁶⁰ Restrictions on Jewish clothing would bar them from fully participating in the visual display of fashion that swept through medieval Europe in successive centuries.

THE FOURTEENTH CENTURY

The fourteenth century witnessed significant changes in the construction of clothing, a wider variety of garments as well as noticeable changes among royalty and aristocracy every few decades. This is the period to which historians such as Daniel Delis Hill ascribe the origins of fashion, when it is defined as an ideal and exclusive entity. For the first time, we have expanding and economically diverse cities housing a middle class of merchants and craftspeople. The middle class used their expendable income to purchase goods, including fine clothing that had only been available to the nobility in previous centuries. The nobility, in turn, strove to differentiate themselves with new forms of dress. Continual change in dress, including headgear and the accompanying styling of hair, flourished, as each group strove to outdo or imitate the other in sartorial elegance. Styles in edgings and excesses changed by the decade as opposed to by the century. The fashions spread to lower classes and rural areas as well.[61] A greater number of visual and written sources such as illuminated manuscripts and wardrobe accounts also allow historians to trace the changing nature not only of clothing, but of the accompanying hairstyles and hair care.[62] Manuscript illustrations portrayed great detail in textiles, and a few valuable examples, such as the Luttrell Psalter, illustrated everyday life for a variety of social classes.

The drive for fashionable novelty as well as new methods in tailoring led to a greater variety of garments and silhouettes.[63] Although throughout the century, fashionable women kept a basic silhouette of looped braids worn over their ears, their hairstyles reflected changing fashions through veils, ribbons, and other accessories.[64] The Luttrell Psalter, created for Sir Geoffrey Luttrell during the late 1320s or 1330s, depicts his wife and his daughter-in-law with these looped braids. Both wear jeweled bands around their heads that hold their delicate veils in place. The veils may be symbolic of married modesty, but given their transparency as well as how far back they are placed, they do almost nothing to cover the hair or the forehead.[65] The loops could be doubled, as in the Neville of Hornby Hours from 1335.[66] Lady Neville has completely eschewed even a diaphanous veil and wears her hair uncovered. In the *Coronation Book of Charles V of France* (1365), two profile views suggest an elaboration on this style, with two braids pinned in back in addition to the side loops.[67] An English poem, "Against the Pride of the Ladies" (ca. 1340) satirizes this hairstyle, comparing the hair loops to "clogs which hang by their jowls," and criticizes women for their uncovered hair. Instead of tucking their hair modestly under linen veils, "they sit like a slit swine which hangs its ears."[68]

Another style involved coiling up the braids into wire mesh covers, known as a *crespine*. The stone image of Jeanne de Bourbon on the chimney-piece of the Great Hall in the Palais de Justice from Poitiers (ca. 1360), wears a *crespine* elaborately decorated with tiny flowers under her crown.[69] As mentioned earlier, an illustration in the Luttrell Psalter catches a lady in the middle of arranging this style, giving us a rare glimpse at hair and the mechanics of the *crespine*. She is in the process of completing one braid while her maid coils up the other braid into the stiff casing (Figure 3.1).[70] In another image, we see Sir Geoffrey's daughter-in-law and wife both wearing the looped braids without the *crespine*, suggesting they were both fashionable concurrently.

The Luttrell Psalter also depicts lower-class women, including the aforementioned maid, as well as peasant women working in the fields and feeding animals. If the illustrations are accurate, we see the huge gulf in hairstyles between noble and peasant women, whose hair is completely covered in white wimples quite similar to the Anglo-Saxon style of previous centuries. The maid helping to arrange her mistress's hair is somewhere in-between: she still covers her hair, but her wimple is starched and crimped and reveals her neck.

An image of St. Ursula and the Virgins from the Hours of Bertrando dei Rossi (ca. 1380–1385) shows a variety of hairstyles available to Italian women.[71] One woman wears a shortened version of the looped braids more popular in England. Most of St. Ursula's maidens wear their hair bound over their forehead and woven through with either ribbons or strings of pearls. The hair at their temples is curled and occasionally cut short into bangs. Any of the fourteenth-century styles required long thick hair, and again women used hairpieces to fill out the necessary length and width of the braids (Figure 4.5). It is from the second quarter of the fourteenth century that we have examples of false hair (real human hair mixed with silk) found in London.[72] In Italian cities, we can see the popularity of false hair though the condemnations of clergy and the sumptuary laws prohibiting it. In the city of Modena between 1327 and 1336, servants and lower-class women were forbidden to wear false braids of silk.[73] In 1310, Antonio d'Orso Bilotti, bishop of Florence and Fiesole, forbade the use of false hair, specifically *zazzerris* (long falling hairpieces) and *casciettis* (strands of hair or curls). However, it was clearly the fashions rather than the falsity of the hair itself to which he objected, as he also allowed women with thinning hair to wear false braids as long as they attempted to appear natural.[74]

The length of men's hair and the popularity of beards varied by region, decade, and also by personal preference. Two English manuscripts from within a few years of each other depict different styles of facial hair. In the Neville of Hornby Hours (ca. 1335), Robert de Neville wears a full beard, while the noblemen in the Luttrell Psalter are uniformly clean-shaven in contrast to the serving men and cooks, who have short or forked beards. The *Coronation Book of Charles V of France*, from 1365, depicts the king and his men with longer loose hair hanging to just above their shoulders. Charles himself and the Duke of Bourbon are clean-shaven, but several of the other men wear short, round beards. And in the *Roman du Roi Meliadus de Leonnoys* (Book of the King Meliadus of Lennoys), from Naples (ca. 1352), a scene at a royal court reveals a room full of diverse styles—from clean-shaven to forked beards and mustaches, and hair in a variety of lengths from just under the ears to hanging almost to the shoulders.[75]

The same image also illustrates a new fashion in men's hoods; the point had grown so long that it developed into a tail long enough to be tucked into a waistband. The tail was known as a liripipe in English and a *cornette* in French.[76] Manuscript images from around Europe depict this style. Several of the human figures and the grotesques in the margins of the Luttrell Psalter wear hoods with liripipes in bright colors. Fashion brought an accompanying element of play, as people adorned themselves with decorative elements serving absolutely no practical purpose. The liripipe is a good example, as are the tippets (ribbons hanging off of sleeves) and the dagging (scalloped edging) that accentuated fashionable garments.[77] Any such extreme in fashion brought condemnation. The author of the mid-century passages of the *Grandes Chroniques de France* (Grand Chronicles of France), who wrote between 1344 and 1350, included the absurd length of the liripipes among the young as one of the youthful fashions responsible for the destruction of the French knighthood at the Battle of Crecy (August 26, 1346).[78] An English chronicler, John of Reading, also referenced the length of the liripipes as one of several excesses in men's fashion, along with the length of sleeves, the points of shoes, and tunics that were too short and too tight.[79] Moving into the fifteenth century, the playful excesses of fashion would only increase, literally and figuratively, to greater heights.

THE FIFTEENTH CENTURY

As Theodore Child so quaintly explained in his book *Wimples and Crisping Pins*, "In the history of feminine coiffure there is to be noted a perpetual and inevitable hostility between the ornament and the thing adorned, between the hair and the veil and its developments, between the natural elements of coiffure and the artificial elements."[80] By the end of the fourteenth century, extravagance had become the order of the day for female headdresses, to the point that the hair itself was completely obscured. Women plucked hair along their foreheads and eyebrows to achieve a clean smooth rounded head, known as a *grand front* or *front bombé* (Figure 8.5). In the *Book of the Knight of the Tower* (1484), Geoffrey de la Tour Landry, a vituperative antagonist of all lady's fashions, orders his daughters, "Do not pluck your eyebrows, nor your temples, nor your foreheads," indicating, of course, that many women were doing just that.[81]

Fashions in headgear favored the tall, the wide, and the attention-getting. One version of a headdress consisted of short veils pinned and held between two horns. The V-shape it formed mirrored the V-shape of the *cote hardie*, a tight outer garment now fashionable since the fourteenth century.[82] In the illustrations to the *Book of the City of Ladies* (ca. 1415), Christine de Pisan wears a version of this style that appears relatively simple (Figure 3.3).[83] In the *Histoire d'Alexandre le Grand* (History of Alexander the Great),

FIGURE 3.3 Detail of a miniature of Christine de Pisan, presenting her manuscript to Queen Isabeau of Bavaria, Paris (ca. 1410–1414). Harley 4431, fol. 3. © The British Library Board.

dating to the late 1420s, we see the extremes to which the same style could reach, with the length of the horns almost doubled from Christine's. In her *Treasury of the City of Ladies*, she critiques non-noble women who tried to dress above their station by adopting the most ostentatious styles. Of one "ordinary lady" who had ordered a *cote hardie* with a train dragging across the ground and floor-length sleeves, she writes, "God only knows how correspondingly large the headdress is and how high the points are! It is actually an extremely ugly and unbecoming outfit, as anyone who really looks at it will agree."[84] De la Tour Landry warns his daughters against the extravagance of the horns with a cautionary tale against "the new headdresses that are shaped like two horns."[85] Florence went so far as to ban horned headdresses, both in 1449 and in 1556.[86]

In Jan van Eyck's portrait of his wife Margaret (Bruges, Groeningemuseum, 1439), the detailed attention to dress reveals the mechanics of the style (Figure 3.4). Her hair is coiled into metal horns decorated with a geometric pattern. Over the horns, her veil is crisped and crimped, possibly with starch or gum. Absolutely no hair is visible, indicating that she has plucked the hair around her forehead with tweezers to achieve the grand front.[87]

FIGURE 3.4 Jan van Eyck, *Portrait of Margaret van Eyck*, painting (1439). Groeningemuseum, Bruges, Belgium. Photo: The Archive at Art Resource, NY.

The other style of headdress was the padded and stuffed *bourrelet* (from *bouret*, meaning "to stuff") that formed the shape of a heart. The horns acted as the base to add even greater height. Depicted in a Book of Hours from Paris (ca. 1435), a woman kneeling at communion has a green and gold *bourrelet* atop her geometrically patterned horns.[88] And in the Bedford Hours, Anne of Burgundy, the sister of Philip the Good, kneels before St. Anne, the Virgin, and Christ while wearing horns easily as long as her face, decorated with jewels, and held together with a central metal band at the top of her forehead.[89] All these hairstyles required numerous tiny pins to keep them in place, made of brass wire, pewter, bronze, and silver, with heads of glass and coral.[90] Queen Isabeau of Bavaria, wife of Charles VI, bought 9,800 pins in 1391.[91] She wears her own opulent *bourrelet* in her depiction in Christine de Pisan's collected works, in contrast to Christine's simple horns and white kerchief (Figure 3.3).[92] Of course, practicality would have to be a consideration even for a queen. The headdresses portrayed in manuscripts and portraits were so cumbersome that they may have been reserved for public occasions. Even a privileged nobleman or woman may not have worn the most fashionable headdress while out hunting or charging into battle.

There was a sense that fashion changed more quickly in France and that the more scandalous of new styles were "French."[93] Christine de Pisan praised the women of Italy for wearing clothing of finer quality that lasted longer than the fickle French fashions. She also suggested that the headdresses of Italian women were always more becoming because more of them were blonde, "for there is nothing in the world lovelier on a woman's head than beautiful blonde hair."[94] The lovely blonde hair may have been the result of hair dye, as the *Trotula*, a collection of writings on women's medicine from Salerno, indicates that a variety of blonde hair dyes existed, utilizing ingredients from crocus to white wine to henna.[95]

Christine may also have been critiquing the French fashion for completely obscuring women's hair in comparison to the Italian fashions. Italian portraits and descriptions of the early fifteenth century suggest that more hair was revealed even while wearing elaborate headdresses. Pisanello's painting *Portrait of a Princess* (Louvre, Paris, ca. 1430s) depicts either the wife of Lionello D'Este, the Marquis of Ferrara, Margarita Gonzaga, or else his sister, Ginevra. The unknown subject has plucked her forehead, but her blonde hair is entirely uncovered, bound tightly back in a white ribbon wound around a bun. In Fra Filippo Lippi's double portrait *Portrait of a Woman with a Man at a Casement* (New York, Metropolitan Museum of Art, ca. 1440), the woman's blonde hair is peaking out from beneath her headdress—in this case a rich and elegant *sella* (saddle), so-called because of its curved dip in the center (Figure 9.7). It resembles the French horned style, as it has an embroidered red veil overtop a horned cap, with the addition of a padded red band.[96] The visibility of Italian hair may explain the controversy surrounding hairpieces, which sumptuary laws tried to regulate. In 1326, Florentine women had petitioned the Duchess of Calabria to intercede with her husband on their behalf so they could wear false hair, forbidden by sumptuary law.[97] In 1440, the pope issued a statement that a woman could wear false hair (along with jewels and elaborate clothing) provided that she was attempting to please her husband.[98]

Italian women also contended with sumptuary legislation regarding the style of their headdresses. The Florentine Statutes of 1322 to 1325 attempted to crack down on foreign styles, known as *alla di là*, meaning "from beyond." That didn't prevent Italians from ignoring the laws, petitioning to change them or altering fashions just enough to get around them. Certainly by the mid-fifteenth century, as families competed for public recognition, Italian women wore headdresses to rival anything produced beyond their borders. In 1447, the Florentine Catarina Strozzi wore a *ghirlando* (garland) of peacock feathers and pearls to her wedding to Marco Parenti. Her bridegroom kept detailed accounts of the wedding clothes: this *ghirlando* embroidered with silver and pearls and decorated with silver tinsel roses came to slightly less than 60 florins.[99] But that wasn't everything—Parenti also had a set of pearl braids made to be wound around a *mazocchio* (a padded roll) which would hold the *ghirlando* in place. This added another 61 florins to the headdress alone.[100] Between the *ghirlando* and the *mazocchio*, Catarina's headdress cost more than the annual incomes of most Florentines. For instance, the wealthiest earners in fourteenth-century Florence, successful lawyers and university professors, earned between 200 and 500 florins a year while bank managers brought home only 100–200 florins.[101] And of course, the 121 florins only accounts for Catarina's headgear. Her wedding gowns, a *cioppa* and a *cotta* (an overdress and an underdress) cost another 174 florins.[102] No portrait exists of Catarina in her wedding finery, but we can see a *ghirlando* in a fifteenth-century drawing currently in the Uffizi Gallery. Not without cause, her mother Alessandra Strozzi bragged in a letter to her son that his sister would wear "the most beautiful clothes in Florence."[103]

Aristocratic and royal men also strove for the smooth hairless forehead as well as the neck. During the first part of the century, men at the French and Burgundian courts cut their hair evenly around in a bowl shape above the ears, with the neck entirely shaved.[104] Raymond of Poitiers demonstrates the bowl style in the Flemish manuscript of the *Roman de Mélusine* (ca. 1445–1450).[105] The style spread to the courts of England and Spain, although notably not Italy. By the second half of the century, even the chopped bowl-length of hair disappeared, and men appeared entirely hairless. King Charles VII of France's portrait (Paris, Louvre, ca. 1445 or 1450), depicts him as thoroughly clean-shaven. He has absolutely no visible hair, having also shaved or plucked his hair from his forehead. Anything that may be on the top of his head is concealed by a wide-brimmed hat. Similar styles appear on noblemen in manuscripts such as the *Très Riches Heures*, created for John, the Duke of Berry between around 1412 and 1416. In lieu of hair, the men wear eye-catching hats in a variety of shapes, including wide-brimmed beaver-fur hats, floppy straw hats, and towering black hats. In an indoor scene where the duke's household exchanges New Year's gifts, the shaved necks are visible on the men without hats.[106] The peasants in the manuscript, on the other hand, have more of a variety in facial hair: some are clean-shaven, wearing hats similar to the aristocracy, while others go about hatless or with loose hair visible beneath a cap, and some have beards. Of course, it is difficult to know how accurate the artists desired to be in their depictions of peasants' hair, as they also depicted them with fine scarlet fitted clothing.

In addition to hats, men still wore hoods, although with the long tails looped up and pinned or tucked into elegant artistic shapes. Two images illustrate the fantastic shapes of the fifteenth-century hood. Jan van Eyck's *Portrait of a Man*, possibly a self-portrait, from 1433 (London, National Gallery) and the image of Louis d'Orléans receiving a copy of Christine de Pisan's book from the author herself in the illustrated manuscript of her works (ca. 1415).[107] In the Van Eyck portrait, the ends of the man's hood are wrapped around themselves to achieve the width and height of a turban. Louis's hood appears to be first wrapped around his head and then flatly folded into wings, the ends secured with a golden ring. Just a small fringe of hair is visible. Both hoods are a bold rich red, dyed with the expensive kermes, the leading sources of scarlet, imported from the Mediterranean.

As we move into the latter half of the fifteenth century, we see a greater gulf between the hairstyles of northern and southern Europe. At the courts of England, Burgundy, and France by the mid-fifteenth century, the extravagance of the headdress had replaced the decoration and arrangement of the hair itself. Women continued to pluck to achieve the smooth pale forehead, as in the well-known image of Rogier van der Weyden's *Portrait of a Lady* (London, National Gallery, 1450–1460) (Figure 4.7). By the end of the century, *bourrelets* had rounded into hats shaped like pillboxes. They were heightened even further by conical forms and veils suspended from the end, a fashion popularized in twentieth-century fairy-tale illustrations. Italian women, in contrast, appear in portraits with loose hair, uncovered, curled, and occasionally entwined with ribbons, as in Piero della Francesco's painting *Portrait of Battista Sforza, Duchess of Urbino* (Florence, Uffizi Gallery, ca. 1467–1470) (Figure 3.5). Giovanna Tornabuoni wears absolutely no visible hair ornaments in her portrait by Domenico Ghirlandaio (Madrid, Museo Thyssen-Bornemisza, 1488). The top half of her hair is braided and coiled up in the back of her head, with an underlayer of ringlets.

By the end of the fifteenth century, we see that fashion trumps modesty as well as practicality. For women, the ubiquitous veil of the early Middle Ages only appeared in stylized forms attached to larger headpieces. The invisibility of hair had come full

FIGURE 3.5 Piero della Francesco, *Portrait of Battista Sforza, Duchess of Urbino* (ca. 1465). Uffizi, Florence, Italy. Photo: Scala/Art Resource, NY.

circle, although it was due to the extravagance of headdresses, rather than religions injunctions to keep hair covered. The popularity of hair dyes and treatments indicates that women still sought to improve upon their natural color and texture, regardless of whether their styles would be visible to the general public. Fashionable men, who had never covered their hair for religious reasons, also displayed a propensity for colorful and eye-catching headgear. Although keeping up with the latest novelties of fashions acted as a form of social expression, it also allowed men and women room to play. By the later Middle Ages, enough varieties of style existed that people could express individuality through their personal preferences. Christine de Pisan, thus, could wear what she deemed as a modest version of the fashionable horned headdress and avoid the extremities she found unattractive. While no doubt some people enjoyed the continual reinvention of fashion, for many, as with the Parenti and Strozzi families, appearing publicly in the most desirable trends was a necessary matter of family honor. It is important to remember, of course, that access to fashion was limited to the wealthy, although the definition of who possessed wealth had certainly expanded. The majority of Europeans couldn't afford *bourrelets* and *ghirlandas* and could hardly wear a hennin into a pasture. As the female maid wearing a crimped wimple in the Luttrell Psalter suggests, however, people could imitate styles even if they couldn't afford to replicate them exactly. Other people, such as monks and nuns, would have deliberately avoided any kind of adherence to fashion. But regardless of whether medieval Europeans strove to follow fashions, they made conscious and unconscious decisions every day about how to dress their hair before stepping out into their complex social networks.

ACKNOWLEDGMENTS

Images cited in this chapter are generally available via online searching or through an online database such as ARTstor.org (many libraries provide access); for others I have indicated sources.

CHAPTER FOUR

Production and Practice

LAURA MICHELE DIENER

The study of medieval hair occurs at the intersection of hygiene, ritual, and beauty. Medieval people needed to clean their hair to keep it free of dirt and vermin. How they arranged it depended on an almost infinite variety of factors such as social class, wealth, religious affiliation, gender, region, and cultural ideals of beauty. Chapter Three on fashion and adornment in this volume discusses several of these aspects further. Gender outweighed many of these determinants, as women were generally expected to wear their hair long and covered, while the length of men's hair changed more frequently. Religious requirements provided the exception, of course, as monastic men and women kept their hair ritually shorn in ways that changed little over the entire medieval period. Other chapters in this volume fully address issues of health, hygiene, and ritual, although it is impossible to write about hair without at least touching upon them. This chapter will focus on the material reality of hair and how medieval people confronted the hair on their bodies as an organic entity, as well as how they cut, dyed, curled, trimmed, and removed it.

In medieval Europe, the professionalization of hair care was divided generally along gender lines. Barbers and barber shops were a feature of medieval cities as they had been in Roman cities, and urban men who could afford it could rely upon them for a shave and a trim as well as for certain medical services. Barber services were also available inside monasteries in order to keep religious men in line with the current standards for hair length and style. Women, for the most part, dressed and treated their hair in domestic settings, with the wealthy utilizing the help of servants. Those servants could possess great expertise in adornment of the kind we would associate with a trained salon hairdresser today. In addition, hair coloring and treatment fell under the heading of cosmetology, which was the purview of women's medical practitioners. Recipes for hair dyes, depilatories, cleansers, and lice removal were included in medical texts for women alongside gynecological advice.

By the mid-thirteenth century, multiple texts on women's health care and cosmetics were available to a Mediterranean and European audience in Latin, Hebrew, and Arabic. Much of the knowledge they contained had originated in the Iberian Peninsula, Provence, and southern Italy, where members of the same faith lived together.[1] During the twelfth century, several of the texts from Italy, probably from the medical school in Salerno, were gathered into the *Trotula* compendium, which deals with cosmetics and hair care in the third section, *De ornatu mulerium* (The Ornamentation of Women). *Sefer ahavat nashim* (Book of Women's Love), written in Hebrew in the second half of the thirteenth century, is another compendium on health and body care. Both texts show the definite influence of Greco-Arabic medical traditions, and they frequently reference the practices of "Saracens" and "Ishmaelites."

As Carmen Caballero-Navas has pointed out, these texts and others demonstrate that the care of women's health and beauty was an experience shared by medieval Jewish, Arabic, and Christian women. Women may have exchanged these recipes by word of mouth in public and private gatherings. The proliferation of medical texts that include sections on cosmetics and hair care may be the written legacy of innumerable female conversations in bedrooms and kitchens across social and cultural boundaries. Even if they were eventually written down by men, they allude to female authority.[2]

The types of sources we have to examine medieval hair practices provide an intriguing look at the way cultural imaginations can gender everyday grooming objects. The work of archaeologists throughout Europe indicates that combs, mirrors, tweezers, razors, and other grooming artifacts belonged to both men and women. Conduct books, romances, sermons, and artistic images, however, portrayed these objects as almost exclusively feminine and equated them with vices such as vanity, lust, and idleness. These objects, alluding as they do to rituals of intimacy, could also act as potent symbols of eroticism for both sexes.

Medievalists have analyzed the extremely mixed messages aimed at medieval men and women regarding their physical appearance. Literature and art could equate beauty with moral goodness, and ugliness with moral failings. In the thirteenth-century romance *Le Roman de la Rose* (Romance of the Rose), the dreamer envisions all the negative aspects of human behavior such as Sorrow, Poverty, and Avarice as unhealthy and unattractive figures, while Generosity of Spirit is a beautiful blonde maiden.[3] As Montserrat Cabré explains, "Human beauty was conceived of as a state of harmony with nature; beautiful and desirable bodies belonged to people who acted appropriately and according to their inner character."[4] These values were shared by Christian, Muslim, and Jewish cultures. Along with physical beauty, they also connected cleanliness and health to internal goodness, understanding all these qualities as manifestations of each other.[5] At the same time, at least in Christian texts, literature and clergymen condemned excessive care of appearance as vanity and, even worse, as a temptation to sexual sin. Roberta Milliken enumerates how these contradictions played out for women in the specific realm of hair. Books on courtly love as well as romances seem to encourage women to improve their appearance through enhancements such as cosmetics, hairpieces, and hair dye. Yet conduct books and sermons castigated them for these same practices. Both sets of sources sent messages to men that women's beauty might be based on artifice and, like their general characters, could not be trusted.[6] Men likewise operated under social codes that equated copious head and beard hair with virility, although too much hair carried associations with wild antisocial behavior as well as with outsiders such as Jews, Arabs, Celts, and pagans.

It is within this bewildering context that we can read the material, artistic, and literary evidence about practices relating to medieval hair care. Recipes for hair care carried social codes about standard definitions of beauty as well as the moral qualities of the men and women who might employ them. At the same time, they offer a glimpse into the lived experiences of medieval people and the choices they made about their bodies.

HAIR CARE AND TOOLS

Women and men regularly combed their hair throughout the entire medieval period. Combs acted as important tools for hygiene as well as style, as people used them to remove dirt and lice in lieu of regular hair washing. Combs of bone and antler are common artifacts for the early Middle Ages (Figure 4.1).[7] Most combs were composite, made up of different pieces riveted together, and could have teeth on one or both sides, although others were carved from a single piece of bone. They could be artistic as well as utilitarian, with decorations of dragon heads being particularly popular.[8] Antler combs became rare by the twelfth century, possibly due to hunting restrictions and decreased deer populations.[9]

Ivory combs were already luxury items by the early seventh century when, according to Bede, Boniface sent one to the Queen of Northumbria, and they remained so until the fifteenth century when boxwood became the material of choice.[10] King Edward I of England acquired two ivory combs in Paris in 1278. They were generally constructed with two sets of teeth on either side of a crossbar. The finer set of teeth removed lice and dirt while the wider set smoothed and untangled the hair. The preciousness of ivory derived from its rarity, its durability, and its color. Its unblemished whiteness inspired thoughts of both purity and beauty, calling to mind the equally unblemished souls of virgin saints. As such, it was ideal for liturgical combs whose purpose was both functional and spiritual; they physically cleaned the hair of priests before the Mass as they symbolically purified their minds (Figure 5.7). It is not a coincidence that the souls of virgin saints were often considered as pure white as ivory. Ivory combs also combined multiple hallmarks of femininity—white skin, long hair, the intimacy of personal grooming—making them an ideal gift for lovers as well as a literary and artistic trope of eroticism.[11]

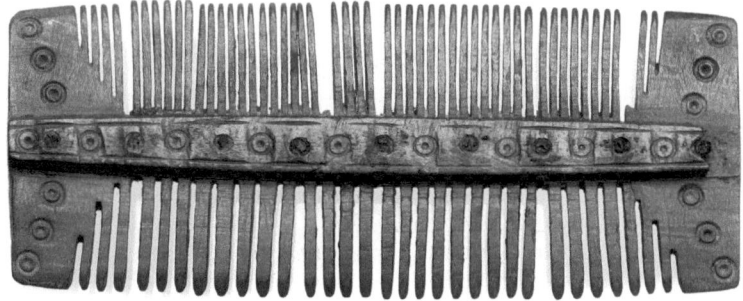

FIGURE 4.1 Bone double-sided composite comb with matching carrying case, Saxon-Norman (tenth to eleventh century). Museum of London.

The texture of ivory was also conducive to fine carving, and the crossbar structure provided a surface for painting, all adding to the personalization of combs.[12] During the fourteenth century, Parisian workshops produced ivory combs with decorated carvings developed from the style of religious ivories. One double-sided ivory comb from Paris around 1320, now in the Victoria and Albert collection, is decorated with lovers in a garden at three different stages of their courtship (Figure 4.2).[13] Combs could also be painted on the sidebar with images of love from courtly and classical traditions as well as personal monograms. One comb from around 1400 belonging to Margaret of Flanders, Duchess of Burgundy, bears her monogram and initials.[14] The inscriptions could be intimate, indicating the erotic nature of combs as a gift between lovers. "Ayesde moi merci" (Have mercy on me) reads one ivory comb from northern France around 1500. During the fifteenth century, boxwood combs also became objects of luxury. The tone of the inscriptions remains the same: "Pren-nes plaisir" (Take pleasure) and "Amorr placet" (love pleases).[15] Parisian comb makers also produced ivory *gravoirs*, a stick for parting hair. During the twelfth through the fourteenth centuries, women's hairstyles involved a neat center part, as well as careful even braiding. *Gravoirs* could be decoratively topped with carved images, such as one in the Victoria and Albert with a tiny Phyllis riding Aristotle.[16] They could also serve as large hairpins, although by the thirteenth century, the styles favored smaller more delicate pins suitable for holding lightly woven veils.[17]

Combs are ubiquitous enough as artifacts to indicate that both men and women possessed them for grooming purposes. Yet in art and literature they functioned more

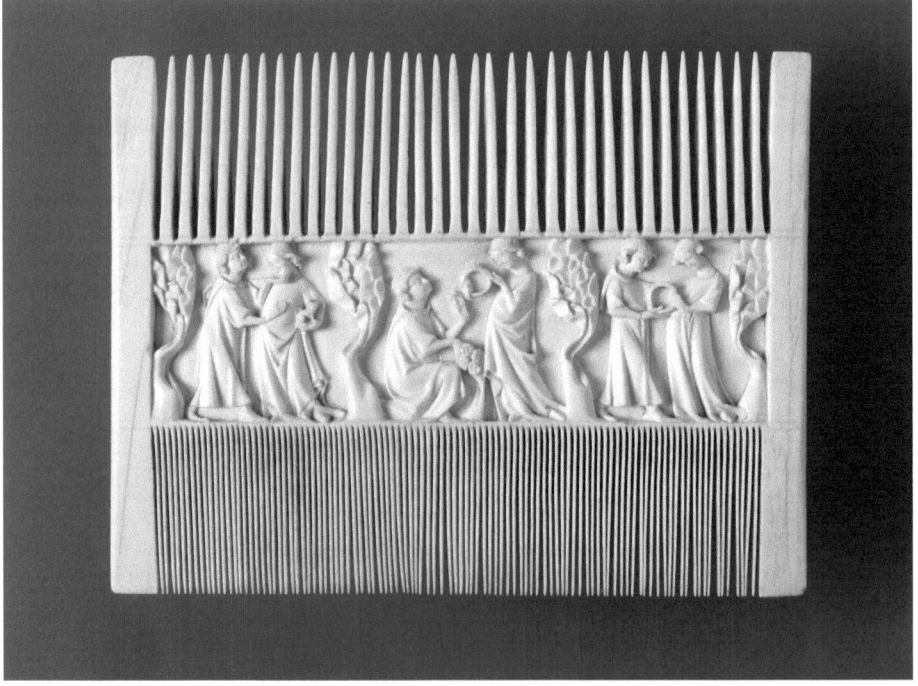

FIGURE 4.2 Comb, Lovers in a garden (ca. 1320). Ivory. Paris, France. © Victoria and Albert Museum, London.

often as symbols of eroticism, as in Chrétien de Troyes' *Lancelot: The Knight of the Cart*. While searching for the kidnapped queen whom he loves, Lancelot finds an ivory and gold comb tangled with her hair, and almost faints from sadness.[18] In other literary moments, combs signify vanity, idleness, and lust. Idleness in *Le Roman de la Rose* is personified as a lovely but empty-headed maiden who gaily proclaims, "I have no care but to enjoy and amuse myself, and to comb and braid my hair."[19] An illustration from a manuscript of *Le Roman de la Rose*, around 1380, appropriately depicts Idleness combing her hair while gazing into a mirror.[20] Mermaids, popular representations of feminine lust and the dangers it posed to men, were frequently depicted with a comb in one hand and a mirror in the other.[21] In the French romance of *Mélusine* by Jean d'Arras, Raymond, the Count of Poitou, discovers the horrific truth about his wife's fairy origins when he encounters her combing her hair in the bath while revealing a mermaid-like tail.[22] As Diane Wolfthal notes, combs are one of the few objects whose symbolism crossed gender boundaries. The lid of a Flemish casket (ca. 1400) portrays a pair of lovers, with the woman tenderly combing the man's hair.[23] And in a fifteenth-century illuminated image of the seven deadly sins owned by the Duke of Berry, a young boy combing his hair personifies lust.[24] Despite the ambiguity associated with combs in artistic images, the material evidence indicates that combing one's hair was part of basic hygiene for Europeans of both genders during the Middle Ages.

CLEANING HAIR

Medieval people kept their hands, faces, and teeth clean, and could bathe in urban bathhouses, private baths, and natural bodies of water.[25] Charlemagne, for example, loved taking steam baths at Aachen and invited his family, friends, and bodyguards to join him.[26] The unpopular and generally unlikable King John took more baths than any English king before him. In "Equitan," a *lai* of Marie de France, two illicit lovers attempt to murder the lady's husband by scalding him in his bath.[27] At the other end of the social scale, peasants, as Barbara Hanawalt has noted in her study of coroner's reports from medieval England, utilized streams, pits, and rivers for bathing, sometimes leading to accidental drownings.[28] Cities such as London, Florence, and Paris also possessed public baths for both sexes.[29] The spirit of the dead husband in Boccaccio's *Corbaccio* (ca. 1353–1355) complains that his widow spent all her time at the public steam baths, returning "even greasier than before."[30] A visit to the baths didn't necessarily indicate hair washing, however, as the dead husband reveals his widow experimented with washing her hair in multiple kinds of ashes in addition to going to the baths, indicating that the hygienic rituals occurred separately. Some visual evidence supports this division of hair washing and body washing. In an illuminated manuscript image from late fifteenth-century Burgundy, men and women bathe together entirely naked except for turbans covering their hair (Berlin, Staatsbibliothek, MS. Dep. Brelau 2, vol. 2, fol. 244, ca. 1470). Hans Memling's painting of Bathsheba (Stuttgart, Staatsgalerie, ca. 1485) stepping out of her bath likewise depicts her wearing a turban (Figure 4.3). On the other hand, a twelfth-century illustration from the Salernitan *Antidotarium magnum* (Large Antidotary) depicts a lady with long unbound hair soaking in a private steam bath. Whether hair was washed while bathing could have been a matter of local custom, personal preference, or even determined by the weather and the amount of time available to the individual since hair takes far longer to dry than skin, and the feel of long wet hair in cold weather is a distinctly unpleasant sensation.

FIGURE 4.3 Hans Memling. *Bathsheba bathing* (1485). Mixed Media on oak. Staatsgalerie, Stuttgart, Germany. Photo: bpk Bildagentur/Art Resource, NY.

How often did medieval people wash their hair? The amount of time anyone devoted to cleanliness probably depended upon a variety of factors: wealth (the aid of servants, the money for public baths), location (access to urban baths, private baths in homes or monasteries), and the effect bathers desired. As I discuss in the section "Hair Dyeing" below, certain recipes for hair dye required extensive washing: up to two or three times a day over three months![31] Religious rituals also came into play. At the end of each menstrual cycle, Jewish women washed their hair as well as their bodies before entering the *mikveh*, a purifying ritual bath. Only after the double-bathing could they resume sexual relations with their husbands.[32]

Baths and servants may have cost money, but soap was available to all but the poorest medieval Europeans. The most inexpensive soaps were mixed from animal fat and ashes, and they worked for both skin and hair.[33] The *Trotula* also suggests a simple cleanser of hot water, natron, and wood bitter-vetch, a wild plant native to Britain.[34] Natron, another kind of ash, more commonly known as soda ash, softens water and is an ingredient in laundry detergent today. More expensive soaps could contain spices for scent. For example, in Boccaccio's *Decameron*, Madame Jancofiore washes her lover "from head to toe" with soap steeped in musk and cloves.[35] Medical texts and conduct books describe cleansers specifically for hair that augment the basic ingredients of fat and ash for shine, thickness, and color. According to Hildegard of Bingen's mid-twelfth-century *Physica* (Physical Things), people could get beautiful hair (and also cure pockmarks) by washing their hair with lye derived from ashes made from plum bark and plum leaves.[36] In his 1484 conduct book, *The Book of the Knight of the Tower*, Geoffrey de la Tour Landry warns his daughters against washing their hair in wine, indicating it was a popular practice for women, and in characteristically lurid language, describes an incident at a church where "ladies who washed their hair in wine and other things to color their hair other than the way God had made it" could not enter until they had cut off their offending tresses.[37] While de la Tour Landry cautions against vanity, he doesn't object to cleanness, as he does recommend that they wash their hair in water and lye, which would be the equivalent of using basic soap.

Washing hair with water-based cleansers or ointments not only cleaned the hair but hopefully got rid of lice and other irritants, as did combing the hair with the fine teeth of a double-sided comb.[38] The *Trotula* offers two hair applications to get rid of "itch-mites eating away at the hair." Both utilize vinegar, a common cleansing agent. The first one mixes the vinegar with myrtle-berry, known for its antiparasitic properties and the second one, with bitter lupins, a Mediterranean legume.[39]

HAIR DYEING

When the dreamer of *Le Roman de Rose* encounters Beauty, he finds her to be "not dark or Brunette," but rather with "long blond hair falling to her heels."[40] In *Le Roman de la Rose* and most other works, the literary ideal of hair was golden for both men and women. Going as far back as the Carolingian court, the poet Sedulius Scottus (writing ca. 840–860) praises Irmingard, wife of Lothar I: "Your fair head is crowned with golden hair."[41] Romances of the twelfth and thirteenth centuries extolled the beauty of blonde hair in both men and women. Chrétien de Troyes praised the "golden tresses" of his heroine Enide, and one of his male heroes, Cligés, possessed "locks [that] seemed made of fine gold."[42] The general emphasis was on the long flowing hair of women, however. In her *Treasury of the City of Ladies*, Christine de Pisan declared that "there is nothing in the world lovelier on a woman's head than beautiful blonde hair."[43] Blonde hair was a sign not only of beauty but of youth, which was prized as an ideal of physical attractiveness as it is in contemporary western cultures. When the dreamer in *Le Roman de la Rose* describes Old Age as one of the negative aspects of the human condition, along with avarice, poverty, envy, hate, covetousness, and religious hypocrisy, he dwells on the ugliness of her white hair.[44] The secular French text, *La Clef d'Amors* (The Key of Lovers), recommends that women with gray hair should dye it.[45] So hair dye could help women not only achieve a more desirable color, but also cover up gray hair.

The Hebrew *Sefer ahavat nashim* (Book of Women's Love), a compilation of texts from Catalonia or Provence, contains no less than five recipes for blonde hair:

> To dye the hair blond: Make a cleanser from the ashes and bark of white ivy wood; wash your head [with it] two or three times a day during three months. Another [remedy]: Anoint your head with ginger oil and [the hair] will turn blond. Another

remedy: Boil large nettles in red vinegar and add a full bowl of water once they are cooked; wash your hair with this during nine days, and not with anything else. Another remedy: Take a fresh pumpkin and perforate it; pour salt and some iron shavings into the orifice and gold-like water will flow [from it]. Another remedy: Take burning water [alcohol], dry false ginger to a powder and put it in a glass vessel with the mentioned water during one or two nights, and [then] wash the hair; it has been tried and tested. Another remedy: Take vine shoot ashes, put them into a cauldron filled with rainwater and boil over the fire until one half of it [is left]. Then take the clean water out of the cauldron, put [it] on the fire together with crushed hard white natron and boil it until it has been reduced by half. Add some saffron if you wish; when it first boils pour into the cauldron two pěshīṭīn [a small coin] of cumin bound in a cloth; wash your head with this soap and after being washed your hair will be like gold.[46]

Unlike the basic soaps described above, these hair dyes could cost medieval women dearly. Some of the ingredients were exotic imports, such as saffron, derived from crocus flowers, which Crusading soldiers brought back from the Middle East. After its popularity as both a cooking spice and an agent of golden dye for both hair and fabric took off, Italian merchants began importing it through central Asia.[47] Even after Europeans began cultivating it closer to home in southern France, Italy, and Spain, it remained expensive, as the harvesting process produces a notoriously small yield.[48] The amounts women were willing to pay for saffron and other imported ingredients such as cumin indicate the extreme desirability of blonde hair and its associations with wealth and breeding in literature. Books such as the *Book of Women's Love* and the *Trotula* recognized that women on the other end of the social scale may also have longed for blonde hair. To that end, they include multiple recipes whose ingredients cover a variety of income levels, from the pricy saffron to common nettles, which could be gathered wild throughout Europe. Other ingredients that appear throughout the *Trotula*, such as walnut shells, oak apples, willow roots, cabbage stalks, and dried roses, were often cultivated in royal and monastic gardens.[49]

It is interesting, as Carmen Caballero-Navas notes, that the majority of the recipes come from Hebrew, Arabic, or Saleritan texts from the southern Italian and Iberian Peninsula, areas where the predominant number of women were unlikely to have naturally blonde hair.[50] Some texts include recipes for lightening or whitening skin, so at least a portion of Jewish and Arabic women were attempting to significantly alter their appearance. In her survey of medieval Andalusian and Arabic literary texts, Claudia da Soller did find that black curly hair surpassed blonde as the height of beauty.[51] But medieval Spanish literature in general upholds the ideal of blonde hair. Juan Ruiz's *Libro de buen amor* (Book of Good Love) probably composed around 1343, describes the ideal lovely woman as a blonde "without henna," presumably meaning naturally blonde, while unattractive women have short black hair.[52] Darker hair in medieval Spain might indicate either Moorish blood or lower-class outdoor work, both being possible reasons for its negative connotations.

The *Trotula* does preserve recipes for black hair dye as well, however. Possibly these were for the benefit of brunettes who wished to cover up gray hair, as opposed to blondes who wanted to dye their hair. A "proven Saracen preparation" for black hair dye requires a green lizard, ground sweet pomegranate, oak apples, and alum."[53] The one color not sought after was red apparently, although possibly some of the ingredients for blonde hair, such as madder and brazilwood, would add a reddish tint to the hair.

How effective were these hair dyes and how long could they last? As with modern hair dyes, the length of time between washings no doubt extended the vibrancy of the color. Some of the most effective recipes involved fixers, such as alum, that would alter the hair's acidic balance to absorb the dye. Europeans may have learned this from fabric dyeing techniques that utilized alum as a mordant to fix colors.[54] A recipe "to make the hair golden," required pretreating the hair (for three days!) with a mixture of alum, oak apples, walnut shells, and walnut bark before applying a concoction of saffron, henna, brazilwood, and dragon's blood (red gum resin).[55] This kind of recipe, which affected the hair's pH balance and utilized the most expensive and exotic ingredients, may have been worth the time and money. Another far simpler recipe for blonde hair which involves a combination of honey and white wine may have produced less dramatic results, but the vinegar in the wine would have left the hair clean and shiny.[56]

As with modern hair-care products, some of the elements listed throughout the recipes—for instance, egg yolks, honey, vinegar, and bear fat—possess smoothing and cleansing qualities as well as or instead of color properties, and they would have acted as a rinse and conditioner during the dyeing process.[57] In the *Corbaccio*, the regretful narrator accuses brunette women of using sulphur to dye their hair blonde.[58] While sulphur does have bleaching properties, and medieval women utilized it on both hair and wool, it also promotes hair growth and treats skin disorders such as dandruff and psoriasis. Boccaccio may not have known exactly why women applied sulphur treatments, or that women may have enjoyed its multiple benefits.[59] Italian women, in particular, had easy access to sulphur, as mines throughout Italy had supplied it, primarily for military purposes, since the Roman Empire.[60]

HAIR ACCESSORIES AND FALSE HAIR

This section will focus primarily on women, as they wore the more elaborate hairstyles that required the most accessories, especially the veil and its accompanying trimmings. Although it varied in length, shape, and arrangement, the veil was a staple of hairstyles for women for most of the Middle Ages. Until about 1100, it covered almost all of the hair and forehead, as well as the shoulders and arms. It could be beautifully decorated or functional, woven or embroidered in elaborate patterns and made of silk, linen or wool. During the twelfth century, veils, known as *couvre-chefs* hung more loosely and could reveal long braids. By the end of the century, the style of the *couvre-chef* evolved into the wimple that draped over the shoulders and around the chin. During the fourteenth century the *couvre-chef* shortened into a diaphanous square fluttering over coiled braids. The veils could be perfumed for effect, as the *Trotula* recommends, "the veil with which the head is tied should be put on with cloves and musk, nutmeg, and other sweet-smelling substances."[61]

Pins were the most ubiquitous and the most significant accessory for dressing the hair in the Middle Ages, and they evolved along with the veil. During the early Middle Ages, pins were made of metal and bone. The shanks tended to be large enough to fasten the voluminous veils of linen and wool and could be carved with decorated heads. The pins held the folds in place to form different shapes, from hoods to wrapped scarves to wimples.[62] During the twelfth century, bone pins gave way to pins of brass wire, pewter, bronze, and silver, with smaller glass, jasper, and coral heads, although a long thin bone pin from the fourteenth century in the collection of the Museum of London indicates that they didn't disappear completely (Figure 4.4).[63] The pins were made finer and smaller

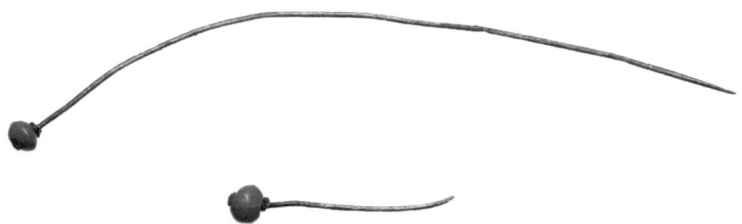

FIGURE 4.4 Copper pins with stone (probably red jasper) heads. Museum of London.

specifically to fasten the diaphanous veils popularly worn with the fillet (a stiffened crown-like band that encircled the head), the barbette (a linen band that wrapped around the head and chin), and the *crespine* (wire and silk cauls worn on both sides of the head).[64] One headdress could use multiple tiny pins. When Princess Joan, the daughter of Edward III, was married in 1348, 12,000 pins were ordered for veils. According to Geoff Egan and Francis Pritchard, "The virtual absence of bone pins after the early thirteenth century appears to have been because they could not compete in fineness with metal pins which were essential for use with fine veiling."[65] They also kept the braids looped into place, as was popular during the fourteenth century.

Other hair accessories included ribbons, hairnets, and mesh coverings. During the twelfth century when female hair became more visible, wealthy women began employing ribbons and hairpieces to achieve the length and fullness of the ideal silhouette, as discussed in Chapter Three of this volume. Artistic depictions of women's hair favored elongated styles based on a center part and two braids hanging down from under a veil. Women could lengthen their braids by weaving them through with ribbons or capping them off with silk tubes or metal cylinders. False hair could have been used as well, especially as styles continued to favor thick braids worn coiled under wimples or bound by bands across the forehead and chin. By the early fourteenth century, most English women braided their hair and looped and pinned the braids over their ears toward the front of their head.[66] Another style involved coiling up the braids into wire or silk meshed *crespines*, as can be seen in an image of a lady and her maid from the Luttrell Psalter (Figure 3.1).[67] In fact, most of our evidence for this style comes from illuminated manuscript illustrations, but four hairnets made of silk thread with a netting needle have been recovered from London.[68] Italian women wore the looped braids or else bound coils of their hair over their foreheads with pearls and ribbons, as in the image of St. Ursula's virgins from the Hours of Bertrando dei Rossi (ca. 1380–1385).[69]

Any of these fourteenth-century styles required long thick hair, and upper-class women used hairpieces to fill out the necessary length and width of the braids. They also required servants to properly arrange the hairpieces for the most natural and becoming effect as well as to secure their veils to hair real and false. A glimpse of this is reported in Boccaccio's the *Corbaccio* where the despotic widow terrorizes her poor maid as she tries to pin her mistress's veil to her hairpiece, referred to as "a tangle of silk."[70] Actual archaeological evidence of such hairpieces is scarce, but one has been recovered from London dating to the second quarter of the fourteenth century. The piece consists of two braids made from blonde human hair, bound with cords to hold them in place. One of the braids is incomplete, but the longer one is bent in two,

PRODUCTION AND PRACTICE 81

indicating it was worn doubled up and hanging to just below the ear, which would be consistent with fourteenth-century looped up braids. Both are stitched to a silk braid decorated with metal that would have been worn across the head as a headband, like a fillet (Figure 4.5).[71]

False hair was so popular in Italian cities that clergy condemned it from the pulpit, and sumptuary laws, laws designed to regulate luxury, attempted to eradicate it. Legislative records illustrate the methods and materials women employed to achieve the latest fashions in hair. For example, in the city of Modena between 1327 and 1336 servants and lower-class women were forbidden to wear false braids of silk.[72] In 1310, Antonio d'Orso Bilotti, the bishop of Florence and Fiesole, forbade the use of false hair, specifically *zazzerris* (long falling hairpieces) and *casciettis* (strands of hair or curls).[73] The responses to such edicts varied: people ignored the sumptuary laws, paid for exemptions, or simply developed new styles in an effort to get around them.[74]

The *Roman de la Rose* describes other ways a woman might compensate for thinning hair.[75] The Old Woman offers this advice for a woman whose hair is lacking:

> And if she sees that her beautiful blond hair is falling out (a most mournful sight), or if it has to be cropped as a result of a serious illness and her beauty thus spoiled too soon ... so that there is no way in which she can regain her thick tresses, she should have the hair of some dead woman brought to her, or pads of light-colored silk, and stuff it all into false hair-pieces. She should wear such horns above her ears that no stag or goat or unicorn should surpass them, not though his head were to burst with the effort.

FIGURE 4.5 Matthew Daniel, plaited hairpiece with silk, drawing (mid-fourteenth century). Museum of London.

AUGMENTING TEXTURE, THICKNESS, AND LENGTH

False hair was one way to achieve long thick hair. Some women hoped to improve the texture of their hair through medicinal treatments. *L'Ornament des Dames* (The Ornament of Ladies) is an anonymous Anglo-Norman treatise written in the thirteenth century. It includes the following recipe attributed to an Arabic woman:

> Certainly, the Saracen woman from Messina cured, in front of my eyes, a young woman who was completely bald and had lost the hair of the eyebrows. She took parsley and sage, crushed them hard and boiled them with white wine and pig's fat. When it was well boiled, she put the fat that floated in another pot; she took cumin and mastic and crushed them with boiled egg's yolk. She boiled together both preparations and anointed the head. You may do this whenever you want that your hair to grow.[76]

The Book of Women's Love recommends a recipe "to make hair grow anywhere," the ingredients of which are similar enough to suggest a strongly cross-cultural influence. These include pig juice and white wine, this time mixed with honey and parsley juice.[77]

The *Trotula* weighs in on hair growth with a recipe of barley, salt, and bear fat. It also recommends treatments for thickening, smoothing, curling, and lengthening hair. The ingredients are similar to other dye and growth recipes that make use of "egg yolks, cumin, wine and pork grease." For curls, it suggests to "Grind root of danewort with oil and anoint the head, and tie it on the head with leaves."[78] There are no correlations in modern herbals, although presumably the danewort acted as a paste and the leaves as curling papers.

As discussed in Chapter Three of this volume, men did wear hats, hoods, and helmets, depending on rank and function in society. They didn't require copious amounts of hair for many of their styles, which were generally simpler and shorter, although they may have attempted to remedy baldness. Medieval medical theory attributed hairiness to the hotter nature of men and considered it a primary marker of sexual virility. Baldness, therefore, indicated not only age but a corresponding lack of sexual vigor, and some medieval men understandably must have desired to recover their lost hair.[79] The thirteenth-century Dominican scholar Albertus Magnus recommended a mixture of burned female goat excrement, vinegar, and honey applied topically. Also in the thirteenth century, the encyclopedist Vincent of Beauvais also credited goat excrement with a variety of medicinal properties, including curing baldness, as well as easing the pain of snake bites, wasp stings, burns, and arthritis. Goats possessed associations with sexuality, perhaps explaining the connection.[80]

HAIR REMOVAL

As much effort as women expended on keeping the hair on their head colored, luxuriant, shiny, and thick, they also sought to remove unwanted hair from other areas of their bodies, such as their armpits, eyebrows, foreheads, and pudenda. The people living in medieval Europe were almost exclusively of Caucasian origin, be they European, Middle Eastern, or Mediterranean, and Caucasians have more body hair than any other race with the exceptions of the Ainu in northern Japan.[81] While the presence of tweezers in early medieval graves indicates that both male and female Europeans had always practiced some limited form of hair removal, women, in particular, seemed more willing to endure pain and expense to tame this body hair according to contemporary ideals of beauty. The fashion for smooth skin, particularly in women's pubic areas, took hold in Europe after Crusading soldiers' encounters with depilated Middle Eastern women.[82] The newfound popularity of hairlessness actually coincided with long-held medieval views on female bodies. As with concepts of male baldness, these views can be traced back to classical medical writers such as Galen and Aristotle, who described women as colder and wetter than men. Body hair was the result of these excess fluids. Men, who were thought naturally hotter and dryer, could cook their fluids into semen while women expurgated them into menstrual blood and hair.[83] Pubic hair especially, due to its proximity to the sexual organs and menstrual discharge, possessed negative, unattractive, and even dangerous properties. A late medieval medical text related that buried pubic hair mixed with menstrual blood would transform into venomous beasts.[84] The dreamer in *Le Roman de la Rose* is horrified by the hair that grows in the ears of Old Age.[85] In Juan Ruiz's *Libro de buen amor* (Book of Good Love), a medieval Spanish text composed around 1343, Don Amor offers advice on how to choose a woman: "Take care that your lady is not hairy or bearded; may Hell rid us of such a half-devil as that!"[86] Pubic hair also carried associations with original sin, so that at times it appeared on artistic images of Eve, for example, Lorenzo Maitani's Genesis reliefs in Orvieto Cathedral, around 1310, and Jan van Eyck's 1432 Ghent Altarpiece (Figure 4.6.).[87]

FIGURE 4.6 Jan van Eyck, Eve, with the slaying of Abel. Wing from the Ghent Altarpiece. Cathedral of St. Bavo, Ghent, Belgium. Photo: Scala/Art Resource, NY.

There were no salons with trained professionals to assist medieval women in waxing, shaving, and plucking their unwanted body hairs. Most women would do this at home, either by themselves or with a servant's help. One of the responsibilities of the poor maid of the wealthy wife in Boccaccio's *Corbaccio* was to remove stray hairs from her mistress' cheeks.[88] Another passage in the same work indicates that hair removal was a fledgling trade among older women, at least in medieval Florence. The narrator describes "certain old biddies, of whom there are a great many around our city, who go about peeling other women, plucking their eyelashes and brows, shaving their cheeks with thin glass, smoothing the hide on their necks, and removing little whiskers."[89] What might one of these old biddies have carried with them when they visited the homes of wealthy Florentine ladies? Tweezers were a popular cosmetic item that women used for eyebrow shaping. Alison, the attractive and fashionable wife in *The Miller's Tale*, plucks her eyebrows: "Plucked to a slender line were her eyebrows, / And they were arched, and black as any sloes (blackthorn berries)."[90] Geoffrey de la Tour Landry also warns his daughters of the horrible afterlife of the woman who had vainly plucked her eyebrows: one devil held her by her hair and put burning needles into her brows while another devil thrust burning brands into her face in every place where she had plucked.[91] Despite his dire warnings, tweezers were considered a commonplace hygiene item for men as well as women and were usually included in cosmetic sets. Cosmetic sets excavated in London dating from the thirteenth and fourteenth centuries include tweezers, earscoops, and toothpicks, all riveted together at one end. The three items fold into each other and could fit neatly into leather cases. Tweezers could be made of bone, copper, bronze, and brass.[92]

Depending on the fashion, women could utilize tweezers to pluck larger areas as well. During the fifteenth century, women plucked the hair on their foreheads as well as their eyebrows in order to achieve a smooth high brow with a minimum of hair visible beneath headdresses and hats. The *Portrait of a Lady* by Rogier van der Weyden (London, National Gallery, 1450–1460) is one of the most iconic images of the hairless brow under a crisp white veil (Figure 4.7).

While plucking would certainly rid women of unwanted hairs, depilatories could cover more ground with longer-lasting results. Henry de Mondeville, a surgeon from fourteenth-century Paris, described women with fingers covered in pitch to remove body hair.[93] The author of the *Book of Women's Love* had advised the following depilatory to "a woman who had hair growing on her forehead since she was born":

> Take some mice and put them into a vessel; take a sponge and sew every one at the back; put some more sponges in the vessel and feed them oils, perfume, and spices in order to make them very thirsty and then give them water to drink. Afterwards squeeze the sponge and anoint the chosen place with the water that flows out; [the hair] will never flow again.[94]

Although this recipe seems somewhat nonsensical, other depilatories from the *Book of Women's Love* involve ingredients such as wax, gum arabic, orpiment (an arsenic compound), aloe, and quicklime that possess more obvious depilatory and soothing qualities.

The *Trotula* includes three recipes for full-body depilatories. One begins, "in order that a woman might become very soft and smooth and without hairs from her head down."[95] All involve several steps, beginning with steaming and cleansing at public baths if possible, indicating the Middle Eastern origins of these recipes. After bathing, an abrasive ointment is applied, with ingredients such as quicklime, galbanum (a plant-derived gum resin), and

FIGURE 4.7 Rogier van der Weyden, *Portrait of a Lady*, painting (ca. 1460). Courtesy National Gallery of Art, Washington.

orpiment. The *Trotula* suggests mixing these harsh substances with soothing additives such as almond milk and cucumber leaves (popular skincare ingredients today) or heading off irritation with a pre-application of oil or honey. If a woman incurs burns during the process, there are recipes for two healing unguents, one of henna and egg whites, and one of poplar buds and rose or violet oil. The repeated warnings against rubbing too hard or sitting too long indicate the risk, discomfort, and downright pain involved with large-scale depilation.[96] Women were willing to endure physical suffering to achieve the ideal smooth skin.

In addition to cosmetic purposes, depilatories may have helped medieval women and men avoid lice that gather in hairy areas. One recipe, which involves myrtle oil and natron (a baking soda–soda ash), "prevents lice from proliferating and armpit hair from growing."[97] The *Trotula* also recommends ointments specifically for "lice which arise in the pubic area and armpits."[98]

Head hair could be more easily removed via shaving and cutting. Secular women may not have required shears as a regular hair accessory since they grew their hair long. Most hairstyles of the high and late Middle Ages relied upon long hair, so much so, as we have seen, that women resorted to false hair when their own proved less than sufficient. For monastic women, on the other hand, access to shears would have been a necessity. Cutting off one's hair signified visibly and dramatically that a woman was leaving behind the earthly world of sexuality, marriage, and childbearing. The moment of hair cutting figures as a point of no return in saint's lives, such as the *Life of Catherine of Siena*, who cuts off her hair to avoid marriage despite the wishes of her family.[99] The Rule of Clare of Assisi, approved in 1253, includes laying aside secular dress and hair cutting as the irrevocable moment before a woman entered her novitiate, after which "she may not go outside the monastery except for some useful, reasonable, evident, and approved purpose."[100] A fourteenth-century manuscript of *Lancelot du Lac* (Lancelot of the Lake) depicts an abbess cutting off the long hair of a novice with a ferocious pair of shears (Figure 4.8).[101] Vowed women would maintain this short hair for the rest of their lives, which would require regular hair cutting. Peter Abelard's suggested Rule for Heloise's nuns at the Paraclete includes the provision that women could wear caps of lambs' wool, as their cropped heads might be more susceptible to cold.[102]

Men never practiced full-body depilation, but the question of whether or not to have a beard and mustache, and what forms they should take, was always relevant among the fashionable, the law-abiding, and the vowed. The length of hair and the exposure of the scalp also varied. Monastic styles remained the most static, with men shaving their heads according either to the Celtic tonsure (shaving the top of the head and letting the bottom layer of hair hang long) or the Roman tonsure (shaving most of the head except

FIGURE 4.8 Miniature of the abbess of the White Nuns cutting the hair of a novice, from *Lancelot du Lac* (ca. 1316). MS Add. 10293, fol. 261. © The British Library Board.

for a short ring all the way around). Early medieval manuscripts typically depict monks as clean-shaven, and clerical regulations required shaving, such as the Council of Aachen (816) which mandated that monks shave every fifteen days.[103]

Razors were an ancient tool, utilized by the Egyptians and Greeks among multiple other cultures, and the professional barber was a feature of Greek and Roman society. They belonged exclusively to the public world of men, as women performed their own hair care at home with the help of servants and slaves.[104] The barber shop itself declined after the Roman Empire split into kingdoms ruled by Germanic chiefs. Barbers emerged again, however, during the eleventh century, as the regulations for shaving among the clergy barbers themselves emerged again during the eleventh century specifically for monastic circles.[105] An image from an English manuscript of *Similitudines* (Likenesses) by Anselm of Canterbury dating to the first half of the thirteenth century illustrates one monk tonsuring another, but certainly by 1163, when the Council of Tours forbade the clergy from shedding blood, the barber developed into a separate and secular profession (Figure 4.9).[106] Medieval barbers also performed medicinal functions, including bloodletting and dentistry, and over the next centuries we see them forming schools and guilds.[107] During the mid-thirteenth century, Parisian barbers formed the Brotherhood of St. Cosmos and St. Domain which organized the first barber training courses. The majority of the training probably dealt with the surgical end of the profession but no doubt included the rudiments of shaving and hair cutting. In London, the Worshipful Company of Barbers formed in 1308.[108]

Shaving kept secular men fashionable as well as clergy regulated. During the fifteenth century, for example, male fashions for smooth hairless foreheads mirrored those of women. In *Très Riches Heures*, created for John, the Duke of Berry between around 1412

FIGURE 4.9 Anselm of Canterbury, a monk receiving the tonsure, from *Similitudines* (Likenesses) (first half of the thirteenth century). MS Cotton Cleopatra, C. XI, fol. 27v. © The British Library Board.

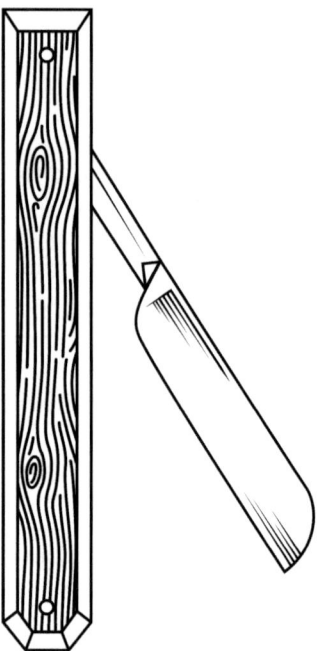

FIGURE 4.10 Matthew Daniel, fifteenth-century men's razor, drawing from Richard Corson's *Fashions in Hair: The First Five Thousand Years*.

and 1416, the noblemen reveal almost no hair under towering hats. Another fashion, the popular "bowl cut" style, which originated in Burgundian and French courts and soon after spread to aristocratic men in England and Spain, required men to shave the back of their necks and sideburns. The portrait of Henry V of England (London, National Portrait Gallery, late sixteenth or early seventeenth century) and the illustration of Raymond de Poitiers in the *Roman de Mélusine* (Romance of Mélusine) illustrate this hairstyle respectively in Flemish and English aristocratic circles.[109] Richard Corson, in his overview of hair fashions, provides an illustration of a fifteenth-century men's razor, a straight blade attached to a wooden sheath with a pin that typically would have been employed to achieve such fashionable styles (Figure 4.10).[110]

CONCLUSION

When considering the development of hair care during the Middle Ages, the twelfth century stands out as pivotal. The Crusades exposed northern Europeans to the wide variety of cosmetic treatments practiced in the Middle East, as well as introduced them to a new world of herbs and spices. During the same century, compilations of female medical texts made their way north from Spain and southern Italy in new Latin and vernacular translations. We also see the beginnings of professionalization during this period, as barbers begin to set up shop in urban areas. The growth of guilds during the thirteenth and fourteenth centuries accelerated the scope of the barber trade. Men and women also worked in soap-making and comb-making as well as apothecary shops, all of which contributed to the variety of tools and ingredients. Female hair care still occurred in private spaces, although certainly by the mid-fourteenth century, some women were earning money performing depilations.

Although medieval conceptions of hygiene may not be stringent enough for modern sensibilities, medieval people attempted to keep their hair reasonably clean and their scalp healthy. Many of the ingredients they used are found today in organic products and were discovered through tried and true practice. Cleanliness was one aspect of hair care, beauty another. Women, in particular, strove for the eternally youthful golden tresses and hairless bodies, although misogynistic texts mocked them for their vanity. At the same time, the play of color and scent may have provided pleasure and added a sense of individuality.

ACKNOWLEDGMENTS

Images cited in this chapter are generally available via online searching or through an online database like ARTstor.org (many libraries provide access); for others I have indicated sources.

CHAPTER FIVE

Health and Hygiene: Hair in the Medical Traditions

FERNANDO SALMÓN AND MONTSERRAT CABRÉ

In medieval Latin Europe, hair was a common object of interest for both health practitioners and the lay public alike. From a theoretical and an empirical point of view, hair was connected to health and disease, and practices involving its care were the concern of a wide range of medical practitioners—physicians, surgeons, barbers, and other healers—as well as women and men without a significant specialization in medical issues. Conceptualizations of hair in the medieval period were formed with the remnants of Hippocratic and Galenic medicine that, recorded in Greek and Arabic, were available in Latin translations dating from the early Middle Ages. During the long twelfth century, western Europe witnessed an explosion in the production and circulation of medical literature. The translations of Arabic authors in particular considerably enriched the accessible medical learning and gave a new impetus to the investigation of practical and theoretical aspects of health care. As a result of this development, an increase in the preoccupations around human hair is noticeable in western medical and surgical literature, as it was particularly relevant in the Arabic traditions, both learned and empirical. Concurrently, the care and practical handling of all types of bodily hair emerged with new force within the context of health-care texts.[1]

During the thirteenth century, the gradual incorporation of medicine as a part of the institutional knowledge taught at the universities enlarged the complexity of the inquiry around human hair. However, the basic notions about hair remained the same as in the earlier period and were remarkably congruent to the practices and ideas displayed by the lay. This is not striking if we recognize that within the Mediterranean basin and beyond, people from diverse cultural, linguistic, and geographical locations were able to share a common understanding of the workings of the body in health and disease, one defined by a conceptual framework dominated by humoralism. Traditionally, humoralism has been defined as a holistic healing system that affirmed that health and disease were part of a continuum conditioned by the balance or imbalance, flux or stagnation of some natural bodily fluids: the humors.[2] This is not the place to describe humoralism in detail, but some basic ideas need to be outlined in order to better understand the shared framework of discourses and practices involving male and female hair that developed along the ancient and medieval Mediterranean, all of which derived from a successful model of understanding of the body in health and disease.

Despite the various ambiguities and contradictions that shaped its long history from the fifth century BCE to the standardization proposed by Galen in the second century CE, the concept of humoralism consistently appeared linked to an idea that each and every individual was a microcosm that echoed the composition of the universe. Nature was composed of four elements (fire, water, air, and earth) that were also characterized by two pairs of opposing qualities. These elements were reflected in each of the four humors that formed the human body (phlegm, blood, yellow bile, and black bile) as these humors displayed qualities of the element that dominated in its composition. Thus the cold and the wet were the qualities that characterized the phlegmatic humor, the hot and the wet the blood, the hot and the dry the yellow bile, and the cold and the dry the black bile since water, air, fire, and earth dominated in each of them respectively. It was thought that the humors derived from the second digestion of the food (the first happened in the stomach to produce chyle) that took place in the liver and was specifically linked to some organs: the phlegm in the brain; the blood in the heart, veins, and arteries; the yellow bile in the gallbladder; and the black bile in the spleen. Through a third digestion produced within the various bodily members, the humors contributed to the nutrition of each of the members and by so doing became their own substance.[3] The humors were also linked to the seasons of the year, astrological planets, different climates, and the regional winds, as Figure 5.1 shows with a diagram of the four elements and the winds from a fifteenth-century medical miscellany. And it seems that this humoral organization of bodily resources provided a convincing rationale that fulfilled expectations regarding the maintenance of health and the prevention and cure of disease.

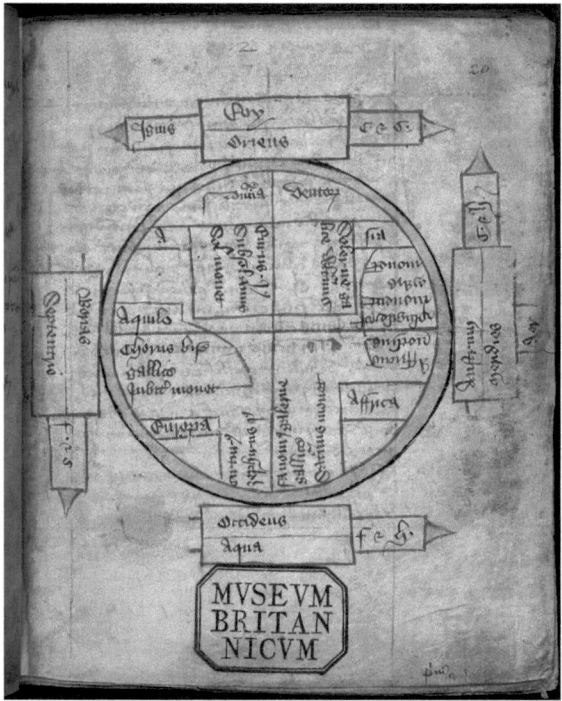

FIGURE 5.1 Diagram of the four elements and the regional winds. John of Ardene, *Medical treatises* (fifteenth century). London, British Library, Sloane 795, fol. 20r. © The British Library Board.

Recently, historians have noted the fact that in medieval Europe and more broadly in the Mediterranean area there were few direct references to the humors as such in medical practice; instead references to the complexions or temperaments abound that reflected the balance or imbalance of the aforementioned qualities in an individual or in each of his or her parts.[4] This important reflection might wisely advise that we talk about humoralism with circumspection in regard to its name, but it does not invalidate the particular epistemological framework that humoralism designates since in medieval medical theory, qualities, temperaments, and humors were part of the same continuum and most of the time synecdochically interchangeable.

Each individual would have a particular temperament that varied according to different features such as age, sex, place, time of birth (geographical and astral), and so on. At the same time, each body part was endowed with a particular temperament that would ensure the fulfillment of its purpose. The brain, for example, was thought to be cold and moist in order to facilitate—among others—the mental functions. The ideal temperament that guaranteed health was the temperate, that is, the well-balanced, but this was always itself still a relative category, both for every particular individual and also for each body part. A healthy woman, for example, was always thought to be colder than a healthy man, or an Ethiopian hotter than a Slav. The departure from this ideal did not inevitably suggest disease but, rather, a tendency toward it. For instance, a particular human brain could be colder and wetter than that ideally temperate but, within a certain latitude, it would still remain healthy even if producing much more mucus. If the balance of cold and wet went beyond that certain limit, however, that brain could end up producing a cold and wet pathology, such as a catarrh (cold).

Medieval medicine and natural philosophy adopted a system that divided the human body into nine temperaments: one perfect and eight imperfect. The imperfect were four simple and four compound, depending on if a single quality (simple) or a pair of them (compound) dominated in a particular temperament. In theory, a person's temperament was physically perceptible and could be discerned directly by touch, particularly by the fingertips that, according to ancient Galen, were the most temperate part of the human body. However, there were other indirect ways that helped the observer to ascertain the general temperament of an individual or of his or her external and internal parts. For example, as discussed more fully later, the various traits of a person's hair were significant indicators of health and illness and thus were often considered in both prevention and therapy.[5]

It is important to highlight that a body conceptualized in this fashion was far from an abstract theoretical construction. It was the locus where medieval medicine acted, and at the same time, it was also the experiential body of the patient. It was a body mediated by sensuous experiences that could be seen but also smelled, touched, and listened to—a body where there was no separation between the somatic and the psychic and where its different parts were in dynamic exchange with each other and with all that surrounded them. Medieval medicine built its approach to human hair within this general frame that abounded in the use of analogies and metaphors of transformation such as processes of concoction, evaporation, and filtering in which the intangible theoretical niceties of the four qualities become very real, as they are embedded in common and basic experiences coming from daily life activities. As with any symbolic representational system—dominated in this case by opposing dualities—medieval approaches to hair in relation with health and disease did also laden these embodied qualities with cultural values that shaped both its conceptualizations and practices.

WAS HAIR A PART OF THE MEDIEVAL BODY?

During the twelfth century, the new educational institutions adopted a fairly stable medical syllabus throughout Europe. In one of its core texts, Galen's *Tegni* (Art), known also as *Microtegni* (Little Art), the body was divided into members that were classified in a fourfold ordering according to their relation with the various powers or faculties that ensured human life. Some, for example, were the roots of those powers, namely the heart, the liver, the brain, and the testicles and thus were named principal members. Other members served the principal members and received their powers from those, for example, the arteries from the heart, the veins from the liver, the nerves and medulla from the brain, and the *vasa seminaria* from the testicles. Still others were defined according to an innate power that was neither influenced nor influencing other members, for instance, the bone, flesh, or fat. A fourth group was defined as having both innate powers and also powers received from others, such as the stomach or the lung. In this account, hair and nails were explicitly set apart from the body members as a different category.[6]

Haly Ibn Ridwan (d. 1068), one of the earliest commentators of the *Tegni*, mused over the possibility of proposing a fifth place for the hair and nails within the classification of body members, but he finally ruled it out on the basis that hair and nails have no relationship with any of the bodily powers, so they could not be considered as proper body members.[7] His judgment was influential, since in the collection of the five to seven texts that formed the basis of medical education, the so-called *Articella*, the *Tegni* was usually read with the interpretation given by Haly in its Latin translation. The subsequent incorporation of a bulk of Galenic works in medical teaching during the thirteenth century and the increased influence of the interpretations provided by the Persian physician Ibn Sina (Avicenna, d. 1037) in his huge synopsis of medical knowledge, the *Canon*, did not challenge this view.

The puzzling position of hair within the body's economy was investigated by various medieval authors. Taddeo Alderotti (1215–1295), the influential thirteenth-century medical master of the Bolognese studium, discussed the possibility of hair having some powers, at least those of nutrition and of generation, since, together with other authors, Galen affirmed that hair was nurtured and that it seemed an obvious fact that it had been generated. Alderotti, however, posited that Galen was wrong because if hair was generated, it happened without the influence of a generative power. Thus even though hair seems to obviously grow, it does so not as a result of any kind of nutrition.[8] Some years later (before 1319), physician and philosopher Pietro Torrigiani (d. ca. 1320) went even further confirming this view. In his self-acclaimed *Plusquam commentum* on the *Tegni*, he asserted that since hair did not participate in any of the body powers, strictly speaking, neither should it be considered as part of the body nor as one of her members.[9] What both Taddeo and Turisanus were reflecting upon was a common tenet held by both natural philosophers and physicians alike. In collections of recipes, medical handbooks, or more theoretically complex treatises, hair was thought to be the product of the exhalation of bodily vapors that emanated through skin pores and were then dried by the surrounding air.[10] The same logic explained its mode of growth that was not attributed to nutrition—as it happened with other body parts—but an ordered addition of dried-up fumes.[11]

In the medieval medical tradition, hair is thus considered a superfluity, one of the by-products of the Galenic bodily functions that emerges from the so-called third digestion.[12] As in any process of concoction, this digestion—that provides the true nutrition for all the bodily members as discussed earlier—generates fumes that naturally ascend to the upper parts of the body.[13] This explained the abundance of hair in the head, in that it would work much as a foundry furnace to channel all bodily vapors that emerged through the skin pores. The movement of the generating fumes runs naturally from the bottom up, not from side to side, and that was used to justify the fact that humans do not have hair on the palms of the hands or on the soles of the feet.[14] The hardness of the skin membranes was also often invoked as a cause for the hairlessness of palms and soles, but in addition, and significantly, a teleological argument was called forth asserting that the presence of hair in those places would interfere with the functions for which human hands and feet were created.[15] This type of thinking was at the heart of medieval Aristotelianism and informed approaches to the human body in the medical traditions.

HAIR AND THE ORDERED WISDOM OF NATURE

The wisdom of Nature was behind the reasoning that sustained the various characterizations of the body parts. To the modern reader, the definition of a body part would suffice with the description of its structure and function—from the macro to the molecular level. However, for a medieval reader, knowledge of a part of the human body required one more step, that of an understanding of what that part had been made for.[16] This approach reflected the teleological thought of the ancients when studying the works of a provident Nature, an approach that was easily translated in medieval Latin Europe into a Creator God that showed his wisdom through an ordered creation.[17]

What was the place of hair within such a systematic understanding of the human body? Despite its humble origins from the fumes of a digestion, most of the natural philosophical and medical sources understood that human hair fulfilled various important functions. The two more commonly mentioned were defense and adornment. However, not all the hair on the body was created for accomplishing both of these functions. The hair of the head, for example, was conceived of as having a function of adornment and also of defense by protecting from the excess of environmental coldness, heat, and dryness. The eyebrows and eyelashes follow the same pattern, as they were interpreted as being important for the decorative purpose of the face but also for the protection of the eyes since they served as barriers to objects that might fall inadvertently into them. But other types of body hair only bore a function of adornment. Nonetheless, it is important to stress that the decorative function of the hair was thought to be as important as the defensive faculty, in particular because it was openly attached to the need of telling the sexes apart (*ad sexus discretionem*).[18]

Hair was considered a basic expression of sexual difference. The unequal distribution of heat in the body explained either the presence or the lack of hair in various areas, and it was identified as the reason behind the different patterns of hairiness on female and male bodies. Heat was the most fundamental physiological difference between the sexes, and male temperaments were considered much hotter and drier than females. It was thought that the coldest man was still warmer and drier than the warmest and driest woman. Heat in combination with dryness allowed the male body to make his superfluities into body hair and beards. In areas such as the chest and the pubis, hair grew due to its proximity to sources of heat like the heart or the testicles. By contrast, women's superfluities were also transformed into hair, but their lesser innate heat as well as the ability of the female body to cleanse out these superfluities through menstruation, explained why women grew hair in fewer regions than men.[19] But if heat and dryness accounted for the geography of hair, humidity gave the reason for its abundance and length on the head. Women's wetter temperaments helped to grow longer hair that more densely covered the scalp; men's dryness was the cause for its lessening and thinness.[20]

Hair was at the center of the physiological explanation of sexual difference, but it was also paramount in the characterization of the feminine, the masculine, and the non-masculine. Losing the hair of the head—hair that had the functions of defense and adornment, as we saw earlier—was thought of as particularly dishonorable for women, as some medical sources stated.[21] The beard and body hair of men only bore the function of adornment, but their features were important in conveying the true mark of masculinity associated with sexual virility and the stages of male maturity as it is portrayed in the depiction of two kings from different generations in Figure 5.2. In the Hippocratic and Aristotelian traditions, they distinguished the male from the female, differentiated the child from the adult as well as the human from the animal.[22] Men of different temperaments would present different patterns of hairiness according to their own degrees of masculinity. Eunuchs and children of both sexes as well as women shared the inability to produce semen that deprived them of growing beards, a phenomenon particularly apparent in the case of eunuchs.[23]

Any sort of body hair was also important in the cleansing of bodily vapors, and some medical authors advised against the practice of blocking these natural gates for the elimination of superfluities. For example, Bernard of Gordon (1283–1308), in his early fourteenth-century medical compendia, the *Lilium medicinae* (Lily of Medicine), denounced those who recommended the use of narcotics or cautery to prevent the growth of pubic hair in young girls on the grounds that the held-back fumes could cause disease.[24]

Adornment, defense, cleansing of the bodily impurities, or sexual difference were listed in the arguments that explained why the Creator endowed the human body with hair that is—when analyzing hair's purpose—its intrinsic *causa finalis* (final cause). However, for a medical audience, the importance of the hair did not stop here. Indeed, the longest

FIGURE 5.2 Old King James I of Aragon (left) and younger King Alfonso of Castile (right) before the representatives of the aljama of Murcia. *Cantigas de Santa María* (Castile, ca. 1280–1284). El Escorial, Madrid, San Lorenzo del Escorial, T I 1, Cantiga 169, fol. 226v, 3–4. © Patrimonio Nacional.

theoretical discussions on hair touched upon its usefulness as a diagnostic sign in a body defined by the balance of the four qualities and the movements and transformations of the humors. For some authors, this was precisely the reason that justified why the ancients mentioned hair when discussing the parts of the body.[25]

HAIR AS A DIAGNOSTIC SIGN OF BRAIN TEMPERAMENT

Hair gave information of the balanced or imbalanced temperament of the brain as other superfluities did, such as the watery mucus eliminated through the palate or those superfluities that emerged from unnatural places as head ulcers.[26] Even if in most cases the distinctive traits of the hair to be considered were just those of the head and the information obtained was useful in relation to the complexion of the brain, authors such as Gentile da Foligno (ca. 1280/1290–1348) argued that the particular features of the head hair of an individual reflected his or her general temperament.[27] The reason given was that the head acted as a chimney for the fumes of the whole body.[28] In his *De complexionibus* (On the Temperaments), Galen (129–210 CE) had openly expressed his opinion about the impossibility of knowing the temperament of a whole body through the analysis of one part and denied as well the physiognomers' claim that from such judgment the character of the person could be inferred. Being part of the Latin medical syllabus, Galen's text was well known in the medieval classroom, and it was often quoted in scholastic literature. Nonetheless, medical masters did not take the opportunity to follow the overt criticism of physiognomy presented in *De complexionibus* nor commented upon the examination by Rhazes (865–ca. 925) in book II of his influential *Liber ad Almansorem*. Until the fifteenth century, medical engagement with the science of physiognomy was limited, and its goals seemed different from purely medical interests; the interactions between the two traditions are few, and they mostly seem to run parallel to each other.[29]

By the late thirteenth century, the main traits to be evaluated when considering hair as a sign of temperament and their meanings were already known and shared with slight differences in the medical schools of Montpellier, Paris, or Bologna. They were described in treatises of natural philosophy such as Aristotle's *De generatione animalium* (On the Generation of Animals) or in works of the traditional medical syllabus such as the *Tegni*, Avicenna's *Canon*, or in some of the newly adopted texts by Galen that were lectured upon in the medieval classroom.[30]

According to Taddeo Alderotti, the three features of hair more commonly thought of as useful diagnostic tools were color, form (straight or curly), and the time that baldness occurred. But he also thought that three other features would complete the list: the time of appearance of hair after birth, its texture (thick or fine), and its quantity (plenty or scarce).[31] Others would append additional signs as well, like the appearance of gray hair, but there was no basic disagreement in their thinking.[32] The interpretation of the particularities of these traits should take into account variations due to the geographical peculiarities or the age of the individual considered. However, despite the well-known temperamental differences between men and women, sexual difference was scarcely mentioned, and it is clear that the whole discourse was built around the temperamental varieties of the male brain. This androcentric rationale was congruous with contemporary learned discourses and is evident if we think of the preeminent significance given to the appearance of baldness as a sign when analyzing each of the brain temperaments, as baldness is hardly a common female characteristic to evaluate.

The more theoretically complex the treatise, the more elaborate the explanation that justified the connection of any of these traits with the underlying temperament. However, from sketchy compendia to long university commentaries, the basic reasoning was consistent and reflected the action of hot, cold, dry, and wet in domestic processes such as concoction, burning, drying, tanning, or rotting, that created easy analogies with the materiality of daily life, analogies that sustained the validity of the inferences relating physically apparent traits with unseen physiological processes. Generally speaking, the signs revealing an underlying temperament, whether single or compound but defined by the hot and the dry qualities, received more attention than the rest when analyzing the temperamental features of the brain. And there was a practical logic in this interest, at least at a rhetorical level. The temperate brain was thought to be one in which the four qualities were in a balance that ensured the best performance of the brain functions. Balance did not mean the same proportion of the four qualities but one in which the cold and the wet were slightly higher than the others. The cold was needed to guarantee the cooling of the heat that emanates from the heart and the wet to avoid a risk of dryness that would impede the functions of thought, sensitivity, and movement.[33] Within a healthy latitude a brain with a temperament that exhibited an excess of dryness and heat would be more opposed to the temperate brain and, for this reason, more prone to disease.[34]

The color of the hair always varied in a spectrum that ran from almost white to deep black, with various middle degrees of blonde and brown depending on the underlying amount of heat. Hair that was typically black would characterize individuals with a hot or a hot and dry brain temperament. The explanation given in these cases was that the excess of heat provoked an intense burning and thus more—and for some authors also darker—fumes; as a result, hair produced under these circumstances was darker than hair produced under the predominance of mild heat, as it happened to those who had a brain of a cold, or of a cold and wet, temperament.[35] The same argument was used to explain the darkening of the hair color over life spans, with a maximum of color intensity in the early adult age at the peak of the relative dominance of the hot quality even if the temperament of the brain was temperate.[36] The whitening of the hair in old age followed the same causal pattern. Grayness, however, usually received a slightly different explanation that entailed the putrefaction of humors poorly cooked due to the decrease or lack of heat. Thus a temperament in which cold dominates could be recognized because it would be marked by an early appearance of gray hair that was generally defined as the product of a certain putrefaction of phlegm that could not be properly cooked due to the relative lack of heat.[37]

It is interesting to note that the interplay of the various qualities and their actions took place in a body where there was no divide between the physical and the psychological; the changes of the temperamental qualities that had physical effects on the body could happen due to emotional disturbances. While lecturing on the *Canon* in the first half of the fourteenth century, Gentile da Foligno reminded his students of the possibility of a sudden occurrence of the whitening of the hair due to extreme fear or sadness, and as seen in Figure 5.3, medieval allegories represent Sorrow as a pale character that has lost all color.[38] Some years earlier, Arnau de Vilanova (ca. 1240–1311) in his ambitious medical compendium, *Speculum medicine* (The Mirror of Medicine) went even further, recognizing the possibility of the same whitening effect but due to an intense fear just dreamed while sleeping.[39]

FIGURE 5.3 Representation of Sorrow (*Tristece*) with grey hair, detail from Guillaume de Lorris and Jean de Meun, *Roman de la Rose* (Paris, ca. 1320–1340). London, British Library, Royal 19 b XIII, fol. 7r, detail. © The British Library Board.

The effect of the various qualities sometimes overlapped, as it happened with the heat that produced not only a warming effect but also a drying one. This becomes apparent in the explanation given to the significance of the form of the hair. Curly hair was always connected to a process of drying, but it could also be the result of a heating action or a combination of both heating and drying. It is not by chance that the common analogy used to explain the curling of hair was the observation that leather straps wrinkled under the sun, providing evidence for the twisting effect.[40]

The temperamental significance of curly or straight hair, as represented in Figure 5.4, was not restricted to the intensity of the drying of fumes but extended to the explanations of the characteristics of the skin's pores through which the fumes emerged to form hair. The dry temperament that removed the humidity from the fumes would also affect the skin, producing twisted pores that shaped the vapors into the curly forms that emerged through them. On the contrary, a wet temperament would produce a wider pore, and a more malleable fume would come out without any contortion to create a straight hair. This general explanation that emphasized the form of the skin pore was given by Galen in the *De complexionibus* and was followed by many medieval medical authors.[41] Some even boasted about the possibility of distinguishing between a type of curly hair

FIGURE 5.4 Adam and Eve nude in the garden of delights. He has curly hair and wears no beard, while she has wavy hair. Eve's hair is ostensibly longer, as female hair was supposed to be. Ibn Butlan, *Tacuinum sanitatis* (fragments, Bavaria, first half of the fifteenth century). Granada, Biblioteca Real, Universidad de Granada, Códice C- 67, fol. 99r. Courtesy of the Royal Library of the University of Granada.

due to a dry and hot temperament and another due to a twisted pore. In the latter case, the curly hair remained curly even in old age, while in the former, the temperamental changes of the aging process were thought to be responsible for gradual loosening of the curl.[42] Others preferred to follow the explanation given by Aristotle in *De generatione animalium*, who contended that due to the excessive evaporation of the humidity there was a tension between the movement of the fumes upwards (due to the heat) and downwards (due to the dominance of earth materials, as a result of the drying process), resulting in curly hair.[43]

The lack of remarkable differences in the features of hair congruous to hot and dry temperaments is also evident in the descriptions and explanations offered about when it first grows and then the time of its loss. The initial growth of hair was consistently recorded as happening at a very early age, after birth or even in the womb due to the fact that both dryness and heat facilitated a strong production of fumes that was hair's *causa materialis* (material cause).[44] In the same vein, the two qualities of hot and dry were thought to be responsible for a certain removal of the minimum humidity necessary for the production of fumes and the excessive dryness of the skin that resulted in the typical early appearance of baldness in these temperaments.[45] So similar were the effects of the hot and dry temperaments thought to be on the hair that an author as meticulous as Taddeo Alderotti advised not paying too much attention to their differences. In his view, establishing which temperament was responsible for the earliest and widest baldness was of a limited interest to a physician, who would be satisfied with knowing that early and extensive baldness could be the sign of any of the three brain temperaments dominated by the hot and dry qualities.[46]

It is important to note that physicians' interest in human hair and their complex theoretical disquisitions about the balance or imbalance of the four qualities as well as their practical advice on how to ascertain those from empirical observation and reasoning was focused on the handling of a healthy brain. The consideration of hair as a useful sign to evaluate diseases affecting the brain or affecting the whole body was much more restricted. In the case of general diseases such as hectic fevers, hair loss was usually considered a sign that spoke of a great diminution of the bodily nutrition and moisture.[47] In the cases of brain diseases—from a violent frenzy to an unnerving migraine—the characteristics of the hair were not taken into account as relevant signs of the underlying pathological temperament.[48] Furthermore, among physicians, hair in itself could be both the locus of disfiguring diseases and also the subject of procedures of embellishment that could heavily mark the individual in a positive or in a negative way. For a modern reader it might seem that only the diagnostic, prognostic, preventive, and therapeutic measures about hair disease would be the object of medical interest. But an analysis of medical compendia and collections of recipes shows that beautifying processes and care for alleviating painful afflictions of the scalp were intermingled as part of the same realm in the Middle Ages.

HAIR CARE AND THE ADORNMENT OF WOMEN AND MEN

Often under the interchangeable rubrics *De ornatu* or *De decoratione* (On adornment), many learned medical and surgical compendia offered a wide variety of hair treatments, including remedies to prevent, to delay, or to reverse the appearance of baldness and gray hair.[49] In a collection of *experimenta* (tested remedies) attributed to Arnau of Vilanova, it is stated that he himself successfully used a certain water to grow his hair after having lost it as a consequence of a continuous fever he had suffered for a month.[50] Health practitioners of diverse status were involved in hair treatments, advising patients to take particular measures to grow, lengthen, or thicken hair—like applying ointments on a shaved head—or for changing its color with dyes.[51] However, neither gray hair nor—in most cases—baldness were considered a health problem; they were seen as an indication of the natural process of aging or as signs of a certain temperament still within the realm of health, even if they appeared earlier than expected. Other changes to hair, nevertheless, were unmistakably thought to be evidence of diseases. Explained within the same temperamental framework, most of them were characterized by a local corruption of the humors that were improperly cooked, the result of which usually also included skin alterations of the scalp (see, for example, Figure 5.5).

Continuous or sudden loss of hair could happen without any other symptoms, but what was named *alopecia* was allied with skin ulcers, flakes, and scales. The *favus* (a certain type of ringworm) was characterized by the honey-crusted lesions, and the *tinea* (general ringworm) by the patchy distribution of the hair loss, by the flakes and crusts, and by a characteristic foul odor. Those who suffered from such conditions were often stigmatized not just because of their disgusting aspect but also because of the fear of contagion. Once the conditions were diagnosed, pessimism about a person's ability to recover was widely shared even if some measures were recommended and used, like purging the corrupted humors or applying ointments locally.[52]

102   A CULTURAL HISTORY OF HAIR IN THE MIDDLE AGES

FIGURE 5.5 A male patient showing his diseased scalp to a physician, detail from the French version of Mattheus Platearius, *Circa instans* (Amiens, first quarter of the fourteenth century). London, British Library, Sloane 1977, fol. 50v, detail. © The British Library Board.

FIGURE 5.6 A woman removing lice with a brush from the scalp of a kneeling man holding a bowl, detail from *Hortus sanitatis* (Mainz: Jacob Meydenbach, 1491), unnumbered. London, Wellcome Library, EPB 5.e.12.

HEALTH AND HYGIENE 103

The possibility of getting rid of lice that were thought to be produced at the skin pores between the skin and the flesh from spontaneous generation by the corruption of the humors—namely phlegm and yellow bile—was viewed more favorably.[53] In such cases, purging measures and the application of unguents were also advised; practical handbooks included some specifically intended for the pubic area and the armpits as well as for lice that resided around the eyes.[54] However, personal hygiene was also highly recommended, including the regular bathing and changing of clothes since it was also thought that sweat and the lack of cleanliness facilitated the generation of lice. Owing to their lifestyles some social groups, such as wild men or poor and religious people, were targeted as being more prone to generating lice because of either their sloth, their excessive consumption of phlegmatic and melancholic foodstuff, or their deficient attention to their personal body care.[55] As Figure 5.6 vividly shows, a brush was used for an immediate delousing of the head.

According to current ideas on its physiology, the ordinary caring of the hair had a significant impact on an individual's health. This is the reason why medical advice concerning the periodical routines to maintain health and prevent illnesses included washing the head at least once every three weeks and, after drying it up well, combing it to open the pores in order to help eliminate the ascending fumes. Additionally, combing the hair was part of the daily grooming practices that physicians recommended to undertake every morning after sleeping in order to clean all the superfluities generated and kept inside the body during the night. Regular combs could have the same double-sided teeth shape as the liturgical combs that were used ritually by priests and often beautifully decorated (see Figure 5.7).[56]

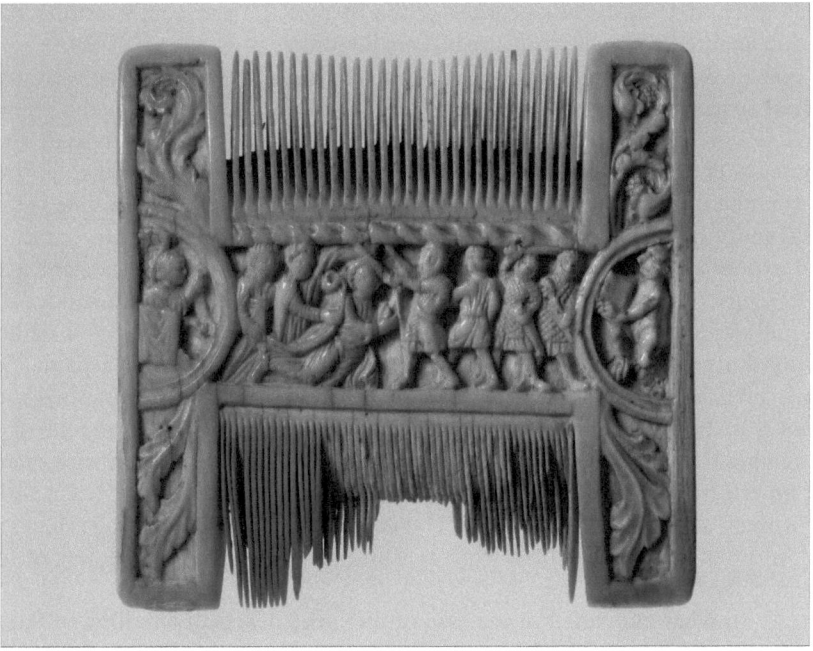

FIGURE 5.7 Liturgical comb (ca. 1200–1210). Ivory. Canterbury, England. New York, The Metropolitan Museum of Art, Accession number 1988.279. Courtesy of The Metropolitan Museum of Art. www.metmuseum.org.

Among the counsels contained in the *Regimens of health* written by physicians for the well-being of men, the care and the shaving of the beard were considered, as well as the depilation of certain hairy parts of the body, such as the armpits if they generated bad smells.[57] Nevertheless, the practical ordinary handling of male hair was not in the charge of physicians but lay within the wide spectrum of functions that in the later Middle Ages were left in the hands of practitioners of lower ranks, namely surgeons and barbers. The new rational surgery that developed at the end of the thirteenth century took on cosmetics as part of its art, and this involved a wide range of hair-care treatments, from softeners to depilatories and from dyes to procedures to stimulate hair growth. Learned surgeons competed with healers of lower status and claimed their superior knowledge to supervise these treatments by stressing the potential dangerous effects inadequate applications could have.[58]

Although it was not always easy to determine the exact status of the different healers, especially those of the inferior levels, the rules governing certain royal households that established a barbership as a particular office clearly distinguished it from the tasks to be undertaken by the court's physicians and surgeons. The barber was explicitly entrusted to care for the king's hair and to serve his most intimate grooming needs, and statutes stressed the royal barber's obligation to keep the instruments of his office clean.[59] More generally, whether in their own shops or in itinerant practices, barbers were responsible for shaving and cutting men's hair; however, surgeons and barber-surgeons also provided hair treatments, and house inventories attest to the overlap of the two occupations. Items such as combs, scissors, copper razors, iron basins, small mirrors, brass bowls, whetstones, crystal thimbles, aprons, and towels were the instruments of the barber's art, but they are also found in the hands of surgeons.[60] Barbery was an eminently male occupation, and although some female barbers have been identified—particularly widows that kept practicing after their husband's deaths—at the turn of the thirteenth century there is a further documented decline in the already small number of women barbers.[61]

The care of women's hair did not take place in barber's shops; these were primarily male social spaces. Instead women's hair care took place at homes in the company of other women, as shown in Figure 5.8, sometimes after consulting with male or female practitioners. The medical handbooks written and used by physicians, surgeons, or barbers contained significant sections on beautifying procedures directly aimed at women. A popular genre of women's health-care texts evolved in Latin and in the vernaculars that included prominent portions devoted to cosmetics.[62] Hair was an important feature of women's beauty, and beauty itself was a gendered ideal whose pursuit demanded different practices of women and of men. They should all act in accordance to their natures, and that involved accommodating the divergent patterns of distribution of hair that resulted from their predominantly wet or hot physiologies.[63] For women, this implied ostensibly the removal of body and facial hair, and texts dealing with the adornment of women contain recipes to make depilatories, often to be applied in combination with steam baths to be more effective.[64] The French royal surgeon Henry de Mondeville (ca. 1260–1320) warned women about the difficulty of adequately preparing and applying recipes for hair removal in order to dissuade them from consulting with unqualified healers or trying to do it themselves.[65]

Contrary to what happened in the case of men, the practical handling of female hair does not seem to have developed into a specialized occupation—as was often the case in regards to women's activities—and there is little information on how such work was commonly carried out.[66] Among the higher ranks of society, ladies-in-waiting and female

FIGURE 5.8 Queen Semiramis in her room, attended by two courtesans and combing herself while receiving a messenger, detail from the French version of Giovanni Boccaccio *De claris mulieribus* (Paris, ca. 1410). London, British Library, Royal 20 C V, fol. 5ra. © The British Library Board.

attendants may have been in charge of washing, cutting, and dyeing women's hair as well as depilating facial and body hair with tweezers and with the variety of procedures recorded in recipe collections; more than likely, women of lesser status also helped each other to care for their hair. Nonetheless, we know that certain individual healers were associated with the administration of useful hair treatments to women, and their practices were of enough merit to be acknowledged in cosmetic texts. This is the case of an unnamed Saracen woman from Messina whose treatments on the prevention of hair loss, on dyes for making hair blonde, as well as her recipes for curing baldness and making the eyebrows grow again, among other procedures, were recorded by an anonymous male author in a thirteenth-century Anglo-Norman recipe collection.[67] Additionally, women who were not identified as healers were randomly singled out as having particular talents such as those involved with delousing or making hair thicker. The great number of such attributions attests to the collective knowledge that women treasured on the practical handling of hair.[68] Indeed, attending to hair was part of the cosmetic domain where women enjoyed the highest degree of independence within the realm of health care.[69]

CONCLUSION

In the Middle Ages, hair was a matter of theoretical investigation as well as a common ordinary preoccupation for women and men. Whether inside university classrooms, at patient's bedsides, in royal courts, at barber's shops, or within the home, it played an important role in people's everyday concerns. For most, it was an ongoing issue all throughout the life cycle and a frequent focus of practical attention that played a significant role in the embodiment of gender. For elite learned men, hair was a bodily expression of human nature in need of explanation and deserving of meticulous reflection. To modern sensibilities, these subtle interpretative efforts to investigate the epistemological status of hair, its place within the body's functions, or its diagnostic value as a physiological sign are striking and alien. However, far from being rhetorical exercises, this chapter has attempted to show that these intellectual investigations were in keeping with the humoral understanding of the human body that imbued the health-care and hygienic culture of the Middle Ages.

ACKNOWLEDGMENTS

Research leading to this chapter has been generously funded by HAR2015-63995-P (MINECO/FEDER).

CHAPTER SIX

Gender and Sexuality

MARTHA EASTON

A fourteenth-century German panel painting depicting an incident from the life of Saint Clare is instructive in understanding the different ways that hair could signify in medieval society and culture (Figure 6.1). The panel, probably created for a convent of Poor Clares

FIGURE 6.1 *The Bishop of Assisi Giving a Palm to Saint Clare,* Germany (ca. 1360). The Cloisters Collection, 1984.343, www.metmuseum.org.

in Nuremburg, illustrates an event that took place on Palm Sunday in the year 1212, when Saint Francis arranged for the bishop of Assisi to hand a palm to Clare. All three figures have different hairstyles that serve as markers of identity. The bishop is depicted with a beard and chin-length hair topped with a miter. Behind him stands Saint Francis, recognizable because of his brown tunic and rope belt, the visible stigmata on his hands, and his clean-shaven face and tonsured head. Clare wears a luxurious dress and crown, denoting her noble status, and her long, flowing hair identifies her as an unmarried woman. However, this scene represents the transformational moment when Clare gives up her life of privilege in order to follow Francis. This transition was marked by cutting her long hair with the large pair of scissors held in his hands and ultimately led to the establishment of the community of religious women bearing her name. In the Middle Ages, hair could be a marker of class, occupation, gender, and sexuality. Depending on whether hair was short or long, light or dark, present or absent, confined to the head or sprouting in other places on the body, it created identity for its owner and for others, and as is the case with Saint Clare, it was sometimes the change from one sort of hair to another that created the most significant meaning in medieval culture.

Ancient and medieval beliefs about the generation of hair reveal broader attitudes, drawn from philosophy, science, and theology, about gender and sexuality.[1] The views of Aristotle and Galen in particular provided the basis for medieval views about gender based on physiological differences. Hair was the result of excess bodily fluids, "gross humors," which were extruded through the pores of the skin. Men were by nature hot and dry (and therefore superior), and they could be characterized by shorter hair and the ability to grow beards, while women were colder and moister, the hair on their heads grew longer, and their faces were smooth and hairless. In Aristotelian thought, beards became associated with masculine virility, and this thought prevailed throughout the Middle Ages; for example, in the twelfth century, Hildegard of Bingen in her *Causae et curae* concurred that a man's ability to grow a beard was due to his greater warmth, and that "woman is without a beard because she is formed from the flesh of man and is subordinate to man and lives in greater quiet."[2] In addition to this scientific evidence, the words of Paul in Corinthians are often invoked as the basis for Christian attitudes about gender and hair. Paul admonishes, "Doth not even nature itself teach you, that, if a man have long hair, it is a shame unto him? But if a woman have long hair, it is a glory to her: for her hair is given her for a covering."[3] For Paul, men had short hair and women had long hair, and any deviation from that prescription was a violation of God and nature.

Despite Paul's words, during the Middle Ages the marker of masculinity for men was not always short hair. The Merovingians, the ruling dynasty of the Latin area known as Francia from the fifth to the eighth century, were popularly known as the "long-haired kings," and their unshorn, flowing locks were a symbol of virility and fierceness (although it should be noted that this long hair was usually shoulder-length, rather than the waist-length hair favored by women). It also distinguished ruler from the ruled; their subjects could not grow their hair beyond a certain length. Despite the Greco-Roman association of long hair with Germanic "barbarians," for the Merovingians, long hair distinguished the free man from the slave.[4]

However, the next ruling dynasty of the Franks, the Carolingians, wore their hair short. In fact, Einhard, the biographer of Charlemagne, takes pains to mention explicitly the long hair of the deposed Merovingian leader Childeric III as if it is yet another characteristic of his ineffectual rule: "The King, contented with the mere royal title, with long hair and flowing beard, used to sit upon the throne and act the part of a ruler."[5] After the Carolingians came to power Childeric's hair was cut off and he was forced into a monastery. This was deeply humiliating, since for the Merovingians the cutting of hair was fraught with symbolic significance; only deposed leaders and other disgraced men had their hair shorn as a form of punishment and exile. There is a biblical parallel with the Old Testament figure of Samson, who was rendered powerless when the temptress Delilah seduced him into revealing that the source of his strength was his hair, and he became impotently unable to defend himself when she cut it off. In contrast, the Franks ritually cut the hair of their boys; Charles Martel sent his son to the Lombard King Liutbrand for his first haircut, thereby solidifying them into a near-familial bond.[6]

And yet, there were times and places during the Middle Ages when long hair for men was decidedly back in fashion for secular men, especially its upper-class members. In the eleventh and twelfth centuries, there are several instances when the clergy condemned men who, in the words of Anselm, the archbishop of Canterbury, "grew their hair like girls."[7] On an Easter Sunday, the men of Henry I's court in England were criticized by the bishop of Séez, who stated, "Those who ... copy women in their flowing hair will be no better than women in defending their country ... You all have long hair like women, which is not right for you who are made in the image of God and ought to act with manly strength."[8] He went so far as to produce a pair of scissors and cut their hair right then and there. At least in the eyes of the bishop, long hair was associated with femininity and, thus, was problematic for the men of the English court. William of Malmesbury, a Benedictine monk who wrote both history and hagiography, also criticized the fashion for long hair at the Anglo-Norman court and suggested that such men were not fully masculinized.[9] The dismay about groups of men with long hair seems to suggest an anxiety not just about hair length but also about the potential for transgressive sexual behavior.

In the Pauline tradition, long hair was a glory for women alone, in part because it served as a veil of modesty. These prescriptions about women and their hair were extended by the early Christian Church Father Tertullian, who dictated that hair by itself was not an adequate covering. In his "On the Veiling of Virgins," Tertullian admonished women, both unmarried and married, to veil their hair, primarily so that the sight of their unbound locks would not excite temptation in men.[10] Yet despite Tertullian's strictures about women and exposed hair, by the later Middle Ages a clear distinction developed between married women, who kept their hair under cover, and unmarried women, who did not. Long, flowing hair became a symbol of maidenhood and, by extension, of availability for marriage. Once a woman married, she concealed her hair in a variety of ways, depending on her status and the fashions of the period. Medieval tomb sculptures, for example, often depict married women with some type of head covering concealing their hair.[11] The well-known *Le Ménagier de Paris*, written in the fourteenth century as if it is a handbook prepared by a bourgeois Parisian husband for his fifteen-year-old wife, contains all sorts of advice about the proper running of a household but also includes information about proper attire. The author admonishes his young wife to avoid looking like

> drunken, foolish, or ignorant women who do not care about their own honor or the good repute of their estate or their husband, and go with ... their hair in disarray spilling from their coifs ... Be careful then, my dear, that your hair, your headdress, your kerchief, your hood and the rest of your garments be neatly and simply arranged, so that anyone who sees you will not be able to laugh or mock you.[12]

Whether Tertullian writing in the second century or Le Ménagier de Paris in the fourteenth, clearly women were meant to keep their hair under control, not only to preserve their own reputations but also to ensure that the men who saw them or lived with them could avoid temptation or disgrace.

The ultimate model of proper behavior and modest appearance for medieval women to emulate was the Virgin Mary, even if they could not possibly achieve her degree of sanctified virtue. She was by far the most represented woman in medieval art and the source of fervent devotion by both genders. The very nature of her role in the Christological narrative demanded a consideration of gender and sexuality. She was the quintessential marriage of body and spirit, the stainless vessel through which the word became flesh, both virgin and mother. Medieval images of the Virgin Mary can vary depending on date, function, and historical context, but in most images, the appearance of Mary's hair helps to identify her either as a virtuous maiden with smooth, flowing, uncovered hair, or as a wife and mother with her hair modestly concealed.

A large number of sculptures depicting the Virgin Mary survive from the eleventh and twelfth centuries, called Thrones of Wisdom (Figure 6.2). These wooden sculptures of

FIGURE 6.2 *Enthroned Virgin and Child*, France (1150–1200). The Cloisters Collection, 67.153, www.metmuseum.org.

the seated Virgin with the Christ Child on her lap were usually held in monasteries and often used in church processions; some of them held relics.[13] Similar to the majority of the Byzantine images of the Virgin, in these sculptures, Mary's hair is usually completely covered, or with perhaps just a small portion visible beneath her head covering.[14] Typically there are few indications of her gender; there is little sense of the curves of a feminine body beneath the drapery that covers it in abstract folds. There are varying interpretations of this sort of presentation of the Virgin; it can be seen as typical of Romanesque art in general, with an overall privileging of abstraction and symbolism over realism. This sort of gender-neutral depiction of the Virgin Mary can also be interpreted as appropriate for the monastic context within which most of these sculptures operated, and the complicated theological work that they did, with Mary functioning not only as a seat for Christ as Solomonic judge but also as a human altar, presenting the body of Christ for visual and spiritual consumption.

Yet later in the Middle Ages, the Virgin Mary began to be represented not only with her hair uncovered but with luxurious tresses flowing down her back. Here, her hair connotes both purity and innocence. Representations of the Virgin Mary sometimes followed the trajectory of her narrative, depicting her with unbound hair in her youth and with a covered head during scenes of the Passion, when she might be present at the foot of the cross. But in the later Middle Ages, it could be argued that one of the most commonly depicted scenes of the Virgin, in both the private devotional space of the opening prayer in the Book of Hours and the public space of the church altarpiece, was the Annunciation, where typically she was represented with uncovered hair.

Almost without exception, that long, flowing hair is blonde. Long, blonde hair has a rich and multilayered significance in medieval culture, and above all it was a signifier of feminine attractiveness. For the Virgin Mary, her blonde hair and her physical beauty connoted her purity and state of spiritual grace, but in more secular contexts, long blonde hair could have decidedly more erotic connotations. Beautiful women in medieval love poetry and romances were often described as possessing flowing, flaxen hair, along with other descriptions of a codified beauty that included small breasts set high up on the chest, softly swelling bellies, and pale skin. Yet in these more secular contexts, long tresses inspire erotic desire. As just one example, the love interest of the thirteenth-century courtly love poem *Roman de la Rose* is described in these terms, and her physical beauty inspires her pursuit and ultimate seduction/rape. The incredible popularity of this thirteenth-century work is evident in that more than three hundred manuscripts of the text still survive. Despite the fact that the late medieval writer Christine de Pisan vehemently objected to the misogyny of the *Roman de la Rose*, particularly the section added by Jean de Meun, in her own instructional book for women she cautions against quickly changing, extravagant fashions and writes that, "Nothing, after all, is a more beautiful headdress for a woman than fine blond hair, as St. Paul bears witness when he says, 'Hair is a woman's capital ornament.'"[15] It seems that medieval women may have taken these ideas about the superiority of blonde hair to heart. In the *Trotula*, a collection of texts on women's medicine, there are a series of recipes that focus on the adornment and enhancement of hair, including several for dye to make it blonde.[16]

The connection between physical attraction and women's hair is also apparent in biblical narratives such as David and Bathsheba. David is seduced by the sight of Bathsheba in the bath, to the point that he arranges for her husband to be sent into battle and killed so that he can have her instead. This scene commonly illustrated the Penitential Psalms in Psalters and Books of Hours, since David repented of his sin. While it may be Bathsheba's nudity that is the main source of her seductive appeal, her long, flowing, usually blonde hair is part of the visual construction of her dangerously tempting appearance, even though her hair is not mentioned in the biblical account. Ironically, David's transgressive gaze is continually repeated by the viewer of these scenes, and some of them can be so erotic in the private context of the illuminated manuscript that they could lead to temptations seemingly at odds with the devotional function for which the manuscript was intended. A particularly eroticized image from the Hours of Louis XII depicts Bathsheba with shimmering golden hair cascading down her back (Figure 6.3).[17] This connects her to other eroticized images of female bathers, especially popular in fourteenth-century Netherlandish painting, and also to objects associated with the toilette.[18] Diane Wolfthal has explored the varying associations of the ivory combs that survive, particularly from the fourteenth century. Images that depict men watching women comb their long hair, as well as the imagery of courtly love that appear on the combs themselves, underscore that feminine hair and its arrangement had associations with erotic suggestion.[19] The image of the harlot of Babylon seated upon the waters in the fourteenth-century Angers Apocalypse tapestry depicts her

FIGURE 6.3 Jean Bourdichon, *Bathsheba Bathing*, Tours, France (1498–1499). The J. Paul Getty Museum, Los Angeles, Ms. 79, recto.

in a gown girdled with a belt so tight over her breasts that she appears to be naked from the waist up, and combing her hair while looking at her reflection in a mirror (Figure 6.4).[20] She is the embodiment of vain self-involvement—and yet she bears a striking visual similarity to a depiction of Saint Catherine in the *Belles Heures* belonging to John, the Duke of Berry (Figure 6.5). This remarkable image, one from a cycle of twelve miniatures of the saint, is a frankly sensuous depiction of Catherine in prison, with her drapery slipping off her body, her breasts exposed, and her long, blonde hair flowing down her back.[21]

The connections between long, blonde hair and eroticism can complicate viewer response to images of female saints, especially virgin martyrs. On the one hand they are connected to the Virgin Mary through their own virginity and their function as witnesses to Christ through their martyrdom. And yet the descriptions of their appearance in hagiographic texts, and their representation in medieval art, often make them indistinguishable from the heroines of medieval romances. In Jacobus de Voragine's thirteenth-century compendium of saints' lives, the extremely popular *Legenda aurea* (Golden Legend), he often describes the youth and beauty of the virgin martyrs, particularly since their physical attractiveness (and their rejection of the pagan men attracted to them) propels them on the path to martyrdom. To underscore this focus on feminine beauty, medieval images of virgin martyrs usually depict them with long, blonde hair. These textual and visual connections between the holy saint and the literary heroine are also interesting in thinking about how both types of women might have functioned as models for the physical appearance and prescribed behavior of medieval women in general. For example, there seems to be a clear connection between the appearance of the reliquaries of the Holy Virgins of Cologne and the fashions of contemporary women of the city. Joan Holladay has posited that the discovery of a Roman cemetery in Cologne, and the subsequent identification of the bones as those belonging to the martyred Saint Ursula and her eleven thousand virgin companions, led to an increase in devotional fervor for the saint and her cult in the thirteenth century.[22] This coincided with rising anxiety in the

FIGURE 6.4 Jean Bondel and Nicolas Bataille, *the Great Whore of Babylon* (Rev. 17:3–6) in the *Apocalypse d'Angers* (1373–1387), a series of tapestries woven for Louis I, Duke of Anjou. Angers, Musée des Tapisseries. Photo: Erich Lessing/Art Resource, NY.

FIGURE 6.5 Paul Herman and Jean de Limbourg, *Saint Catherine Tended by Angels*, from The *Belles Heures* of John, Duke of Berry, France (1405–1408/9). New York, The Cloisters Collection, 1954, MS. 54.1.1, fol. 17v. www.metmuseum.org.

city about the extreme asceticism of the city's Beguine population, and the Ursula-busts, with their contemporary hairstyles and headdresses (Figure 6.6), might have provided the young women of Cologne with an alternative model of spirituality, fulfilled through marriage and family.

The women discussed thus far, whether the sacred (the Virgin Mary and other biblical figures, female martyrs) or the secular (literary heroines, wives, and unmarried maidens) might be portrayed with hair that is covered or uncovered, but it is always neatly arranged. When long, flowing hair is disheveled, it connotes something quite different in medieval culture and society. This has already been alluded to by *Le Ménagier de Paris* in its criticism of the ignorant wives who parade about with "their hair in disarray." Hair that is both uncovered and uncontrolled was an outward sign of immoderate behavior and immoral thoughts; loose hair equated to a loose woman. Thus, a wide variety of female figures were often depicted in medieval art or described in medieval texts as having wild, unkempt hair, including biblical women such as Eve and Mary Magdalene. Particularly for the latter, the emphasis on her hair can have multivalent meanings, alluding to her sensual past, as well as her devotional act of washing Christ's feet with her tears and drying them with her hair, although at times she is depicted with her hair covered, especially in scenes where she is serving as the 'Apostle to the Apostles' announcing the resurrection of Christ to his disciples. Other female figures typically represented with

FIGURE 6.6 Reliquary bust of a companion of Saint Ursula, Germany (sixteenth century, ca. 1520–1530). Oak, polychromed and gilt on plaster ground; glass opening for relic. Gift of J. P. Morgan, 1917 (17.190.728) Photo © The Metropolitan Museum of Art. Image source: Art Resource, NY.

uncovered and often unkempt hair included mythological women such as Venus and female personifications such as Luxuria. A particularly well-known images of the latter appears on a side panel of the entrance portal at the church of Saint-Pierre at Moissac.[23] Luxuria's hair flows over her shoulders in wavy, uncombed clumps, taking the same shape as the serpents that chew on her naked breasts. Other women depicted with wild, untamed hair include monstrous and/or marginalized women such as sirens, mermaids, prostitutes, and witches. A panel from the pulpit at the Church of San Pietro in Gropina, probably dating from the twelfth century, depicts a woman with wild, uncontrolled hair holding up the split ends of a tail; above her, a male figure holds his ankles in a similar position, while serpents chew on the sides of his face (Figure 6.7). The man appears to be wearing either some sort of loincloth or, since it is carved in a similar fashion to the female figure's hair, it may be an exuberant growth of pubic hair providing a frame for his dangling penis. This seems a surprising selection of imagery for a pulpit, and it has usually been interpreted as signifying the evils of temptation. Depicting a woman with disheveled hair was also a way of signifying the ostracized Other and, thus, Jewish women and Muslim women were sometimes represented with uncovered, wild hair, even though in both religions women customarily covered their heads as signs of female modesty and reverence for God. (In actuality, prostitutes, Jews, and Muslims were sometimes required to wear identifying clothing in order to distinguish them.[24]) One example of a woman with exposed, unkempt hair, the female figure on the Puerta de las Platerías at Santiago de Compostela (Figure 6.8), was so striking in its own time that it warranted a mention in the Pilgrim's Guide to Santiago de Compostela, making it one of the rare cases where a contemporary medieval viewer describes a monument and recommends that other people pay particular attention to it. He writes, "Nor should be forgotten the woman who stands next to the Lord's Temptation, holding between her own hands the stinking head of her lover, cut off by her rightful husband, which she is forced by her husband to kiss

FIGURE 6.7 Figural tribune (left side) on pulpit in the Church of San Pietro, Gropina, Loro Ciuffernna, Arezzo, Italy (twelfth century). Photo: Syrio. Public domain.

FIGURE 6.8 *Woman with a Skull*, Cathedral of Santiago de Compostela, Puerta de las Platerías, left tympanum, Spain (early twelfth century). Photo: Scala/Art Resource, NY.

twice a day. Oh, what ingenious and admirable justice for an adulterous wife; it should be recounted to everyone!"[25] Since the present location of the sculpted figure is not its original one, this figure has been interpreted in a variety of ways by modern scholars; most recently it has been suggested that she was meant to be seen in conjunction with a figure of David and Bathsheba.[26] Regardless of her specific identity, it is clear that her uncovered, tousled hair in conjunction with her partial nudity coded her as a figure of sexual temptation.

This emphasis on hair and unbridled sexuality is also evident in images and descriptions of the wild men and women, members of a mythological monstrous race who lived on the outskirts of society.[27] This type of uncivilized, marginalized group has a variety of sources, stories, and interpretations, but they were often characterized as being naked, and yet completely covered with body hair (in addition to long hair for the women, and long beards and shoulder-length hair for the men), as if they occupied some liminal space between human and animal. The wild people were often described as sexually promiscuous and indiscriminate, and yet because they lived outside the confines of society, later in the Middle Ages they were also understood as naïve innocents.

Just as the virgin martyrs become visually and textually entangled with the heroines of secular romances, the appearance of wild women is very reminiscent of the way that a few hermit female saints were depicted, particularly in the later Middle Ages. These women grew hair in unconventional places, most notably Mary of Egypt and Mary Magdalene.[28] The hagiographies of both saints described them as spending time in the desert, where they subsisted on diets provided through miraculous means and where their clothes rotted away. To retain their modesty, both of them grew luxurious tresses of hair. In medieval images of the saints, their hair is represented in conventional ways, flowing from their heads down to cover their bodies, but sometimes it sprouts out all over their bodies. In the miniature of Mary of Egypt carried to heaven by angels from the *Prayer Book of Charles the Bold*, the saint's body is completely covered with short hair, with just her face, breasts, knees, hands, and feet left bare (Figure 6.9). She can be contrasted with the hybrid half-woman, half-animal that appears in the left margin, combing her long hair and looking into a mirror, in a bestial depiction of sinful Vanity. And yet, Mary of Egypt's furry appearance makes her virtually indistinguishable from wild women, such as the one with a unicorn in her lap depicted in a fifteenth-century German playing card (Figure 6.10).[29] Emphasizing her hair seems to foreground her earlier life as a prostitute instead of the repentance and asceticism of her later sojourn in the desert.[30] Some of the late medieval images of furry wild people and hirsute female saints are similar to certain depictions of Satan in hell or, even more surprisingly, giant female pudenda, underscored by their visual connection to objects like the medieval metal badges in the shape of genitalia, such as the walking vulva on a pilgrimage (Figure 6.11).[31]

The ample pubic hair evident on the vulvic badge, and perhaps on the pulpit at San Pietro in Gropina, introduces another type of body hair and its relationship to gender and sexuality. Penny Howell Jolly has examined the presence, and absence, of pubic hair depicted on European nudes from the thirteenth through the sixteenth centuries.[32] While earlier in the Middle Ages, pubic hair tends to be absent, it becomes more visible on both genders in later centuries. Surprising to a modern audience, Christ is often represented with visible pubic hair, perhaps because Christ's human nature became more and more important in late medieval devotion.[33] Pubic hair could have a variety of meanings, depending on the context, but pubic hair on men had the possibility of suggesting mature masculine power and virility. For the most part, images of female nudes in medieval art

FIGURE 6.9 *Saint Mary of Egypt, Prayer Book of Charles the Bold,* Rouen, France (1480–1990). The J. Paul Getty Museum, Los Angeles, Ms. 37, fol. 153v.

FIGURE 6.10 Master E. S., playing card with wild woman with unicorn, Germany (fifteenth century). Engraving: second state. Harris Brisbane Dick Fund, 1922 (22.83.16) © The Metropolitan Museum of Art. Image source: Art Resource, NY.

FIGURE 6.11 Vulva figure depicted as a pilgrim, Arnemuiden, the Netherlands (1425–1475). Van Beuningen Family Collection, Langbroek, the Netherlands.

continued the classical tradition of representing them devoid of any pubic hair, so when it was present it was almost always a signifier of lust, temptation, and even prostitution.

Some women did remove their pubic hair; the practice spread to western Europe by men returning from the Crusades, where they were introduced to the fashion in eastern brothels since Muslim women typically removed their body hair.[34] In the later Middle Ages, a more immediately visible form of feminine hair removal became fashionable; a high forehead was a symbol of beauty and, thus, women would pluck their hairlines back and gather their hair into elaborate head coverings. A notable depiction of two different sorts of female hair appears in a miniature from the *Hours of Mary of Burgundy* (Figure 6.12).[35] A noblewoman, very likely Mary of Burgundy herself, sits holding her Book of Hours, dressed in the height of fashion with a high plucked hairline and her hair concealed in an elaborate hennin, a cone-shaped headdress especially worn by members of the nobility. While this scene has been variously interpreted, it seems that her devotional focus has resulted in the visionary scene visible behind her through a window-like opening, where she appears again with other court ladies, all dressed in fashionable gowns with their hair invisible underneath their hennins. In contrast, the Virgin Mary, Mary of Burgundy's named saint, is depicted with her long, blonde, uncovered hair flowing unencumbered down her back.

Whether hair grew from their heads or on their bodies, was covered or removed, or grew long or short, a marker of femininity was a smooth, beardless face. Men might be bearded or beardless, depending on age, religious vocation, and fashion. The Anglo-Saxon King Harold's scouts famously identified the invading Normans as an army of priests since they wore their hair short and were clean-shaven, as was the practice in the Latin Church; in the Greek Church, it was more common for priests to have beards.[36] While at different times the fashion for beards might vary, it was often the case that cultural practices surrounding the presence of facial hair for men were dictated by class, so that if upper-class men wore beards, lower-class men did not, and vice versa. In western European art, beards could signify the wisdom generally associated with the elderly, or in conjunction with exotic-looking headgear and clothing, could identify someone as from the "East" (specifically as a Jewish or Muslim man). Yet whether bearded or shaved, it was understood that the ability to grow a beard was a physiological

FIGURE 6.12 *Maximilian and Mary of Burgundy in front of the Virgin*, miniature from the *Hours of Mary of Burgundy*, manuscript, France (fifteenth century). Österreichische Nationalbibliothek. © DeA Picture Library/Art Resource, NY.

indication of mature masculinity. A man seemingly incapable of producing facial hair might be mocked, and his sexuality perhaps called into question, as Chaucer seems to do in his description of the Pardoner in the Prologue of *The Canterbury Tales*: "He had no beard, nor was he like to have; / Smooth was his face, as if he had just shaved. I took him for a gelding or a mare."[37] A man who could not grow a beard veered dangerously close to feminine physiology. And yet even this gender boundary could be transgressed, particularly by female saints such as Saint Wilgefortis, who miraculously sprouted a beard in order to thwart the advances of an unwanted suitor and retain her virginity.[38] After a series of tortures by both her father, who had promoted the marriage, and her intended bridegroom, Wilgefortis was crucified. In fact, one theory about the origin of her legend is that it developed in order to provide an explanation for images of the crucified Christ wearing a tunic, in contrast to the loincloth that he usually wore in most medieval representations of the scene. Interestingly, the combination of bearded face and long tunic apparently was more logically explained as a miraculous and protective growth of facial hair by a woman, rather than by a man wearing seemingly feminine attire. This corresponds with medieval attitudes about potential slippages in gender binaries; both medieval hagiography and literature have a number of examples of women performing and "passing" as men for a variety of religious, political, and social reasons.[39] The *Legenda aurea* included several examples of women who dressed as men to enter monasteries, usually to escape marriage to a pagan man. The opposite, men performing as women, almost never happened, except in carnivalesque situations when the absurdity of such a situation was underscored.

Part of "passing" as a man meant cutting one's hair. Because long hair was so synonymous with femininity, cutting it off was a dramatic move and was fraught with significance.[40] Although the hirsutism of particular female saints signified their extreme spiritual asceticism, the cutting of hair functioned as a way of transitioning from one state to another, usually a move from a secular identity to a spiritual one. A woman who cut her hair and gave up her socially prescribed roles as wife and mother was moving from the body to the spirit, the change of her outward appearance signifying her interior transformation. In short, cutting a woman's hair was a method of masculinization. Even so, a leitmotif in the stories of the cross-dressing saints is that their "true" genders are revealed, often upon their deaths. In the case of cross-dressing heroines in medieval romances, such as the *Roman de Silence*, the hint of same-sex desire present when another woman falls in love with female Silence (dressed as a man to protect her father's estate) is eradicated when Venus intervenes and miraculously turns Silence into an actual man.[41]

The potentially transgressive nature of a woman with short hair is evident in the case of Joan of Arc. After she was captured by the Burgundians and handed over to the English to be tried for heresy, her transvestism became a significant part of her trial, not just her decision to wear men's clothing but also her short hair. According to the transcript of her trial, her accusers state, "Likewise, you have said that you wore and still wear men's clothing at God's command and at his good pleasure, and because you had orders from God to wear this habit, you have put on a short tunic doublet, and boots tied up with many pointed laces. You even wear your hair cut round above the ears."[42] In order to eliminate her problematic appropriation of masculine appearance, at one point Joan's head is shaved. While a woman with short hair may be masculinized to either positive or negative effect, a woman with no hair at all becomes nearly monstrous, like the Sheela-na-gigs with their bald heads and splayed vaginas.[43] Even in the modern era, the forcible shaving of a woman's head is a form of punishment and humiliation; French women who slept with German soldiers during World War II had their heads shaved and were paraded through the streets.

Shaving the head completely seems to have been a humiliating experience for medieval men as well as women. Some scholars have suggested, following Freud and Lacan, that cutting the hair, and especially shaving the head, is a symbolic form of castration and, thus, a forcible shearing of the hair might signify not just a stripping of masculine power but a complete loss of gender.[44] Baldness due to the natural process of aging could also be interpreted in a negative fashion, as a loss of masculinity and virility.

One exception to the negative associations of shaving the head is the tonsure, the hairstyle adopted by men when they left the outside world for the religious life. In the German panel painting discussed at the outset of this chapter (Figure 6.1), Saint Francis is recognizable as a monk because of his so-called Roman tonsure, shaved on top with a fringe of hair on the sides; the exact form of the tonsure varied in different times and places, but always involved the removal of hair.[45] Women joining religious communities, such as Saint Clare, also either cut off or veiled their hair, thereby eliminating its associations with beauty, vanity, and sexual availability, and signaling that they were now Brides of Christ rather than brides of men. But the tonsure served as an even more obvious marker of religious and social identity. Its meanings were somewhat ambiguous; while it served as an indication of the piety and learnedness associated with monasticism, it also retained some of the more negative implications of masculine hairlessness.[46] For both men and women passing from a secular to a spiritual world, cutting the hair signified a rejection of sexuality, and by extension, a disavowal of socially prescribed gender roles.

During the Middle Ages, hair served as an important indicator of social class, religious status, age and maturity, and secular fashion. In medieval scientific, philosophical, theological, and social practice, women wore their hair long, and men wore their hair short. Long hair connoted femininity, and by extension, sexuality. For women, their hair was a source of beauty and romance, but depending on its appearance, it could also indicate vanity, pride, and temptation. Yet there were certainly times during the Middle Ages when long hair was fashionable for both sexes, although men who adopted this fashion were often criticized. In fact, the importance of hair in medieval culture is underscored by the way it reflects social attitudes, particularly expectations about gender, and thus women and men with hair more closely associated with the opposite sex occupied a transgressive space in medieval culture. The rich and subtle ways that hair could create meaning are especially apparent when a transition is in process: when a Merovingian king is forced to cut his long hair as punishment; when a female saint miraculously grows hair on her body or face; when a man entering a monastery tonsures his head, and a woman joining a convent veils, or cuts off, her hair. The appearance of hair—whether it is long or short, carefully combed or unkempt, veiled or exposed, on the head or elsewhere on the face or body—helped to shape gender identity, both in artistic representation and in real life.

ACKNOWLEDGMENTS

I would like to thank Roberta Milliken for inviting me to participate in this volume, and to acknowledge that her own work, especially *Ambiguous Locks: An Iconography of Hair in Medieval Art and Literature* (Jefferson, NC: McFarland and Company, 2012), is a rich source of information on hair as a signifier of gender and sexuality in the Middle Ages. Many of the topics in this chapter are addressed there.

CHAPTER SEVEN

Race and Ethnicity: Hair and Medieval Ethnic Identities

KIM M. PHILLIPS

Hair types, hairstyles, facial hair, and hair coverings all feature among medieval markers of ethnic difference. During the period ca. 800 to ca. 1450, medieval Europeans formulated divisions between peoples that encompassed both cultural and bodily attributes. Where cultural distinctions were more often emphasized in the early medieval era, over the longer period and especially from the late twelfth century there was a gradual shift toward greater emphasis on physical markers of difference—including skin color, hair color and texture, facial features, height, and body shape. Yet the body did not at this time occupy the dominant place in anthropological distinctions that it came to possess in the modern era. Head, facial, and body hair make for an interesting focus in histories of medieval ideas of human difference, as they are the product as much of cultural practices as of natural variation.[1] The aim of this chapter is to offer a brief and necessarily selective view of hair's role in medieval constructions of human differences, especially between the Christian peoples of the hegemonic centers of Latin Christendom (that is, many of the regions now occupied by the nation-states of modern Western Europe) and peoples perceived as foreign or different, whether in their midst, on their periphery, or in lands far distant.

HAIR AND ETHNICITY: MEDIEVAL CONCEPTS AND CONTEXTS

Patrick Geary argued in an important article on early medieval contexts that ethnicity is situational. He drew on work in sociology to explain that rather than existing as an entity "out there," ethnicity is a process through which individuals and groups achieve self-identity and identify others as different from themselves. Given this, the primary task for historians is to "determine by what criteria individuals and groups might be so identified and, equally important, under what circumstances ethnicity was perceived at all." We should ask "in what situational contexts ethnicity becomes a relevant issue."[2] In subsequent decades, these foundational ideas have become embedded. For example, Geraldine Heng, surveying themes concerning medieval race asserts, "Race-making ... operates as specific historical occasions in which strategic essentialisms [that is, traits perceived as natural and intrinsic] are posited and assigned through a variety of practices and pressures, so as to construct a hierarchy of peoples for differential treatment."³ Robert Bartlett takes the idea as read, stating "the general point that ethnicity is 'situational' ... has been made often enough."⁴ Nonetheless, it bears repeating. Ethnic or racial differences, rather than existing as objective phenomena, are in effect called into being in response to perceived needs and power struggles. In specific historical moments, it becomes tactically compelling to draw lines of distinction around groups of individuals and designate them as possessing an internal coherence. The bases for such distinctions are varied, and usually more than one category may be invoked.⁵

It has been widely accepted that cultural factors including religion, myths of origin, shared territory, military organization, customs, language, and legal identities prevailed in early medieval societies as markers of group difference, while somatic elements such as body, skin, and hair type were less frequently remarked. Geary finds that, although a few normative and scholarly texts offered clear guidelines, many sources paid limited attention to ethnic identities. While there are key exceptions, such as Regino of Prüm's (ca. 900) claim that origin (or descent), customs, language, and law (*genere, moribus, lingua, et legibus*) formed the key points of division between "nations of peoples" (*nationes populorum*), in early medieval narrative sources ethnic identity features only rarely in accounts of individuals.⁶ The standard Latin terms such as *gens, natio*, and *populus* (broadly, nation, tribe, and people) were more often used of groups than individuals, and most especially of groups of warriors. Indeed, alongside designations of social elites and groups linked by seeming "out of place" in a geographic or religious sense, ethnic identification had greatest early medieval utility in creating bonds of military organization and, by implication, political affiliation. According to Geary, "One finds a contradiction between the articulated criteria by which peoples were to be differentiated [origins, customs, language, and law], and the circumstances in which these differentiations actually took place ... [that is, essentially] 'ethnicity in the service of politics'." Ethnicity, then, is more than situational, it is also functional: it is always "*for* something."⁷

Hair types and hairstyles always had a role to play in deployments of perceived ethnic difference. Walter Pohl, concentrating on the period from late antiquity to the ninth century, finds language, military methods, clothing, hairstyles, and other body signs the most telling signs of ethnic identity employed among peoples we would now term "European" but who would have perceived profound differences among themselves.⁸ Their use of ethnic markers, including hair and beard styles, appears to have been designed as much to designate "self" as much as "other": to create an in-group, and sense of functional cohesion, as much if not more than to articulate an "out-group" to which caution or suspicion might apply. Bartlett, in his broader study of hair meanings, which takes in status, gender, nationality, and religious status as well as ethnicity, finds that "one of the oldest and most general functions of hair treatment was to distinguish ethnic groups." He cites Tacitus on the knotted hair of the Suevi, the Byzantines on the hairstyles of diverse peoples such as the Avars, and the contrast between the long-haired, bearded Anglo-Saxons and their crop-headed, clean-shaven Norman foes.⁹

Isidore of Seville's *Etymologiae* (ca. 620–636) was arguably the most influential book in the Latin West, apart from the Bible, from the time it was written until the early sixteenth century. The learned Bishop of Seville paid little attention to hair in describing the world's peoples (*gentes*), where *gens* is defined by shared origin or self-identification in distinction from others, though he observes that the Scythians, known as "Albanians," take their name from the white (*albus*) hair that results from a snowy climate.¹⁰ While

Isidore's method is primarily linguistic, the influence of climate that would later become more prominent is here glimpsed. His chapter on the clothing of different nations ventures more physical details, expressed as cultural habits and natural traits, among which references to head and facial hair types and styles are scattered:

> We see the curls (*cirrus*, perhaps "topknot") of the Germans, the mustaches and goatees of the Goths, the tattoos of the Britons. The Jews circumcise the foreskin, the Arabs pierce their ears, the Getae with their uncovered heads are blond, the Albanians shine with their white hair. The Moors have bodies black as night, while the skin of the Gauls is white. Without their horses, the Alani are idle. Nor should we omit the Picts (*Pictus*), whose name is taken from their bodies, because an artisan, with the tiny point of a pin and the juice squeezed from a native plant, tricks them out with scars to serve as identifying marks, and their nobility are distinguished by their tattooed (*pictus*) limbs.[11]

No single method or principle is applied here: even etymology is deployed haphazardly. If ethnicity is *for* something, in the case of Isidore, its role is as a minor element in a vast compendium of knowledge that aimed to preserve classical learning to demonstrate the diversity of God's creation within a unified Catholicism.

Such diffuse notions of human difference remained in place until the late twelfth century. From then, and especially in universities, ancient notions of climatic, geographic, and other environmental influences upon human types experienced a sharp revival. Peter Biller identifies several foundational Greek texts translated into Latin either via Arabic or, in some cases, directly from Greek, between the late eleventh and early thirteenth centuries. These include the Hippocratic *Airs, Waters, Places*, Aristotle's *Politics*, Galen's *On Complexions*, Haly Abbas's *Liber pantegni*, Avicenna's *Canon*, Pseudo-Aristotle's *Problems*, and Aristotle's *On Animals*. He further suggests that mendicant friars may have spread their ideas beyond relatively narrow university circles and curricula.[12] Claire Weeda develops Biller's ideas, arguing for a "twelfth-century outburst of ethnic stereotyping." This occurred within a broader context of strengthened ethnic consciousness and renewed pride and confidence among the intellectuals of late twelfth- and thirteenth-century Europe, along with the effects of centralizing state bureaucracies and greater mobility of certain social and occupational groups such as merchants, pilgrims, intellectuals, migrants, and settlers.[13] Environmental determinism and the revival of humoral theory (see Chapter Five of the present volume) contributed to a transformation in learned thinking on ethnicity and began to place increased emphasis on the body and character. However, "scientific" thinking did not affect all later medieval uses of ethnic divisions, as will be glimpsed below in sections on the Irish and peoples of Asia.

The renewal of ancient interest in bodily distinctions and associated theories about mental and moral qualities propelled the thirteenth-century emergence of proto-racial thought. From the thirteenth to mid-fifteenth centuries the shift toward an emphasis on descent or origin was intensified by processes of colonization felt in Ireland, the Baltic, Poland, and Bohemia, where "birth" or "blood" came increasingly to serve as the boundary marker between colonists asserting rights of lordship and native populations subject to dispossession and legal exclusion. Around the same time, Christian prejudice against Jewish people was intensifying and taking on new, and long afterwards shockingly persistent, physical dimensions. In learned circles around 1300, Jewish men were viewed as unnaturally "melancholic" in humor and prone to menstruation, as exuding a noxious odor, and as possessing a reviled physiognomy. The consequences of intensified focus on descent and bodily distinctions were felt in many contexts, but perhaps most especially later fifteenth-century and sixteenth-century Iberia where the *limpieza de sangre* (purity of blood) statutes, first enacted in Toledo in 1449, were brought to bear against Jewish and Saracen populations, and to justify persecution and expulsion of *conversos* and *moriscos* (respectively, Jewish and Muslim converts to Christianity).[14]

Bartholomaeus Anglicus's *De proprietatibus rerum* (On the Properties of Things; ca. 1240) included many descriptions of parts of the human body and diversity among nations in chapters that bear witness to the powerful influence of climate and humoral theory in his own time and depart markedly from the etymologically founded explanations of Isidore, whose *Etymologiae* was one of his chief sources.[15] His chapter on hair, "De capillis," begins by invoking Isidore but quickly turns to the work of Constantine the African (d. before 1098), a convert from Islam to Christianity whose medical writings helped to revive humoral theory in western learning:

> And Constantine saith that head hair comes from thick and great fumosity and heat, and that fumosity comes from fire and kindling of humours, and passes out at the pores of the head, and is dried with air that is without, and so turned into the substance of hair. While this humour grows, hair grows that is bred and comes thereof and is nourished therewith. Whoever that loses this fumosity loses also the hair of the head. Also the hair hath the quality of this fumosity, for if this fumosity is black the hair is black, and much hair if the fumosity is much, and scarce hair if it is scarce.

Many hair-associated conditions such as baldness and grayness are caused by deficient heat, while heat excess could cause *alopecia*.[16] Bartholomaeus also makes several uses of climate and humoral theory to explain bodily differences among peoples, including hair types, as will be seen in the next section.

HAIR IN DEPICTIONS OF OUTSIDERS: IRISH, JEWISH, SARACEN, AFRICAN, ASIAN, AND THE MONSTROUS

The illustration depicting two men of Connacht in a curragh from Bodleian Library (MS Laud misc. 720) offers a concise set of images relating to perceived primitivism, of which hair is a vital component (Figure 7.1). It falls within the third section of Gerald of Wales's *Topographia Hibernica* (The Topography of Ireland), which provides a detailed description of Irish people who had been perceived since antiquity as rustic and indeed barbaric. The allegedly backward state of the Irish is evident through perceived cultural and physical defects. Their primitive dress, horse management, weaponry, land husbandry, and many other customs all serve for Gerald as testament to their idle and undeveloped state: "The Irish are a rude people, subsisting on the produce of their cattle only, and living themselves like beasts—a people that has not yet departed from the primitive habits of pastoral life."[17] In person, the Irish are said to possess a remarkable vigor, height, ruddiness of face, and an attractive appearance that owes nothing to their efforts and everything to gifts of Nature. In remarking on their hair and beards, Gerald employs the etymological method: "This people, then, is truly barbarous, being not only barbarous in their dress, but suffering their hair and beards (*barbis*) to grow enormously in an uncouth manner, just like the modern fashion recently introduced."[18] His final comment echoes contemporary English monastics decrying the scandalous fashions for long hair and beards, thus serving to denigrate the courtiers who had adopted such a fad by unfavorable comparison with the wild Irish.[19] Gerald was far from novel in connecting

FIGURE 7.1 Two Connacht men sitting in a curragh holding paddles. Late-thirteenth-century manuscript of *Topographia Hibernica* by Giraldus Cambrensis (Gerald of Wales) (ca. 1147–ca. 1220). Laud Misc. 720 fol. 226v. Photo: Bodleian Libraries, University of Oxford/The Art Archive at Art Resource/Art Resource, NY.

masculine Gaelic hairiness to barbarism. In the sixth century Gildas (d. 570) called Picts and Scots (Irish) "worms" with boorish, bearded faces who came out of holes to ravage England.[20]

Several images in the four surviving illustrated copies of the *Topographia* portray the typical hirsute Irishman, including the illustration of two men from an offshore island. In the context of explaining the faulty and as yet incomplete state of Christianity in the country, despite its early implantation, he relates a story heard from some sailors who had taken refuge by an island off the shore of Connacht during a ferocious storm and were approached by two men in a curragh. The men were "stark naked, except that they wore broad belts of the skin of some animal fastened round their waists. They had long yellow hair, like the Irish, falling below the shoulders, and covering great part of their bodies."[21] The manuscript illuminator has closely followed the text, yet adds further details such as the finely shaded musculature, a hint of hair on the forearms, and faces featuring hooked, bumpy noses, and strongly marked downturned mouths.

With colonization, Irish men's hair remained central to the differentiation of Gaelic inhabitants and English settlers. To the ancient stereotype of the savage Irish was added a new dimension, the Irish as enemy. By the end of the thirteenth century and enduring until the Tudor era, lawmakers began to express anxiety about English settlers' "degeneracy," qualms first formally expressed in the 1297 enactment against English adoption of Irish clothing and hairstyles: "Also, in modern times, Englishmen, as if degenerate, wear Irish clothing and having their heads half-shaved, grow their hair long at the back of the head and call it a *culan*, conforming to the Irish both in dress and appearance."[22] According to the text, the trouble was that "some Englishmen are killed and taken to be Irishmen, although the killing of Englishmen and Irishmen requires to be punished in different ways." Englishmen must wear on their heads "the custom and tonsure of the English," on pain of arrest, imprisonment, and confiscation of property.²³ Contrary to the sense of the legislation, however, the *culan* (Irish *cúlán*) was a style associated not with native Irish in general but with a dedicated warrior band in particular.²⁴ In the early sixteenth century the glib, an Irish military hairstyle almost the opposite of the *culan*, in that the back of the head was shaved and a shaggy mass of hair hung over the forehead, often accompanied by a long drooping handlebar mustache, was described and pictured by authors including traveler Laurent Vital and depicted by Albrecht Dürer. Vital, who mentions that Irishmen in general go bareheaded, also comments on women's hairstyles, saying many crop their hair at the front and back apart from two long plaits at either side which are looped on top and hang in front to the waist where they are clipped to the tassels of headdresses. Though we will see a few relevant exceptions below, Vital's comment is unusual in that women's hair is only rarely remarked in medieval ethnic descriptions.²⁵ The glib hairstyle, along with various items of Irish clothing, was banned for English subjects by a statute of Henry VIII, 1537.²⁶ If ethnicity is situational and functional, then English misgivings about Irish hair may be firmly located within the history of English colonization, where early connections with barbarity helped to justify incursion and later identification of Irish military masculinities served to demarcate rulers and enemies and to punish Englishmen for national treachery.

Gerald's accounts of the Welsh in his *Journey Through Wales* and *Description of Wales* lack the same degree of vitriol, no doubt partly because of his own quarter-Welsh heritage. He describes the nobleman Cynwrig ap Rhys as "tall and handsome, with fair curly hair," though dressed in the minimalist fashion typical of his countrymen, with bare legs and feet: "He had a natural dignity, which owed nothing to affectation: he was, as it were, a man adorned by nature, not by art."²⁷ Gerald's general account of Welsh men and women takes in haircuts and coverings:

> Both the men and the women cut their hair short and shape it round their ears and eyes. Like the Parthians the women cover their heads with a flowing white veil, which sticks up in folds like a crown … The men shave their beards, leaving only their mustaches. This is not a new habit, but one which goes back to time immemorial. You can find it in the book which Julius Caesar wrote about his exploits, for there we read: the Britons shave their whole body except their upper lip [*De bello Gallico* V.14]. Sometimes they shave their heads, too, so that they can move more freely, for, when they run through the forest groves, they want to avoid the fate of Absalom [2 Samuel 18:9]. Of all the people I have seen the Welsh are the most particular in shaving the lower parts of the body.²⁸

Gerald displays his Parisian university education when using climate theory in his *Description of Wales*, stating "the Saxons and the Germans derive their cold nature from the frozen polar regions which lie adjacent to them," and "the English, although they now live elsewhere, still retain their outward fairness of complexion and their inward coldness of disposition from what nature had given them earlier on." To the contrary, the Britons, including the Welsh "transplanted from the hot and arid regions of the Trojan plain, keep their dark colouring, which reminds one of the earth itself, their natural warmth of personality and their hot temper, all of which gives them confidence in themselves."²⁹ In his many-layered account, Gerald employs the latest in Parisian scientific thinking to compile imagery of ethnic types that resists any straightforward reading of Latin Christian prejudice or partiality.

Turning to medieval representations of Jewishness, we must take into account the complex and ambiguous position of Jewish people in medieval Christian thought. On the one hand, Jews—especially those of the Old Testament—were Christian forebears, recognized as God's chosen people, and bearers of Christian prophecy. On the other, they were condemned as Christ-killers and as blind, obstinate, and hard-hearted in their ongoing refusal to accept Christ as the Messiah. Complicating this apparently dichotomous portrayal, furthermore, were concepts of Jews as "witnesses" to Christian faith and of the necessity of safeguarding them from harm in expectation of their mass conversion in the prelude to Christ's second coming, while from the twelfth century and after their frequent association with moneylending at interest made them at once essential and reviled within some Christian communities.[30] While Jews received little in the way of distinctive visual treatment before the later twelfth century, from that time forward a rising tide of Christian anti-Jewish prejudice began to impact upon textual description and artistic representation. Nonetheless, portrayals remained multifarious; as Sara Lipton argues, ambiguity in medieval Christian representation of Jews is both "intentional and meaningful," and she extends her analysis through consideration of the widespread exemption of Jewish women from negative iconography.[31]

Head hair and hairstyles constitute a relatively minor aspect of Jewish portrayals, although dark hair was commonly featured.[32] More important were the colors red and yellow, especially associated with Jewish garments; yellow stars and other identifying badges, used after the Lateran Council edicts of 1215; distinctive physiognomy, including large eyes and mouths but especially the allegedly Jewish nose; grotesque features and distorted body shapes; dark complexion; grimacing expressions; blindfolds, especially in depictions of Synagoga, to indicate alleged failure to recognize the Messiah; moneybags; the presence of demons; and engagement in idolatry. However, three common elements in representation deserve our notice: headwear, beards, and, in some instances, red hair.

The so-called Jewish hat (*pileum cornutum*) frequently signals Judaism in medieval art, although it could take diverse shapes.[33] The *Martyrdom of Simon of Trent* (an 1849 copy of a 1493 original from Hartmann Schedel's *Liber chronicarum*, also known as the *Nuremberg Chronicle*) (Figure 7.2) portrays late medieval anti-Judaism at its harshest, depicting as it does a notorious instance of alleged "blood libel" in which Jews were maliciously accused of murdering Christian boys for the imagined purpose of reenacting the crucifixion, obtaining blood for ritual purposes or to replace the blood supposedly lost as a result of "Jewish male menstruation."[34] Like many other such cases, the Trent episode had very real and tragic outcomes, with the arrest and trial of the whole local Jewish community and the execution by burning of several Jewish men. In the image, identified by the *rouelles* (circular yellow badges) attached to their garments as well as by individual Jewish names, the imagined perpetrators drain blood from the boy's penis in a perverse circumcision. The figure of "Israhel" wears a version of the "Judenhut" commonly depicted in anti-Semitic art, a funnel cap surmounted by a knob. Others wear versions of the Phrygian cap, loose turbans, or scholars' caps.

Also significant are the beards of four of the male figures, particularly the forked and straggly beards of Israhel, Thobias, and Angelus.[35] Beards, unlike hooked noses, had by no means solely pejorative connotations, and even forked beards could be worn by authoritative Christian men. Some contemporary portraits of Geoffrey Chaucer showed him with a short forked beard, while Edward III of England was usually depicted with flowing wavy hair, long divided beard, and trailing mustache.[36] Beards and long hair were subject to the whims of fashion among Christian men. In elite English contexts, the hirsute preferences of Anglo-Saxon men gave way to the cropped heads and clean-shaven militaristic styles preferred by the Normans; the pendulum swung back to full facial hair

FIGURE 7.2 *The Martyrdom of Simon of Trent*, 1493 (1849). A nineteenth-century version of a fifteenth-century manuscript illustration in *Liber chronicarum* (the Nuremberg Chronicle) by Hartmann Schedel. Cabinet des Estampes, Bibliothèque Royale, Brussels, Belgium. Photo: HIP/Art Resource, NY.

and long locks in the fourteenth century, and back again to beardless faces and shorn heads in the fifteenth. Male hair and beardedness were also strong markers of religious function in the Latin Church, with shaved faces and short tonsured hair required of men in holy orders. Bartholomaeus explains beards in terms of body heat, dry complexion, and gender, as a beard is "token of virtue and strength of kind [natural] heat." Men, he says, as hotter and drier than women, grow beards, although some hot and moist women sprout whiskers and cold and dry men have little beards. Men of moist regions grow smooth lustrous beards, as do the men of Thrace, while men with dry brains living in hot regions have the opposite.[37] As we have seen, classically influenced scholarship argued for the dominance of melancholy in Jewish men, which could produce hairiness.[38] Yet in the case of Jewish men, long, straggly, and/or forked beards were not adequate in themselves to signify religious identity or deviance, but contributed to the overall iconography of Jewish men.

Medieval depictions of Judas, especially in German art from the fourteenth to sixteenth centuries, frequently portray the treacherous disciple with red hair and/or beard, along with a ruddy complexion. Alone among the disciples, Judas is shown as a typical caricature, his ruddy coloring serving to emphasize associations with the sins of deceit and treachery.[39] Late medieval German art and literature also developed the theme of the so-called "Red Jews," an idolatrous tribe anticipated to rise in the east in the prelude to the apocalypse and sometimes depicted with red hair.[40] Bartholomaeus claimed that a "hot" body could be the cause of black or red hair in large quantity—"colde is the mother of whiteness and of paleness, as heat is the mother of blackness and of redness"—which again suggests a scientific explanation for Jewish red hair, though the broader association with perfidy might have been more decisive.[41]

The dark dawn of the crusading era from the end of the eleventh century brought another enemy figure to the forefront of Christian minds: the Muslim or "Saracen," often imagined as a heretic and/or idolater rather than as a practitioner of an independent faith more unambiguously monotheistic than Christianity itself. Geographically associated with the south and east, Saracens shared several physical features with Africans. Medieval artists developed visual shorthands, enabling instant viewer recognition of subjects as Saracens, namely the turban or knotted headband (*tortil*), long beard, swarthy complexion, and curved sword. Bulbous noses, thick lips, and distorted features were also frequently employed, while in some cases Muslims were more fully associated with demons through being endowed with horns, grimacing visages, and hybrid or quasi-monstrous bodies.[42] As with portrayals of Irish and Jews, it is noticeable that the typical Saracen was male.

Climate theory and other environmental factors were widely employed to account for the bodies of Saracens. As Suzanne Conklin Akbari writes, "the Saracen body was constructed as the product of an Oriental climate, nourished by alien and exotic foodstuffs."[43] The hot climates of Saracen homelands were alleged to produce dark skin, frizzy hair, lecherous and belligerent disposition, and cowardly conduct. While high and late medieval authors drew extensively on ancient texts to explicate theories of bodily difference, the shift of academic inquiry from a Mediterranean to a northwest (especially Parisian) setting required a corresponding transference of climatic explanation. The formerly idealized "middle" climate of the Mediterranean was reimagined as the southern and (middle) eastern zone of excessive heat.[44] The portrait of the Andalusian Muslim philosopher Ibn Rushd (known to the west as Averroës) in Gozzoli's rendition of *The Triumph of Saint Thomas Aquinas* (detail, 1470–1475) (Figure 7.3) depicts an esteemed

FIGURE 7.3 Benozzo de Lesse Gozzoli (ca. 1420–1497). The Arab philosopher Averroës, from *The Triumph of Saint Thomas Aquinas*, detail (1470–1475). Musée de Louvre, Paris. Photo: Gianni Dagli Orti/The Art Archive at Art Resource, NY.

thinker in a humiliating posture, vanquished along with his book and prostrate at the feet of his Christian successor. Richly dressed with a brimless roll-edged cap, similar to some Persian headwear, the philosopher presents a quite different image from the turbaned armed warriors more often typical of Saracen imagery. But the long corkscrew curls of his hair and beard, now turned gray to befit his venerable status, are indicative of the hot climate of his homeland as well as his age. Bartholomaeus drew on Aristotle to explain that when "the humour is smoky, hot, and dry, the hair of the beard and of the head shall be crispy and curled," while "in the elderly the beard hoareth [turns gray] for feebleness of heat and plenty [abundance] of cold."[45]

Hot climate was, however, more regularly associated with Africans, as Bartholomaeus details in a number of passages. His chapter on Europeans gives an especially clear description of the differences between Africans, people of the far north, and Asians, the latter illustrative of a medium type between two extremes:

> For the sun abideth long over the Affers, men of Affrica, and burns and wastes humours and makes [them] short of body black of face, with crisp hair. And because spirits pass out at pores that be open, so they be more cowards of heart.
>
> And the contrary is of men of the north land: for the coldness that is without stops the pores and breeds humours of the body [and] makes men more full and huge; and cold that [is] the mother of whiteness makes them more white in face and [in] skin, and vapours and spirits be smiten [driven] inward and make hotter within and so the more bold and hardy. And the men of Asia be moderately disposed in that.[46]

Debra Higgs Strickland enumerates the typical features of peoples grouped under the name "Ethiopians" as seen in medieval art, including "woolly or tightly coiled hair."[47] An Apulian capital from ca. 1230 depicts an African head with tight curling hair (Figure 7.4).

FIGURE 7.4 Capital (ca. 1230) Limestone. Apulia, Italy. Overall: 35.9 × 33 × 33 cm. Base: Diam. 19.7 cm. Hole for Pin Mount: Diam. 1.4 × 5.5 cm. Gift of James Hazen Hyde, 1955 (55.66). The Metropolitan Museum of Art. Image © The Metropolitan Museum of Art. Image source: Art Resource, NY.

An apparently Muslim head is portrayed on the left of the pillar. Within his unusually severe description of the black people of Zanzibar, whose appearance he likens to devils, Marco Polo remarks that the men have "hair so crisp it cannot be straightened even with water."[48] Homogenizing and demonizing depictions of sub-Egyptian Africans did not depend on the rediscovery of humoral theory, however, as they were well known in early and high medieval texts and imagery.[49] Scientific theories supplied an apparent explanation.

We can see that portrayals of Irish, Jews, Muslims, and black Africans had long histories by the mid-thirteenth century, although the revival of Greek humoral and climatic theory produced a number of new elements. In the mid-thirteenth century, however, entirely new (from a European perspective) groups sprang into view. The long-distance journeys into Asia that were prompted by Mongol domination from the early thirteenth to later fourteenth centuries allowed European travelers a view of the peoples of Mongolia, China, Southeast Asia, and India who had previously been imagined, when at all, only through scanty and distorted Roman sources. The first to travel into the heart of Mongolia and return to write detailed reports were Franciscan friars John of Plano Carpini and William of Rubruck. Both supplied brief but vivid physical descriptions of their hosts.

Carpini's description was not meant to serve a primarily ethnographic purpose but to enable identification of Mongol warriors if taken as prisoners of war. In addition to comments on facial bone structure, eyes, cheeks, nose, eyelids, height, waists, and feet, he remarks,

> Hardly any of them grow beards, although some have a little hair on the upper lip and chin, and this they do not trim. On the top of the head they have a tonsure like clerics, and as a general rule all shave from one ear to the other to the breadth of three fingers, and this shaving joins on to the aforesaid tonsure. Above the forehead also they all likewise shave to two fingers' breadth, but the hair between this shaving and the tonsure they allow to grow until it reaches their eyebrows, and, cutting more from each side of the forehead than in the middle, they make the hair in the middle long; the rest of their hair they allow to grow like women, and they make it into two braids which they bind, one behind each ear.[50]

Rubruck's description from a few years later is very similar, though he adds that women, too, shave the middle of their heads to their foreheads on the day after marrying. Women's heads are not usually seen, given their distinctive tall headdresses, but Rubruck reported seeing the head of Möngke Khan's Christian wife in church: "She began to take off her head-dress, which is called a *bocca*, and I saw her bare head."[51] Riccold of Monte Croce a few decades later included thin beards in a highly derogatory description of Mongols, especially old men, as resembling apes.[52]

Carpini, too, was perhaps the first European to offer an authentic description of Chinese men ("Kitayans") whom he saw at the Mongol court: "They seem to be most affable and kindly men. They have no beard and their physiognomy is much like that of the Mongols, though they are not so broad in the face."[53] Beardlessness was also remarked as a feature of Tibetans, although Carpini says this is due to cultural practices as well as nature: "They do not grow beards, indeed they carry in their hands, as we saw, an iron instrument, with which they always pluck their beards if any hair happens to grow there." The "Kergis" (Kyrgyz) are also said to have "no beards."[54] Marco Polo says little about the hair of Asian peoples, though notes that the attractive women of "Ergiuul" on the western edge of China are black-haired—as too are the men—but also free of body hair and well made in every way.⁵⁵

Yet the foreign could be comprehended in familiar terms as well. Rubruck found the shaven-headed Buddhist monks "looked to me like Frenchmen," and at Möngke's court after their long journey, Rubruck and his fellow Franciscans shaved (and went barefoot) because they wanted to appear in front of the Khan as they would look in their own homeland, but Nestorians there thought they might be "tuins" (east Asian monks, either Taoists or Buddhists).⁵⁶ In a different vein, manuscript illuminators who endeavored to portray east Asian peoples often depicted the women in particular as indistinguishable from idealized European models, their blonde hair arranged artfully around fair-skinned faces. Mongolian or other north or east Asian men were differentiated from European counterparts largely by their headgear, although the scene of the banquet of the Great Khan from the *Livre des merveilles*, ca. 1410 (Figure 7.5) also grants the khan and his guests bushy beards and somewhat bulbous noses.⁵⁷ These features are not found in all contemporary versions of this scene. Ambrogio Lorenzetti's depiction of a Mongol in a detail from the fresco of the *Martyrdom of the Franciscans of Tana* (ca. 1336–1340), though somewhat earlier than the French manuscript, shows a more realistic figure, neither Europeanized, idealized, nor demonized (Figure 7.6). Between the mid-thirteenth and late fifteenth centuries, European views of Asia were scattered and in formation, so general patterns do not emerge; moreover, lacking either the power or the motive to conquer or dominate eastern realms, fixed or phobic stereotypes had not yet taken hold.

FIGURE 7.5 Master of Egerton (fl. 1405–1420). Banquet of the Great Khan. From Marco Polo (1254–1324), *Livre des merveilles* (Paris, 1410?–1412?) Français 2810 fol. 39r. Bibliothèque Nationale de France (BnF). © BnF, Dist. RMN-Grand Palais / Art Resource, NY.

FIGURE 7.6 Ambrogio Lorenzetti (fl. ca. 1311–1348). Head of a Tartar. Detail from the *Martyrdom of the Franciscans* at Tana. S. Francesco. Photo: Scala/Art Resource, NY.

Long shaggy hair and beards retained their associations with primitivism, as they did in Riccold's description of the Kurds as "a fierce, monstrous tribe whose wickedness and savagery exceeds that of all the other barbarous nations we found. They live in the mountains and steep locations like wild goats ... They walk around half naked and unkempt, with long hair and beards."[58] Given the widespread association of wildness with hairiness, it is not surprising that among the so-called "monstrous" peoples associated with the eastern and southern reaches of the inhabited globe, some were hirsute. For example, in the popular alleged memoir *The Book of Sir John Mandeville*, the author describes imagined monsters of eastern islands as "all hairy except for the face and the hands. This people move as well under the sea as they do on dry land, and they eat meat and fish completely raw."[59] Closer to home, many European cultures drew on biblical, classical, and Celtic precedents in imagery of the wild man and wild woman— "wodewose" in Middle English: naked, irrational, sometimes libidinous forest-dwelling peoples, representing the archetypical antithesis of civilization; from the twelfth century both male and female of the quasi-human species were regularly portrayed as covered in hair. These were not necessarily phobic images, however. The engraving *The Savage Family* of the late fifteenth century (Figure 7.7) is almost tender in its vision of wild parents and their infants, dwelling in a rough rocky landscape by a winding stream. The image represents a late medieval turn away from fear to envy of the savage: "The characteristic late medieval image of a free and enlightened creature living in complete harmony with nature reflects not the mythic wild man as the embodiment of all that man should eschew but, on the contrary, the wild man as a symbol of all that man should strive to achieve."[60] Though associations with disorder and the bestial endured, by the fifteenth century wilderpeople could be seen to embody an idyllic prelapsarian condition.

FIGURE 7.7 Master BXG (1466–1490), *The Savage Family*. Engraving. Collection Rothschild. 288LR. Photo: Tony Querrac. Musée de Louvre, Paris. © BnF, Dist. RMN-Grand Palais /Art Resource, NY.

CONCLUSION

Hair played a relatively minor, yet regular, role in medieval constructions of ethnic difference. Distinctions of culture and religion outweighed perceptions of bodily difference in early medieval constructions of ethnicities, although the revival of humoral and climatological theory in twelfth- and thirteenth-century universities saw increasing interest in the body. As both an outgrowth of the body and a feature uniquely suited to modification, hair was regularly featured in descriptions of ethnic groups, and could serve to define the "in" as well as the "out" groups, and to be deployed in relatively neutral contexts as well as those featuring vitriol and persecution. Yet I would like to end on a note of caution. A chapter such as this is necessarily highly selective, in both its choices of illustrative examples and the huge matters it must omit. On the latter point, it should be emphasized that any detailed inquiry into medieval concepts of ethnicity and proto-race needs to place findings into context. Here I have selected passages and images that mention or depict hair or beards. Yet medieval descriptions of ethnic groups, apart from those which fall under the heading of medical or scientific writings, remained overwhelmingly interested in cultural differences. Thus while we will find important and interesting remarks on hair types as well as skin color, physiognomy, body height and shape, and so forth, we often must search for those comments embedded within long and detailed accounts of religious beliefs and practices, living arrangements, military organization, governance, marital and sexual customs, and foodways. Ultimately, a more important matter than which elements of ethnic difference are featured is the question of function: when, where, and why are differences between peoples highlighted, exaggerated, or invented, and for whom?

CHAPTER EIGHT

Hair and Social Class

JOHN BLOCK FRIEDMAN

In the stratified society of medieval Europe from about 800 to about 1450 a person's social rank was determined by birth. In the later Middle Ages sumptuary laws closely regulated how members of each of the classes should dress with regard to color, cut, fabric, ornament, hairstyle, and the like, so that a person's place in society could be immediately determined at a distance, and that person not be confused with someone of higher or lower status.[1] For example, in Peter Idley's *Instructions to his Son*, written in 1450, this hierarchical conception of society is clearly laid out for the young man: "each man is to know himself and his better: a page from a groom, and a groom from a yeoman as is right. As the A.B.C. is made in order by letter, a yeoman from a squire, and a squire from a knight. And so to the highest and mightiest. And as they are arranged in order of rank, so shall their clothing and ornament be."[2] This class identification was considered so intrinsic to social order that moralists regarded attempts to seem of a higher class through changes in clothing, hairstyle, and other accepted visual social identifiers as transgressing the natural order, attacking the very fabric of society.

Hair—its length as well as its absence—plays a role in such class identification. Though in different periods and in different places attitudes toward the presence or absence of hair conflicted, generally speaking, two basic patterns emerge in the western European Middle Ages: for men, hair grows longer as men rise—or wish to be seen doing so—in social class. And conversely, though female hair on the head remains long according to St. Paul's precept in 1 Corinthians 11:14 that a woman's glory lies in her hair, the reduction of hair through plucking the eyebrows, hairline and temples, and even genitalia marks a similar real or pretended rise in social status.

Broadly speaking, for most of early and late medieval history, young men associated with royal courts prized long hair though Catholic moralists inveighed against this fashion. How did long hair on men become associated with the aristocracy and its wearing become a specific privilege allowed only to that class? Long hair on rulers becomes customary in the time of the Merovingian or long-haired kings, the *Reges Criniti*.[3] Oddly, however, the Carolingian dynasty's most famous ruler, Charlemagne, and those kings who followed him, in the spirit of contradiction remarked on above, prided themselves on short hair. Charlemagne's long white beard is frequently mentioned in the *Song of Roland* even though, according to Giles Constable, "none of the Carolingian [rulers] including Charlemagne, had a beard, and the typical male style during the Carolingian period was to have a mustache and a clean shaven chin."[4] Indeed, beards and mustaches played little part in determining medieval social class, though long beards tended to mark outsiders such as pagans, Muslims, Jews, and sinners.[5]

Geoffrey Chaucer in the *Canterbury Tales* (ca. 1380–1390) shows the range of meaning associated with male and female hair length and style, describing people from all walks of life on a pilgrimage to the shrine of St. Thomas in Canterbury. He depicts some of the elaborate hairstyles of the aristocracy just mentioned as defining features of male status. For example, in *The Knight's Tale*, Arcite, a noble young knight, mentions his uncut hair and beard as signs of his personal importance: "My beard, my hair that hang down very long and have never felt a razor or scissors."[6] A similarly aristocratic young man, the Knight's Squire in the *General Prologue*, has "hair curled by a hot iron."[7]

In England, as Robert Bartlett notes, moralists criticized long hair, indicating how fashionable and widespread and accordingly irritating it was.[8] For even if long hair indicated an upper-class status at the court, many clerical writers, again following Saint Paul's teaching "if a man have long hair, it is a shame unto him," considered it vain, feminine, and even un-Christian.[9] One of the most vituperative of these early critics of male long hair was Orderic Vitalis, whose *Ecclesiastical History* laments effeminacy at the court of King William II of England. He speaks of how the nobility now "parted their hair from the crown of the head to the forehead, grew long and luxurious locks like women." Youths now "shave the front part of their head, like thieves, and let their hair grow very long in the back, like harlots ... They curl their hair with hot irons ... Scarcely any knight appears in public ... decently shorn according to the Apostle's precept."[10]

Though Leviticus 19:27 and 21:5 specifically forbade the shaving of the head ("ye shall not round the corners of your heads ... they shall not make baldness upon their head") the characterizations of Absalom in 2 Samuel 14:26 and Samson in Judges 16:17 contributed to the clerical condemnations of long hair for men. These Old Testament characters were cautionary illustrations of male vanity and sexual subjection: Absalom was vain about his long, luxuriant hair, which contributed to his death, while Samson allowed Delilah to cut his seven locks of hair, telling her he had never yet cut it, and so lost the source of his strength to a woman.

Both Absalom and Samson appear frequently as exempla in medieval vernacular literature. Geoffrey Chaucer, again, for example, in *The Miller's Tale* in the *Canterbury Tales* names a vain and silly young village clerk with long blond hair Absolon. Medieval commentators on scripture such as Peter of Riga in his *Aurora* fostered the belief that Absalom's hair was golden and especially luxuriant, and Chaucer, ironically, plays on the idea that Absolon's hair was associated with sexual success and disaster.[11]

So too, the Samson story became a staple in misogynistic literature, associating the cutting of hair by women with the loss of male sexual and political power. In overly trusting Delilah and succumbing to her charms, Samson relinquished his male dominance and consequently was ruined. Thus he often served as a model of love sickness or excess attraction to the female form,[12] a view further strengthened by medical authorities following the Pseudo-Aristotelian *Problemata* (Problems), that warned that excessive sexual intercourse and contact with the female genitalia caused male baldness and thus loss of social status.[13] For instance, the Iberian writers Jacme Roig (ca. 1400–1478) in *The Spill* and Alfonzo Martinez de Toledo (1398–1470) in *El Corbacho de Reprobación del amor mundano* (The Crow or the Reprobation of Worldly Love) use this belief to dissuade men from loving women by pointing out their moral and physical flaws. Both allude to the story of Samson, in presenting this medieval belief about baldness—available to the Spanish in a translation of the physician Bernard of Gordon's *Lilium medicinae* (Lily Flowers of Medicine).[14]

If long hair marked the aristocratic man, then short or cropped hair and baldness became specific signs of the lower-class man, signifying servitude, outrageousness, and folly. By the twelfth century we begin to find hair length—especially its absence—clearly associated with social transgressivity. For example, in the scene of the mocking of Christ from the right-hand leaf of the altar triptych in the church in Idar-Oberstein, painted around 1390, Christ is shown having a lock of hair yanked out; a grotesquely bald and lower-class tormentor leans on him (Figure 8.1). In an engraving by the Master E.S. from Germany made in 1460, a scene of feasting and sexual revelry in a Garden of Love is commented on by the presence of a bald fool, with the belt of whose robe one of the festive women suggestively toys (Figure 8.2).[15]

In England and on the continent, by the late fourteenth century, the opposition between short-haired servile men and long-haired aristocratic men was clearly established by law and custom. This applied to both rural and urban men of low social station. For example, a law promulgated in thirteenth-century Bavaria stated that "peasants and their sons should cut their hair to the ears."[16] And apprentices in fifteenth-century London were routinely shorn. A Mercer's Guild document remarks of a condition for admission to the company that the apprentice should behave in a serious manner and have appropriate dress and hair length and not go about like a playboy or a man of the king's court.[17]

By the end of the Middle Ages, then, the convention that short hair characterized male peasants or villagers, even relatively wealthy or important ones, was well established. Thus in Chaucer's *General Prologue* of the *Canterbury Tales*, the Squire's Yeoman is described as having a "close cropped head" and the manorial Reeve has short hair: "his hair was shorn high above his ears" in illustration of the Bavarian sumptuary law just mentioned.[18]

For men, then, it would seem that to lose hair was to lose social status, to move downward in class, and to grow hair was to move upward socially. Yet the cultural and social tensions that distinguished many parts of medieval Europe often erupted into

FIGURE 8.1 Master of the Mainz Mocking, *Mocking of Christ* (ca. 1390). Upper right-hand wing of the Idar-Oberstein Altar-Triptych, "Crag-Church" or Felsenkirche, Idar-Oberstein, Germany. Photo: John Block Friedman.

FIGURE 8.2 Master E.S., *Love Garden with Bald Fool* (1460). Cleveland Museum of Art 1993.161. Courtesy of the Cleveland Museum of Art.

transgressions of these traditional principles. The rise of a money economy that raised the power of cities and that of the merchant and artisanal bourgeoisie, challenged the traditional feudal agrarian income of the nobility. This resulted in a conflict between the struggling and increasingly disclassed economically and politically depressed small aristocracy and the upwardly mobile and financially powerful peasantry that was widespread throughout Europe. After the Black Death, particularly with the shortage of workers, peasants commanded more pay for their work and had a higher standard of material culture. Rising to positions of significant manorial responsibility and wealth, they often married upward into the minor nobility. Not surprisingly, this newly upwardly mobile population also suddenly had the means to dress and adopt the appearances of the nobility, though this caused considerable worry as it threatened the basic understanding of social order established by the class-stratified society.

These threats to order were implicit in the social commentary of such writers as Seifried Helbling, who describes in about 1300 how peasants acquired prerogatives of lesser knights in his *Der kleine Lucidarius* (The Small Enlightener) where a peasant rises through his administrative skills, sending his son to court and his daughters to serve as seamstresses for women of the court; in time, the nobleman's son marries the wealthy daughter of this peasant official for her dowry and their children are granted knighthoods.[19] However, this fear of and contempt for upwardly mobile rustics and even the smaller bourgeoisie is perhaps nowhere better seen than in the songs of the Middle High German Neidhart (1190–1240) and in *Meier Helmbrecht*, by Wernher the Gardener, who show the age's preoccupation with peasant "up-classing" and the problems this poses to a hierarchical society. Both poets take the modification of traditional hairstyles—namely the supposed penchant of the higher peasants for imitating the style of the nobility through their elaborate long hair—as a symbol of what they see as the faults and failures of their age, blaming peasants for contemporary social disorganization.

Neidhart's adversarial relation to such wealthy and stylish peasants whom he views as a threat to social order can be seen in his thirty-seven Winter Songs.[20] Accordingly, waved and overly long blonde hair on rustics is one of Neidhart's most common topics for satire, particularly when worn under a fancy cap. For example, in Winter Song 24, he writes, "Listen to how these rustics are dressed. Their clothes are above their place. Tight tunics, and short cloaks, red hoods, buckled shoes, and black hose. They wear silk pouches, and in them put bits of ginger to make themselves sweet to the girls. They wear their hair long—a privilege of good birth."[21] No doubt it is just such transgressive hair that is intended in a satiric pen-and-ink drawing from a south German "labor of the months" scene of 1475, showing a peasant binding sheaves in a field. He has long and elaborately curled hair.[22]

Neidhart contrasts such hair with the Carolingian moral rejection of long hair and sometimes forcibly cutting it as a sort of moral control that was mentioned earlier. In Winter Song 36, foppish villagers are warned "one will cut your hair off / Next to the ears above the curls / You peacocks will lose your tails," and the speaker pines for a stricter time under Charlemagne, when the "long curled blonde hair" of one peasant would have been cut off. "One shall prescribe hair ... according to the old customs, as one wore it in the time of Karl der Grosse [Charlemagne]."[23]

The speaker laments as well not only the hair of the young villagers but also their caps that call attention to it. He says, for example, of the cap of a village dandy, Hildemar "that it [the hair] is tied up inside / And outside there are embroidered birds with silk thread / For this many little hands have moved their fingers / To ornament it so." He goes on to curse the vain hairstyle of the cap's peasant owner: "Haven't you seen his long spiral curls, / That hang down below the chin? / At night they lie gathered in the cap / The hair ... in the cap would span a palm if set free."[24] A miniature showing Neidhart and such transgressive peasants appears in the famous Codex Manesse in Heidelberg, dating from about 1315 (Figure 8.3). The miniature depicts the poet as a tall (his height shows his superiority to those around him) graceful figure in an old-fashioned long gown beset by cruder sword-bearing rustics, one of whom has hair to his shoulders (swords were prohibited to peasants by sumptuary laws) and wears the offensive cap satirized in the song. Their short tunics expose striped or parti-colored hose, further emphasizing the point that those surrounding the poet were not conforming to social conventions. Such striped and parti-colored garb at this period commonly appeared on socially undesirable characters such as pagans, fools, and tormentors of Christ.[25]

Wernher the Gardener (ca. 1230–1240) is another writer who in his poem *Meier Helmbrecht* focuses on the social disorder arising from attempts to up-class oneself through altered appearance and through marriage. Helmbrecht, the main character, attempts to change his agricultural "nature" through hair length and style that leads him to become a false knight-robber and oppressor of his own class. Alluding to Neidhart as an influence on his poem, Wernher takes from the older poet a central symbol, the cap enclosing Helmbrecht's long hair, which features prominently in a painting of the hero on the first page of the manuscript now in the Austrian National Library (Figure 8.4). Indeed, the poem's speaker characterizes the ambitious young peasant who symbolically rejects his peasant life by his fashion excesses, most of which involve his hair: "I saw—this is really true— / a farmer's son who had a head of hair / that was curly and blond. It fell long and full / right down over his shoulders. / He decked it with a cap / covered with splendid pictures."[26] Such a cap is probably modeled on the one in Neidhart's portrait of the boorish and upwardly mobile Hildemar of Winter Song 29. And then, when the young Helmbrecht announces to his father his intention to go to court because he is tired of rustic life, he says,

FIGURE 8.3 The Poet Neidhart besieged by peasants (1315). Codex Manesse, Heidelberg Universitätsbibliothek MS Cod. Pal. Germ. 848, LXIII, fol. 273r. Courtesy of Heidelberg University Library.

> may God hate me
> if I should ever yoke up your oxen for you
> If I should drive your steers once more
> and sow your oats.
> That really wouldn't suit
> my long blond hair
> and my curly locks
> … and my splendid cap.[27]

What is interesting to note is after his career as a knight-bandit, the younger Helmbrecht is seemingly taught a lesson about his pretentious behavior, as he suffers the symbolic humiliation of having the *visibilia* of his social supremacy, his cap and his long hair

> now completely torn to bits.
> It was a gruesome scene.
> Nothing so big as a penny
> was left in one piece …
> Here lay a lock of hair, over there a piece
> of the cap … You've never seen a scalp so bald
> … You could see his curly blond hair
> now of little consequence,
> lying on the ground.[28]

FIGURE 8.4 Ambras Heldenbuch, Hans Ried and others, Helmbrecht with long hair (1517). MS A, Vienna, Österreichische Nationalbibliothek, MS Cod. S.N., 2663, fol. 225. Courtesy of the Austrian National Library.

At the same time that traditions regarding male hair were observed whereby longer hair became an outward symbol of a man's high birth and social status, we see the absence of facial and body hair signaling aristocratic status for women. Therefore, by the twelfth century, depilation, removal of hair at brows and hairline, and lightening dark hair were among the means of attaining ideal aristocratic female beauty, particularly in medieval romances and lyrics. The removal of female pubic hair also signaled beauty and high status. Lower-class women, then, were typically regarded as darker and hairier than their upper-class counterparts. Accordingly, women sometimes sought to up-class themselves (or are up-classed by others) through the removal of hair or alteration of hair color through dyeing or wigs.

The ideal for medieval female beauty was blonde hair framing a wide, high, somewhat bulged brow, called the *front bombé* (bulged forehead), with thin, high, arched dark eyebrows.[29] Blondeness even becomes a topos in rhetorical manuals such as Matthew of Vendôme's *Ars versificatoria* (The Art of Versification) composed around 1175, where the student employs model exercises such as the *ordo effictionis* (order of features) showing how to portray through words ideal female beauty by presenting physical features one by one beginning at the top of the head and working down to the feet. Matthew, for instance, established Helen of Troy's legendary beauty by first describing her lovely blonde tresses:

"Her golden hair, unfettered by any confining knot, / cascades quite freely about her face, / ... Her dark eyebrows, neatly lined twin arches."[30]

Vernacular poets quickly appropriated these techniques of Latin schoolroom description as well as the beauty canons they offered. For example, in an *effictio* (portrait) closely modeled on Matthew's, Boccaccio, in the *Teseide*, shows Emilia, the beautiful noblewoman who attracts the affections of the two male protagonists, with hair "long and plentiful and [it] could truly be described as golden ... I say that her hair seemed to be of gold, and it was not worn tightly in braids but loose and well combed."[31]

Such blonde hair becomes the standard for courtly beauty. Obviously, whatever their hair color, noble women had more of the time, the means, and the servants to ornament their hair through dyeing, elaborate braiding, weaving in of silk, wearing of coifs, circlets, and garlands, often of peacock feathers, with the result that these ornaments became marks of nobility. By the twelfth century, the *De ornatu mulierum* (The Ornamentation of Women) in the *Trotula*, a treatise on women's medicine, shows that blonde hair was important to the upper-class woman; the work gives her a recipe for a hair preparation involving a lime bleach. After use, "her hair will be golden and shimmering."[32] For example, in Giovanni Boccaccio's misogynistic dream vision *Il Corbaccio* (The Crow), written in 1365, the practices by Florentine upper-class brunettes of dyeing their hair blonde and arranging it elaborately to attract men are noted as a female vice at several points. The narrator declares, "Most of them make their hair, produced black from their pates, like spun gold, sometimes with sulfur, sometimes with rinse-waters, and most often with the rays of the sun. They arrange it in tresses behind their backs, now loose upon their shoulders, or now twisted upon their heads, depending on the way they think they look the most charming."[33]

Elsewhere the speaker comments satirically on the elaborate hair arrangement of upper class women:

> After she had herself diligently combed and had twisted her hair upon her head, she placed on top of it a certain tangle of silk which she called her "tresses," and attached it with a net of the finest silk; having been handed the appropriate garlands and flowers, placing these first on her head and distributing little blossoms everywhere, she would deck out her head just as she had sometimes seen a peacock's tail painted with eyes.[34]

Florentine sumptuary laws of 1356 attest to the practices described, for they forbade any woman below the rank of wife of a knight to wear in the city "any crown of gold, silver, pearls, precious stones, mother of pearl." Those of lower rank, however, could wear a "garland or circlet ... of gold, silver, or pearls, gilded, silver plated or imitation, with enamels ... [but it must] not be valued at over ten gold florins."[35]

In contrast to such flower-bedecked wealthy beauties, peasant or rustic women were typically imagined as dark, dirty, and hairy of body and face, as in the Occitan mock *pastourelle* "Mentre per una ribiera" (While along a bank) of about 1320 to 1333, and their hair and its treatment differs accordingly. The traditional *pastourelle* is largely a French poetic form popular in the twelfth and thirteenth centuries describing a romantic encounter between a lovely shepherdess tending her flock and a roving knight from a noble court who comes upon the young rustic by chance while seeking adventure.[36] In this comic or mock *pastourelle* example, however, instead of being lovely, the peasant "piggirl" according to the knight is "wild and ugly, / Swarthy, black as pitch." When she agrees to make love with him and the knight sees her genitalia, he runs off.[37] In Juan Ruiz's *Book of Good Love,* written in 1343, the hideous mountain shepherdess Alda is even hairy of hands.[38] In a comic poem by Luigi Pulci (1432–1484) the more urban "beloved" is "hairy around her little mouth and she really looks like a barbel" (catfish), while Giovanni Mauro (1490–1536) wrote a burlesque poem about some mountain women of extreme ugliness who were the exact opposites of courtly beauties in depilation, speaking, for example, "of the dark forests of their eyebrows."[39]

In the traditional northern French *pastourelle* such rustic women though generally attractive were typically portrayed as brunettes and/or having darker features in keeping with their social class.[40] Accordingly, in one such poem dating from the thirteenth century, a girl recognizes that her coloring fatefully defines her social position in life but has still managed to attract the knight. When overheard singing by the narrator, she says, "In God's name, I have a handsome friend, / Charming and attractive, / *Even though* I'm a brunette," while another *pastourelle* comments on how the coarse, dark peasant appearance can be redeemed by the single courtly detail of uncharacteristically light hair. Here the girl sings, "I know I am not pretty, but at least I am a blonde."[41]

Class mobility is also implicit in *pastourelle* structure. The upper-class suitor wishes to down-class himself and live with the girl with whom he is immediately smitten. Given the nature of the gulf between classes in *pastourelle*, the woman has to be up-classed in some way—in other words, given attributes more of the woman of the court than of the fields to be suitable for the knight. Descriptions of the shepherdess' hair and eyebrows play an important role in this process and are far less broadly treated than in the mock *pastourelles* noted earlier. So whereas in courtly lyric or narrative poetry the woman almost always is fair, with northern French or Norman blonde hair and blue eyes, in contrast, the heroine of *pastourelle* is usually dark haired. And if by chance she is blonde, then she has dark eyes and skin. These "mixed" characteristics fix her peasant nature.

The shape and fullness of a woman's eyebrows and hairline played another important role in distinguishing a woman's class and beauty. Generally speaking, especially in the later Middle Ages, an upper-class woman's eyebrows should be artfully shaped by removing hair. For example, in Juan Ruiz's *Book of Good Love* the ideal girl is clearly one with such plucked and shaped courtly eyebrows, a feature that by implication lower-class women lack. The sage advice offered in the work, then, is to "look for a beautiful woman … / And try not to fall in love with a peasant girl … Look for a woman with / Eyebrows … long and arched," specifying their aristocratic thinness and making an interesting contrast with the "dark forests" of eyebrows mentioned above.[42]

Toward the second half of the fourteenth century and well into the fifteenth century, perhaps responding to the same Gothic taste for "verticality" appearing in architecture and in aristocratic male fashion that had something of a stovepipe look, particularly noticeable at the court of the Burgundian Duke Philip the Good, aristocratic women also plucked their hairlines and temples to increase the expanse and curvature of their foreheads, to achieve an effect that one fifteenth-century French poem enumerating twenty-three characteristics of beautiful women called a *grand front* (a broad, high forehead).[43] Women, then, intentionally modified their faces through depilatory practices in order to conform to courtly standards of beauty.

A good illustration of such a fashionable woman is Jean Fouquet's Melun diptych leaf of King Charles VII's mistress Agnès Sorel (1420–1450) pictured as the Virgin Mary (Figure 8.5) that clearly associates this depilatory style with royalty. In short, Agnès Sorel has exactly the sort of noble look to which many women would aspire. Indeed, most late Gothic depictions of the Virgin Mary feature it as well.

FIGURE 8.5 Jean Fouquet, Agnès Sorel as the Virgin (1420–1450). *Melun Diptych*, right leaf. Antwerp, Musée Royal des Beaux-Arts. Courtesy of the Musée des Beaux-Arts.

Such literary and cosmetic references to female eyebrows and hairlines associate high social class and beauty with art, the depilation done manually or by chemical means. Thus, not only does the removal of hair become a way of identifying an aristocratic woman at a distance but it also reflects medieval beauty canons. That such cosmetic practices were early considered routine for female beauty is clear from the *De ornatu mulierum* (The Ornamentation of Women) attributed to the Spanish physician Arnold of Villanova (1240–1311), which was, as its title suggests, modeled on the *Trotula*. Arnold mentions in his introduction that "depilation and whitening are vital to women either by necessity or because they consider it suitable to have clear, shining, and beautiful faces."[44]

Vernacular as well as learned southern Mediterranean and Iberian culture was particularly rich in discussions of female depilation and recipes for it. A rather general reference which could apply to the forehead or the pubic regions of upper-class women appears in the late fourteenth-century vernacular adaptation of the *De ornatu mulierum* written by a Catalan named only Joan who also titled his work *Trotula*.[45] Additionally, there were recipes and allusions to the process in similar treatises, though the social rank of the women was not always indicated. The fifteenth-century *Vergel de señores* (Garden of gentlemen), a Spanish health manual, gives several recipes.[46] *El Corbacho*, mentioned earlier, also refers to "pins, mirrors, make-up boxes, combs, sponges with gum to use as a fixer for laying hair … silver tweezers to pull out some little hair or other if it shows itself, a steel mirror to study her face" as implements for following up on such recipes.[47]

The author of *El Corbacho* is probably alluding to the discussion of depilation in its Italian source, Boccaccio's *Il Corbaccio*. Apparently in Florence there was a group of house-call-making beauticians, lower-class women who had the skills to depilate upper-class women. The woman described in *Il Corbaccio* as bleaching and elaborately ornamenting her hair frequents "certain old biddies, of whom there are a great many around our city, who go about peeling other women, plucking their eyelashes and brows, shaving their cheeks with thin glass ... and removing little whiskers."[48]

Yet if the previously discussed cultural and social tensions that characterize late medieval Europe erupted into transgressions of the traditional male principles of class distinction, not surprisingly, they also erupted into the same kind of class transgressions among women. There are many examples of lower-class women, then, emulating the beauty practices of their upper-class counterparts. For instance, as early as the thirteenth century one cosmetic method of achieving the *front bombé* was practiced among village women, as indicated by a description of the cosmetic items offered by a traveling mercer or seller of sewing and cosmetic supplies in the anonymous French "Dit du Mercier" (Song of the Mercer). The speaker in his *boniment* (sales pitch) to the villagers remarks that "I have much finery for women: / Everything necessary to the toilette: / razors to shave the hairline, tweezers."[49] However, perhaps the best-documented example of the practice of female facial depilation as an instance of up-classing is that of Chaucer's Alison in *The Miller's Tale*, the eighteen-year-old wife of a much older wealthy Oxford carpenter. She is relatively urbanized—Helen Cooper calls her a "city wife"—and stylish, belonging to the new money economy developing at the end of the fourteenth century in England.[50] Her transgressive attire, includes silk, forbidden by sumptuary law to those of her station, and her eyebrow and hairline treatments reflect her position in the emerging urban class. Though Alison's shining countenance is compared to a newly minted gold coin, the noble, her roots in the peasant class are clearly shown through her association with animal husbandry, dairying, and agriculture.

Although Chaucer leaves vague details of Alison's given features such as her hair color, we do learn several important things about the "accidentals" of what she has done to her features, modifying them to make her look more like a woman of the court. He highlights the expanse and character of Alison's forehead and hairline and the cosmetic treatment and color of her eyebrows. That Alison imitates the style of women above her in the social order in her treatment of these features is clear from the very first line of her portrait: "Her broad silk headband sat high on her head / ... Her two eyebrows were closely plucked, / And they were as black as a sloe berry."[51] When she goes to church "her forehead shone as bright as day," suggesting that her hairline had been plucked, shaven, or otherwise depilated in the fashionable aristocratic *front bombé* style of the late fourteenth and fifteenth centuries.[52] Again, the poet calls attention to this part of her face, the expanse of her forehead, to establish that she is not "low browed" with a low hairline, a specific peasant or villainous facial detail. Overall, that she has been dressing and getting herself up above her station as the *faux* courtly woman of high romance is a point noted, for example, by James Morey who has even seen hints of *Tristan*'s Iseult, a famous courtly beauty, in Alison's description.[53]

Such fashionable practices—whether among upper- or lower-class women—were largely condemned by clerics who spoke of them as signs of pride, vanity, and other worldly vices that led both the artificially beautified women and the men who were attracted by them astray. Moreover, Geoffrey de la Tour Landry, in composing in 1372 a conduct manual called *Livre du Chevalier de la Tour Landry* (The Book of the Knight of la Tour Landry) for his daughters to ease their entry into the urban elite, was particularly concerned that the girls not ape the fashions of those socially higher than themselves or indeed vainly run after new fashions. He tells a monitory tale about a knight who had a vision of his dead wife's torment in hell by devils who stuck burning needles into her eyebrows, temples, and forehead. The angel who was explaining the vision to the widower-knight said the punishment was because she "had shaved her eyebrows and her temples, and plucked out her hairs to make herself more beautiful and pleasing to the world." Geoffrey then warns his daughters, "do not change your faces nor pluck your eyebrows or foreheads."[54] Obviously these strictures for the daughters indicated that girls of similar social station—or somewhat lower, such as Chaucer's Alison—were doing exactly what the father warned against.

This focus on controlling and shaping female hair through cosmetic art as a social class identifier expresses a male medical and cultural fear of female hair where, for example, conventional descriptions of the extremely ugly woman such as those found in Juan Ruiz's *Book of Good Love*, often mention low brows and excess facial hair as inspiring horror in male observers, who seem to have tied dark female body hair to low social status. Ugly as well as beautiful women have antecedents in the medieval rhetorical tradition. For instance, Matthew of Vendôme's model description for the famous beauty, Helen of Troy, noted earlier, has a counterpoint in the model for the hideous woman called Beroe; her *effictio* mentions her "bushy brows bristling."[55]

With the codification and diffusion of canons of both beauty and ugliness in the fourteenth century, attitudes more or less concealed in folklore and the cultural imagination begin to appear openly in the works of sophisticated writers. It is no wonder, then, that even female pubic hair becomes connected with social class, and the common practice of removing it among upper-class women is suggested by numerous cosmetic recipes widely available for doing this, though with more reticence of terminology than with that applied to facial depilation. The *De ornatu mulierum* in the *Trotula* ensemble advises on the preparation of a specific potion for *nobilibus* (upper-class women): let the woman take a very hot steam bath after anointing herself with it. "When she has stayed there a little while, try to pull out the hairs from the pubic area. If they do not fall out easily, let her have hot water poured over her and let her wash herself all over."[56] There were also various vernacular adaptations of the *De ornatu*; the late fourteenth-century Catalan *Trotula*, for instance, promised to show every woman "how to take good care of her hair, and how to remove it from the places it should not be, either for awhile or for ever ... or to change to any desired colour."[57]

If depilation of pubic hair was linked to high social class, abundant pubic hair was a common characteristic of lower-class women. The sight of pubic hair triggered such class associations but also combined with negative connotations such as ugliness, animal urges, and/or disease. A comic example of the association of pubic hair and class appears in Chaucer's *The Miller's Tale*, a work which we already noted as preoccupied with social change among villagers and wealthier peasants, and whose primary female character is Alison, the rustic who has married well enough to imitate some of the noble fashions. Through the fortuitous circumstances of a dark night, a small window at near ground level, and the malicious prank of Alison and her lover Nicholas, the love-struck parish clerk Absolon inadvertently kisses Alison's bottom (which she sticks out the window for this purpose) thinking it was her mouth: "but with his mouth he juicily kissed her naked ass before he was aware of it and jumped back, thinking something was wrong—he knew a woman had no beard—and he had felt something very rough and longhaired."[58] This episode focuses on Alison's profuse pubic hair, which reveals her villager origins however much she appears to be "of the town," and, as we saw earlier, had plucked her brows and hairline extensively.[59]

The folkloric male fear of female pubic hair undoubtedly influenced female attitudes toward its removal. The fear is rationalized, especially in fifteenth-century Iberian misogynistic medical and moralizing writers, by the quasi-scientific belief already noted that women are inherently diseased, and transmit to men a variety of maladies such as loss of hair through sexual intercourse and contact with their menstrual blood. Pubic hair, then, is just one aspect of this clerical and medical horror of the female genitalia as disease-bearing and status-destroying.

This horror can be seen in descriptions of lower-class women in later *pastourelle* variants, where an urban and or upper-class narrator comments on a peasant woman. Niccolò Campani (1478–1523) ridiculed rustics by ironically praising their values, lifestyle, speech, and appearance. One of his poems describes an encounter between a peasant (who takes Niccolò's point of view) and a miller's daughter whom he spies while on his way home. The miller's daughter has her skirt hoisted up letting the peasant look at her thighs. What follows is the poet's self-conscious reversal of the conventional order of description in that he works from the bottom up, not the top down:

She was showing me her two large feet,
That looked like freshly turned-over sods.
And a little higher up
Were two big legs straight, and long as two pilings,
Mottled white and olive, they looked like two firebrands.
And going up a bit … Her hams were gleaming up there like a lantern
And they were much hairier than I can tell you—
So think what that other thing must have been like.[60]

It is clear that the hairiness of the miller's daughter, so closely related to her undescribed but presumably frightening genitalia, is intended to stir the audience's fear of hirsute peasant women, sexual contact with whom can lead to male hair loss.

Another comparable commentary on the pubic hair of peasant girls that expands the dangerous effects of its exhibition is found in Oswald von Wolkenstein's *pastourelle* variant "Ain Grasserin durck külen tau" (A girl mowing the grass in the cool dew), associating female pubic hair with danger to the upper-class male lover. Using agricultural metaphors the poet cleverly describes a sexual encounter between an upper-class male lover and a rustic girl. The male narrator speaks wittily of his partner's "brown-haired sickle" that first gives him "delight" but eventually incites fear as the peasant girl's appetite is insatiable.[61] In this instance, then, the pubic hair of the worker is potentially damaging as it is linked ironically to the male lover's loss of self if not castration.

In Mediterranean folklore this fear of female pubic hair, particularly that of peasant women, was very early harnessed to its display and removal as an apotropaic gesture. A folk belief involved the act of lifting the skirts and showing the genitalia to frighten off evil, as did the miller's daughter in Campani's poem, for female genitalia were so "potent" that bad fortune could be deterred by their exhibition. Medieval town and city gates were liminal sites for statuary imagined to bring good luck or ward off bad fortune from entering. A marble bas-relief carved in 1185, once in the wall of Milan's Porta Tosa, depicts a rustic woman lifting her skirts and trimming her pubic hair with a large pair of shears, presumably to bring genital power more in view (Figure 8.6).[62]

A full-length bridal portrait of an aristocratic or at least decidedly upper-class couple, painted on a panel in about 1470 in southern Germany brings into sharp focus many of the themes we have treated in this chapter on hair and social class (Figure 8.7). While there is much to be said about the floral symbolism of the young man's gift of chicory to

FIGURE 8.6 Apotropaic carving from the Porta Tosa, Milan (ca. 1185). Milan, Castello Sforzesco Museum of Ancient Art, number 528. Photo: Penny Howell Jolly.

FIGURE 8.7 Anonymous, *Bridal Portrait* (1470). Oil on panel. South German. Cleveland Museum of Art 1932.179. Courtesy of the Cleveland Museum of Art.

his bride, the matching colors of their clothing and the like in the bridal portrait, it is the couple's hair and the woman's arched eyebrows and high broad forehead that capture the viewer's attention. Here we see displayed many of the traditions we have been tracing that associate long hair on men with aristocratic status and thin arched eyebrows and a shaved or plucked hairline on women with beauty and nobility. Many of the socially emerging figures discussed earlier aspired in various ways to look like—if they could not be—this couple. The attempts—and the way society regarded these as transgressive—by many of the figures mentioned in this chapter to resemble the people featured in the panel have in various ways shown us something of the power of the cultural imagery of hair in the Middle Ages.

ACKNOWLEDGMENTS

I am grateful to Linde Brocato, Farrell Brody, Montserrat Cabré, Timothy Carroll, Kristen Figg, Paul Freedman, Kathrin Giogoli, Ana Grinberg, Jacqueline Leclercq-Marx, Roberta Milliken, Linda Parshall, Melanie Schuessler-Bond, Claudio da Soller, Michael Twomey, and Karen A. Winstead for advice, information, help with translations, photography, and stylistic suggestions in the preparation of this chapter.

CHAPTER NINE

Cultural Representations: Head and Body Hair in Medieval Art

PENNY HOWELL JOLLY

Hair's malleability makes it a perfect medium for establishing identity, whether of one's ethnic or racial origin, gender, class status, or religious persuasion. But even more manipulable are visual representations of hair. We will never know for certain how successfully fifteenth-century Italian women made their hair fit Petrarch's golden ideal, but their painted portraits depict these usually dark-haired women as blonde beauties. Red hair marks fools, so some images of Judas show him red-haired or even red-bearded. Throughout history, art has constructed realities rather than just recording them; images convey meaning, offering models for ideal behaviors or prescriptive warnings and cautionary examples. Yet conventions regarding hair also reflect the capriciousness of changing fashion and are deeply contextual; meanings become unstable, linked to a particular locale, class of people, or moment in time, and simple "difference" often creates meaning. One category of men might appear bearded because another appears clean-shaven. In the twelfth century, priests and peasants shaved, while young aristocrats grew beards and long hair; a century later, beards became passé, appearing typically on unfashionable, older men. Throughout medieval art, visible head and facial hair helps define their wearers' status or significance, and by the late Middle Ages, artists also begin depicting normally private body hair, to signify age, gender, sexuality, and even character.

Far from being essentially a woman's issue, in the Middle Ages men's hair, not only on their heads but also on their faces and bodies, played significant political, social, and religious roles. Paul Dutton writes that portraits of Charlemagne (742–814) show him in short hair and a mustache (Figure 9.1), thus distinguishing him from his Merovingian predecessors—the famous "long-haired kings"—and from other equally hair-conscious Germans, whose long hair, sometimes gathered in a topknot, differentiated them from more closely shorn slaves. Charlemagne's neatly coiffed hair acknowledged his restoration of the glorious Roman past, while his non-Roman mustache confirmed his ties to Theodoric the Great and the Carolingians' place within civilized, Christian society; for Charlemagne, long hair and beards marked pagan enemies. Dutton notes even Charles the Bald (823–877) appears with a full head of short hair and a mustache; whether he was actually bald is unknown, but his hirsute imagery reaffirmed his ties to his grandfather Charlemagne, to Rome, and to the civilized, Christian German world.[1]

FIGURE 9.1 *Charlemagne*, detail (ninth century). Paris, Louvre. Photo: Erich Lessing/Art Resource, NY.

The Bayeux Tapestry, embroidered around 1070, most likely for the Norman Bishop Odo, similarly uses head and facial hair to distinguish the superior Normans from the Anglo-Saxons. Mustaches and longer hair mark the defeated Harold and his Anglo-Saxon troops, and their dying king, Edward the Confessor, wears additionally a long shaggy beard (Figure I.9). The victorious Normans, led by William the Conqueror, appear clean-shaven and short-haired; contemporaries believed this style demonstrated their superior virtue, while the defeated Anglo-Saxons' hirsuteness confirmed their effeminacy.[2] Indeed, Harold's scouts, upon seeing William's shaved and short-haired soldiers advance in 1066, mistook them for priests.[3] When English and French courtiers begin growing long hair and beards later in the eleventh century and early twelfth, complaints of effeminacy reappear. Orderic Vitalis, a monastic reformer complaining about the fashion, writes in his ca. 1135 *Historiae ecclesiasticae*,

> At that time effeminate men had dominion throughout the world ... They rejected the ways of heroes, ridiculed the counsel of priests, and persisted in their barbarous style of dress and way of life. They parted their hair in the middle, they let it grow long, as women do, and carefully tended it, and they delighted in wearing long and excessively tight undershirts and tunics.[4]

The figure slaying a dragon in the initial "R" of a Cistercian manuscript from 1111 exemplifies the new style: he wears a tightly fitted tunic with trailing sleeves, long hair, and beard.⁵ While secular writers praised the fashionable courtly aesthetic, others like Orderic judged it as dangerously countermanding the lessons of the Battle of Hastings and the Norman victory: it rejected "the ways of heroes."

While beards were long an important sign of masculinity, they became suspect, probably due to their ancient association with sexuality. Widely believed classical theories of the four humors posited that beards resulted from the body's "cooking" of excess semen; therefore, beards reflected surplus sexuality.⁶ Already by the ninth century, clerics were required to shave their beards and wear short hair, though practices were inconsistent, leading the 1031 Church Council of Bourges to mandate all should have "an ecclesiastical tonsure, that is, a shaven beard and a circle on the head."⁷ Clerical hair removal suggests virtuous obedience and renunciation of worldly pleasures, or possibly a sort of castration, marking clerical celibacy.⁸ Orderic again complains regarding twelfth-century lay practices: "[A]ll our fellow countrymen are crazy and wear little beards, openly proclaiming by such a token that they revel in filthy lusts like stinking goats."⁹ Pauline Stafford sees these as rival masculinities in Norman England, as clergy condemned beards and effeminate hairstyles while asserting the virility of their own tonsured heads and faces.¹⁰ Furthermore, eleventh- and twelfth-century Crusaders were urged to shave in order to distinguish themselves on the battlefield from the infidels: long beards became associated with pagans, Muslims, and Jews (Figure I.3).¹¹ The 1337 *Roman de Godefroi de Bouillon* depicts neatly helmeted Crusaders—contemporary armor also discouraged beard-wearing—attacking Saracens who wear beards and head ties, and carry shields marked with heads of kinky-haired black men.¹² Well into the Renaissance and later, long beards remained associated with easterners, whether Greek clergy, who still today do not tonsure, or infidels. In Europe, the twelfth-century hirsute fashion quickly subsided, and, except for periods in the fourteenth century, beards did not enjoy widespread popularity until the sixteenth, when they became one of the most important markers of virile masculinity.

Even though beards were rarely fashionable from the ninth through the fifteenth centuries, their appearance—or absence—in art continued to signify, with meanings shifting from context to context. Giles Constable notes shaving was neither easy nor often practiced; twelfth-century Cistercians were required to shave only seven times per year and Carthusians only six, so short beards would have often adorned "clean-shaven" monastic faces. Older clerics of rank, despite rules, wore beards to signify dignity and elevated positions.¹³ Visual imagery thus generally presents a more distinctly ordered world of tonsured, clean-shaven clerics, obedient and celibate, but Andrea da Firenze's *Way to Salvation* (Florence, Santa Maria Novella Chapter House, ca. 1365) stands as an exception. Its depiction of heavy five-o'clock shadows on the Dominican saints in the foreground may offer a rare representation of those intermittent monastic beards, and the enthroned pope and older clerics appear with full beards. Art can also revise history, adding beards to make heroes older and wiser: Charlemagne's image alters greatly in the later Middle Ages, when he appears with a beard he never wore, visually affirming his experience and wise authority.¹⁴ In the case of Old Testament prophets, lengthy beards recall their Otherness, for they were Jews living in a distant place and time. Yet despite Christianity's fraught relationship with its Hebrew roots, these men are positive figures whose beards also mark their advanced age and its attendant authority and wisdom, qualities associated with their identities as prophets and God's chosen.

Although beards can represent authority and virility, these values can be undermined, and facial hair made to suggest negative qualities. In Pacino di Bonaguida's ca. 1325 *Tabernacle* with *Christ in the Temple among the Doctors* (University of Arizona Museum of Art), the supposedly older and wiser Hebrew scholars appear with long facial and head hair while Christ represents the *puer senex*, the spiritually old youth.[15] His short hair and lack of beard emphasize his heroic youthfulness, even as he sits frontally enthroned above the doctors, his scale dwarfing theirs; they drop their books in astonishment as he confounds them with his knowledge and wisdom. The adolescent Daniel, another *puer senex*, defends the innocent Susanna from the corrupt Elders in Domenico di Michelino's mid-fifteenth-century *cassone* panel (Avignon, Musée du Petit Palais).[16] Well-dressed, with white hair and beards declaring their authority, their purported wisdom as judges, *and* their identity as Jews, the Elders are nonetheless outwitted by young Daniel, shown blond and smooth-cheeked. Very different in meaning, among the recurrent types of sculpted figures appearing particularly in eleventh- and twelfth-century Romanesque churches, are single figures who pull their own beards and pairs of fighters who pull each others'. One example juxtaposes the latter aggressors with the virtue Concord, clarifying their role as personifications of the vice Discord, while the single male figures who stare frontally and fiercely pull their own beards to either side relate formally to spread-legged Sheela-na-gig figures and likely serve a similar apotropaic function, reconfirming their threatening beards' powerful virility.[17]

Because beards and extensive body hair can express virility as well as maturity, they most significantly distinguish men from women. Inspired by Aristotle and other ancient writers, medieval and Renaissance scientists believed men, hot and dry by nature, better cooked their excess bodily fluids into head hair and body hair; wider pores on their heads, armpits, chests, and pubic areas allowed for more luxuriant growth in those areas, while the palms or soles of their feet remained hairless. Women, by contrast, were cold and wet; dangerous superfluities exited their bodies through pores in their hottest and, therefore, hairiest regions—their heads and pubic areas—but otherwise were expelled monthly via menstruation, explaining their comparative hairlessness.[18] Thus, not just facial but body hair distinguished men from women, with pubic hair appearing on images of mature male nudes in thirteenth-century Italy, probably influenced by classical art. Pubic hair appears, for example, on Nicola Pisano's highly classicizing and muscular ca. 1260 Pisa Pulpit's *Fortitude*, a figure derived from a Greco-Roman Hercules sculpture, as well as on various classically inspired nudes by Italian artists from Lorenzo Maitani to Jacopo della Quercia, Lorenzo Ghiberti, and Donatello.[19] With rare exception, nude female bodies in art remain hairless until the sixteenth century.

Pubic hair also distinguishes men from boys, as depictions of mature male nudes, including Jupiter, Neptune, and Hercules, not only wear beards but genital hair, while youthful figures generally do not.[20] This again reflects classical ideas of gender as a continuum, with "fully cooked" men at one end, and incomplete, deficient, colder figures—that is, women—at the other. Young men were situated part way along this continuum: not yet fully cooked, they represented an intermediary position, combining features of the two extremes.[21] In art, youthful males such as Ganymede, Bacchus, Mercury, and even Apollo typically appear beardless, without pubic or torso hair, important markers of full manhood. Donatello's mid-fifteenth-century bronze *David*, influenced by both classical ideas and sculpture, exemplifies these distinctions. As many have noted, his figure appears erotic yet of ambiguous gender. Adrian Randolph suggests viewers from the two major viewing perspectives in the Medici Palace courtyard saw the sculpture very differently, creating a "mobile configuration of gender." The frontal public view displayed David's male genitals, confirming his masculinity and contrasting with the private rear view; there he appeared with "luxuriant shoulder-length tresses," "plump buttocks," and a long fingerlike feather that caresses his thigh, all suggesting feminine characteristics.[22] However, Donatello challenges David's masculinity from both viewing positions. The rear view emphasizes the figure's sinuous effeminate form and long hair, but the front also fails to establish his full masculinity, which here remains latent: he lacks pubic hair, and his smooth face contrasts with Goliath's heavily bearded head at his feet.

By the second half of the thirteenth century, artists begin depicting chest and axillary (underarm) hair on men, most commonly in Italy on depictions of the suffering Christ. Especially in Crucifixion and Man of Sorrows imagery, this very ordinary detail of Christ's anatomy expresses his humble humanity and hints at his vulnerability to human sin, since *copious* chest and axillary hair typically appears on degenerate sinners.[23] For example, in the early 1420s Fra Angelico depicts one of Christ's detractors at the Crucifixion—the sponge-bearer—with abundant chest hair (Figure 9.2), and the pagan governor in Lukas Moser's 1432 Tiefenbronn Altarpiece (Figure 9.3), another reprobate who as yet remains unresponsive to Mary Magdalene's entreaties, sleeps nude but with prolific axillary hair, a shaggy beard, and a night cap over his unkempt hair. A 1340s miniature in Justinian's *Codex* includes an arrested thief, bald and almost naked, with prominent axillary and chest hair.[24] Baldness, discussed below, generally implies negative characteristics, while unkempt or excessive facial and body hair similarly indicates a base nature. Thus, Christ's more subtle body hair, even pubic hair, like his shame*less*ly naked genitals in Renaissance art, expresses visually his fully human nature.[25]

FIGURE 9.2 Fra Angelico, *Crucifixion*, detail (ca. 1420–1423). New York, The Metropolitan Museum of Art, Maitland F. Griggs Collection, Bequest of Maitland F. Griggs, 1943 (43.98.5). Photo © The Metropolitan Museum of Art.

FIGURE 9.3 Lukas Moser, Tiefenbronn Altarpiece, detail (1432). Tiefenbronn, St. Maria-Magdalena. Photo: Erich Lessing/Art Resource, NY.

Visual conventions regarding women's hair during these centuries are in some ways less complicated and remain remarkably consistent. Young unmarried women show their hair to publicly advertise their virginity, fertility, and availability, while married women and widows claim moral control and modesty by appearing with their long hair bound up and hidden under a veil or headdress. While aristocratic women such as Yolande de Soissons cleverly begin wearing diaphanous veils in order to show off their beautiful tresses, as seen in her ca. 1190 prayer-book portrait, these conventions of decorum remain in place throughout the Middle Ages and beyond.[26] Ambrogio Lorenzetti's *Effects of Good Government in the City of Siena*, from 1338 to 1342, exemplifies a range of these practices (Figure 9.4) and offers a revelation. At the right, just inside the city wall, one older peasant woman, properly veiled and presumably married, carries a hen while below her a youthful unmarried girl exposes her hair. At the far left, a bride publicly acknowledges her marriage by riding a horse to her new home, her long, uncovered hair topped by the traditional marriage crown. Typically brides' exposed hair at weddings symbolizes virginity, similar to our modern tradition of wearing white.[27] Hair and dress cues reveal the central ring of dancers—surprisingly, to twenty-first-century eyes—as male not female, possibly a troupe of traveling players. As Jane Bridgeman first noted, they wear short, center-parted hair rolled under, high on their necks, and expose their ankles; women wore longer hair, generally plaited at the sides, and even the peasant women at the far right wear gowns that cover their ankles, while men throughout the scene expose theirs.[28] Scholarship on hair and dress fashions has thus revised our interpretation of this important fresco.

FIGURE 9.4 Ambrogio Lorenzetti, *Effects of Good Government in the City of Siena* (1338–1342). Siena, Palazzo Pubblico. Photo: Scala/Art Resource, NY.

Understanding the conventions of women's hair leads to other surprises, including recognition of a miracle. For example, among *married* women, only one circumstance allows public exposure of hair: queens at their coronations; this may express their role as brides "marrying" their nations.[29] These three conditions for uncovering women's hair—identifying young virgins, brides, and queens—enrich the interpretation of Jan van Eyck's ca. 1436 *Madonna and Child* (Figure 9.5) by creating visual contradictions. Mary, shown here with long hair cascading over her shoulders, sits enthroned under a regal canopy while wearing a jeweled diadem and nursing the infant Christ. Jan's original audiences must have been struck by the paradoxes suggested by her hair and position. Her coronet-adorned hair expresses youthfulness and virginity, promised fertility and marriage, and queenship. Her long tresses and enthronement as Queen of Heaven remind viewers of her Coronation when she, Christ's mother, became his Bride. But this young Virgin and Bride has already borne a child and breastfeeds him, confirming her very human status; breast milk was believed to be "cooked" menses, heated up by pregnancy and birth. Nursing thus confirmed Mary's fully human status: contrary to the then-proposed but not yet accepted dogma of Mary's Immaculate Conception, she menstruated, as did normal mothers, as a result of Original Sin. Further, in this time period queens would not nurse but instead would employ midwives; thus Mary's humility seemingly contradicts her exalted position as Bride and Queen.[30] While today's viewers may simply see one of many seemingly formulaic *Madonnas*, past audiences, understanding Mary's hair, would marvel

FIGURE 9.5 Jan van Eyck, *Madonna and Child* (ca. 1436). Frankfurt, Städeliches Kunstinstitut. Photo: Foto Marburg/Art Resource, NY.

at her simultaneously regal status and humble humanity, as well as see confirmation of the miracle of a young unmarried virgin giving birth.

Eve's hair reveals both positive and negative aspects of her nature. Even though medieval science believed women's hair naturally grew longer than men's, many images of Adam and Eve include equal-length hair, perhaps suggesting the couple's initial sinlessness and close affinity at creation. For example, in the ninth-century Touronian Bibles and the 1015 Hildesheim Doors, both Adam's and Eve's hair trails down their backs, Adam is beardless, their bodies hairless and—at least until Eve sins—they seemingly remain anatomically indistinguishable.[31] But in later medieval art, gender distinctions increasingly appear, and longer hair on Eve marks her deficient and sinful nature. Gislebertus's ca. 1130 *Eve* from Autun Cathedral's north portal slithers along the ground like a snake while accepting the fruit from the serpent's claw behind her, her long tresses caressing her shoulders. The ca. 1244–1254 Morgan Crusader Bible's *Temptation and Fall* (Figure 9.6) includes a virile Adam with shorter hair and full beard and an Eve sporting long tresses. The serpent also appears distinctly female, wearing a proper married woman's hair-covering headdress with wimple as it tempts Eve, directly contradicting Peter Comestor's commonly accepted explanation that the serpent beguiled Eve because it had the "countenance of a virgin, because like favors like."[32] Does the matron's headdress partially exonerate Eve by suggesting the latter's innocent youthfulness, implied by her long hair, was no match for

FIGURE 9.6 *Temptation and Fall*, Morgan Crusader Bible, detail of fol. 1v, MS M. 638 (Paris, France, ca. 1244–1254). The Pierpont Morgan Library, New York. Purchased by J. P. Morgan (1867–1943) in 1916. Photo: The Pierpont Morgan Library, New York.

the older, wiser woman-serpent, her headdress falsely claiming wifely propriety? Or does the serpent's headdress foreshadow the consequences of Eve's act: that women will need to cover their "glory" to protect men from such temptation as seen here?

In Jan van Eyck's 1432 Ghent Altarpiece Adam and Eve appear unusually positive in their postlapsarian condition, partly due to Jan's interest in the natural state of their bodies.[33] Unfashionable Adam seems never to have shaved or cut his hair, and Eve's even longer unruly locks similarly suggest a world before combs. Adam also represents one of the most remarkable depictions of body hair in medieval and Renaissance art: his convincingly human appearance surely derives from Jan's first-hand observation of eyelashes and leg, arm, chest, and pubic hair, each strand painted with a single-hair brush. Viewers could readily identify with this very human man. Eve's nudity, however, remains more idealized, her high forehead and slim eyebrows reflecting the fashion for plucking or singeing facial hairs, her body smooth and hairless except for her prolific pubic bush. While this last looks less convincingly natural in its continuation up her body midline toward her navel, a hair display more normally seen on male bodies, it reasserts her closeness to nature rather than culture. The *Trotula*, a twelfth-century treatise on women's medicine, advises a noblewoman should be "soft and smooth and without hairs from her head down," so to please fashion, women typically plucked hairs and used depilatories, even for pubic hair, in order to create smooth expanses of skin.[34] The desire for women's pubic depilation in Europe may well have originated among the Crusaders returning from the East, as Muslims practiced removal of body hair, and the *Trotula* specifically refers to a depilatory used by "Saracen noblewomen"; visual evidence of such aristocratic practices, however, remains elusive.[35] The *Trotula* advises avoiding eyebrows when removing unwanted facial hair, but in the 1320s, high hairless foreheads became fashionable and remained so for centuries (e.g. Figure 9.7).[36] The many representations of totally hairless fifteenth- and sixteenth-century female nudes— "from her head down"—may reflect real practices or at least satisfy this bodily ideal. Moralizers naturally judged such cosmetic procedures sinful, and in 1371 to 1372, the Knight of La Tour Landry reported a holy man's dream of a woman tortured in Hell by a devil who "thrust in her brows, temples, and forehead, hot burning awls and needles, into the brain ... because she had ... plucked her brows, front and forehead, to have away the hair."[37]

FIGURE 9.7 Fra Filippo Lippi, *Portrait of a Woman and Man* (ca. 1440). New York, The Metropolitan Museum of Art, Marquand Collection, Gift of Henry G. Marquand, 1889 (89.15.19). Photo © The Metropolitan Museum of Art.

Because depilation was an upper-class practice, visible pubic hair on women in visual imagery became associated with improper or excessive sexuality and power. A rare medieval example of a woman displaying pubic hair is the unusual twelfth-century relief from Milan's Porta Tosa of a woman raising her skirts and cutting her pubic hair (Figure 8.6). Demonstrating the female body's destructive power—a medical text asserts, "And whosoever were to take a hair from the pubic of a woman and mix it with menses and then put it in a dung-heap, would at the end of the year find wicked venomous beasts"—this relief likely served an apotropaic function, protecting the portal into the city from penetration.[38] Yet, while I know of only rare depictions of pubic hair on women until Jan's *Eve*, visual metaphors for it abound in Gothic manuscripts in the form of small, furry animals. Lucy Freeman Sandler offers a telling discussion of a bawdy image in an early fourteenth-century psalter, noting that, as with our slang term "pussy," these creatures functioned as surrogates for female pudenda; Madeline Caviness similarly analyzes the cats, squirrels, and rabbits in the *Book of Hours of Jeanne d'Evreux* from the period 1323–1326.[39] By the sixteenth century, when pubic hair on women becomes much more commonly depicted, it typically marks highly eroticized figures, including witches, Venus, prostitutes, and other sexual predators.[40] Women's pubic hair thus retained negative associations, even while these "beards," as they were frequently called, indexed women's fertile and sexual natures just as men's facial hair did.

Women's head hair was associated with beauty throughout the Middle Ages, yet could signal either hair's dangerous ability to arouse desire and sin or its power to elevate men to a higher spiritual realm.[41] Already in the late first century, Paul asserted woman's hair was her "glory," yet he concludes it must therefore be veiled (1 Corinthians 11:2–16); thus respectably married medieval women covered their hair in public.[42] The late fourteenth-century German, Heinrich von Langenstein, added, "the veil ... is a symbol of her subservience. The woman wears a headdress so that it may be recognized that she is subordinate to the man, who ranks above her. The veiled head is also a sign that woman transgressed the first commandment and violated its terms."[43] In this way, covering women's hair, while protecting men from its dangers, constantly reasserted woman's inferior and sinful nature. But courtly love traditions and Neoplatonic discourses celebrated hair as woman's crowning glory, a positive attribute that offered beauty with all its attendant *virtuous* qualities: idealized women's beautiful exteriors revealed their beautiful interiors.[44] In Sonnet 159, Petrarch (1304–1374) acknowledges this well-established Neoplatonic trope of idealized beauty's divinely transformative power, even as he challenges it. He asks from what "Platonic heaven" could come such a perfect face, with "such golden hair" and a heart "home to so many signal virtues that I esteem"; he first responds, "For those who believe that beauty is divine, / the search ends here," yet then concludes, "Such perfection as I have here extolled / carries danger. I feel my spirits decline / that her laughter can revive a hundredfold."[45] Hair's connections with vanity and sin could be tempered by its associations with ideal virtue, yet women's beautiful hair remained ambiguous, uplifting, and inspirational but seductive and dangerous.

Real women struggled to meet the ideals of poets like Petrarch, who repeatedly extolled the virtues of "golden hair."[46] While the twelfth-century *Trotula* offers no special praise for fair hair—it includes formulas for both black and blonde dyeing[47]—by the thirteenth century and for the succeeding three centuries, the fashionable ideal generally meant blondeness. In fifteenth-century Italy, where most women were naturally dark-haired, this of course presented challenges. While women's success using concoctions of lemons, tree bark, or walnut shells might be fleeting, painters could create blondeness for posterity, as numerous fifteenth-century portraits reveal. Fra Filippo Lippi's ca. 1440 portrait of a Florentine woman shows a striking blonde, her hair caught up high in cauls to either side of her head in fashionable French style (Figure 9.7).[48] Blondeness became a sign particularly of upper-class beauty, and gold dust, hairpieces of false or natural hair, and other costly treatments for lightening became available to the leisured nobility.[49]

Critics mocked women's efforts, condemning deceptive coloring and artificial hair as attempts to seduce men and lead them to sin. For example, from the late thirteenth through the early fifteenth centuries, high fashion decreed upper-class women wear their hair coiled or braided at the sides of their heads in a succession of styles sometimes padded with silk or purchased hair and often crowned with elaborate headdresses. The *Roman de la Rose*, completed between 1269 and 1278, called such styles "horns that … could not be surpassed by stag, billy goat, or unicorn," and the derogatory term *"corne"* (horn) continued in use in the fourteenth and fifteenth centuries, even as hair styling varied.[50] For example, the 1381 tomb sculpture of Marie de France (Figure 9.8) depicts her fashionable courtly hair with braided plaits hanging straight down on either side of her head; having died young and unmarried, she wears these so-called *cornes* uncovered.[51] In the 1420s, bourgeois women in Flanders wore a different version of *cornes*, as seen on

FIGURE 9.8 Jean de Liège, *Bust of Marie de France* (1381). New York, The Metropolitan Museum of Art, Gift of George Blumenthal, 1941 (41.100.132). Photo © The Metropolitan Museum of Art.

FIGURE 9.9 Workshop of Robert Campin, Merode Triptych, detail of the donors (ca. 1427–1432). New York, The Metropolitan Museum of Art, The Cloisters Collection, 1956 (56.7). Photo © The Metropolitan Museum of Art.

the female donor in Robert Campin's Merode Triptych (Figure 9.9) and portraits by Jan van Eyck. Though modestly covered with a veil and wimple, this hairstyle with pointy, horn-shaped cauls above the ears led to comparisons with devils and "senseless beasts."[52] Hugo van der Goes's ca. 1470–1475 *Fall of Adam and Eve* (Vienna, Kunsthistoriches Museum) makes the allusion unmistakable by depicting a salamander-like serpent with two upward pointing braids of hair, alluding to devils' horns. Women, however, seem to have largely ignored these critics; horned styles remained fashionable, especially in the North but—as we have seen—also on stylish Florentine beauties (Figure 9.7).

Women's hair fashions, like men's, could also declare natal origins or create political alliances. Barbara von Hohenzollern, German and, therefore, possibly naturally fair-haired, married and moved to Mantua's Gonzaga court in 1433. Avoiding northern Italian hair fashions, she retained the then-fashionable French double-horned hairstyle even as late as Andrea Mantegna's 1465 to 1474 frescoes in the *Camera Picta*, by which time it was out-of-style in the North; she may have retained the fashion as significant to her identity. Evelyn Welch notes that women shared hairstyles to demonstrate alliances and create female networks; Barbara's intimate friend, the Duchess of Milan, Bianca Maria Visconti, also adopted the French fashion, and generations of later northern Italian women continued cementing friendships via hairstyles.[53]

Long hair, unkempt or unrestrained, could express the inherent sinfulness of an individual's body or mark it as undergoing a transient state of discord or disruption. Hair's danger and sexuality emerge not just in images of Eve but in those of other innately evil figures: hair cascades down the body of the twelfth-century personification of *Luxuria*, the sin of lust, at Moissac, while the seductive Whore of Babylon in the Angers Tapestry (1373–1387) sits and combs her long hair, erotically enticing viewers to follow her (Figure 6.4).[54] Her vanity contrasts clerics' use of liturgical combs to part their hair prior to saying Mass, an act that symbolizes the priest's ordering and focusing of his thoughts on the liturgy.[55] Similarly Ambrogio Lorenzetti's frescoed Eve, lying seductively below the upright, enthroned Madonna in the chapel of San Galgano (Montesiepi, 1334–1336), wears both braids and long, serpentine tresses that contrast the Virgin's neatly veiled hair; Lorenzetti thus clarifies their opposing natures.[56] Twelfth-century church capitals reveal the inherent evil of devils through their wildly flame-like hair that recalls Hellfire, while nearby depictions of dutiful monks include neat monastic tonsures.[57] Roberta Milliken notes devils often torture women in Hell by pulling their hair, suggesting the sexual nature of their sins.[58] All these beings' degenerate natures are revealed by their locks, yet hair can also indicate transitory mental states and fleeting disorder. Female mourners pull their hair and rip their clothing to express their minds' temporary alteration by grief, and grieving widows traditionally wear their hair down and exposed; they briefly function outside of socially accepted norms.[59] Emotionally charged fourteenth-century Italian images of the Lamentation over the Dead Christ often include Mary Magdalene as chief mourner, exposing her own hair in grief-stricken disarray; she was even called Christ's widow.[60] Like personifications of the vices of Despair and Anger at Giotto's Arena Chapel in Padua (ca. 1305), she indicates her mental state via unkempt hair.

However, Mary Magdalene's long, uncovered hair, one of her chief attributes, prompts complex, multivalent interpretations. Beyond her sorrowful mourning over Christ, it represents her preconversion vanity and lust when, as a prostitute, she dressed it with perfumes. But it also provides the means of her penitential conversion when she uses it to wipe Christ's feet at the House of Simon, and following Christ's death, her hair grows miraculously to clothe her nakedness during her last thirty years of life in ascetic isolation in the wilderness. In this late thirteenth-century Florentine panel (Figure 9.10) the standing Magdalene has seemingly become her hair: it totally encompasses her body while angels miraculously lift her to heaven and feed her, and later when she takes her final communion from Bishop Maximinus and then dies. At all these moments, her long hair paradoxically recalls her vanity and promiscuousness, but also her renunciation, conversion, and penitence. As with other ascetics—St. Mary of Egypt, Anthony, Paul— excessive or even miraculous hair growth signals rejection of the worldly life and acceptance of the contemplative.[61] Mid-fifteenth-century examples by Donatello and Antonio Pollaiuolo emphasize Mary Magdalene's spiritual union with God and rejection of earthly values by depicting her advanced in age, with weathered skin, while others depict her having grown a pelt of hair, like the fabulous wild men and wild women discussed below, thus emphasizing both her potent sexuality and her outcast nature.[62]

Hair symbolism, however, is rarely stable, and so an antithetical hair practice also signals Mary Magdalene's renunciation and penance: in an unusual late fourteenth-century illumination, she cuts off her hair following her conversion to symbolize her rejection of her luxurious preconversion life and her new acceptance of Christ.[63] Orderic, writing in the early twelfth century, complains about his contemporaries' inconsistent hair practices: "Up to now penitents and prisoners and pilgrims have normally been unshaven,

FIGURE 9.10 Magdalene Master, *St. Mary Magdalene* (late thirteenth century). Florence, Accademia. Photo: Scala/Art Resource, NY.

with long beards, and in this way have publicly proclaimed their condition of penance or captivity or pilgrimage."[64] Enforced cutting of hair by another often meant punishment, humiliating the party involved; Samson's shearing by Delilah (Judges 16:4–22) furthered his emasculation by depriving him of his great strength.[65] But voluntary cutting—like clerical tonsure—could indicate personal sacrifice and penance. When St. Clare follows St. Francis into his new order, she willingly lets him cut her hair, as depicted in the Altarpiece of St. Clare (1280s, Sta. Chiara, Assisi); there she kneels before an altar surrounded by Franciscan friars while Francis crops her tresses.[66] Nuns typically cut their hair and cover their heads during their consecration ceremony, leading to its common name of "taking the veil"; the ceremony marks their new status as Brides of Christ, but unlike secular brides, their transformation is marked by shorn hair.[67] Once again, meanings of hair remain deeply contextual: *not* cutting hair can signal penance and renunciation of the worldly realm, but so can cutting or covering it. Rogier van der Weyden eliminates ambiguity regarding the Magdalene's hair in his ca. 1435 *Christ's Descent from the Cross* (Madrid, Prado); as she stands in a posture of extreme mourning, her veil hangs down long over her shoulder, serving as a modest surrogate for her beautiful hair.

Baldness, while natural in many men, acquires particular meaning when it results from human agency, that is, from head-shaving as involuntary public humiliation and punishment. Thus in Justinian's *Codex*, noted above, the arrested thief with excessive body hair appears with a shaved head; like his axillary and chest hair, baldness declares his deficient character. Persecutors of Christ also appear with stubbly shaved heads or as balding men; sometimes their hair loss reveals sores or deformations on their skulls, further signs of degeneracy.[68] Slaves and prisoners were often shaved, and so images of the Bad Thief crucified alongside Christ can display the thief's public humiliation as hair loss, in some cases contrasting with the hirsute Good Thief.[69] Women judged guilty of particularly heinous moral crimes could be punished by hair cutting, and Anu Korhonen points out their hair loss was a more drastic humiliation than for men;[70] perhaps this explains why I know of no medieval images of shaved or crop-haired women other than those who sacrificed their hair voluntarily, like Mary Magdalene and St. Clare. Finally, a shaved head could connote a fool.[71] Illustrations for the opening verse of Psalm 53, "The fool says in his heart, 'There is no God,'" traditionally depict a bald man; an example from ca. 1270 to 1280 (Figure 9.11) shows not only his shaved head with prominent stubble, confirming he does not suffer from natural baldness, but also stubble in his shaved pubic region, another sign of his lack of respectability and low status.

Yet, as with hair, the meanings of baldness remain unstable. While hair growth signals the onset of adolescence, hair loss signals the advent of old age, particularly in men. It was believed men's hotter natures produced more hair, but later-in-life cooling led to its loss; illness and excessive sex could also promote baldness.[72] Images of the Adoration of the Magi frequently portray the three kings as embodying the universality of humanity coming to Christ by representing not just the three known continents but also the three ages of man. Gentile da Fabriano's 1423 Strozzi Altarpiece (Florence, Uffizi) demonstrates this exactly by depicting the most-honored magus as white-haired, balding, and exhibiting a long white beard while he kneels, touching and kissing Christ's foot; the second magus's dark hair and beard demonstrate his mature manhood; the third and youngest king appears smooth-cheeked and blond, a hair color associated with youthfulness. Old Testament prophets, New Testament saints like Paul, and even God the Father can appear as balding men, their advanced ages and sometimes grey or white hair suggesting wisdom and authority.[73] Indeed, when the bald Elisha, after receiving the mantle from

FIGURE 9.11 *Psalm 53*, Bible, Garrett 28, detail of fol. 224r, English (1270–1280). Manuscripts Division, Department of Rare Books and Special Collections, Princeton University Library, Princeton. Photo: Princeton University Library.

Elijah, is mocked by children who shout *"Ascende calve"* ("Go up, baldy"), God sends two she-bears to tear them apart (2 Kings 2:1–13, 23–4). Patricia Rose, thus, identifies Donatello's *Lo Zuccone* (1435–1436) sculpture for the Florence Cathedral Campanile as Elisha, based on the excessive fabric of his over-sized mantle and his bald head: he even leans forward, emphasizing the expanse of his mostly hairless pate.[74] Elisha's baldness also carried typological associations and was interpreted metaphorically. As Amy Neff explains, Augustine interpreted the mocking of Elisha as anticipating that of Christ in the same way that *"calve"* (bald) foreshadows "Calvary": "For he [Christ] was mocked as if bald by the jeering Jews because he was crucified in the place of Calvary."[75] She further attributes *spiritual* baldness to St. Francis when he renounces his parents and earthly goods while children mock him and throw stones, as in the late thirteenth-century *St. Francis's Renunciation* fresco in the Upper Church of Assisi, or that by Giotto in the Bardi Chapel (Sta. Croce, Florence): he thus becomes not only the "other Christ," but the "new Elisha." A ca. 1280 text, now identified as by John of Wales, explains, "Truly he [Francis] too is 'bald,' he too is without hair, he too is denuded of all things of the world."[76] Like voluntary clerical tonsure, here baldness signals renunciation.

Finally, hair stigmatizes the Other. As mentioned above, beards separate Jews and Saracens from Christians, facial hair and the length of head hair distinguish Anglo-Saxons from invading Normans, and untamed hair identifies ascetics living exiled from normal society. As early as the twelfth century, furry full-body pelts mark the medieval wild men and women, a legendary race of monstrous outcasts who promised fertility, sexual prowess, and supernatural strength; thus they appear on shields and in architectural settings as apotropaic figures.⁷⁷ Yet their excessive hair simultaneously identified them as savage outsiders—libidinous, untamed, and dangerous. Sometimes shown as giants or with enlarged male genitals, wild men were known to abduct civilized women, often while brandishing a large club (Figure I.1). Their hairiness confirmed other bestial and ungodly qualities: immoral and impaired mental abilities, associations with violent and aggressive acts, and even cannibalism. However, by the later fifteenth century, ideas about the noble savage and urban dwellers' idealistically positive assessments of rural life helped to redefine wild men and women: seen as close to nature, they came to represent innocence even while retaining their negative stereotypes.⁷⁸

Hair color and type also reveal difference. Red hair, the least common human variety, which Aristotle in his *Physiognomics* compares to red foxes' fur, also denoted negative character traits, and Ruth Mellinkoff traces its particular connections to Judas, beginning in the later twelfth century. While red hair did not consistently mark Christ's betrayer, she notes other sometimes redheaded shameful characters, including the Bad Thief, Cain, and Malchus, Caiaphas's servant whose ear is cut off during Christ's arrest.⁷⁹ Alternatively, artists sometimes demonstrate the evil nature of Malchus by depicting him as bald or as an African with kinky black hair, as in Jean Le Noir's mid-fourteenth-century *Arrest of Christ* in the *Hours of Jeanne de Navarre*; any of these visual signs clarifies Malchus's outsider status relative to civilized Christianity.⁸⁰ The Bari Throne (Figure 9.12), commissioned by Pope Urban II ca. 1098, shows from the front three crouching Atlas figures supporting a seat that Archbishop Elias would occupy during the liturgy at the new pilgrimage site of

FIGURE 9.12 Bari Throne, detail (1098). Bari, Basilica of San Nicola. Photo: Scala/Art Resource, NY.

San Nicola in Bari. The two outermost figures are bare-chested and bare-headed, and both grimace as they struggle to uphold the throne. While their identity remains uncertain, that to the right has tightly curled hair: clearly a black African. Likely both represent uncivilized heathens, Others to the European population, here subjected to the superior power of Christianity; this theme of conquest repeats at the throne's rear, where two lions devour two kinky-haired men, again with contorted faces. By contrast, the center front figure supports his burden easily, his face remains undistorted as he looks upward, and he wears a tunic and hat and uses a walking stick. His identity is disputed, but based on his dress's similarity to that of figures on the *Last Judgment* tympanum's lintel at Ste.-Lazare, Autun, I identify him as a pilgrim. Thus the episcopal throne honors Christian pilgrims newly visiting Bari while simultaneously condemning the grimacing pagans; indeed, Bari was also the launching site for Crusaders in 1096 after Urban II declared the First Crusade against the heathens.[81] Nevertheless, not all Africans are depicted as unrepentant infidels. By the later Middle Ages St. Maurice routinely appears as a black man with kinky hair, while in mid-thirteenth-century Italian *Adorations*, black attendants begin to participate in the Magi's retinue, and the first incontrovertible example of a Black Magus accepting Christ appears in Hans Multscher's 1437 Wurzach Altarpiece.[82]

Medieval art presents multiple semiotic systems for expressing meaning via head and body hair, often overlapping and sometimes contradictory. Nonetheless, exploring the role of hair in imagery offers viewers powerful tools to better understand gender, sexuality, religion, class, and, above all, the human spiritual condition in the Middle Ages.

ACKNOWLEDGMENTS

Images cited in this chapter are generally available via online searching or through an online database such as ARTstor.org (many libraries provide access); for others I have indicated sources.

NOTES

Introduction

1. Jacques Le Goff eloquently discusses such issues in his book *Must We Divide History Into Periods?*, trans. Malcolm DeBevoise (New York: Columbia University Press, 2017). The focus of this work is the distinction between the Middle Ages and the Renaissance, a distinction that Le Goff questions as he sees more continuity between these time periods than differences.
2. John Arnold attributes the term to several important intellectuals including Petrarch (1304–1374), Pierre Pithou (1539–1596), and William Camden (1551–1625). See *What is Medieval History?* (Cambridge: Polity Press, 2008), 8–10.
3. This term was used to commonly denote the fifth through the eleventh centuries. However, because the centuries fall within the span of time making up the Middle Ages, the label "the Dark Ages" is often used as a synonym for the medieval period as a whole.
4. The second definition of the adjective "medieval" in the *Merriam-Webster's Collegiate Dictionary* is "having the quality (as cruelty) associated with the Middle Ages" and the third definition is "extremely outmoded or antiquated."
5. For more, see Régine Pernoud, *Those Terrible Middle Ages: Debunking the Myths*, trans. Anne Englund Nash (San Francisco: Ignatius Press, 1977).
6. For more on sumptuary legislation limiting social mobility, see Clare Sponsler, "Narrating the Social Order: Medieval Clothing Laws," *CLIO: Journal of Literature, History, and the Philosophy of History* 21, no. 3 (1992): 265–83.
7. For more on sumptuary legislation, see Alan Hunt, *Governance of the Consuming Passions: A History of Sumptuary Laws* (London: Macmillan, 1996).
8. Tertullian, *The Apparel of Women*, in *Disciplinary, Moral, and Ascetical Works*, trans. Rudolph Arbesmann, Sister Emily Joseph Daly, and Edwin A. Quain (Washington, DC: Catholic University of America with Consortium Books, 1959), bk. 2, chap. 7, 138.
9. Ibid., chap. 8, 140.
10. For a useful overview of the development of medieval historiography, see Arnold, *What is Medieval History?*
11. There are many that could be named here; some include Johan Huizinga, Marc Bloch, Jacques Le Goff, Jean-Claude Schmitt, Erwin Panofsky, Aaron Gurevich, Georges Duby, Michelle Perrot, Michael Baxandall, Emmanuel Le Roy Ladurie, and Caroline Walker Bynum.
12. "Culture" is a difficult term to define; it eludes pat definitions, as understandings of the term shift over time. For more on this, see Peter Burke, *What is Cultural History?* (Cambridge: Polity Press, 2008), 29–30.
13. Ibid., 51–2.
14. The work of theorists such as Mikhail Bakhtin, Norbert Elias, Michel Foucault, and Pierre Bourdieu has been particularly important in exploring/revealing the intricacies of the interactions between authority, privilege, control, progress, social identity, civilization, and culture. By questioning and revealing traditional paradigms, these thinkers steered the

attention of cultural historians toward the history of practices and representations. For more on this, see Burke, *What is Cultural History?*, especially 51–76.

15. James George Frazer, *The Golden Bough: A Study in Magic and Religion*, 3 vols. (New York: Macmillan and Company, 1935), especially vol. 3.
16. Charles Berg, *The Unconscious Significance of Hair* (Washington, DC: Guild Press, 1951).
17. E.R. Leach, "Magical Hair," *The Journal of the Royal Anthropological Institute of Great Britain* 88, no. 2 (1958): 147–61.
18. C.R. Hallpike, "Social Hair," *Man* 4, no. 2 (1969): 256–64.
19. I do not mean to suggest by this that the earlier scholars did not note the complexity of hair symbolism, for they did. Nonetheless, they did also tend to strive to offer universal grammars for the language of hair through their works.
20. Raymond Firth, *Symbols: Public and Private* (Ithaca, NY: Cornell University Press, 1973).
21. P. Hershman, "Hair, Sex and Dirt," *Man* 9, no. 2 (1974): 274–98.
22. Ibid., 296.
23. Anthony Synnott, "Shame and Glory: A Sociology of Hair," *British Journal of Sociology* 38, no. 3 (1987): 381–413.
24. Robert Bartlett discusses hair as a language complete with a grammar albeit a basic one as he focuses on its various meanings throughout the Middle Ages: Bartlett, "Symbolic Meaning of Hair in the Middle Ages," *Transactions of the Royal Historical Society* 4 (1994): 43–60.
25. Simon Coates, "Scissors or Sword? The Symbolism of a Medieval Haircut," *History Today* 49, no. 5 (1999): 7–13.
26. Averil Cameron, "How Did the Merovingian Kings Wear Their Hair?" *Revue Belge de Philologie et d'Histoire* 43, no. 4 (1965): 1203–16; Maximilian Diesenberger, "Hair, Sacrality and Symbolic Capital in Frankish Kingdoms," in *The Construction of Communities in the Early Middle Ages: Texts, Resources and Artefacts*, eds. Richard Corradini, Max Diesenberger, and Helmut Reimitz (Leiden: Brill, 2003), 173–212; Paul Edward Dutton, *Charlemagne's Mustache and Other Cultural Clusters of a Dark Age* (New York: Palgrave Macmillan, 2004); Erik Goosmann, "The Long-haired Kings of the Franks: 'Like so Many Samsons?'" *Early Medieval Europe* 20, no. 3 (2012): 233–59; Jean Hoyoux, "Reges Criniti: Chevalures, Tonsures et Scalps chez les Mérovingians," *Revue Belge de Philologie et d'Histoire* 26, no. 3 (1948): 479–508; and Peter H. Johnsson, "Locks of Difference: The Integral Role of Hair as a Distinguishing Feature in Early Merovingian Gaul," *Ex Post Facto* 19 (2010): 55–68.
27. Conrad Leyser, "Long-haired Kings and Short-haired Nuns: Writing on the Body in Caesarius of Arles," *Studia Patristica* 24 (1993): 143–50.
28. Carl Phelpstead, "Hair Today, Gone Tomorrow: Hair Loss, the Tonsure, and Masculinity in Medieval Iceland," *Scandinavian Studies* 85, no. 1 (2013): 1–19; William Sayers, "Early Irish Attitudes Toward Hair, Beards, Baldness and Tonsure," *Zeitschrift für Celtische Philologie* 44, no. 1 (1991): 154–89; H. Platelle, "Le Problème du Scandale: Les Nouvelles Modes Masculines aux XIe et XIIe Siècles," *Revue Belge de Philologie et d' Histoire* 53, no. 4 (1975): 1071–96; and Pauline Stafford, "The Meanings of Hair in the Anglo-Norman World: Masculinity, Reform, and National Identity," in *Saints, Scholars, and Politicians*, eds. M. van Dijk and R. Nip (Turnhout: Brepols, 2005): 153–71.
29. Ilse Friesen, "Saints as Helpers in Dying: The Hairy Holy Women Mary Magdalene, Mary of Egypt, and Wilgefortis in the Iconography of the Late Middle Ages," in *Death and Dying in the Middle Ages*, eds. E. DuBruck and B. Gusick (New York: Peter Lang, 1999), 239–53; and Roberta Milliken, *Ambiguous Locks: An Iconology of Hair in the Art and Literature of the Middle Ages* (Jefferson, NC: McFarland Publishers, 2012).

30. Laura Clark, "Fashionable Beards and Beards as Fashion: Beard Coats in Thomas Malory's *Morte D'Arthur*," *Parergon* 31, no. 1 (2015): 95–109; Giles Constable, "Introduction: Beards in the Middle Ages," in Burchard of Bellevaux, *Apologiae duae, Corpus Christianorum Continuatio Mediaevalis*, LXI (Turnhout: Brepols, 1985); Zehava Jacoby, "The Beard Pullers in Romanesque Art: An Islamic Motif and Its Evolution in the West," *Arte Medievale* 1, no. 1–2 (1987): 65–85; Penny Howell Jolly, "Pubics and Privates: Body Hair in Late Medieval Art," in *Meanings of Nudity in Medieval Art*, ed. Sherry Lundquist (Farnham: Ashgate, 2012): 183–206; and Margaret Sleeman, "Medieval Hair Tokens," *Forum for Modern Language Studies* 17, no. 4 (1981): 322–36.
31. Robert Mills, "The Significance of the Tonsure," in *Holiness and Masculinity in the Middle Ages*, eds. P.H. Cullum and Katherine J. Lewis (Toronto: University of Toronto Press, 2004), 109–26; Edward James, "Bede and the Tonsure Question," *Peritia* 3 (1984): 85–98; and Daniel McCarthy, "On the Shape of the Insular Tonsure," *Celtica* 24 (2003): 140–67. For a history of the tonsure practice, see also Louis Trichet, *La Tonsure: Vie et Mort d'une Pratique Écclésiastique* (Paris: Les Éditions du Cerf, 1990).
32. Paul E. Belcher, "Absalom's Hair," *Mediaeval Studies* 12 (1950): 222–33; Susan Wade, "Gertrude's Tonsure: An Examination of Hair as a Symbol of Gender, Family and Authority in the Seventh-century Vita of Gertrude of Nivelles," *Journal of Medieval History* 39, no. 2 (2013): 129–45; Lewis Wallace, "Bearded Woman, Female Christ." *Journal of Feminist Studies in Religion* 30, no. 1 (2014): 43–63; and Karen Winstead, "St. Katherine's Hair," in *St. Katherine of Alexandria: Texts and Contexts in Western Medieval Europe*, eds. Jacqueline Jenkins and Katherine Lewis (Turnhout: Brepols, 2003), 171–99.
33. Chantal Connochie-Bourgne, ed., *La Chevalure dans la Littérature et l'Art du Moyen Âge* (Provence: Publications de l'Université de Provence, 2004).
34. See, for example, Theodore Child, *Wimples and Crisping Pins* (New York: Harper and Brothers, 1895); Wendy Cooper, *Hair, Sex, Society, Symbolism* (New York: Stein and Day, 1971); Richard Corson, *Fashions in Hair: The First Five Thousand Years* (New York: Hillary House, 1971); Georgine De Courtais, *Women's Headdress and Hairstyles in England from AD 600 to the Present Day* (London: Batsford, 1986); Penny Howell Jolly, *Hair: Untangling a Social History* (Saratoga Springs, NY: Frances Young Tang Teaching Museum and Art Gallery, Skidmore College, 2004); Allan Peterkin, *One Thousand Beards: A Cultural History of Facial Hair* (Vancouver: Arsenal Press, 2001); Reginald Reynolds, *Beards: Their Social Standing, Religious Involvements, Decorative Possibilities and Value in Offence and Defence Through the Middle Ages* (New York: Doubleday and Company, 1949); Victoria Sherrow, *Encyclopedia of Hair: A Cultural History* (Westport, CT: Greenwood Press, 2006); Mary Trasko, *Daring Do's: A History of Extraordinary Hair* (Paris: Flammarion, 1994); and Marie De Villermont, *La Histoire de la Coiffure Féminine* (Paris: Librarie Rénouard, 1892).
35. Examples include Geoff Egan and Frances Pritchard, *Dress Accessories c. 1150–1450* (Woodbridge: Boydell Press, 2008); Eric Silverman, *A Cultural History of Jewish Dress* (London: Bloomsbury, 2013); Louise Sylvester, Mark Chambers, and Gale Owen-Crocker, eds., *Medieval Dress and Textiles in Britain: A Multilingual Sourcebook* (Woodbridge: Boydell, 2014); James Laver, *Costume and Fashion* (London: Thames and Hudson, 1995); Margaret Scott, *Medieval Dress and Fashion* (London: British Library, 2009); and Phyllis Tortora and Keith Eubank, *A Survey of Historical Costume* (New York: Fairchild, 1989).
36. Wolfthal, Diane. "The Sexuality of the Medieval Comb," in *Thresholds of Medieval Visual Culture: Liminal Spaces*, eds. Elina Gertsman and Jill Stevens (Woodbridge, NY: Boydell Press, 2012), 176–94; Scott, *Medieval Dress and Fashion*; Elizabeth Kuhns, *The Habit: A History of the Clothing of Catholic Nuns* (New York: Doubleday, 2003), especially

53–61, 64–89, and 103–04; and Désirée Koslin, "Manifest Insignificance: The Consecrated Veil of Medieval Religious Women," in *Sacred and Ceremonial Textiles*, Proceedings of the Fifth Biennial Symposium of the Textile Society of America (Chicago: Textile Society of America, Inc., 1996), 141–7, and "Robe of Simplicity: Initiation, Robing, and Veiling of Nuns in the Middle Ages," in *Robes and Honor: The Medieval World of Investiture*, ed. Stewart Gordon (New York: Palgrave, 2001), 255–74.

37. Mary Rose D'Angleo, "Veils, Virgins, and the Tongues of Men and Angels," in *Off With Her Head: The Denial of Women's Identity in Myth, Religion, and Culture*, eds. Howard Eilberg-Schwartz and Wendy Doniger (Berkeley: University of California Press, 1995), 131–64; J. Duncan M. Derret, "Religious Hair," *Man* 8 (1973): 100–03; and Gabriela Signori, "Veil, Hat, or Hair? Reflections on an Asymmetrical Relationship," *The Medieval History Journal* 8, no. 1 (2005): 25–47.

Chapter One

1. This chapter primarily focuses on Christian culture; Jewish and Muslim approaches to hair in religion and ritual are deserving of chapters unto themselves.
2. All biblical citations are from the Douay-Rheims edition (English translation of Latin Vulgate), http://www.drbo.org/index.htm.
3. Clement of Alexandria, *The Instructor*, trans. William Wilson, in *Ante-Nicene Fathers*, vol. 2, eds. Alexander Roberts, James Donaldson, and A. Cleveland Coxe (Buffalo, NY: Christian Literature Publishing Co., 1885; Rev. and ed. for New Advent by Kevin Knight), http://www.newadvent.org/fathers/0209.htm (accessed May 8, 2016).
4. Elisheva Baumgarten, *Practicing Piety in Medieval Ashkenaz: Men, Women, and Everyday Religious Observance* (Philadelphia: University of Pennsylvania Press, 2014), 179–81.
5. See Jussi Hanska, "Sermons on the Tenth Sunday after Holy Trinity: Another Occasion for Anti-Jewish Preaching," in *The Jewish-Christian Encounter in Medieval Preaching* (Routledge Research in Medieval Studies, no. 6), eds. Jonathan Adams and Jussi Hanska (New York: Routledge, 2015), 195–214.
6. See Jace Crouch, "The Judicial Punishment of *Decalvatio* in the Visigothic Spain: A Proposed Solution Based on Isidore of Seville and the *Lex Visigothorum*," *The Mediterranean Review* 3, no. 1 (June 2010): 59–77.
7. Erik Goosmann, "The Long-haired Kings of the Franks: 'Like So Many Samsons?'" *Early Medieval Europe* 20, no. 3 (2012): 233–59, especially 248–54.
8. See Greti Dinkova-Brun "Biblical Thematics: The Story of Samson in Medieval Literary Discourse," in *The Oxford Handbook of Medieval Latin Literature*, eds. Ralph Hexter and David Townsend (Oxford: Oxford University Press, 2012), 356–75.
9. Geoffrey Chaucer, *The Monk's Tale*, in *Canterbury Tales*, trans. David Wright (Oxford: Oxford University Press, 1985), 382.
10. Images cited in this chapter are generally available via online searching or through online databases like ARTstor.org, Wikimedia, the Web Gallery of Art (wga.hu), and museum websites. Where possible, I have listed museum accession numbers to ease searching.
11. See Leslie Brubaker, *Vision and Meaning in Ninth-Century Byzantium: Image as Exegesis in the Homilies of Gregory Nazianzus* (Cambridge: Cambridge University Press, 1999), 92–5.
12. See Kirk Ambrose, *The Nave Sculpture of Vézelay: The Art of Monastic Viewing* (Toronto: Pontifical Institute of Medieval Studies and University of Toronto Press, 2006), 84, n. 73.
13. Earlier depictions of Absalom's fate, such as the fresco at Mustair, in Switzerland (ca. 800), depict Absalom hanging by his neck, rather than his hair.

14. C.R. Dodwell, *The Canterbury School of Illumination*, 1066–1200 (Cambridge: Cambridge University Press, 1954), 42.
15. Augustine, *Expositions on the Psalms*, Digital Psalms Version 2007, compiled by Ted Hildebrant, https://faculty.gordon.edu/hu/bi/ted_hildebrandt/otesources/19-psalms/text/books/augustine-psalms/augustine-psalms-web.htm (accessed May 15, 2016).
16. Alcuin, letter to King Athelred, 793, trans. Dorothy Whitelock, in *The Viking Age: A Reader*, eds. Angus A. Somerville and R. Andrew McDonald (Toronto: University of Toronto Press, 2010), 233.
17. Madeline Caviness, "Norman Knights, Anglo-Saxon Women, and the 'Third Sex': The Masculinization of England After the Conquest," in *Reframing Medieval Art: Difference, Margins, Boundaries*, http://dca.lib.tufts.edu/caviness/chapter2.html (accessed September 2, 2015).
18. See Leila Leah Bronner, "From Veil to Wig: Jewish Women's Hair Covering," *Judaism* 42, no. 4 (1993): 465–77; Marc Michael Epstein, "Clothing: Jewish," in *Medieval France: An Encyclopedia*, ed. William Kibler (New York: Routledge, 1995), 449–50; and Eric Silverman, *A Cultural History of Jewish Dress* (London: Bloomsbury, 2013), 90–1.
19. Diane Wolfthal, *Images of Rape: The "Heroic" Tradition and its Alternatives* (Cambridge: Cambridge University Press, 1999), 43, 164.
20. Roberta Milliken, *Ambiguous Locks: An Iconology of Hair in Medieval Art and Literature* (Jefferson, NC: McFarland and Company, 2012), 109–10.
21. Matthew 28:1–8; Mark 16:9–10; Luke 8:2, 24:10; John 20:18.
22. See Theresa Coletti, *Mary Magdalene and the Drama of the Saints: Theater, Gender, and Religion in Late Medieval England* (Philadelphia: University of Pennsylvania Press, 2004), 209–11.
23. Katherine Ludwig Jansen, "Mary Magdalen and the Contemplative Life," in *Medieval Religion: New Approaches*, ed. Constance Berman (New York: Routledge, 2005), 249–71, at 259.
24. Jacobus de Voragine, *The Golden Legend: Readings on the Saints*, vol. 1, trans. William Granger Ryan (Princeton, NJ: Princeton University Press, 1993), 96.
25. See Katherine Ludwig Jansen, *The Making of the Magdalen: Preaching and Popular Devotion in the Later Middle Ages* (Princeton, NJ: Princeton University Press, 2000), 37–8, 132–4.
26. Xavier Barbier de Montault, "L'Eglise Royale et Collegiale de Saint Nicolas, à Bari (Deux-Sicilies), fin," *Revue de l'Art Chrétien* 2 (1884): 305–14.
27. Patrick Demouy, "Le trésor de la cathédrale," in *Reims: La grâce d'une cathédrale*, ed. Thierry Jordan (Strasbourg: Édition La Nuée Bleue, 2010), 316.
28. De Voragine, *The Golden Legend*, vol. 1, 103.
29. Elizabeth Nightlinger, "The Female *Imitatio Christi* and Medieval Popular Religion: The Case of St Wilgefortis," in *Representations of the Feminine in the Middle Ages*, ed. Bonnie Wheeler (Dallas, TX: Academia Press, 1993), 291–328; Ilse E. Friesen, *The Female Crucifix: Images of St. Wilgefortis Since the Middle Ages* (Ontario: Wilfrid Laurier University Press, 2001); Lewis Wallace, "Bearded Woman, Female Christ: Gendered Transformations in the Legends and Cult of Saint Wilgefortis," *Journal of Feminist Studies in Religion* 30, no. 1 (2014): 43–63.
30. Thomas Mathews, *The Clash of Gods: A Reinterpretation of Early Christian Art*, revised and expanded ed. (Princeton, NJ: Princeton University Press, 1993), 108–9, 126–7.
31. For a critical edition of the Latin text, see Ernst von Dobschütz, *Christusbilder: Untersuchungen zur christlichen Legende* (Leipzig: J.C. Hinrichs, 1899), 308–24; see also

Cora Lutz, "The Letter of Lentulus Describing Christ," *The Yale University Library Gazette* 50, no. 2 (1975): 91–7.
32. Lutz, "The Letter of Lentulus Describing Christ," 93.
33. On the Holy Face tradition, see Herbert Kessler and Gerhardt Wolf, eds., *The Holy Face and the Paradox of Representation: Papers from a Colloquium Held at the Bibliotheca Hertziana, Rome, and the Villa Spelman, Florence, 1996* (Bologna: Nuova Alfa Editoriale, 1998).
34. Giles Constable, *Crusaders and Crusading in the Twelfth Century* (Farnham: Ashgate, 2008), 333.
35. Sara Lipton, *Dark Mirror: The Medieval Origins of Anti-Jewish Iconography* (New York: Metropolitan Books, 2014), 48–54.
36. Clement of Alexandria, *The Instructor*, bk. 3, chap. 3, "Against Men Who Embellish Themselves," http://www.ccel.org/ccel/schaff/anf02.vi.iii.iii.iii.html (accessed December 8, 2015).
37. Thomas of Celano, *The First Life of Saint Francis of Assisi*, trans. Christopher Stace (London: Society for Promoting Christian Knowledge, 2000), 78. For the original Latin, Thomas of Celano, *Vita prima di S. Francesco d'Assisi*, ed. Leopoldo Amoni (Rome: Tipografia della Pace, 1880), 132; de Voragine, *The Golden Legend*, vol. 1, 165–6.
38. Robert Mills, "The Signification of the Tonsure," in *Holiness and Masculinity in the Middle Ages*, eds. P.H. Cullum and Katherine Lewis (Toronto: University of Toronto Press, 2004), 111.
39. Hucbald, "Ecloga de Calvis," trans. Thomas Klein, "In Praise of Bald Men: A Translation of Hucbald's Ecloga de Calvis," *Comitatus: A Journal of Medieval and Renaissance Studies* 26, no. 1 (1995): 1–9.
40. Désirée G. Koslin, "*He hath couerd my soule inward:* Veiling in Medieval Europe and the Early Church," in *The Veil: Women Writers on Its History, Lore, and Politics*, ed. Jennifer Heath (Berkeley: University of California Press, 2008), 162–3.
41. Joan Mueller, *A Companion to Clare of Assisi: Life, Writings, Spirituality* (Leiden: Brill, 2010), 34.
42. Milliken, *Ambiguous Locks*, 72–3.
43. See Koslin, "*He hath couerd my soule inward*," as above, note 40.
44. Aelred of Rievaulx, "The Nun of Watton," in *Women and Writing in Medieval Europe: A Sourcebook*, ed. Carolyne Larrington (London: Routledge, 1995), 130–5. The episode is cited: *Patrologia Latina*, ed. J.P. Migne (Paris, 1841–1864), vol. 195, col. 791–6, trans. O. Gutman.
45. See Julia Bolton Holloway, Joan Bechtold, and Constance S. Wright, introduction to chap. 5, "Holy Disobedience," in *Equally in God's Image: Women in the Middle Ages*, eds. Holloway, Bechtold, and Wright (New York: Peter Lang, 1990), 220–1.
46. John Anson, "The Female Transvestite in Early Monasticism: The Origin and Development of a Motif," *Viator* 5 (1974): 1–32.
47. Jane Tibbetts Schulenburg, *Forgetful of Their Sex: Female Sanctity and Society, ca. 500–1100* (Chicago: University of Chicago Press, 1998), 161–4.
48. See Régine Pernoud, *The Retrial of Joan of Arc: The Evidence for Her Vindication*, trans. J.M. Cohen (San Francisco: Ignatius Press, 1983).
49. John T. McNeill and Helena M. Gamer, *Medieval Handbooks of Penance: A Translation of the Principal 'Libri Poenitentiales* (New York: Columbia University Press, 1938, rep. 1990), 358.
50. Ruth Mazo Karras, *Common Women: Prostitution and Sexuality in Medieval England* (Oxford: Oxford University Press, 1996), 15.

51. Mills, "The Signification of the Tonsure," 109–26.
52. See Julia Barrow, *The Clergy in the Medieval World: Secular Clerics, their Families, and their Careers in North-Western Europe, c. 800—c. 1200* (Cambridge: Cambridge University Press, 2015), 33.
53. Guillaume Durand, *The Rationale Divinorum Officiorum: The Foundational Symbolism of the Early Church, Its Structure, Decoration, Sacraments and Vestments* (Louisville, KY: Fons Vitae, 2007), 257. For a scholarly edition of the Latin source text, see *Guillelmi Duranti Rationale divinorum officiorum*, eds. Timothy Thibodoeau and Anselm Davril (Corpus Christianorum, Continuatio Mediaevalis), vol. 140 (Turnhout: Brepols, 1995).

Chapter Two

1. Marina Warner, *From the Beast to the Blonde: On Fairy Tales and Their Tellers* (New York: Farrar, Straus & Giroux, 1995), 371.
2. His full name in Welsh: *Ieuan Goch Benllwyd ap Bedo Benllwyd ap Gruffudd ap Maredudd Ddu.*
3. For the original text, see Siôn Ceri, *Gwaith Siôn Ceri*, ed. Cynfael Lake (Aberystwyth: Canolfan Uwchefrydiau Cymreig a Cheltaidd, 1996), 10.5–14. Translations are my own unless noted differently.
4. Ibid., 15.55–8.
5. Guto'r Glyn, "Moliant i wallt du Harri Gruffudd o'r Cwrt Newydd," ed. Barry J. Lewis, gutorglyn.net, Poem 33, lines 17–20, http://www.gutorglyn.net/gutorglyn/poem/?poem-selection=033&first-line=%23 (accessed January 10, 2016). All English translations of Guto'r Glyn's work are from this online edition.
6. Ibid., lines 6–16.
7. *Pedeir Keinc y Mabinogi*, ed. Ifor Williams, 2nd ed. (Cardiff: University of Wales Press, 1951), 23.16. "They had the boy baptized in the way it was done at that time. This was the name that they gave him, Gwri Wallt Euryn: all the hair on his head was as yellow as gold." This translation comes from *The Mabinogion*, trans. Sioned Davies (Oxford: Oxford University Press, 2007), 18.
8. *Breudwyt Ronabwy*, ed. Melville Richards (Cardiff: University of Wales Press, 1948), 2.6; and *Culhwch and Olwen: An Edition and Study of the Oldest Arthurian Tale*, eds. Rachel Bromwich and Daniel Simon Evans (Cardiff: University of Wales Press, 1992), 25.663.
9. William Sayers, "Early Irish Attitudes toward Hair and Beards, Baldness and Tonsure," *Zeitschrift für Celtische Philologie* 44, no. 1 (January 1991): 154–89 (quote p. 162).
10. *The Mabinogion*, 71. For the original Welsh, see *Historia Peredur vab Efrawc*, ed. Glenys Goetinck (Cardiff: University of Wales Press, 1976), 16.30–17.1–3.
11. Robert Bartlett, "Symbolic Meanings of Hair in the Middle Ages," *Transactions of the Royal Historical Society* s. 6, 4 (1994): 43–60 (see p. 45).
12. Ibid., 45.
13. Ibid., 46. See also *Statutes and Ordinances and Acts of the Parliament of Ireland: King John to Henry V*, ed. Henry F. Berry (Dublin: Her Majesty's Stationery Office, 1907), 210.
14. Bartlett, "Symbolic Meanings," 46.
15. Ibid., 46. See also *Parliaments and Councils of Medieval Ireland*, 1, eds. Henry G. Richardson and George O. Sayles (Dublin: Stationery Office, 1947), nos. 13, 17.
16. *Táin bó Cúailnge: Recension I*, ed. Cecile O'Rahilly (Dublin: Dublin Institute for Advanced Studies, 1976), 1. Translation in O'Rahilly, *Táin bó Cúlainge*, 125.
17. Herwig Wolfram, *History of the Goths*, trans. Thomas J. Dunlap (Berkeley: University of California Press, 1988), 301, 103; J.M. Wallace-Hadrill, *The Long-haired Kings: And*

Other Studies in Frankish History (London: Methuen, 1962), 156–7; 232–3; 245–6; Averil Cameron, "How did the Merovingian Kings wear their Hair?" *Revue belge de philologie et d'historie* 43, no. 4 (1965): 1203–16. See also Bartlett, "Symbolic Meanings," 44.
18. Ibid., 44. See also W. Sayers, "Early Irish Attitudes toward Hair and Beards, Baldness and Tonsure," *Zeitschrift für Celtische Philologie* 44, no. 1 (1991), 154–89.
19. *Sachsenspiegel, Landrecht* I, ed. Karl Eckhardt (Göttingen: Musterschmidt-Verlag, 1956), 104.
20. *The Law of Hywel Dda: Law texts from Medieval Wales*, ed. and trans. Dafydd Jenkins (Llandysul: Gomer Press), 142. For the original Welsh, see *Damweiniau Colan*, ed. Dafydd Jenkins (Aberystwyth: Cymdeithas Lyfrau Ceredigion, 1974), 45.2–4.
21. *Táin bó Cúailnge from the Book of Leinster*, ed. Cecile O'Rahilly (Dublin: Dublin Institute for Advanced Studies, 1967), 27.735; and O'Rhailly, *Táin bó Cúailnge: Recension I*, 45, 58.
22. Sayers, "Early Attitudes toward Hair and Beards," 166.
23. Jenkins, *The Law of Hywel Dda*, 53. For the original Welsh, see Dafydd Jenkins and Morfydd E. Owen, eds., *The Welsh Law of Women* (Cardiff: Cardiff University Press, 1980), 170.
24. Williams, *Pedeir Keinc y Mabinogi*, 47.10–11; Goetinck, *Peredur*, 37.5.
25. Thomas of Malborough, *History of the Abbey of Evesham*, eds. and trans. Jane Sayers and Leslie Watkiss (Oxford: Clarendon Press, 2003), 81.
26. *The Laws of the Earliest English Kings*, ed. and trans. Frederik L. Attenborough (Cambridge: Cambridge University Press, 1922), 8–9.
27. Jenkins, *The Law of Hywel Dda*, 198.
28. Attenborough, *The Laws of the Earliest English Kings*, 79.
29. Geoffrey of Monmouth, *The History of the Kings of Britain: An Edition and Translation of De Gestis Britonum*, ed. Michael D. Reeve and trans. Neil Wright (Woodbridge: Boydell Press, 2007), 226; Geoffrey of Monmouth, *Brut Dingestow*, ed. Henry Lewis (Cardiff: Cardiff University Press, 1942). See Chris Grooms, *The Giants of Wales: Cewri Cymru* (Lampeter: Mellen, 1993), 214–18.
30. Grooms, *The Giants of Wales*, 214–15.
31. Gruffudd Llwyd, *Gwaith Gruffudd Llwyd a'r Llygliwiaid eraill*, ed. Rh. Ifans (Aberystwyth: Centre for Advanced Welsh and Celtic Studies, 2000), 16.9–12.
32. See Bartlett, "Symbolic Meanings," 48.
33. In Bromwich and Evans, *Culhwch and Olwen*, xxxii. For the original Latin, see Nennius, *The Historia Brittonum*, ed. David N. Dumville (Cambridge: D.S. Brewer, 1985), 90.
34. *The Mabinogion*, 183. For the original Welsh, see Bromwich and Evans, *Culhwch and Olwen*, 7.166–7.
35. Molly Myerowitz Levine, "The Gendered Grammar of Ancient Mediterranean Hair," in *Off with Her Head! The Denial of Women's Identity in Myth, Religion, and Culture*, eds. Howard Eilberg-Schwartz and Wendy Doniger (Berkeley: University of California Press, 1995), 76–130 (quotation on p. 100). See also Roberta Milliken, *Ambiguous Locks: An Iconology of Hair in Medieval Art and Literature* (Jefferson, NC: McFarland & Company, 2012), 70–1.
36. Bartlett, "Symbolic Meanings," 54.
37. Ibid., 54.
38. *The Mabinogion*, 125. For the original Welsh see *Owein or Chwedyl Iarlles y Ffynnawn*, ed. R.L. Thompson (Dublin: Institute of Advanced Studies, 1968), 14.353–6.
39. Margaret Scott, *Medieval Dress and Fashion* (London: The British Library, 2009), 112–13.
40. Christine de Pisan, *The Treasure of the City of Ladies or The Book of the Three Virtues*, trans. Sarah Lawson (London: Penguin, 1985), 135.

41. Geoffrey Chaucer, *The Riverside Chaucer*, ed. Larry D. Benson (Oxford: Oxford University Press, 2008).
42. *The Mabinogion*, 192. For the original Welsh, see Bromwich and Evans, *Culhwch and Olwen*, 18.487–90.
43. Matthew of Vendôme, *Ars versificatoria*, trans. Roger P. Parr (Milwaukee: Marquette University Press, 1981).
44. Ibid., 81.
45. Geoffrey de la Tour Landry, *The Book of the Knight of La Tour Landry*, ed. G.S. Taylor (London: Verona Society, 1930), 45.
46. For the development and relationship between sirens and mermaids, see Meri Lao, *Sirens: Symbols of Seduction*, trans. John Oliphant of Rossie (Rochester, VT: Park Street Press, 1998); and Gwen Benwell and Arthur Waugh, *Sea Enchantress: A Tale of the Mermaid and Her Kin* (London: Hutchinson, 1965).
47. Lao, *Sirens: Symbols of Seduction*, 20.
48. Brunetto Latini, *The Book of the Treasure (Li Livres dou Tresor)*, trans. Paul Barrette and Spurgeon Baldwin (New York: Garland, 1993), 107; bk. 1, chap. 136, sec. 2.
49. Milliken, *Ambiguous Locks*, 123–33.
50. See Barbara G. Walker, *The Woman's Dictionary of Symbols and Sacred Objects* (London: Pandora, 1995), 129, 263.
51. Quoted in Ann Marie Rasmussen, *Mothers and Daughters in Medieval German Literature* (Syracuse, NY: Syracuse University Press, 1997), 143.
52. Shulamith Shahar, *The Fourth Estate*, trans. Chaya Galai (London: Routledge, 2003), 108. See also Madeline H. Caviness, *Visualizing Women in the Middle Ages: Sight, Spectacle, and Scopic Economy* (Philadelphia: University of Philadelphia Press, 2001), 113, fig. 50.
53. Vern Bullough, "The Prostitute in the Early Middle Ages," in *Sexual Practices and the Medieval Church*, eds. James Brundage and Vern Bullough (Amherst, NY: Prometheus Books, 1994), 36. See also Ruth Mazo Karras, *Common Women: Prostitutes and Sexuality in Medieval England* (Oxford: Oxford University Press, 1996), 15.
54. Milliken, *Ambiguous Locks*, 155. See also Barbara Hanawalt, *"Of Good and Ill Repute": Gender and Social Control in Medieval England* (New York: Oxford University Press, 1998), 27.
55. Geoffrey de la Tour Landry, *The Book of the Knight of La Tour Landry*, 55.
56. Raymond of Capua, *Life of St. Catherine of Siena*, trans. George Lamb (New York: P.J. Kennedy, 1960), 41.
57. Iolo Goch, *Iolo Goch: Poems*, ed. and trans. Dafydd Johnston (Llandysul: Gwasg Gomer 1993), 128–9; Dafydd Nanmor, *The Poetical Works of Dafydd Nanmor*, ed. Thomas Roberts and rev. Ifor Williams (Cardiff: University of Wales Press, 1923), 92.
58. Milliken, *Ambiguous Locks*, 177.
59. Marina Warner, *Alone of All Her Sex: The Myth and Cult of the Virgin Mary* (London: Picador, 2000).
60. For the formation of the Immaculate Conception, see Miri Rubin, *Mother of God: A History of the Virgin Mary* (London: Penguin Books, 2010), 173–6 and 303–5; Donna Spivey Ellington, *From Sacred Body to Angelic Soul: Understanding Mary in Late Medieval and Early Modern Europe* (Washington, DC: Catholic University of America Press, 2001), 52–60 and 171–7; and Warner, *Alone of All Her Sex*, 236–54.
61. Iorwerth Fynglwyd, *Gwaith Iorwerth Fynglwyd*, eds. Howell L. Jones and E.I. Rowlands (Cardiff: University of Wales Press, 1975), 96; Gruffudd ap Maredudd, *Gwaith Gruffudd ap Maredudd 2: Cerddi Crefyddol*, ed. Barry J. Lewis (Aberystwyth: Canolfan Uwchefrydiau Cymreig a Cheltaidd Prifysgol Cymru, 2005), 75.

62. Jenkins, *The Laws of Hywel Dda*, 54. See also Aled Rhys Wiliam, ed., *The Book of Iorwerth (Llyfr Iorwerth): A Critical and Definitive Text of the Gwynedd (Venedotion) Code of Medieval Welsh Law* (Cardiff: University of Wales Press, 1960), 51.
63. Jenkins, *The Laws of Hywel Dda*, 54.
64. Jacques Rossiaud, *Medieval Prostitution*, trans. Lydia G. Cochrane (Oxford: Blackwell, 1998), 57.
65. Étienne De Bourbon, *Anecdotes historiques, legends et apologues tires du recueil inedit d'Etienne de Bourbon, Dominicain du XIHe siècle*, ed. A. Lecoy de la Marche (Paris: Société de l'histoire de France, 1877), 230 no. 276, 238 no. 285; Karras, *Common Women*, 111. See also Theodore Child, *Wimples and Crisping Pins* (New York: Harper and Brothers, 1895), 75: "Even the veil, the emblem of modesty, destined to conceal, is made a flag and banner of coquetry, and in its various innumerable transformations it becomes wimple, turban, coif, or bonnet, and in the end mere pretext for ornamentation."
66. Warner, *From the Beast to the Blonde*, 371.

Chapter Three

1. Margaret Scott, *Medieval Dress and Fashion* (London: The British Library, 2007), 8.
2. Joanne Entwistle, *The Fashioned Body: Fashion, Dress, and Modern Social Theory* (Cambridge: Polity Press, 2015), 2, and discussion 1–8.
3. Scott, *Medieval Dress and Fashion*, 8.
4. See Ilya Parkins, *Pioriet, Dior, and Schiaparelli: Fashion, Femininity and Modernity* (New York: Bloomsbury Publishing, 2012), especially the introduction. For discussions of the fashion as a marketable concept in the eighteenth century, see Jane Ashelford, *The Art of Dress: Clothes Through History 1500–1914* (London: The National Trust, 2011); and Valerie Steel, *Paris Fashion: A Cultural History* (New York: Oxford University Press, 1988).
5. James Laver, *Costume and Fashion* (London: Thames and Hudson, 1995).
6. Daniel Delis Hill, *History of World Costume and Fashion* (Upper Saddle River, NJ: Prentice Hall 2011), 320–2.
7. See Roberta Milliken, *Ambiguous Locks: An Iconology of Hair in Medieval Art and Literature* (Jefferson, NC: McFarland and Company, 2012), 54–69.
8. Valerie Garver, *Women and Aristocratic Culture in the Carolingian World* (Ithaca, NY: Cornell University Press, 2009), 32.
9. Ibid., 35.
10. Gillian Vogelsang-Eastwood and William Vogelsang, *Covering the Moon: An Introduction to Middle Eastern Face Veils* (Leuven: Peeters, 2008), 35–9.
11. Gale Owen-Crocker, *Dress in Anglo-Saxon England* (Woodbridge: Boydell Press, 1980), 219.
12. Ibid., 221.
13. C.R. Dodwell, *Anglo-Saxon Art: A New Perspective* (Ithaca, NY: Cornell University Press, 1985), 129–87.
14. *Bible of San Paolo*, Rome, Church of San Paolo fuori le Murs, fol. 1r; and for a discussion of the veil, see Scott, *Medieval Dress and Fashion*, 17.
15. New Minster Charter, London, British Library, MS Cotton Vespasian MS A VIII, fol. 2v.
16. *Karolus Magnus et Leo Papa* in *Poetry of the Carolingian Renaissance*, trans. Peter Goodman (Norman: University of Oklahoma Press, 1985).
17. Gale Owen-Crocker, "Brides, Donors, Traders: Imports into Anglo-Saxon England," in *Textiles and the Medieval Economy: Production Trade, and Consumption of Textiles, 8th–16th Centuries*, eds. Angela Ling-Huang and Carsten Jahnke (Oxford: Oxbow Books, 2015), 64–77, especially 66.

18. Owen-Crocker, *Dress in Anglo-Saxon England*, 225–6.
19. Garver, *Women and Aristocratic Culture*, 52.
20. Ibid., 203; and in Hugh Magennis, "Gender and Heroism in the Old English Judith," in *Writing Gender and Genre in Medieval Literature: Approaches to Old and Middle English Texts*, ed. Elaine M. Treharne (Cambridge: D.S. Brewer, 2002), 14.
21. Ibid., 226.
22. *Aldhelm: The Prose Works*, trans. Michael Lapidge and Michael Herren (Cambridge: D.S. Brewer, 1979), 127–8.
23. Owen-Crocker, *Dress in Anglo-Saxon England*, 225–6.
24. *Liber Vitae*, London, British Library, MS Stowe 944, fol. 6r.
25. Owen-Crocker, *Dress in Anglo-Saxon England*, 224.
26. Dorothy Whitelock, ed. and trans. *Anglo-Saxon Wills* (Cambridge: Cambridge University Press, 1930), 15.
27. *Njal's Saga*, trans. Robert Cook (London: Penguin Classics, 2001), 28.
28. Owen-Crocker, *Dress in Anglo-Saxon England*, 230; and Elizabeth Wincott Heckett, "Some Silk and Wool Headcoverings from Viking Dublin; Uses and Origins—an Enquiry," in *Textiles in Northern Archaeology* NESAT III, eds. Penelope Walton and John Peter Wild (London: British Council for Archaeological Research, 1990), 85–96.
29. Peter Sawyer, *The Wealth of Anglo-Saxon England* (Oxford: Oxford University Press, 2013), 66.
30. Howard Williams, "Transforming Body and Soul: Toilet Implements in Early Anglo-Saxon Graves," in *Anglo Saxon Studies in Archaeology and History* 14, eds. Sarah Semple and Howard Williams (Oxford: Oxford University School of Archaeology, 2007), 66–91.
31. *Liber Vitae*, fol. 6r and *New Minster Charter*, London, British Library, MS Cotton Vespasian A VIII, fol. 2v.
32. *San Paolo Bible*, fol. 1r and *Codex Aureus of St. Emmeram*, Munich, Bayerische Staatsbibliothek, MS. Clm. 14000, fol. 5v.
33. Owen-Crocker, *Dress in Anglo-Saxon England*, 20.
34. For a classic description of the tonsure debate as well as the Synod of Whitby, see bk. III of Bede's *Ecclesiastical History of the English History*, trans. Leo Sherley-Price (London: Penguin, 1968).
35. Maximilian Diesenburger, "Hair, Sacrality, and Symbolic Capital in the Frankish Kingdoms," in *The Construction of Communities in the Early Middle Ages: Texts, Resources, and Artifacts*, eds. R Corradini, M. Diesenburger, and H. Reimitz (Leiden: Brill, 2003), 173–212, especially 909.
36. Joan Evans, *Dress in Mediaeval France*, (Oxford: Clarendon Press, 1952), 11.
37. *The Complete Romances of Chrétien de Troyes*, trans. David Staines (Bloomington: Indiana University Press, 1990), 6.
38. *The Trotula: A Medieval Compendium of Women's Medicine*, ed. and trans. Monica H. Green (Philadelphia: University of Pennsylvania Press, 2001), 115.
39. Scott, *Medieval Dress*, 45.
40. Eunice Rathbone Goddard, *Women's Costume in French Texts of the Eleventh and Twelfth Centuries* (Baltimore: Johns Hopkins University Press, 1927), 125.
41. Janet Snyder, "From Content to Form: Court Clothing in Mid-Twelfth-Century Northern French Sculpture," in *Encountering Medieval Textiles and Dress: Objects, Texts, Images*, eds. Désirée G. Koslin and Janet E. Snyder (New York: Palgrave Macmillan, 2002), 99.
42. *Alphonso Psalter*, London, British Library MS Add. 24686, fol. 13v.
43. Scott, *Medieval Dress and Fashion*, 72.

44. Gilliaume de Lorris and Jean de Meun, *The Romance of the Rose*, 3rd ed., trans. Charles Dahlberg (Princeton, NJ: Princeton University Press, 1995), 205.
45. Oversang-Eastwood and Oversang, *Covering the Moon*, 64–71.
46. Scott, *Medieval Dress and Fashion*, 40–1.
47. Quoted in Christina Waugh, "'Well-Cut Through the Body': Fitted Clothing in the Twelfth-Century Europe," *Dress* 26, no. 1 (1999): 16.
48. *Moralia in Job*, Dijon, Bibliothèque Municipale, MS 173, fol. 174r; and Shaftesbury Psalter, London, British Library, MS Lansdowne 383, fol. 5r.
49. Evans, *Dress in Mediaeval France*, 4–5.
50. Snyder, "From Content to Form," 93.
51. Evans, *Dress in Mediaeval France*, 12–13.
52. Debra Higgs Strickland, *Saracens, Demons, and Jews: Making Monsters in Medieval Art* (Princeton, NJ: Princeton University Press, 2003), especially 42, 78, 98–108.
53. *Topographica Hibernica*, London, British Library, MS Royal 13 B VIII fol. 28v.
54. *Vie de Saint Louis*, Paris, Bibliothèque Nationale de France, MS Français 13568.
55. Delis Hill, *History of World Costume and Fashion*, 326.
56. Ibid., 328–9.
57. Eric Silverman, *A Cultural History of Jewish Dress* (London: Bloomsbury, 2013), 47.
58. Ibid., 55.
59. Ibid., 58.
60. Ibid., 48.
61. Delis Hill, *History of World Costume Fashion*, 321–2.
62. Scott, *Medieval Dress and Fashion*, 79–80.
63. Delis Hill, *History of World Costume Fashion*, 337.
64. Scott, *Medieval Dress and Fashion*, 88.
65. Luttrell Psalter, London, British Library, MS Add. 42130, fol. 202v.
66. Neville of Hornby Hours, London, British Library, MS Egerton 2781, fol. 35r.
67. *Coronation Book of Charles V of France*, London, British Library, MS Cotton Tiberius BVIII, fol. 67v.
68. "Against the Pride of Ladies," in *Satirical Songs and Poems on Costume from the 13th to the 19th Century*, ed. Frederick W. Fairhold (London: The Percy Society, 1849), 41.
69. Evans, *Dress in Mediaeval France*, plate 29.
70. Luttrell Psalter, British Library, fol. 63.
71. Hours of Bertrando dei Rossi, Paris, Bibliothèque Nationale, MS Lat. 757, fol. 380.
72. Geoff Egan and Frances Pritchard, *Dress Accessories c. 1150–1450* (Woodbridge: Boydell Press, 2008), 292–3.
73. Scott, *Medieval Dress and Fashion*, 88.
74. Stella Marie Newton, *Fashion in the Age of the Black Prince* (Woodbridge: Boydell Press, 1980), 131.
75. *Roman du Roi Meliadus de Leonnoys* London, British Library, MS Add. 12228. fol. 220r.
76. Newton, *Fashion in the Age of the Black Prince*, 11.
77. Delis Hill, *History of World Costume Fashion*, 331–2.
78. Newton, *Fashion in the Age of the Black Prince*, 9–10.
79. Ibid., 9.
80. Theodore Child, *Wimples and Crisping Pins* (New York: Harper and Brothers, 1895), 86.
81. *The Book of the Knight of the Tower*, ed. M.Y. Offord and trans. William Caxton (Oxford: Oxford University Press, 1921), 76–7.
82. Scott, *Medieval Dress and Fashion*, 203.

83. *Collected Works of Christine de Pizan*, London, British Library, MS Harley 4431, fol. 5r.
84. Christine de Pizan, *The Treasury of the City of Ladies or the Book of the Three Virtues*, trans. Sarah Lawson (London: Penguin, 1985), 116.
85. Caxton, *The Book of the Knight of the Tower*, 62–3.
86. Scott, *Medieval Dress and Fashion*, 145.
87. Janetta Rebold Benton, *Materials, Methods, and Masterpieces of Medieval Art* (Santa Barbara, CA: ABC-CLIO, 2009), 223.
88. Book of Hours, London, British Library, MS. Add. 18192, fol. 196.
89. Bedford Hours, London, British Library, MS. Add. 18850, fol. 257v.
90. Egan and Pritchard, *Dress Accessories*, 297.
91. Delis Hill, *History of World Costume Fashion*, 340.
92. *Collected Works of Christine de Pizan*, London, British Library, MS Harley 4431, fol. 3.
93. Scott, *Medieval Dress and Fashion*, 145.
94. Christine de Pizan, *The Treasury of the City of Ladies*, 116.
95. *The Trotula*, 171–3.
96. Carole Collier Frick, *Dressing Renaissance Florence: Families, Fortunes, and Fine Clothing* (Baltimore: Johns Hopkins University Press, 2005), 317.
97. Catherine Kovesi Killerby, *Sumptuary Law in Italy, 1200–1500* (Oxford: Clarendon Press, 2002), 121.
98. Scott, *Medieval Dress and Fashion*, 140.
99. Frick, *Dressing Renaissance Florence*, 127.
100. Ibid.
101. Ibid., 97.
102. Ibid., 127.
103. Ibid., 124–5.
104. Delis Hill, *History of World Costume Fashion*, 335–6.
105. *Roman de Mélusine*, London, British Library, MS Harley 4418, fol. 36r.
106. Très Riches Heures, Musée Condé, Chantilly, France, MS 65.
107. *Collected Works of Christine de Pizan*, London, British Library, MS Harley 4431, fol. 5r.

Chapter Four

1. Carmen Caballero-Navas, "The Care of Women's Health and Beauty: An Experience Shared by Medieval Jewish and Christian Women," *Journal of Medieval History* 34, no. 2 (2008): 146–63, especially 147.
2. Ibid., 161–2.
3. Guillaume de Lorris and Jean de Meun, *The Romance of the Rose*, trans. Frances Hogan (Oxford: Oxford University Press, 1999), 5–9, 19.
4. Montserrat Cabré, "Beautiful Bodies," in *A Cultural History of the Human Body in the Middle Ages*, ed. Linda Kalof (Oxford: Berg, 2010), 134.
5. Ibid., 130.
6. Roberta Milliken, *Ambiguous Locks: An Iconology of Hair in Medieval Art and Literature* (Jefferson, NC: McFarland and Company, 2012), 87–8.
7. Kevin Leahy, "Anglo-Saxon Crafts," in *The Oxford Handbook of Anglo-Saxon Archaeology*, eds. David A. Hinton, Sally Crawford, and Helena Hamerow (Oxford: Oxford University Press, 2011), 449.
8. See the comb at the Victoria and Albert Museum, A.809–1877.
9. Marloes Rijkelijkhuizen, "Dutch Medieval Bone and Antler Combs," in *Written in Bone: Studies on Technological and Social Contexts of Past Faunal Skeletal Remains*, eds. Justyna

Baron and Bernadeta Kufel-Diakowska (Wroclaw: Institute of Archaeology, University of Wrocław, 2011), 203.
10. Diane Wolfthal, "The Sexuality of the Medieval Comb," in *Thresholds of Medieval Visual Culture: Liminal Spaces*, eds. Elina Gertsman and Jill Stevenson (Woodbridge: Boydell Press, 2012), 178; and Bede, *The Ecclesiastical History of the English People*, trans. Leo Shirley-Price (London: Penguin 1990), II.12.
11. Ibid., 177–80.
12. Ibid., 177.
13. London, Victoria and Albert, A.560-1910.
14. Wolfthal, "The Sexuality of the Medieval Comb," 187.
15. Ibid., 180–1; and Geoff Egan and Frances Pritchard, *Dress Accessories c. 1150–1450* (Woodbridge: Boydell Press, 2008), 376.
16. London, Victoria and Albert Museum, A. 286–1867
17. For discussions of ivory combs and *gravoirs*, see Michael Camille, *The Medieval Art of Love: Objects and Subjects of Desire* (New York: Harry N. Abrams, Inc., 1998).
18. Ibid., 243 and Chrétien de Troyes, *Lancelot: The Knight of the Cart*, trans. Burton Raffel (New Haven, CT: Yale University Press, 1997), 46–7.
19. De Lorris and de Meun, *Romance of the Rose*, 11.
20. *Le Roman de la Rose*, London British Library, MS Yates Thompson 21, fol. 165.
21. Milliken, *Ambiguous Locks*, 130.
22. Discussed in Milliken, *Ambiguous Locks*, 126–32, and original reference in Jean d' Arras *A Bilingual Edition of Jean D'Arras's Mélusine or L'Histoire de Lusignan*, ed. and trans. Matthew W. Morris (Lewiston, NY: Edwin Mellen Press, 2007).
23. Wolfthal, "The Sexuality of the Medieval Comb," 187.
24. Ibid., 187–8.
25. For a discussion of medieval bathing practices, see Virginia Smith, *Clean: A History of Personal Hygiene and Purity* (Oxford: Oxford University Press, 2007), 149–80.
26. Einhard, "The Life of Charlemagne," in *Two Lives of Charlemagne*, ed. Peter Ganz (London: Penguin Classics, 2008), 28.
27. Marie de France, "Equitan," in *Marie de France: Poetry*, trans. Dorothy Gilbert (New York: W.W. Norton and Company, 2015), 33–4.
28. Barbara Hanawalt, *The Ties that Bound: Peasant Families in Medieval England* (Oxford: Oxford University Press, 1986), 61.
29. Katherine Ashenburg, *The Dirt on Clean: An Unsanitized History* (New York: North Point Press, 2007), 80.
30. Giovanni Boccaccio, *The Corbaccio or the Labyrinth of Love*, trans. and ed. Anthony Cassell (Binghamton, NY: Medieval and Renaissance Texts and Studies, 1993), 42.
31. Carmen Caballero-Navas, ed. and trans., *The Book of Women's Love and Jewish Medieval Medical Literature on Women, Sefer Ahavat Nashim* (Kegan Paul Library of Jewish Studies) (London: Kegan Paul, 2004), 122.
32. Ashelford, *The Dirt on Clean*, 69–70.
33. Victoria Sherrow, *Encyclopedia of Hair: A Cultural History* (Westport, CT: Greenwood Press, 2006), 347.
34. *The Trotula: A Medieval Compendium of Women's Medicine*, ed. and trans. Monica H. Green (Philadelphia: University of Pennsylvania Press, 2001), 115; and "Vicia orobus (Wood Bitter-vetch)," *Online Atlas of the British and Irish Flora*, http://www.brc.ac.uk/plantatlas/index.php?q=plant/vicia-orobus (Accessed March 1, 2016).
35. Giovanni Boccaccio, *The Decameron*, trans. G.H. McWilliam (London: Penguin Books, 1972), VIII.10, 635.

36. Hildegard of Bingen, *Hildegard von Bingen's Physica: The Complete English Translation of Her Classic Work on Health and Healing*, trans. Priscilla Throop (Rochester, VT: Healing Arts Press, 1998), 113.
37. Geoffrey de la Tour Landry, *The Book of the Knight of the Tower*, ed. M.Y. Offord and trans. William Caxton (Oxford: Oxford University Press, 1921), 78.
38. Wolfthal "Sexuality of the Medieval Comb," 180.
39. Geneta Alem, et al. "Invitro Antibacterial Activity of Crude Preparation of Myrtle (Myrtus Communis) on Common Human Pathogens," *Ethiopian Medical Journal* 46, no. 1 (2008): 63–9; and *Trotula*, 117.
40. De Lorris and de Meun, *Romance of the Rose*, 16–17.
41. Quoted in Valerie Garver, *Women and Aristocratic Culture in the Carolingian World* (Ithaca, NY: Cornell University Press, 2009), 47.
42. Chrétien De Troyes, *Arthurian Romances*, trans. W.W. Comfort (London: Everyman's Library, 1963), 5 and 109.
43. Christine de Pizan, *The Treasury of the City of Ladies or the Book of the Three Virtues*, trans. Sarah Lawson (London: Penguin, 1985), 116.
44. De Lorris and de Meun, *Romance of the Rose*, 7.
45. As discussed in Milliken, *Ambiguous Locks*, 83.
46. *Book of Women's Love*, 122.
47. Pat Willard, *Secrets of Saffron: The Vagabond Life of the World's Most Seductive Spice* (Boston, MA: Beacon Press, 2002), 78–9.
48. Ibid.
49. *Trotula*, 116–17; and see Tania Bayard, *Sweet Herbs and Sundry Flowers: Medieval Gardens and the Gardens of the Cloisters* (New York: Metropolitan Museum of Art, 1985), especially 8–27, and *Book of Women's Love*, 122.
50. Caballero-Navas, "The Care of Women's Health and Beauty," 153–4.
51. Claudio Da Soller, "The Beautiful Woman in Medieval Iberia: Rhetoric, Cosmetics, and Evolution" (PhD Diss. Columbia, University of Missouri-Columbia, 2005), 46–8.
52. Quoted in ibid., 48–9.
53. *Trotula*, 115.
54. Elena Phipps, *Looking at Textiles: A Guide to Technical Terms* (Los Angeles: J. Paul Getty Trust, 2011), 54.
55. *Trotula*, 115.
56. Ibid.
57. *Trotula*, 115–16.
58. Boccaccio, *The Corbaccio*, 25.
59. A.K. Gupta and K. Nicol, "The use of sulfur in dermatology," *J Drugs Dermatol* 3, no. 4 (2004): 427–31.
60. Gerald Kutney, *Sulphur: History, Technology, Applications, Industry* (Toronto: ChemTec Publishing, 2007), 6–7.
61. *Trotula*, 115.
62. Gail Owen-Crocker, "Dress and Identity," in *The Oxford Handbook of Anglo-Saxon Archaeology*, eds. David A. Hinton, Sally Crawford, and Helena Hamerow (Oxford: Oxford University Press, 2011), 103–4.
63. Egan and Pritchard, *Dress Accessories*, 297.
64. Georgine de Courtais, *Women's Headdress and Hairstyles in England from AD 600 to the Present Day* (London: B.T. Batsford, 1973) 18–22.
65. Ibid., 297.
66. Ibid., 88.

NOTES 187

67. Luttrell Psalter, British Library, fol. 63.
68. Egan and Pritchard, *Dress Accessories*, 291.
69. Hours of Bertrando dei Rossi, Paris, Bibliothèque Nationale, MS Lat. 757, fol. 380.
70. Boccaccio, *The Corbaccio*, 44.
71. Egan and Pritchard, *Dress Accessories*, 292.
72. Margaret Scott, *Medieval Dress and Fashion* (London: The British Library, 2007), 88.
73. Stella Mary Newton, *Fashion in the Age of the Black Prince* (Woodbridge: Boydell Press, 1980), 131.
74. Catherine Kovesi Killerby, *Sumptuary Law in Italy, 1200–1500* (Oxford: Clarendon Press, 2002), 121.
75. De Lorris and de Meun, *Romance of the Rose*, 229.
76. Quoted in Caballero-Navas, "Care of Women's Health and Beauty," 53.
77. *Book of Women's Love*, 120–1.
78. *Trotula*, 116.
79. Joan Cadden, *Meanings of Sex Differences in the Middle Ages* (Cambridge: Cambridge University Press, 1993), 181–3.
80. Ruth Mazo Karras, *From Boys to Men: Formations of Masculinity in Late Medieval Europe* (Philadelphia: University of Pennsylvania Press, 2002), 105–6.
81. Wendy Cooper, *Hair: Sex, Society, Symbolism* (New York: Stein and Day, 1971), 20.
82. Cooper, *Hair: Sex, Society, Symbolism*, 114.
83. Penny Jolly, "Pubic and Privates: Body Hair in Late Medieval Art," in *Meanings of Nudity in Medieval Art*, ed. Sherry Lindquist (Farnham: Ashgate Publishing, 2012), especially 185–6 and Cadden, *Meanings of Sex Differences in the Middle Ages*, 171–83.
84. Jolly, "Pubic and Privates," 185–6.
85. De Lorris and de Meun, *Romance of the Rose*, 7.
86. Quoted and translated in Soller, "The Beautiful Woman in Medieval Iberia," 45.
87. Ibid., 188–9.
88. Boccaccio, *The Corbaccio*, 44.
89. Ibid., 42.
90. Geoffrey Chaucer, *The Miller's Tale* in *The Canterbury Tales*, trans. David Wright (Oxford: Oxford University Press, 1985), 84.
91. De la Tour Landry, *The Book of the Knight of the Tower*, 76–7.
92. Egan and Pritchard, *Dress Accessories*, 383.
93. As discussed in Jolly, "Pubic and Privates," 190.
94. *Book of Women's Love*, 119–20.
95. *Trotula*, 113.
96. Ibid., 113–14.
97. Ibid., 140.
98. Ibid., 99.
99. Raymond of Capua, *The Life of St. Catherine of Siena*, trans. George Lamb (Charlotte, NC: TAN Books, 2003), 25–6.
100. "The Rule of Saint Clare," in *Francis and Clare: The Complete Works*, trans. Regis J. Armstrong and Ignatius Brady (New York: Paulist Press, 1982), 212.
101. The *Prose Lancelot Grail*, London, British Library MS Add 10293 fol. 5r.
102. *The Letters of Abelard and Heloise*, ed. M.T. Clanchy and trans. Betty Radice (London: Penguin Books, 2003), 193.
103. Maximilian Diesenburger, "Hair, Sacrality, and Symbolic Capital in the Frankish Kingdoms," in *The Construction of Communities in the Early Middle Ages: Texts, Resources,*

and Artifacts, eds. R Corradini, M. Diesenburger, and H. Reimitz (Leiden: Brill, 2003), 173–212, especially 909.
104. Cooper, *Hair: Sex Society, Symbolism*, 153–4.
105. Ibid., 156–7.
106. Ibid. and *Similitudines Anselmi*, British Library, MS Cotton Cleopatra C. XI, fol. 27v.
107. Ibid. and Sherrow, *Encyclopedia of Hair*, 51–2.
108. Allan Peterkin, *One Thousand Beards: A Cultural History of Facial Hair* (Vancouver: Arsenal Pulp Press, 2001), 70.
109. *Roman de Mélusine*, London, British Library, MS Harley 4418, fol. 36r.
110. Richard Corson, *Fashions in Hair: The First Five Thousand Years* (London: Peter Owen, 2012), 138.

Chapter Five

1. Monica H. Green, "Introduction," *The Trotula: A Medieval Compendium of Women's Medicine*, ed. and trans. Monica H. Green (Philadelphia: University of Pennsylvania Press, 2002), 45–8; Laurence Moulinier-Brogi, "Esthétique et soins du corps dans les traités médicaux latins à la fin du Moyen Âge," *Médiévales* 46 (2004): 55–72; Michael McVaugh, *The Rational Surgery of the Middle Ages* (Florence: Edizioni del Galluzzo, 2006), 215–22.
2. Vivian Nutton, "Humoralism," in *Companion Encyclopedia of the History of Medicine*, vol. 1, eds. William Bynum and Roy Porter (London: Routledge, 1993), 281–91.
3. Juan A. Paniagua, *Studia Arnaldiana: Trabajos en torno a la obra médica de Arnau de Vilanova, c.1240–1311* (Barcelona: Fundación Uriach, 1994).
4. See the contributions in *The Body in Balance: Humoral Medicines in Practice*, eds. Peregrine Horden and Elisabeth Hsu (New York: Berghahn, 2013).
5. For a comprehensive view of medieval medicine, see Nancy Siraisi, *Medieval and Early Renaissance Medicine: An Introduction to Knowledge and Practice* (Chicago: Chicago University Press, 1990); Luke Demaitre, *Medieval medicine. The Art of Healing, from Head to Toe* (Santa Barbara, CA: Praeger, 2013).
6. Galen, *Tegni sive ars parva*, in *Articella*, fols. 158ra–159ra. Venice, 1483.
7. Haly Ibn Ridwan, *Commentum in microtegni Galieni*, in *Articella*, Venice, 1483, com. 31, fol. 159ra.
8. Taddeo Alderotti, *Commentum in microtegni Galieni*, Naples, 1522, II, fol. 40rb/va.
9. Turisanus (Pietro Torrigiani), *Plusquam commentum in parvam Galeni artem*. Venice, 1557, fol. 39v.
10. Gilbertus Anglicus, *Compendium medicinae*. Lyons, 1510, fol. 73va.
11. Bernard de Gordon, *Lilium medicinae*. Paris, 1542, fol. 74v.
12. Bernard de Gordon, *Lilium medicinae*, fol. 76v.
13. Arnau de Vilanova *Speculum medicinae*, in *Opera Omnia*, Basel, 1585, fol. 45.
14. Turisanus, *Plusquam commentum in parvam Galeni artem*, fol. 48r.
15. Taddeo Alderotti, *Expositio in Joannitii Isagogarum lib*. Venice, 1527, fol. 370rb.
16. Fernando Salmón, "The Body Inferred: Knowing the Body through the Dissection of Texts," in *A Cultural History of the Human Body in the Medieval Age*, ed. Linda Kalof (Oxford: Bloomsbury, 2014), 77–97.
17. Roger French and Andrew Cunningham, *Before Science: The Invention of the Friar's Natural Philosophy* (Aldershot: Scolar Press, 1996).
18. Haly Ibn Abbas, *Pantegni (Theorice)*, in Isaac Israeli, *Omnia opera Ysaac ... Galieni a Constantino compositum* (Lyons, 1515), fol. 9rb; Gilbertus Anglicus, *Compendium medicinae*, fol. 74ra/b; Bernard de Gordon, *Lilium medicinae*, fols. 74v–75r.

19. Joan Cadden, *Meanings of Sex Difference in the Middle Ages: Medicine, Science and Culture* (Cambridge: Cambridge University Press, 1993), 170–83; Monica H. Green, "Flowers, Poisons and Men: Menstruation in Medieval Western Europe," in *Menstruation: A Cultural History*, eds. Andrew Shail and Gillian Howie (Basingstoke: Palgrave Macmillan, 2005), 51–64; Katharine Park, "Medicine and Natural Philosophy: Naturalistic Traditions," in *The Oxford Handbook of Women and Gender in Medieval Europe*, eds. Judith Bennett and Ruth M. Karras (Oxford: Oxford University Press, 2013), 84–100.
20. Gilbertus Anglicus, *Compendium medicinae*, fol. 74rb.
21. Haly Ibn Abbas, *Pantegni (Theorice)*, fol. 9rb. The medical sources are dry at providing an explanation for this statement but the wider cultural frame that associates women's hair with sexuality has been analyzed by Roberta Milliken, *Ambiguous Locks: An Iconology of Hair in Medieval Art and Literature* (Jefferson, NC: McFarland, 2012).
22. Helen King, "Barbes, sang et genre: Afficher la différence dans le monde antique," in *Langages et métaphores du corps dans le monde antique*, eds. Jérôme Wilgaux and Véronique Dasen (Rennes: Presses Universitaire de Rennes, 2008), 153–68.
23. Haly Ibn Abbas, *Pantegni (Theorice)*, fol. 9rb; Cadden, *Meanings of Sex Difference*, 181.
24. Bernard de Gordon, *Lilium medicinae*, f. 74v–75r.
25. Turisanus, *Plusquam commentum in parvam Galeni artem*, f. 39v.
26. Gentile da Foligno. *Primus Avi. Canon. Avicenne … cum lucidissima Gentilis Fulgi. expositione* (Venice), 1520, III, fol. 17rb.
27. Gentile da Foligno posed a question about the hair as a sign of the brain complexion or of the complexion of the whole body. He concluded that at least secondarily, hair provided information about the general complexion of the body. Gentile da Foligno. *Primus Avi. Canon. Avicenne*, I, fol. 135rb.
28. Taddeo Alderotti, *Commentum in microtegni Galieni*, fol. 52ra.
29. Galen, *De complexionibus*, in *Opera Omnia (II)* (Venice, 1490), fols. 15vb–17va. Joseph Ziegler has convincingly argued that the fifteenth century witnessed an increase in the medical interest in physiognomy. Despite his suggestion that this concern might have started earlier, he has admitted that with a few exceptions, during the thirteenth and fourteenth centuries medical texts are silent on this theme. Joseph Ziegler, "Médecine et physiognomonie du XIVe au debut du XVIe siècle," *Médiévales* 46 (2004): 89–108. On the other hand, Walton O. Schalick has shown how independent they were from each other the cosmetical and the physiognomic traditions: "The Face Behind the Mask: 13th- and 14th-Century European Medical Cosmetology and Physiognomy," in *Medicine and the History of the Body*, eds. Yasuo Otsuka, Shizu Sakai, and Shigehisa Kuriyama (Tokyo: Ishiyaku EuroAmerica, 1999): 303–4.
30. Luis García Ballester, "The *New Galen*: A Challenge to Latin Galenism in Thirteenth-Century Montpellier," in *Text and Tradition. Studies in Ancient Medicine and its Transmission Presented to Jutta Kollesch*, eds. Klaus-Dietrich Fischer, Diethard Nickel, and Paul Potter (Leiden: Brill, 1998): 55–83. Reprinted in *Galen and Galenism*, eds. Jon Arrizabalaga, Montserrat Cabré, Lluís Cifuentes, and Fernando Salmón (Aldershot: Ashgate Variorum Reprints, 2002), essay V.
31. Taddeo Alderotti, *Commentum in microtegni Galieni*, fol. 53ra.
32. Gentile da Foligno. *Primus Avi. Canon. Avicenne*,III, fol. 9ra.
33. Turisanus, *Plusquam commentum in parvam Galeni artem*, fol. 47r.
34. Haly Ibn Ridwan, *Commentum in microtegni Galieni*, fol. 162rb.
35. Turisanus, *Plusquam commentum in parvam Galeni artem*, fol. 48r.
36. Turisanus, *Plusquam commentum in parvam Galeni artem*, fol. 48r; Gentile da Foligno. *Primus Avi. Canon. Avicenne*, III, fol. 24rb.

37. Bernard de Gordon, *Lilium medicinae*, fol. 80r.
38. Gentile da Foligno. *Primus Avi. Canon. Avicenne*, I, fol. 135vb; Guillaume de Lorris and Jean de Meun, *The Romance of the Rose*, trans. by Charles Dahlberg, 3rd ed. (Princeton, NJ: Princeton University Press, 1993), 34–5, verses 291–338.
39. Arnau de Vilanova *Speculum medicinae,* fol. 159.
40. Taddeo Alderotti, *Commentum in microtegni Galieni,* fol. 57rb
41. Galen, *De complexionibus*, fol. 15rb.
42. Gentile da Foligno. *Primus Avi. Canon. Avicenne*, I, fol. 135vb.
43. Turisanus, *Plusquam commentum in parvam Galeni artem*, fol. 48v.
44. Avicenna, *Liber Canonis tocius medicinae* (Venice, 1527), III, t. I, chap. 17, fol. 135ra/b.
45. Turisanus, *Plusquam commentum in parvam Galeni artem*, fol. 50v–52r.
46. Taddeo posed the *questio*: "Circa hoc queritur an in cerebro sicco vel calido velocior vel maior debeat esse calvities." Taddeo Alderotti, *Commentum in microtegni Galieni*, fol. 57va. And he concluded: "Ad hoc respondeo quod complexio calida et complexio sicca sunt equales in generando calvitium et si est ibi differencia non est tanta de qua sit curandum apud medicum." Ibid., fol. 57vb.
47. Haly Ibn Abbas, *Pantegni (Theorice)*, X, chap. 11, fol. 56vb.
48. Avicenna, *Liber Canonis*, III, t. I, chaps. 16 to 28, fols. 135rb–135vb. Haly Ibn Abbas, *Pantegni (Theorice)*, IX, chaps. 4 to 7, fols. 41va–42va.
49. See, for example Avicenna, *Liber Canonis*, IV, fen. VII, t. I, chaps. 2 and 16, fols. 377r/v and 379ra.
50. Michael McVaugh, "The *Experimenta* of Arnald of Villanova," *Journal of Medieval and Renaissance Studies* 1, no. 1 (1971): 15; English translation in Faith Wallis, ed., *Medieval Medicine: A Reader* (Toronto: Toronto University Press, 2010), 401.
51. See, for instance, Taddeo Alderotti. *I "consilia" di Taddeo Alderotti*, ed. Giuseppe Michele Nardi, pref. Pietro Capparoni (Torino: Edizioni Minerva Medica, 1937), 68–126, and Franck Collard, "Perfidus physicus ou inexpertus medicus: Le cas Jean de Grandville, médecin du comte Amédée VII de Savoie," in *Mires, Barbiers, Physiciens et Charlatans: Les Marges de la Médecine de l'Antiquité au XVIe siècle,* eds. Franck Collard and Évelyne Samama (Langres: Guéniot, 2004), 142.
52. A short description of each of the afflictions and the social and therapeutic attitudes toward them in Bernard de Gordon, Lilium, fols. 74r–85r.
53. Gilbertus Anglicus, *Compendium*, fol. 81vb.
54. *The Trotula*, 136–8.
55. Bernardo de Gordon, *Lilium medicinae*, fol. 84v.
56. Diane Wolfthal, "The Sexuality of the Medieval Comb," in *Thresholds of Medieval Visual Culture: Liminal Spaces*, eds. Elina Gertsman and Jill Stevenson (Woodbridge: Boydell Press, 2012), 176–94.
57. Pedro Gil Sotres, "Introducción," in *Arnaldi de Villanova Regimen Sanitatis ad Regem Aragonum*, eds. Luis García Ballester and Michael R. McVaugh (Barcelona: Fundació Noguera-Universitat de Barcelona, 1996), 759; *Arnaldi de Villanova Regimen Sanitatis ad Regem Aragonum*, 435, l. 87–91.
58. McVaugh, *The Rational Surgery*, 222–5.
59. *Ordinacions de la Casa i Cort de Pere el Cerimoniós*, eds. Francisco M. Gimeno, Daniel Gonzalbo, and Josep Trenchs (València: Universitat de València, 2009), 96–7. We are indebted to Lluís Cifuentes for this reference.
60. Carmel Ferragud, "Barbers in the Process of Medicalization in the Crown of Aragon," in *Medieval Urban Identity: Health, Economy and Regulation*, ed. Flocel Sabaté (Cambridge:

Cambridge Scholars Publishing, 2015), 143–65; Lluís Cifuentes, "La medicina en las galeras de la Corona de Aragón a finales de la Edad Media: la caja del barbero y sus libros," *Medicina e Historia*, 4ª época, 4 (2000): 1–15; Lluís Cifuentes, "La promoció intel·lectual i social dels barbers-cirurgians a la Barcelona medieval: l'obrador, la biblioteca i els béns de Joan Vicenç (fl. 1421–1464)," *Arxiu de Textos Catalans Antics* 19 (2000): 429–79.

61. Monica H. Green, "Documenting Medieval Women's Medical Practice," in *Practical Medicine from Salerno to the Black Death*, eds. Luis García Ballester et al. (Cambridge: Cambridge University Press, 1994), 344–5, reprinted in Monica Green, *Women's Healthcare in the Medieval West: Texts and Contexts* (Aldershot: Ashgate, 2000), essay II; Monica H. Green, *Making Women's Medicine Masculine: The Rise of Male Authority and Pre-Modern Gynaecology* (Cambridge: Cambridge University Press, 2008), 294–5.
62. *The Trotula*, 164–91; Montserrat Cabré, "From a Master to a Laywoman: A Feminine Manual of Self-Help," *Dynamis* 20 (2000): 371–93.
63. Montserrat Cabré, "Beautiful Bodies," in *A Cultural History of the Human Body in the Medieval Age*, ed. Linda Kalof (Oxford: Bloomsbury, 2014), 121–40.
64. *The Trotula*, 166–9.
65. McVaugh, *The Rational Surgery*, 223–4, n. 113.
66. Monica H. Green, "Documenting Medieval Women's Medical Practice," in *Practical Medicine from Salerno to the Black Death*, eds. Luis García-Ballester, Roger French, Jon Arrizabalaga, and Andrew Cunningham (Cambridge: Cambridge University Press, 1994), 322–52, reprinted in Monica H. Green, *Women's Healthcare in the Medieval West: Texts and Contexts* (Aldershot: Ashgate, 2000), essay II; Montserrat Cabré, "Women or Healers: Household Practices and the Categories of Health Care in Late Medieval Iberia," *Bulletin of the History of Medicine* 82, no. 1 (2008): 18–51.
67. Pierre Ruelle, *L'ornement des dames (Ornatus mulierum): Texte anglo-normand du XIIIème siècle* (Brussels: Presses Universitaires de Bruxelles, 1967), 36, 38, 44.
68. For instance, Ruelle, *L'ornement des dames*, 40, 44.
69. Monica H. Green, "The Possibilities of Literacy and the Limits of Reading: Women and the Gendering of Medical Literacy," in Monica H. Green, *Women's Healthcare in the Medieval West: Texts and Contexts* (Aldershot: Ashgate, 2000), first publication, essay VII, 45.

Chapter Six

1. See the discussion in Penny Howell Jolly, "Pubics and Privates: Body Hair in Late Medieval Art," in *The Meanings of Nudity in Medieval Art*, ed. Sherry C.M. Lindquist (Burlington, VT: Ashgate, 2012), 185–6; and Penny Howell Jolly, *Hair: Untangling a Social History* (Saratoga Springs, NY: Frances Young Tang Teaching Museum and Art Gallery, Skidmore College, 2004), 22. For more on medieval attitudes about gender, see Joan Cadden, *Meanings of Sex Difference in the Middle Ages* (Cambridge: Cambridge University Press, 1993).
2. *Hildegard of Bingen: On Natural Philosophy and Medicine*, trans. Margret Berger (Rochester, NY: D.S. Brewer, 1999). See Martha A. Brożyna, *Gender and Sexuality in the Middle Ages: A Medieval Source Documents Reader* (Jefferson, NC: McFarland and Company, 2005), 153.
3. 1 Corinthians 11:14–15. See also Veda Coble-Stevens, "Speech, Gesture, and Women's Hair in the Gospel of Luke and First Corinthians," in *The Symbolism of Vanitas in the Arts, Literature and Music: Comparative and Historical Studies*, ed. Liana De Girolami (Lewiston, NY: Edwin Mellen Press, 1992), 322–9.
4. Paul Edward Dutton, *Charlemagne's Mustache and Other Cultural Clusters of a Dark Age* (New York: Palgrave Macmillan, 2004), 15.

5. Ibid., 17.
6. Robert Bartlett, "Symbolic Meanings of Hair in the Middle Ages," *Transactions of the Royal Historical Society* s. 6, 4 (1994): 48.
7. Ibid., 50.
8. Ibid., 50–1, 58.
9. Kirsten A. Fenton, "Men and Masculinities in William of Malmesbury's Presentation of the Anglo-Norman Court," *Haskins Society Journal* 23 (2014): 115–24.
10. Tertullian, *On the Veiling of Virgins*, Ante-Nicene Fathers, vol. 4, trans. S. Thelwall, *The Ante-Nicene Fathers: Translations of the Fathers down to A.D. 325*, eds. Alexander Roberts and James Donaldson (Grand Rapids, MI: Eerdmans, 1987).
11. For more on the gendering of tomb sculptures, see Rachel Dressler, "Gender as Spectacle and Construct: The Gyvernay Effigies at St. Mary's Church, Limington," *Different Visions: A Journal of New Perspectives on Medieval Art*, no. 1 (2008): 1–24.
12. Gina L. Greco and Christine M. Rose, trans., *The Good Wife's Guide (Le Ménagier de Paris): A Medieval Household Guide* (Ithaca, NY: Cornell University Press, 2009), 57–8.
13. The best-known and most comprehensive examination of these sculptures is still Ilene H. Forsyth, *The Throne of Wisdom: Wood Sculptures of the Madonna in Romanesque France* (Princeton, NJ: Princeton University Press, 1972).
14. Maria Vassilaki, ed. *Images of the Mother of God: Perceptions of the Theotokos in Byzantium* (Aldershot: Ashgate), 2005.
15. Christine de Pizan, *A Medieval Woman's Mirror of Honor: The Treasury of the City of Ladies*, trans. Charity Cannon Willard (Tenalfy, NJ: Bard Hall Press, 1989).
16. *The Trotula: A Medieval Compendium of Women's Medicine*, ed. and trans. Monica H. Green (Philadelphia: University of Pennsylvania, 2001), 175.
17. See Thomas Kren, "Looking at Louis XII's Bathsheba," in *A Masterpiece Reconstructed: The Hours of Louis XII*, ed. Thomas Kren (Los Angeles: Getty Publications, 2005), 42–61.
18. Diane Wolfthal, "Sin or Sexual Pleasure? A Little-Known Nude Bather in a Flemish Book of Hours," in *The Meanings of Nudity in Medieval Art*, ed. Sherry Lindquist (London: Ashgate Press, 2012), 279–97.
19. Diane Wolfthal, "The Sexuality of the Medieval Comb," in *Thresholds of Medieval Visual Culture: Liminal Spaces*, eds. Elina Gertsman and Jill Stevenson (Woodbridge: Boydell Press, 2012), 176–94.
20. See the broader discussion of women combing their hair in Diane Wolfthal, *In and Out of the Marital Bed: Seeing Sex in Renaissance Europe* (New Haven, CT: Yale University Press, 2010), especially in chap. 2, "The Dressing Area of the Home," 43–73.
21. For the manuscript, see especially Timothy B. Husband, *The Art of Illumination: The Limbourg Brothers and the Belles Heures of Jean de France, Duc de Berry* (New York: Metropolitan Museum of Art, 2008). For further discussion about the Catherine cycle, see Martha Easton, "Uncovering the Meanings of Nudity in the *Belles Heures* of Jean, Duke of Berry," in *The Meanings of Nudity in Medieval Art*, ed. Sherry Lindquist (London: Ashgate Press, 2012), 149–81.
22. Joan A. Holladay, "Relics, Reliquaries, and Religious Women: Visualizing the Holy Virgins of Cologne," *Studies in Iconography* 18 (1997): 67–118. See also Scott B. Montgomery, *St. Ursula and the Eleven Thousand Virgins of Cologne: Relics, Reliquaries and the Visual Culture of Group Sanctity in Late Medieval Europe* (Bern: Peter Lang, 2010).
23. For an image, see Marian Bleeke, et al., "Women in/and Visual Culture," in *A Cultural History of Women in the Middle Ages*, ed. Kim Phillips (Oxford: Berg Publishers, 2013), 193, fig. 8.9.

24. Katherine L. French, "Genders and Material Cultures," in *The Oxford Handbook of Women and Gender in Medieval Europe*, eds. Judith M. Bennett and Ruth Mazo Karras (Oxford: Oxford University Press, 2013), 202–3.
25. Paula Gerson, ed. *The Pilgrim's Guide to Santiago de Compostela*, 2 vols (London: Harvey Miller, 1998), ii: 74–7.
26. Claudia Rückert, "A Reconsideration of the Woman with a Skull on the Puerta des las Platerías at Santiago de Compostela Cathedral," *Gesta* 51, no. 2 (2012): 129–46.
27. See Lorraine Kochanske Stock, *The Medieval Wild Man* (New York: Palgrave, 2005); and Timothy Husband, with the assistance of Gloria Gilore-House, *The Wild Man: Medieval Myth and Symbolism* (New York: Metropolitan Museum of Art, 1980).
28. Ruth Mazo Karras, "Holy Harlots: Prostitute Saints in Medieval Legend," *Journal of the History of Sexuality* 1, no. 1 (1990): 3–32. See also Martha Easton, "'Why Can't a Woman Be More Like a Man?' Transforming and Transcending Gender in the Lives of Female Saints," in *The Four Modes of Seeing: Approaches to Medieval Imagery in Honor of Madeline Harrison Caviness*, eds. Elizabeth Carson Pastan, Ellen M. Shortell, and Evelyn Staudinger Lane (London: Ashgate Press, 2009), 333–47.
29. For more on this playing card with additional bibliography, see Husband, *The Wild Man*, 167–9 and color plate V.
30. In the case of Mary Magdalene, her identification as a prostitute developed as various biblical stories began to coalesce around her. For more on Mary Magdalene, see for example Katherine Ludwig Jansen, *The Making of the Magdalen: Preaching and Popular Devotion in the Later Middle Ages* (Princeton, NJ: Princeton University Press, 2000) and Susan Haskins, *Mary Magdalen: Myth and Metaphor* (New York: Riverhead Books, 1993).
31. For more on the vulva on pilgrimage badge, see Sarah Salih, "Female Sexualities," *Different Visions: A Journal of New Perspectives on Medieval Art*, no. 5 (2014): 15–19. For the secular badges in general, see especially Nicola McDonald, "Introduction," in *Medieval Obscenities*, ed. Nicola McDonald (Rochester, NY: York Medieval Press, 2006), especially 2–11; Jos Koldeweij, "Shameless and Naked Images: Obscene Badges as Parodies of Popular Devotion," in *Art and Architecture of Late Medieval Pilgrimage in Northern Europe and the British Isles*, eds. Sarah Blick and Rita Tekippe (Leiden: Brill, 2005), 493–510; and Jan Baptist Bedeaux, "Laatmiddeleeuwse sexuele amuletten," in *Annus Quadrigia Mundi: Opstellen over Middeleeuwse Kunst* (Utrecht: De Walburg, 1989).
32. Jolly, "Pubics and Privates."
33. For more on this, see especially Leo Steinberg, *The Sexuality of Christ in Renaissance Art and Modern Oblivion*, 2nd ed. (Chicago: University of Chicago Press, 1997).
34. Jolly, "Pubics and Privates," 190.
35. *The Hours of Mary of Burgundy*, commentary by Erik Inglis (London: Harvey Miller, 1995). See also Andrea Pearson, *Envisioning Gender in Burgundian Devotional Art, 1350–1530: Experience, Authority, Resistance* (Aldershot: Ashgate, 2005), and Jennifer Kolpacoff Deane, "Pious Domesticities," in *The Oxford Handbook of Women and Gender in Medieval Europe*, eds. Judith M. Bennett and Ruth Mazo Karras (Oxford: Oxford University Press, 2013), 274–5.
36. Bartlett, "Symbolic Meanings of Hair," 45.
37. Geoffrey Chaucer, *The Canterbury Tales*, trans. David Wright (Oxford: Oxford University Press, 1985), 20.
38. Ilse E. Friesen, *The Female Crucifix: Images of St. Wilgefortis Since the Middle Ages* (Ontario: Wilfrid Laurier University Press, 2001); Ilse E. Friesen, "Saints as Helpers in Dying: The Hairy Holy Women Mary Magdalene, Mary of Egypt, and Wilgefortis in

the Iconography of the Late Middle Ages," in *Death and Dying in the Middle Ages*, eds. Edelgard E. DuBruck and Barbara I. Gusick (New York: Peter Lang, 1999), 239–53; Elizabeth Nightlinger, "The Female Imitatio Christi and Medieval Popular Religion: The Case of St. Wilgefortis," in *Representations of the Feminine in the Middle Ages*, ed. Bonnie Wheeler (Dallas, TX: Academia Press, 1993); and Jean Gessler, *La Légende de sainte Wilgeforte ou Ontcommer: La vierge miraculeusement barbue* (Brussels: Editions Universelle, 1938).

39. For more on female cross-dressing, see especially Valerie R. Hotchkiss, *Clothes Make the Man: Female Cross Dressing in Medieval Europe* (New York: Garland, 1996).
40. Jeffrey J. Andresen, "Rapunzel: The Symbolism of the Cutting of Hair," *Journal of the American Psychoanalytic Association* 28 (1980): 69–88.
41. Heldris de Cornuälle, *Le Roman de Silence*, trans. Regina Psaki (New York: Garland, 1991). See the discussion of this in Easton, "Why Can't a Woman...," 341–2. See also Peggy McCracken, "'The Boy Who Was a Girl': Reading Gender in the *Roman de Silence*," *The Romanic Review* 85, no. 4 (1994): 517–36.
42. *Procès en nulité de la condemnation de Jeanne d'Arc*, ed. Pierre Duparc (Paris: Klincksieck, 1977–1989), 1, 432–3, as reproduced and discussed in Hotchkiss, *Clothes Make the Man*, 59. See also Susan Schibanoff, "True Lies: Transvestism and Idolatry in the Trial of Joan of Arc," in *Fresh Verdicts on Joan of Arc*, eds. Bonnie Wheeler and Charles T. Wood (New York: Garland, 1996), 31–60.
43. There are an increasing number of publications exploring the many meanings of Sheela-na-gigs, including Barbara Freitag, *Sheela-na-gigs: Unravelling an Enigma* (London: Routledge, 2004) and Jørgen Andersen, *The Witch on the Wall: Medieval Erotic Sculpture in the British Isles* (Copenhagen: Rosenkilde and Bagger, 1977).
44. See Sigmund Freud, "Fetischismus," in *Gesammelte Werke*, eds. Anna Freud et al. (London: Imago, 1940–1952), 14, 317, as well as the discussion in Hotchkiss, *Clothes Make the Man*, 27, and additional bibliography, 152, n. 66.
45. Victoria Sherrow, *Encyclopedia of Hair: A Cultural History* (Westport, CT: Greenwood Press, 2006), 271–3.
46. For more on this point, see Robert Mills, "The Significance of the Tonsure," in *Holiness and Masculinity in the Middle Ages*, eds. P.H. Collum and Katherine J. Lewis (Toronto: University of Toronto, 1994), 109–26. See also Carl Phelpstead, "Hair Today, Gone Tomorrow: Hair Loss, the Tonsure, and Masculinity in Medieval Iceland," *Scandinavian Studies* 85, no. 1 (2013): 1–19.

Chapter Seven

1. My position differs a little in this respect from Robert Bartlett's: see his "Symbolic Meanings of Hair in the Middle Ages," *Transactions of the Royal Historical Society* s. 6, 4 (December 1994), 43–4; and "Illustrating Ethnicity in the Middle Ages," in *The Origins of Racism in the West*, eds. Miriam Eliav-Feldon, Benjamin Isaac, and Joseph Ziegler (Cambridge: Cambridge University Press, 2009), 137. His point in the latter that "in its malleability and responsiveness to fashion, hair is in fact more like clothes than like the body," holds well for the early and high Middle Ages, but does not convey the entirety of perspectives especially from the late twelfth century and later. In acknowledgment of my scholarly debts in producing this chapter, I should particularly like to thank Roberta Milliken for her wise advice.
2. Patrick Geary, "Ethnic Identity as a Situational Construct in the Early Middle Ages," *Mitteilungen der Anthropologischen Gesellschaft in Wien* 113 (1983): 15–26, reprinted in *Medieval Perspectives* 3, no. 2 (Fall 1988): 3. On early medieval ethnic diversity and problems

of interpretation, see further Walter Pohl, "Conceptions of Ethnicity in Early Medieval Studies," *Archaeologia Polona* 29 (1991): 39–49; explored in detail in Walter Pohl and Helmut Reimitz, eds., *Strategies of Distinction: The Construction of Ethnic Communities, 300–800* (Leiden: Brill, 1998), and Walter Pohl and Gerda Heydemann, eds., *Strategies of Identification: Ethnicity and Religion in Early Medieval Europe* (Turnhout: Brepols, 2013).

3. Geraldine Heng, "The Invention of Race in the European Middle Ages I: Race Studies, Modernity, and the Middle Ages," and "The Invention of Race in the European Middle Ages II: Locations of Medieval Race," *Literature Compass* 8, no. 5 (2011): 324–5; see also 332.

4. Bartlett, "Illustrating Ethnicity," 141.

5. This is not the place for a detailed discussion of terminology, but note that debate exists over whether medievalists should use the term "race" given that physical-anthropological phenotypes began to emerge in human typologies only in the late seventeenth century. In medieval contexts "race" was a late medieval French word meaning "stock," "breed," or "bloodline" used of hunting dogs, falcons, and horses. From the mid-fifteenth century its first uses in describing humans referred not to ethnic types but social rank: they were to identify noble humans and thus make claims for the inborn qualities of aristocracy. See Charles de Miramon, "Noble Dogs, Noble Blood: The Invention of the Concept of Blood in the Late Middle Ages," in *Origins of Racism*, eds. Miriam Eliav-Feldon, Benjamin Isaac, and Joseph Ziegler (Cambridge: Cambridge University Press, 2009), 200–16. Opposing views on terminology include William Chester Jordan, "Why Race?," *Journal of Medieval and Early Modern Studies* 31, no. 1 (2001): 165–73; and Heng, "Invention of Race," while Miriam Eliav-Feldon, Benjamin Isaac, and Joseph Ziegler's, "Introduction," to *Origins of Racism*, 1–31, helps clarify the subject. Also, for the early period, see Stephen J. Harris, "An Overview of Race and Ethnicity in Pre-Norman England," *Literature Compass* 5, no. 4 (2008): 740–54. Less debate, perhaps wrongly, surrounds the validity of "ethnicity," a word deriving from ancient Greek *ethos*. The chief terms for human groupings in medieval Latin texts are *gens, natio, populus,* and *homines*, which do not lend themselves to forming abstract nouns. There is no perfect solution, but this chapter will use "ethnicity" as an umbrella term and "proto-racial" for certain later medieval shifts toward attention to the body especially from the thirteenth century.

6. See Geary, "Ethnic Identity," 4, who describes Prům's passage as already "much discussed" in earlier German scholarship. It also informs Robert Bartlett's discussion in *The Making of Europe: Conquest, Colonization and Cultural Change 950–1350* (Princeton, NJ: Princeton University Press, 1993), 197 and 241, and "Medieval and Modern Concepts of Race and Ethnicity," *Journal of Medieval and Early Modern Studies* 31, no. 1 (2001): 41.

7. Geary, "Ethnic Identity," 7–8 and 10–11 (quoting Sidney Mintz in the latter).

8. Walter Pohl, "Telling the Difference: Signs of Ethnic Identity," in *Strategies of Distinction*, eds. Walter Pohl and Helmut Reimitz (Leiden: Brill, 1998), 17–69 (on hair at pp. 51–61).

9. Bartlett, "Symbolic Meanings of Hair," 45. For early medieval hair see also Paul Dutton, *Charlemagne's Mustache and Other Cultural Clusters of a Dark Age* (New York: Palgrave Macmillan, 2004), 3–42.

10. Isidore of Seville, *Etymologies*, trans. Stephen A. Barney, W.J. Lewis, and J.A. Beach (Cambridge: Cambridge University Press, 2006), "Introduction," 3; and bk. 9, sec. 2, para. 65, p. 195. His book on the parts of the world ("The Globe") echoes that general lack of attention to hair, while also repeating his explanation of Albanians, bk. 14. sec. 3, para. 34, p. 288.

11. Ibid., bk. 19, sec. 23, para. 7, p. 386.
12. Peter Biller, "Proto-racial Thought in Medieval Science," in *Origins of Racism*, eds. Miriam Eliav-Feldon, Benjamin Isaac, and Joseph Ziegler (Cambridge: Cambridge University Press, 2009), 157–80.
13. Claire Weeda, "Images of Ethnicity in Later Medieval Europe" (Unpublished PhD thesis, University of Amsterdam, 2012), 9. For an overview of her main arguments, see Claire Weeda, "Ethnic Identification and Stereotypes in Western Europe, c. 1100–1300," *History Compass* 12, no. 7 (2014): 586–606.
14. Bartlett, *Making of Europe*, 236–42; Peter Biller, "Views of Jews from Paris around 1300: Christian or Scientific?" in *Christianity and Judaism*, ed. Diana Wood (Oxford: Blackwell, 1992), 187–207; Peter Biller, "A 'Scientific' View of Jews from Paris around 1300," *Micrologus* 9 (2001): 137–68; David Nirenberg, "Was there Race Before Modernity? The Example of 'Jewish' Blood in Late Medieval Spain," in *Origins of Racism*, eds. Miriam Eliav-Feldon, Benjamin Isaac and Joseph Ziegler (Cambridge: Cambridge University Press, 2009), 232–64; John Edwards, "Beginnings of a Scientific Theory of Race? Spain, 1450–1600," in *From Iberia to Diaspora: Studies in Sephardic History and Culture*, eds. Yedida K. Stillman and Norman K. Stillman (Leiden: Brill, 1999), 179–96; Helen Rawlings, *Church, Religion and Society in Early Modern Spain* (Basingstoke: Palgrave, 2002), 1–26.
15. Suzanne Conklin Akbari, *Idols in the East: European Representations of Islam and the Orient, 1100–1450* (Ithaca, NY: Cornell University Press, 2009), 42–6, details sections in which Bartholomaeus follows or departs from Isidore on human types.
16. The quotation is from John Trevisa's late fourteenth-century Middle English translation of Bartholomaeus's book, but with spelling updated: John Trevisa, *On the Properties of Things: John Trevisa's Translation of "Bartholomaeus Anglicus, De Proprietatibus Rerum." A Critical Text*, eds. M.C. Seymour et al., 3 vols. (Oxford: Clarendon Press, 1975–1978), 1, 288–90; see also 169–70.
17. Giraldus Cambrensis, *The Topography of Ireland*, trans. Thomas Forester, in *The Historical Works of Giraldus Cambrensis*, ed. Thomas Wright (London: H.G. Bohn, 1863), bk. 3, chap. 10, p. 124. The Bodley MS (ca. 1260) is one of four surviving illustrated copies, all closely related, the earliest of which are dated to around 1200. The Bodley MS appears to be a copy of Dublin, NLI, MS 700, ca. 1200: See Bartlett, "Illustrating Ethnicity," 151.
18. Giraldus, *Topography*, bk. 3, chap. 10, p. 125.
19. The scandal surrounding the courtly fashion for long hair and perceptions of effeminacy is studied in many places, including Frank Barlow, *William Rufus* (London: Methuen, 1983); Bartlett, "Meanings of Hair," 50–2 and 58–9; and Pauline Stafford, "The Meanings of Hair in the Anglo-Norman Worlds: Masculinity, Reform, and Nationality Identity," in *Saints, Scholars, and Politicians: Gender as a Tool in Medieval Studies*, eds. Mathilde van Dijk and Renée Nip (Turnhout: Brepols, 2005), 153–71.
20. Gildas, *The Ruin of Britain and Other Works*, ed. and trans. Michael Winterbottom (Chichester: Phillimore and Co., 1978), bk. 19, chap. 1, pp. 25 and 94–5.
21. Giraldus, *Topography*, bk. 3, chap. 26, p. 139.
22. Philomena Connolly, ed., "The Enactments of the 1297 Parliament," in *Law and Disorder in Thirteenth-Century Ireland: The Dublin Parliament of 1297*, ed. James Lydon (Dublin: Four Courts, 1997), 158–61. For discussion, see Seán Duffy, "The Problem of Degeneracy," in the same volume, pp. 87–106, especially 89; and Bartlett, "Symbolic Meanings of Hair," 46.
23. Connolly, ed. "Enactments," pp. 158–61.
24. Katharine Simms, "Gaelic Warfare in the Middle Ages," in *A Military History of Ireland*, eds. Thomas Bartlett and Keith Jeffery (Cambridge: Cambridge University Press, 1996), 101.

25. Laurent Vital, "Archduke Ferdinand's Visit to Kinsale in Ireland," trans. Dorothy Convery, introduction by Hiram Morgan, for *CELT: Corpus of Electronic Texts: A Project of University College, Cork*, http://www.ucc.ie/celt/published/T500000-001/index.html (accessed June 20, 2016), 284–8; Durer's sketch of three mustachioed galloglass warriors and two kerns with shaggy blond glibs from 1521 is reproduced in Seán Duffy, *The World of the Galloglass* (Dublin: Four Courts Press, 2007), 158.
26. See http://www.english.cam.ac.uk/ceres/haphazard/extra/63-144-57-2/notes.html (accessed June 20, 2016).
27. Gerald of Wales, *The Journey Through Wales*, in *The Journey Through Wales and the Description of Wales*, trans. Lewis Thorpe (Harmondsworth: Penguin, 1978), bk. 11, chap. 4, pp. 178–9.
28. Ibid., bk. 1, chap. 11, p. 238.
29. Ibid., bk. 1, chap. 15, p. 245. For a detailed analysis of Gerald's multifaceted "ethnographic achievement," see Robert Bartlett, *Gerald of Wales, 1146–1223* (Oxford: Clarendon Press, 1982), 178–210; on climate and environment, see 201–5.
30. Among large numbers of works summarizing these themes, see Robert Chazan, *The Jews of Medieval Western Christendom, 1000–1500* (Cambridge: Cambridge University Press, 2006), 43–76.
31. Sara Lipton, *Images of Intolerance: The Representation of Jews and Judaism in the Bible moralisée* (Berkeley: University of California Press, 1999), 16; see also Sara Lipton, *Dark Mirror: The Medieval Origins of Anti-Semitic Iconography* (New York: Metropolitan Books, 2014). Other studies on Jewish people in later medieval artistic representation include Ruth Mellinkoff, *Outcasts: Signs of Otherness in Northern European Art of the Later Middle Ages*, 2 vols. (Berkeley: University of California Press, 1993), passim; Debra Higgs Strickland, *Saracens, Demons, and Jews: Making Monsters in Medieval Art* (Princeton, NJ: Princeton University Press, 2003), 96–155.
32. On dark hair, Lipton, *Dark Mirror*, 10, 118, 120, 175, 185, and 208.
33. Mellinkoff, *Outcasts*, 1:59–94 (vol. 2 contains the associated images); Strickland, *Saracens, Demons, and Jews*, 105–6; problematized in Lipton, *Dark Mirror*, 16–45, 57, 77–80, 158–9, 173.
34. E.M. Rose, *The Murder of William of Norwich: The Origins of the Blood Libel in Medieval Europe* (Oxford: Oxford University Press, 2015); R. Po-Chia Hsia, *Trent 1475: Stories of a Ritual Murder Trial*, 2nd ed. (New Haven, CT: Yale University Press, 1996).
35. On Jewish beards, see Lipton, *Dark Mirror*, 7, 48–50, 59–60, 105–7, 141–5, 151–3.
36. Michael Seymour, "Manuscript Portraits of Chaucer and Hoccleve," *The Burlington Magazine* 124, no. 955 (1982): 618–23; fifteenth-century portraits of Edward III and other English kings from William the Conqueror to Henry V are found on the rood screen of York Minster, ca. 1420, https://yorkminster.org/visit-york-minster/minster-treasures/kings-039-screen.html (accessed June 22, 2016).
37. Trevisa, *On the Properties of Things*, vol. 1, bk. 5, chap. 15, pp. 196–7.
38. Biller, "Scientific View of Jews," 144.
39. Mellinkoff, *Outcasts: Signs*, 1:147–59 on red hair in general and 1:150–4 on Judas's coloring in particular.
40. Strickland, *Saracens, Demons, and Jews*, 232–6.
41. Trevisa, *On the Properties of Things*, vol. 1, bk. 4, chap. 1, p. 133 and bk. 4, chap. 2, p. 136.
42. Strickland, *Saracens, Demons, and Jews*, 165–92.
43. Akbari, *Idols in the East*, 114; see also 155–63. Akbari refines influential earlier studies, such as Jeffrey Jerome Cohen, "On Saracen Enjoyment: Some Fantasies of Race in Late Medieval France and England," *Journal of Medieval and Early Modern Studies* 31, no. 1

44. Biller, "Proto-Racial Thought," 171; Weeda, "Images of Ethnicity," pp. 88–9.
45. Trevisa, *On the Properties of Things*, vol. 1, bk. 5, chap. 15, p. 197.
46. Ibid., vol. 2, bk. 15, chap. 50, pp. 752–3. His subsequent chapter on Ethiopia, "blue men's land," further emphasizes the effects of the hot sun on "toasting" bodies to dark hues, as well as describing some monstrous peoples also to be found there (vol. 2, bk. 15, chap. 52, p. 754). See also vol. 1, bk. 4, chap. 2, p. 136: women of cold lands "bear children with [white] skins, that have long, yellow, soft and straight hair. The contrary is in hot lands there women bear children that be black and have little hair and crisp, as in blue men's land."
47. Strickland, *Saracens, Demons, and Jews*, 79, also 85–6, 88, 89, 90, and 93.
48. Marco Polo, *The Description of the World*, eds. A.C. Moule and P. Pelliot, 2 vols. (London: George Routledge and Sons, 1938), vol. 1 chap. 192, pp. 432–3.
49. For example, see Strickland, *Saracens, Demons, and Jews*, 80–3.
50. John of Plano Carpini, *History of the Mongols*, in *Mission to Asia*, ed. Christopher Dawson, trans. "a nun of Stanbrook abbey" (New York: Harper and Row, 1966), bk. 2, chap. 2, pp. 6–7. Travel writing on Asia is described and analyzed in the present author's *Before Orientalism: Asian Peoples and Cultures in European Travel Writing*, (Philadelphia: University of Pennsylvania Press, 2014), and the many earlier sources cited therein.
51. William of Rubruck, *Journey of William of Rubruck*, in *Mission to Asia*, ed. Dawson, bk. 4, chap. 1–3, pp. 101–2 and bk. 29, chap. 19, p. 162.
52. Riccoldo Da Montecroce, *The Book of Pilgrimage*, in *A Christian Pilgrim in Medieval Iraq: Riccoldo da Montecroce's Encounter with Islam*, trans. Rita George-Tvrtković (Turnhout: Brepols, 2012), 188.
53. Carpini, *History*, bk. 5, chap. 10, p. 22.
54. Ibid., bk. 5, chap. 14, p. 23 and bk. 5, chap. 31, p. 31.
55. Marco Polo, *Description of the World*, vol. 1, ch. 72, pp. 180–1.
56. Rubruck, *Journey of William Rubruck*, bk. 28, chap. 11, p. 153.
57. On the importance of headgear in representations of eastern peoples, see Joyce Kubiski, "Orientalizing Costume in Early Fifteenth-Century French Manuscript Painting (*Cité des Dames* Master, Limbourg Brothers, Boucicaut Master, and Bedford Master)," *Gesta* 40, no. 2 (2001): 161–80. I am grateful to Tania Colwell of the Australian National University for this reference.
58. Riccoldo, *Book of Pilgrimage*, 199–200.
59. "Sir John Mandeville," *The Book of John Mandeville with Related Texts*, ed. Iain Macleod Higgins (Indianapolis, IN: Hackett, 2011), chap. 32, p. 176.
60. Timothy Husband, with the assistance of Gloria Gilmore-House, *The Wild Man: Medieval Myth and Symbolism* (New York: Metropolitan Museum of Art, 1980), 13.

Chapter Eight

1. For a recent survey of sumptuary legislation, see John Block Friedman, "Coats, Collars, and Capes: Royal Fashions for Animals in the Early Modern Period," in *Medieval Clothing and Textiles*, vol. 12, eds. Robin Netherton and Gale R. Owen-Crocker (Woodbridge: Boydell and Brewer, 2016), 61–94.
2. Quoted in Louise M. Sylvester et al., eds. and trans., *Medieval Dress and Textiles in Britain: A Multilingual Sourcebook* (Woodbridge: Boydell Press, 2014), 187.

3. See J.M. Wallace-Hadrill, *The Long Haired Kings* (New York: Barnes and Noble, 1962); and Jean Hoyoux, "Reges Criniti: Chevalures, tonsures et scalps chez les Merovingians," *Revue belge de philologie et d'histoire* 26, no. 3 (1948): 479–508.
4. See Giles Constable, "Introduction on Beards in the Middle Ages," in Burchard of Belleveaux's *Apologia de Barbis*, in Corpus Christianorum, Continuatio Medievalis, LXII, ed. R.B.C. Huygens (Turnholt: Brepols, 1985), 47–150, especially 63–4.
5. Ibid., 69 and 102.
6. Geoffrey Chaucer, *The Canterbury Tales*, in *The Riverside Chaucer*, ed. Larry Benson (Boston, MA: Houghton Mifflin, 1987), I (A) 2415–16.
7. Ibid., I (A) 81.
8. Robert Bartlett, "Symbolic Meanings of Hair in the Middle Ages," *The Transactions of the Royal Historical Society* s. 6, 4 (1993): 43.
9. See particularly Henri Platelle, "Le problème de scandale: Les nouvelles modes masculines aux XIe et XIIe siècles," *Revue belge de philologie et d'histoire* 53, no. 4 (1975): 1071–96. Additional documentation appears in Bartlett, "Symbolic Meanings of Hair," 50–2.
10. Quoted in Sylvester, ed. and trans., *Medieval Dress and Textiles*, 131 and 133.
11. Paul E. Beichner, "Absolon's Hair," *Mediaeval Studies* 12 (1950): 222–33, and the same author's ed., *Aurora Petri Rigae Biblia Versificata*, Vol. 1 (Notre Dame, IN: University of Notre Dame Press, 1965), 273, lines 49–50.
12. See Michael R. Solomon, *The Literature of Misogyny in Medieval Spain: The "Archipreste" de Talavera and the Spill* (New York: Cambridge University Press, 1997), 188, n. 10.
13. Ibid., 72. The connection of sexual activity and male baldness derives from the Pseudo-Aristotelian *Problemata*. See Bruno Roy, "Pilosité et horripilation dans les *Problèmes d'Aristote*, d'Evrart de Conty," in Chantal Connochie-Bourgne, ed., *La chevalure dans la littérature et l'art du Moyen Âge* [Senefiance 50] (Aix-en-Provence: Publications de l'Université de Provence, 2004) 357–63, especially 360. See here John Block Friedman, "Eyebrows, Hairlines, and 'Hairs Less in Sight': Female Depilation in Late Medieval Europe," in Robin Netherton and Gale R. Owen-Crocker, eds., *Medieval Clothing and Textiles*, vol. 14 (Woodbridge: Boydell and Brewer, 2018), 81–111, especially note 54.
14. Bernard of Gordon, *Lilio de medicina*, eds., John Cull and Brian Dutton (Madison, WI: Hispanic Seminary of Medieval Studies, 1991), 75.
15. For the pulling of Christ's hair, see James H. Marrow, *Passion Iconography in Northern European Art of the Late Middle Ages and Early Renaissance* (Kortrijk: Van Ghemmert, 1979), 171–89. For more on baldness, see Ruth Mellinkoff, *Outcasts: Signs of Otherness in Northern European Art of the Late Middle Ages* (Berkeley: University of California Press, 1993), I, 181–94.
16. Pax Bavarica 71, in Ludwig Weiland, ed., *Monumenta Germaniae Historica: Constitutiones et acta publica imperatorem et regum* II (Hanover: Impensis Bibliopoli Hahnianai, 1896) no. 427, 577.
17. Middle English quotation in Sylvia Thrupp, *The Merchant Class of Medieval London 1300–1500* (Ann Arbor: University of Michigan Press, 1962), 150.
18. Chaucer, *The Canterbury Tales*, I (A) 109 and 589–90.
19. Seigfried Helbling, *Der kleine Lucidarius*, in *Peasant Life in Old German Epic*, trans. Clair Hayden Bell (New York: Norton, 1968), 5.
20. Neidhart, *Die Lieder Neidharts*, ed. Edmund Wiessner (Tübingen: Niemeyer, 1984). Translations are by Kathrin Giogoli and Michael Twomey communicated to me by email in 2009.
21. Ibid., 121, stanza 4.
22. Published by Gerhard Jaritz, "The Material Culture of the Peasantry in the Late Middle Ages: 'Image' and 'Reality,'" in Del Sweeney, ed., *Agriculture in the Middle Ages: Technology,*

Practice, and Representation (Philadelphia: University of Pennsylvania Press, 1995), 165–88, especially 168, fig. 21.
23. Wiessner, *Die Lieder Neidharts*, 184–5, stanzas 4–5.
24. Ibid., 66, stanzas 7 and 152, stanza 7.
25. See Heidelberg, Universitäts bibliothek Cpg 848, LXIII, fol. 273r of about 1315. On particoloring associated with social interlopers, see John Block Friedman, "The Iconography of Dagged Clothing and its Reception by Moralist Writers," in Robin Netherton and Gale R. Owen-Crocker, eds., *Medieval Clothing and Textiles*, vol. 9 (Woodbridge: Boydell and Brewer, 2013), 121–38, especially 128 and 134, and Michel Pastoureau, *The Devil's Cloth: A History of Stripes and Striped Fabrics*, trans. Jody Gladding (New York: Columbia University Press, 2001).
26. Wernher the Gardener, *Meier Helmbrecht*, in *Wernher der Gartenere, Helmbrecht*, trans. Linda B. Parshall (New York: Garland, 1987), 3, lines 9–17.
27. Ibid., 19–21, lines 268–73, 275.
28. Ibid., 125, lines 1883–5, 1890–1, 1896, 1898–1900.
29. See Montserrat Cabré, "Beautiful Bodies," in *A Cultural History of the Human Body in the Middle Ages*, ed. Linda Kalof (Oxford: Berg, 2010), 127–47.
30. Matthew of Vendôme, *Ars versificatoria*, in *Matthew of Vendôme: The Art of Versification*, ed. and trans. Aubrey E. Galyon (Ames: Iowa State University Press, 1980), 43, sec. 56.
31. Giovanni Boccaccio, *Teseide*, in *The Book of Theseus: Teseida delle Nozze d'Emilia by Giovanni Boccaccio*, trans. Bernadette Marie McCoy (New York: Medieval Text Association, 1974), 323–24.
32. See Monica H. Green, ed. and trans., *The Trotula: A Medieval Compendium of Women's Medicine*, (Philadelphia: University of Pennsylvania Press, 2001), 169–71 and 173–5. See generally Myriam Rolland-Perrin, *Blonde comme l'or, La chevelure féminine au Moyen Âge* (Aix-en-Provence: Publications de l'Université de Provence, 2010).
33. Giovanni Boccaccio, *Il Corbaccio*, in *The Corbaccio, Giovanni Boccaccio*, ed. and trans. Anthony K. Cassell (Urbana: University of Illinois Press, 1975), 25.
34. Ibid., 44.
35. Ibid., 25, 44, 158–9.
36. For the *pastourelle* genre, see John Block Friedman, *Brueghel's Heavy Dancers: Transgressive Clothing, Class, and Culture in the Late Middle Ages* (Syracuse, NY: Syracuse University Press, 2010), 8–45.
37. "Mentre per una ribiera," in *The Medieval Pastourelle*, ed. and trans. William D. Paden (Garland Library of Medieval Literature 34–5, ser. A) (New York: Garland, 1987), 435 and 437. See also Friedman, *Brueghel's Heavy Dancers*, 93–4.
38. Juan Ruiz, *The Book of Good Love*, trans. Elizabeth O. Macdonald (London: Dent and Tuttle, 1999), 113. See also Friedman, *Brueghel's Heavy Dancers*, 83–7.
39. Quoted in Patrizia Bettella, *The Ugly Woman: Transgressive Aesthetic Models in Italian Poetry from the Middle Ages to the Baroque* (Toronto: University of Toronto Press, 2005), 89. The Mauro poem is quoted in Friedman, *Brueghel's Heavy Dancers*, 95–6.
40. See, for example, Cabré, "Beautiful Bodies," 132; and Herman Braet, "'A thing most brutish': The Image of the Peasant in Old French Literature," in Sweeney ed., *Agriculture in the Middle Ages*, 191–204, especially 195.
41. The first quote is in the anonymous poem "From Saint-Quentin to Cambrai" in *The Medieval Pastourelle*, 229, my emphasis; the second quote is in the anonymous poem "From Metz, in the cool the other day," ibid., 256.
42. Juan Ruiz, *The Book of Good Love*, 113.

43. "Twenty-three Characteristics of Beautiful Women" in *La Parnasse érotique du XVe siècle: Recueil des pièces,* ed. J.M. Angot (Geneva: Slatkine, 1978), 7–9, n. 1. See also Friedman, "Eyebrows, Hairlines, and 'Hairs Less in Sight'," 92 and notes.
44. I use here the edition of Arnold's treatise by Montserrat Cabré i Pairet, "La Cura del Cos Femení i la Medicina Medieval de Tradició Llatina: Els Tractas 'De Ornatu' i 'De decorationibus mulierum' Atribuïts a Arnau de Vilanova, 'Tròtula' de Mestre Joan, i 'Flors del tresor de beutat,' Atribuït a Manuel Díeç de Calatayud (Unpublished PhD diss., University of Barcelona, 1996), 199. "Depilatio et clarificatio dominabus multum sunt necessaria et secundum rationem convenit eastenere faciem claram, fulgentem et pulchram ..." See also Geneviève Dumas, "Le soin des cheveux et des poils: Quelques pratiques cosmétiques (XIII–XVI siècles," in Connochie-Bourgne, ed., *La chevalure dans la littérature et l'art du Moyen Âge,* 129–41.
45. This translation of *De ornatu mulierum* is quoted in Montserrat Cabré, "From a Master to a Laywoman: A Feminine Model of Self-Help," *Dynamis* 20 (2000): 387.
46. *Vergel de señores.* These recipes were kindly supplied me by Montserrat Cabré.
47. Eric W. Naylor and Jerry R. Rank, eds. and trans., *The Archpriest of Talavera by Alonso Martínez de Toledo: Dealing with the Vices of Wicked Women and the Complexions of Men* (Tempe: Arizona Center for Medieval and Renaissance Studies, 2013), 112, 109.
48. Boccaccio, *Il Corbaccio,* 42.
49. Quoted in John Block Friedman, "Chaucer's Pardoner, Rutebeuf's 'Dit de l'Herberie,' The 'Dit du Mercier' and Cultural History," *Viator* 38, no. 1 (2007): 316.
50. Helen Cooper, "The Miller's Tale," in Helen Cooper, ed., *The Canterbury Tales,* Oxford Guides to Chaucer (Oxford: Oxford University Press, 1989), 106.
51. Chaucer, *The Canterbury Tales,* I (A) 3243 and 3245–6.
52. Ibid., I (A) 3310. For more on Chaucer and class, see Derek S. Brewer, "Class Distinction in Chaucer," *Speculum* 43 (1968): 290–305, especially 294, and "The Ideal of Feminine Beauty in Medieval Literature, Especially 'Harley Lyrics,' Chaucer and Some Elizabethans,". *Modern Language Review* 50, no. 3 (1955): 257–69
53. James H. Morey, "The 'cultour' in the *Miller's Tale*: Alison as Iseult," *The Chaucer Review* 29, no. 4 (1995): 373–81.
54. Geoffrey de la Tour Landry, *Le Livre du Chevalier de La Tour Landry, pour l'enseignement de ses filles,* ed. Anatole De Montaiglon (Nendeln: Kraus Reprint, 1972), 109–10.
55. Matthew of Vendôme, *Ars versificatoria,* 44, sec. 57. For fuller discussion of Beroe, see Friedman, *Brueghel's Heavy Dancers,* 88–93.
56. Green, *De ornatu mulierum,* in *The Trotula,* 168–9.
57. Cabré, "From a Master to a Laywoman," 387.
58. Chaucer, *The Canterbury Tales,* I (A) 3734–8.
59. Ibid., I (A) 3380.
60. My translation of Niccolo Campani, "Capitolo delle Bellezze della Dama," in *Poeti del Cinquecento: Poeti Lirici, Burleschi Satirici e Didascalici,* eds. Guglielmo Gorni, Massimo Danzi, and Silvia Longhi (Milan: R. Ricciardi, 2001), 938–40. See also Bettella, *The Ugly Woman,* 192–3.
61. "Ain Grasserin durck külen tau," in *The Medieval Pastourelle,* 483. See Karl Kurt Klein and Hans Moser, eds., *Die Lieder von Oswalds von Wolkenstein* (Tübingen: Niemeyer, 1987), no. 76, 202–3, and Song 76 in Albrecht Classen, trans., *The Poems of Oswald von Wolkenstein* (New York: Palgrave Macmillan, 2008), 158–9, who translates the phrase as "her scythe covered with brown hair," no. 1, 158.

62. See Andrea von Hülsen-Esche, "À propos de la Porta Romana de Milan: Dans quelle mesure la sculpture de l'Italie du Nord reflète-t-elle certains aspects de l'histoire communale," *Cahiers de civilisation médiévale* 38, no. 2 (1992): 147–54, especially 152 and n. 46.

Chapter Nine

1. Paul Dutton, *Charlemagne's Mustache* (New York: Palgrave Macmillan, 2004), 3–42. Long hair was restricted to Merovingian royalty; see ibid., 11–14; and Bonnie Effros, "Appearance and Ideology," in *Encountering Medieval Dress and Textiles*, eds. Désiré Koslin and Janet Snyder (New York: Palgrave, 2002), 13.
2. See Pauline Stafford, "Meanings of Hair in the Anglo-Norman World: Masculinity, Reform, and National Identity," in *Saints, Scholars, and Politicans*, eds. M. van Dijk and R. Nip (Turnhout: Brepols, 2005), 153–71. For Bayeux Tapestry images, see, for example, scenes 38–40 and 51 (Normans), and 1, 4, 13, 25, 27, 28, 30, 51, 53 (Anglo-Saxons).
3. Stafford, "Meanings of Hair," 165. Clerics in the Bayeux Tapestry are distinguished by tonsures and clean-shaven faces.
4. Quoted in Christina Waugh, "'Well-Cut through the Body': Fitted Clothing in Twelfth-Century Europe," *Dress* 26, no. 1 (1999): 16.
5. Ibid., 3–16 and fig. 3; Aileen Ribeiro, *Dress and Morality* (Oxford: Berg, 2003), 34–6 and fig. 10; and Stafford, "Meanings of Hair," 164–8.
6. See Joan Cadden, *Meanings of Sex Difference in the Middle Ages* (Cambridge: Cambridge University Press, 1993), 171 and 181; Will Fisher, *Materializing Gender in Early Modern English Literature and Culture* (Cambridge: Cambridge University Press, 2006), 107–8.
7. Quoted in Giles Constable, "Introduction" to Burchard de Bellevaux's *Apologie de Barbis*, in *Apologiae duae, Corpus Christianorum, Continuatio Mediaevalis*, LXII (Turnhout: Brepols, 1985), 108, where he discusses medieval disputes regarding clerical tonsure. His essay, 47–130, offers the most detailed overview of beards and shaving in the Middle Ages known to me; for clerical hair, see especially 72–85 and 103–30. On the controversy regarding the coronal tonsure versus the Irish tonsure, visible in the ca. 800 Book of Kells, see Daniel McCarthy, "Illustration and Text on the Book of Kells, Folio 114RV," *Studies in Iconography* 35 (2014): 1–38, especially 24–7.
8. Constable, "Introduction," 56–7, 60; and Robert Bartlett, "Symbolic Meanings of Hair in the Middle Ages," *Transactions of the Royal Historical Society*, s. 6, 4 (1994): 57–8, speculate regarding meanings of clerical tonsure.
9. *Ecclesiastical History*, IV; as quoted in Ribeiro, *Dress and Morality*, 35.
10. Stafford, "Meanings of Hair," 167.
11. Zehava Jacoby, "Beard Pullers in Romanesque Art: An Islamic Motif and its Evolution in the West," *Arte Medievale* 1, no. 1–2 (1987): 65–7; and Laura Clark, "Fashionable Beards and Beards as Fashion: Beard Coats in Thomas Malory's *Morte d'Arthur*," *Parergon* 31, no. 1 (2014): 96–7.
12. Paris, Bibliothèque nationale, MS. Fr. 22495, fols. 19 and 147v; in http://library.artstor.org/library/#1, search "Bouillon Saracens 2484" and "Bouillon Saracens 2586."
13. Constable, "Introduction," 61 and 116–18.
14. Dutton, *Charlemagne's Mustache*, 27–30; Clark, "Fashionable Beards," 98–9.
15. At http://www.artmuseum.arizona.edu/, under "Collections," search inv. 1961.013.013. On the *puer senex*, see J.A. Burrow, *Ages of Man: A Study in Medieval Writing and Thought* (Oxford: Clarendon, 1986), especially 95–102.
16. In http://library.artstor.org/library/#1, search "Michelino Susanna."

17. See Jacoby, "Beard Pullers," 65–85, and Christa Sütterlin, "Universals in Apotropaic Symbolism: A Behavioral and Comparative Approach to Some Medieval Sculptures," *Leonardo* 22, no. 1 (1989): 65–74, especially 65, 66, and 73, and 67 on the genital-exposing Sheela-na-gig figures.
18. On hair and gender difference more generally, see Luke Demaitre, *Medieval Medicine: The Art of Healing, from Head to Toe* (Santa Barbara, CA: Praeger, 2013), 111–19; Cadden, *Meanings of Sex Difference*, 169–95.
19. On depictions of pubic hair in art, see Penny Jolly, "Pubics and Privates: Body Hair in Late Medieval Art," in *Meanings of Nudity in Medieval Art*, ed. Sherry Lindquist (Farnham: Ashgate, 2012), 183–206.
20. Ibid., 185 and 187.
21. Cadden, *Meanings of Sex Difference*, 171, 178, and 181; Fisher, *Materializing Gender*, 87–93 and 108–11.
22. *Engaging Symbols: Gender, Politics, and Public Art in Fifteenth-Century Florence* (New Haven, CT: Yale University Press, 2002), 171–3.
23. See Jolly, "Pubics and Privates," 183–5; for additional examples, see Amy Neff, *A Soul's Journey into God: Franciscan Art, Theology, and Devotion in a Late Duecento Manuscript, the* Supplicationes Variae (Toronto: Pontifical Institute of Medieval Studies, forthcoming).
24. In Susan L'Engle, "Ad*dress*ing the Law: Costume as Signifier in Medieval Legal Miniatures," in *Encountering Medieval Dress and Textiles*, eds. Désiré Koslin and Janet Snyder (New York: Palgrave, 2002), 146–7 and fig. 8.3.
25. See Leo Steinberg, *Sexuality of Christ in Renaissance Art and in Modern Oblivion*, 2nd rev. ed. (Chicago: University of Chicago Press, 1996), on Christ's shameless genitals.
26. New York, Morgan Library, M. 729, fol. 232v; in http://library.artstor.org/library/#1, search "1981–42557." Jewish practice similarly prescribed hair coverings; Leah Bronner, "From Veil to Wig: Jewish Women's Hair Covering," *Judaism* 42, no. 4 (Fall 1993): 465–77.
27. Margaret Scott, *Medieval Dress and Fashion* (London: British Library, 2007), 112; see also Rogier van der Weyden's 1445 Seven Sacraments Altarpiece (Antwerp, Musée des Beaux Arts), depicting the sacrament of marriage, or Robert Campin's *Marriage of the Virgin* (ca. 1430, Madrid, Prado).
28. Jane Bridgeman, "Ambrogio Lorenzetti's Dancing 'Maidens': A Case of Mistaken Identity," *Apollo* 133, no. 350 (1991): 245–51.
29. Scott, *Medieval Dress*, 112, who speculates instead it emphasizes virginity and perhaps their entering a "quasi-religious state."
30. For medieval ideas regarding breastmilk, nursing, menstruation, and Mary's human status, see Margaret Miles, *A Complex Delight* (Berkeley: University of California Press, 2008); Megan Holmes, "Disrobing the Virgin: The *Madonna Lactans* in Fifteenth-Century Florentine Art," in *Picturing Women in Renaissance and Baroque Italy*, eds. Geraldine Johnson and Sara Matthews Grieco (Cambridge: Cambridge University Press, 1997), 167–95; Cadden, *Meanings of Sex Difference*, 173–6; Charles Wood, "Doctors' Dilemma: Sin, Salvation, and the Menstrual Cycle in Medieval Thought," *Speculum* 56, no. 4 (1981): 710–27; and William MacLehose, "Nurturing Danger: High Medieval Medicine and the Problem(s) of the Child," in *Medieval Mothering*, eds. John Parsons and Bonnie Wheeler (New York: Garland, 1996), 3–15.
31. In Herbert Kessler, *Illustrated Bibles from Tours* (Princeton, NJ: Princeton University Press, 1977), figs. 1, 3–5; only the San Paolo Bible shows breasts on Eve; the Hildesheim doors clearly distinguish the two only beginning with scene three, *The Fall*.

32. *Historia Scholastica*, in PL 198:1072: "virgineum vultus habens"; translated in Henry Kelly, "Metamorphoses of the Eden Serpent during the Middle Ages and Renaissance," *Viator* 2 (1971): 308.
33. Though see also Linda Seidel, "Nudity as Natural Garment: Seeing through Adam and Eve's Skin," in *Meanings of Nudity in Medieval Art*, ed. Sherry Lindquist (Farnham VT: Ashgate, 2012), especially 213–18.
34. *The Trotula: An English Translation of the Medieval Compendium of Women's Medicine*, ed. and trans. Monica H. Green (Philadelphia: University of Pennsylvania Press, 2001), 113–14 and 118 on depilatories; and Jolly, "Pubics and Privates," 189–90.
35. *Trotula*, 144 and n. 7.
36. Ibid., 118; Richard Corson, *Fashions in Hair* (London: Peter Owen, 1965), 106, claims post-1320 women began plucking or shaving their foreheads.
37. *Book of the Knight of La Tour-Landry*, ed. G. Taylor (London: John Hamilton, 1930), 95–6.
38. From *Women's Secrets*, as quoted in Danielle Jacquart and Claude Thomasset, *Sexuality and Medicine in the Middle Ages*, trans. Matthew Adamson (Princeton, NJ: Princeton University Press, 1988), 76; for the relief, see Jolly, "Pubics and Privates," 200–1 and fig. 6.13.
39. Respectively, "A Bawdy Betrothal in the Ormesby Psalter," in *Tribute to Lotte Brand Philip*, eds. William Clark et al. (New York: Abaris, 1985), 156–9; and "Patron or Matron? A Capetian Bride and a *Vade mecum* for Her Marriage Bed," *Speculum* 68, no. 2 (1993), especially 340–4. See also Malcolm Jones, *Secret Middle Ages* (Phoenix Mill: Sutton Publishing, 2002), 38–43, 51–5, and 57–8; and, for earlier artworks with female pubic hair, consult Jolly, "Pubics and Privates," 187–9.
40. Jolly, "Pubics and Privates," 192–200.
41. On hair's dangers, see Roberta Milliken, *Ambiguous Locks: An Iconology of Hair in Medieval Art and Literature* (Jefferson, NC: McFarland, 2012), 89–159.
42. See Duncan Derret, "Religious Hair," *Man* 8, no. 1 (1973): 100–3; on Paul's medieval reception, consult Gabriela Signori, "Veil, Hat or Hair? Reflections on an Asymmetrical Relationship," *Medieval History Journal* 8, no. 1 (2005): 25–47.
43. As quoted in ibid., 30.
44. On the complex roles of hair and beauty in medieval literature, see Derek Brewer, *Tradition and Innovation in Chaucer* (London: Macmillan, 1982), 30–45; Peggy Knapp, *Chaucerian Aesthetics* (New York: Palgrave Macmillan, 2008), 99–125; and, particularly for Platonist traditions, Victoria Kirkham, "Poetic Ideals of Love and Beauty," 49–61, and Dale Kent, "Women in Renaissance Florence," especially 41, both in *Virtue and Beauty*, ed. David Brown (Washington, DC: National Gallery of Art, 2001).
45. *Sonnets and Shorter Poems*, trans. David Slavit (Cambridge, MA: Harvard University Press, 2012), 136.
46. For example, in Sonnets 59, 67, 90, 157, 213, 218, 220, 253, 348, as well as 159, quoted above.
47. *Trotula*, 115–16.
48. Joanna Woods-Marsden, "Portrait of the Lady, 1430–1520," in *Virtue and Beauty*, ed. Brown, 65–7.
49. Joseph Manca, "Blond Hair as a Mark of Nobility in Ferrarese Portraiture of the Quattrocento," *Musei Ferraresi, Bollettino Annuale* 17 (1990/91): 51–60.
50. Guillaume de Lorris and Jean de Meun, *Roman de la Rose*, trans. C. Dahlberg (Hanover, NH: University Press of New England, 1983), 229. See Mireille Madou, "Cornes et Cornettes," in *Flanders in a European Perspective*, eds. M. Smeyers and B. Cardon (Leuven: Peeters,

1995), 417–26. On moralizers' generalized fears regarding women's hair, see Ribeiro, *Dress and Morality*, 39–53, passim.
51. In *Set in Stone: The Face in Medieval Sculpture*, ed. Charles Little (New Haven, CT: Yale University Press, 2006), 138–40.
52. From a fifteenth-century sermon; see *Medieval Dress and Textiles in Britain: A Multilingual Sourcebook*, eds. L. Sylvester, M. Chambers, G. Owen-Crocker (Woodbridge: Boydell, 2014), 157. Ribeiro, *Dress and Morality*, fig. 24, from 1426, shows women tempting St. Anthony with actual devils' horns coming out of their hair. On the Campin-style hair, see Cheunsoon Song and Lucy Roy Sibley, "The Vertical Headdress of Fifteenth-Century Northern Europe," *Dress* 16, no. 1 (1990): 5–15, especially 10–11.
53. Evelyn Welch, "Signs of Faith: The Political and Social Identity of Hair in Renaissance Italy," in *La Fiducia Secondo i Linguaggi del Potere*, ed. Paolo Prodi (Bologna: Società Editrice il Mulino, 2007), 379–94, especially 388–92; she offers additional examples there and in "Art on the Edge: Hair and Hands in Renaissance Italy," *Renaissance Studies* 23, no. 3 (2008): 241–68.
54. *Luxuria*, ca. 1115, appears in the left side relief, south portal, at Moissac's Church of St.-Pierre; For the eroticism of hair combing, see Diane Wolfthal, "Sin or Sexual Pleasure? A Little-known Nude Bather in a Flemish Book of Hours," in *Meanings of Nudity in Medieval Art*, ed. Sherry Lindquist (Farnham: Ashgate, 2012), 279–97.
55. On early medieval grooming practices, including liturgical combs, see Steven Ashby, "Technologies of Appearance: Hair Behaviour in Early Medieval Europe," *Archaeological Journal* 171, no. 1 (2014): 151–84, especially 176–7; and search The Victoria and Albert Museum website, http://collections.vam.ac.uk/, "A.544–1910 comb" and "A.27–1977 liturgical comb."
56. In http://library.artstor.org/library/#1, search "Lorenzetti monte siepi [sic] maesta."
57. Multiple examples of fiery-haired devils are at the Church of Ste.-Madeleine, Vézelay, and St.-Lazare, Autun.
58. Milliken, *Ambiguous Locks*, 148–53.
59. Bartlett, "Symbolic Meanings," 53–6; and Mosche Barasch, *Gestures of Despair in Medieval and Early Renaissance Art* (New York: New York University Press, 1976), 18, 68, 78, and 88.
60. See Penny Jolly, *Picturing the "Pregnant" Magdalene in Northern Art, 1430–1550* (Aldershot: Ashgate, 2014), 83, on the Magdalene as widow. For the Magdalene's exposed hair while mourning Christ, see, for example, Giotto's *Lamentation* (Arena Chapel, Padua, ca. 1305).
61. See Ilse Friesen, "Saints as Helpers in Dying: The Hairy Holy Women Mary Magdalene, Mary of Egypt, and Wilgefortis in the Iconography of the Late Middle Ages," in *Death and Dying in the Middle Ages*, eds. E. DuBruck and B. Gusick (New York: Peter Lang, 1999), 239–53.
62. For a 1472 anonymous German woodcut example of the latter, go to http://library.artstor.org/library/#1, search "8072.1472/56."
63. Illustrated in Susan Haskins, *Mary Magdalen: Myth and Metaphor* (New York: Harcourt Brace, 1993), plate 21.
64. *Ecclesiastical History*, quoted in *Medieval Dress and Textiles in Britain*, 133. On voluntary long hair versus practices for cutting hair, see C.R. Hallpike, "Social Hair," *Man* 4, no. 2 (1969): 256–64; Constable, "Introduction," 119–24; and Bartlett, "Symbolic Meanings," 52–3.

65. On punishments involving hair, see Milliken, *Ambiguous Locks*, 153–9; and Barbara Hanawalt, *"Of Good and Ill Repute": Gender and Social Control in Medieval England* (New York: Oxford University Press, 1998), 24–7.
66. In Milliken, *Ambiguous Locks*, 72–3 and fig. 4.
67. On nuns' tonsure and veiling rules and ceremonies, see ibid., 69–80.
68. Ruth Mellinkoff, *Outcasts: Signs of Otherness in Northern European Art of the Late Middle Ages*, 2 vols. (Berkeley: University of California Press, 1993), i: 184–6.
69. http://library.artstor.org/library/#1, search "Crucifixion 15356" and "Crucifixion 06550."
70. "Strange Things Out of Hair: Baldness and Masculinity in Early Modern England," *Sixteenth Century Journal* 41, no. 2 (2010): 376–7, where she also notes (381) God's threat to punish proud women by making them bald (Isaiah 3:16–7). L'Engle, "Addressing the Law," 148, cites a 1340s illumination of a nuns' hair-cutting ceremony.
71. Mellinkoff, *Outcasts*, i: 186–8; Jones, *Secret Middle Ages*, 103–5.
72. Demaitre, *Medieval Medicine*, 115–19, passim; and Shulamith Shahar, *Growing Old in the Middle Ages*, trans. Yael Lotan (London: Routledge, 1997), 37–47, passim.
73. Mellinkoff, *Outcasts*, i: 183–4.
74. Patricia Rose, "Bears, Baldness, and the Double Spirit: The Identity of Donatello's *Zuccone*," *Art Bulletin* 63, no. 1 (March 1981): 31–41.
75. *Enarrationes in Psalmos, In Psalmum LXXIV*, as quoted in Amy Neff, "Wicked Children on Calvary and the Baldness of St. Francis," *Mitteilungen des Kunsthistorischen Institutes in Florenz* 34, no. 3 (1990), 215–44 at 216.
76. Ibid., 234; and Neff, *A Soul's Journey*, forthcoming.
77. On wild men and women and for images, see Timothy Husband, *The Wild Man: Medieval Myth and Symbolism* (New York: Metropolitan Museum of Art, 1980), 1–17; Roger Bartra, *Wild Men in the Looking Glass: Mythic Origins of European Otherness* (Ann Arbor: University of Michigan Press, 1994), 85–117; and Jones, *Secret Middle Ages*, 64–5.
78. Husband, *Wild Man*, 14–17.
79. Mellinkoff, *Outcasts*, i: 145–59, with reference to Aristotle on 148.
80. Ibid., i: 192 and 135 respectively; illustrated in François Avril, *Manuscript Painting at the Court of France* (New York: Braziller, 1978), plate 17.
81. See Rowan Dorin, "Mystery of the Marble Man and His Hat: A Reconsideration of the Bari Episcopal Throne," *Florilegium* 25 (2008): 29–51, who contextualizes and reviews controversies surrounding the throne; however, I find his identification of the central figure as a Muslim unconvincing.
82. See Jean Devisse, "A Sanctified Black: Maurice," in *Image of the Black in Western Art*, 5 vols. eds. David Bindman and Henry Louis Gates (Cambridge, MA: Harvard University Press, 2010), ii: pt. 1, 139–94, on Maurice; and Paul Kaplan, *Rise of the Black Magus in Western Art* (Ann Arbor: UMI Research Press, 1985), 7–17, on inclusions of black attendants, and 87–9 on black Magi.

BIBLIOGRAPHY

Abbas, Haly Ibn. *Pantegni (Theorice)*. In Isaac Israeli, *Omnia opera Ysaac ... Galieni a Constantino compositum*. Lyons, 1515.
Akbari, Suzanne Conklin. *Idols in the East: European Representations of Islam and the Orient, 1100–1450*. Ithaca, NY: Cornell University Press, 2009.
Aelred of Rievaulx. "The Nun of Watton." In *Women and Writing in Medieval Europe: A Sourcebook*, edited by Carolyne Larrington, 130–5. London: Routledge, 1995.
Alcuin. Letter to King Athelred, 793. Translated by Dorothy Whitelock. In Angus, *The Viking Age: A Reader*, edited by A. Somerville and R. Andrew McDonald, 233. Toronto: University of Toronto Press.
Alderotti, Taddeo. *Commentum in microtegni Galieni*, lib. II. Naples, 1522.
Alderotti, Taddeo. *Expositio in Joannitii Isagogarum lib*. Venice, 1527.
Alderotti, Taddeo. *I "consilia" di Taddeo Alderotti*. Edited by Giuseppe Michele Nardi. Preface by Pietro Capparoni. Torino: Edizioni Minerva Medica, 1937.
Aldhelm: The Prose Works. Translated by Michael Lapidge and Michael Herren. Cambridge: D.S. Brewer, 1979.
Ambrose, Kirk. *The Nave Sculpture of Vézelay: The Art of Monastic Viewing*. Toronto: Pontifical Institute of Medieval Studies/University of Toronto Press, 2006.
Andersen, Jørgen. *The Witch on the Wall: Medieval Erotic Sculpture in the British Isles*. Copenhagen: Rosenkilde and Bagger, 1977.
Andresen, Jeffrey J. "Rapunzel: The Symbolism of the Cutting of Hair." *Journal of the American Psychoanalytic Association* 28 (1980): 69–88.
Anglicus, Glibertus. *Compendium medicinae*. Lyons, 1510.
Anson, John. "The Female Transvestite in Early Monasticism: The Origin and Development of a Motif." *Viator* 5 (1974): 1–32.
Arnold, John A. *What is Medieval History?* Cambridge: Polity Press, 2008.
Ashby, Steven. "Technologies of Appearance: Hair Behaviour in Early Medieval Europe." *Archaeological Journal* 171, no. 1 (2014): 151–84.
Ashelford, Jane. *The Art of Dress: Clothes Through History 1500–1914*. London: The National Trust, 2011.
Ashenburg, Katherine. *The Dirt on Clean: An Unsanitized History*. New York: North Point Press, 2007.
Augustine. *Expositions on the Psalms*. Digital Psalms, compiled by Ted Hildebrant as an open-access online resource, 2007. https://faculty.gordon.edu/hu/bi/ted_hildebrandt/otesources/19-psalms/text/books/augustine-psalms/augustine-psalms-web.htm. Accessed May 15, 2016.
Avicenna. *Liber Canonis tocius medicinae*. Venice, 1527. Brussels: Medicinae Historia, 1971.
Barasch, Mosche. *Gestures of Despair in Medieval and Early Renaissance Art*. New York: New York University Press, 1976.

Barbier de Montault, Xavier. "L'Eglise Royale et Collegiale de Saint Nicolas, à Bari (Deux-Sicilies), fin." *Révue de l'Art Chrétien* 2 (1884): 305–14.

Barrow, Julia. *The Clergy in the Medieval World: Secular Clerics, their Families, and their Careers in North-Western Europe, c. 800–c. 1200*. Cambridge: Cambridge University Press, 2015.

Bartra, Roger. *Wild Men in the Looking Glass: Mythic Origins of European Otherness*. Ann Arbor: University of Michigan Press, 1994.

Bartlett, Robert. *Gerald of Wales, 1146–1223*. Oxford: Clarendon Press, 1982.

Bartlett, Robert. *The Making of Europe: Conquest, Colonization and Cultural Change 950–1350*. Princeton, NJ: Princeton University Press, 1993.

Bartlett, Robert. "Symbolic Meanings of Hair in the Middle Ages." *Transactions of the Royal Historical Society* s. 6, 4 (1994): 43–60.

Bartlett, Robert. "Medieval and Modern Concepts of Race and Ethnicity." *Journal of Medieval and Early Modern Studies* 31, no. 1 (2001): 39–56.

Bartlett, Robert. "Illustrating Ethnicity in the Middle Ages." In *The Origins of Racism in the West*, edited by Miriam Eliav-Feldon, Benjamin Isaac, and Joseph Ziegler, 132–56. Cambridge: Cambridge University Press, 2009.

Baumgarten, Elisheva. *Practicing Piety in Medieval Ashkenaz: Men, Women, and Everyday Religious Observance*. Philadelphia: University of Pennsylvania Press, 2014.

Bayard, Tania. *Sweet Herbs and Sundry Flowers: Medieval Gardens and the Gardens of the Cloisters*. New York: Metropolitan Museum of Art, 1985.

Bedeaux, Jan Baptist. "Laatmiddeleeuwse sexuele amuletten." In *Annus Quadriga Mundi: Opstellenover Middeleeuwse Kunst opgedragen aan prof Dr. Anna C. Esmeijer*, 16–30. Utrecht: De Walburg, 1989.

Beichner, Paul E. "Absolon's Hair." *Mediaeval Studies* 12 (1950): 222–33.

Beichner, Paul E., ed. *Aurora Petri Rigae Biblia Versificata*, Vol. 1. Notre Dame, IN: University of Notre Dame Press, 1965.

Benson, Larry D. *The Riverside Chaucer*. Boston, MA: Houghton Mifflin Company, 1987.

Benton, Janetta Rebold. *Materials, Methods, and Masterpieces of Medieval Art*. Santa Barbara, CA: ABC-CLIO, 2009.

Benwell, Gwen, and Arthur Waugh. *Sea Enchantress: A Tale of the Mermaid and Her Kin*. London: Hutchinson, 1965.

Berg, Charles. *The Unconscious Significance of Hair*. Washington, DC: GuildPress, 1951.

Bernard of Gordon. *Lilio de medicinae*. Edited by John Cull and Brian Dutton. Madison, WI: Hispanic Seminary of Medieval Studies, 1991.

Bettella, Patrizia. *The Ugly Woman: Transgressive Aesthetic Models in Italian Poetry from the Middle Ages to the Baroque*. Toronto: University of Toronto Press, 2005.

Biller, Peter. "A 'Scientific' View of Jews from Paris around 1300." *Micrologus* 9 (2001): 137–69.

Biller, Peter. "Proto-racial Thought in Medieval Science." In *The Origins of Racism in the West*, edited by Miriam Eliav-Feldon, Benjamin Isaac, and Joseph Ziegler, 157–80. Cambridge: Cambridge University Press, 2009.

Biller, Peter. "Views of Jews from Paris around 1300: Christian or Scientific?" In *Christianity and Judaism*, edited by Diana Wood, 187–207. Oxford: Blackwell, 1992.

Bleeke, Marian, et al. "Women in/and Visual Culture." In *A Cultural History of Women in the Middle Ages*, edited by Kim Phillips, 179–213. Oxford: Berg Publishers, 2013.

Boccaccio, Giovanni. *The Decameron*. Translated by G.H. McWilliam. London: Penguin Books, 1972.

Boccaccio, Giovanni. *Teseide*. In *The Book of Theseus: Teseida delle Nozzi d'Emilia by Giovanni Boccaccio*. Translated by Bernadette Marie McCoy. New York: Medieval Text Association, 1974.

Boccaccio, Giovanni. *Il Corbaccio*. In *The Corbaccio, Giovanni Boccaccio*. Edited and translated by Anthony K. Cassell. Urbana: University of Illinois Press, 1975.

Boccaccio, Giovanni. *The Corbaccio or the Labyrinth of Love*. Translated and edited by Anthony Cassell. Binghamton, NY: Medieval and Renaissance Texts and Studies, 1993.

Braet, Herman. "'A Thing Most Brutish': The Image of the Peasant in Old French Literature." In *Agriculture in the Middle Ages: Technology, Practice, and Representation*, edited by Del Sweeney, 191–204. Philadelphia: University of Pennsylvania Press, 1995.

Breudwyt Ronabwy. Edited by Melville Richards. Cardiff: University of Wales Press, 1948.

Brewer, Derek. "The Ideal of Feminine Beauty in Medieval Literature, Especially 'Harley Lyrics,' Chaucer and Some Elizabethans." *Modern Language Review* 50, no. 3 (1955): 257–69.

Brewer, Derek. *Tradition and Innovation in Chaucer*. London: Macmillan, 1982.

Brewer, Derek S. "Class Distinction in Chaucer." *Speculum* 43 (1968): 290–305.

Bridgeman, Jane. "Ambrogio Lorenzetti's Dancing 'Maidens': A Case of Mistaken Identity." *Apollo* 133, no. 350 (1991): 245–51.

Bronner, Leila Leah. "From Veil to Wig: Jewish Women's Hair Covering." *Judaism* 42, no. 4 (Fall 1993): 465–77.

Brożyna, Martha A. *Gender and Sexuality in the Middle Ages: A Medieval Source Documents Reader*. Jefferson, NC: McFarland and Company, 2005.

Brubaker, Leslie. *Vision and Meaning in Ninth-Century Byzantium: Image as Exegesis in the Homilies of Gregory Nazianzus*. Cambridge: Cambridge University Press, 1999.

Bullough, Vern. "The Prostitute in the Early Middle Ages." In *Sexual Practices and the Medieval Church*, edited by James Brundage and Vern Bullough, 34–42. Amherst, MA: Prometheus Books, 1994.

Burke, Peter. *What is Cultural History?* Cambridge: Polity Press, 2008.

Burrow, J.A. *Ages of Man: A Study in Medieval Writing and Thought*. Oxford: Clarendon, 1986.

Caballero-Navas, Carmen. *The Book of Women's Love and Jewish Medieval Medical Literature on Women, Sefer Ahavat Nashim*. London: Kegan Paul, 2004.

Caballero-Navas, Carmen. "The Care of Women's Health and Beauty: An Experience Shared by Medieval Jewish and Christian Women." *Journal of Medieval History* 34, no. 2 (2008): 146–63.

Cabré, Montserrat. "La Cura del cos femení i la medicina medieval de tradició llatina: Els tractats 'De Ornatu' i 'De decorationibus mulierum' atribuïts a Arnau de Vilanova, 'Tròtula' de mestre Joan, i 'Flos del tresor de beutat,' atribuït a Manuel Díeç de Calatayud." PhD diss., University of Barcelona, 1996.

Cabré, Montserrat. "From a Master to a Laywoman: A Feminine Manual of Self- Help." *Dynamis* 20 (2000): 371–93.

Cabré, Montserrat. "Women or Healers: Household Practices and the Categories of Health Care in Late Medieval Iberia." *Bulletin of the History of Medicine* 82, no. 1 (2008): 18–51.

Cabré, Montserrat. "Beautiful Bodies." In *A Cultural History of the Human Body in the Middle Ages*, edited by Linda Kalof, 121–62. London: Berg, 2010.

Cadden, Joan. *Meanings of Sex Difference in the Middle Ages: Medicine, Science and Culture*. Cambridge: Cambridge University Press, 1993.

Cameron, Averil. "How Did the Merovingian Kings Wear Their Hair?" *Revue Belge de Philologie et d'Histoire* 43, no. 4 (1965): 1203–16.

Camille, Michael. *The Medieval Art of Love: Objects and Subjects of Desire*. New York: Harry N. Abrams, Inc, 1998.

Campani, Niccolo. "Capitolo delle Bellezze della Dama." In *Poeti del Cinquecento: PoetiLirici, Burleschi Satirici e Didascalici*, edited by Guglielmo Gorni, Massimo Danzi, and Silvia Longhi, 938–40. Milan: R. Ricciardi, 2001.

Caviness, Madeline. "Patron or Matron? A Capetian Bride and a *Vade mecum* for Her Marriage Bed." *Speculum* 68 (1993): 333–62.

Caviness, Madeline. *Reframing Medieval Art: Difference, Margins, Boundaries*, online 2001. http://dca.lib.tufts.edu/caviness/chapter2.html. Accessed March 30, 2018.

Caviness, Madeline H. *Visualizing Women in the Middle Ages: Sight, Spectacle, and Scopic Economy*. Philadelphia: University of Pennsylvania Press, 2001.

Ceri, Siôn. *Gwaith Siôn Ceri*. Edited by Cynfael Lake. Aberystwyth: Canolfan Uwchefrydiau Cymreig a Cheltaidd, 1996.

Chaucer, Geoffrey. *The General Prologue*. In *The Canterbury Tales*, translated by David Wright, 3–24. Oxford: Oxford University Press, 1985.

Chaucer, Geoffrey. *The Miller's Tale*. In *The Canterbury Tales*, translated by David Wright, 81–99. Oxford: Oxford University Press, 1985.

Chaucer, Geoffrey. *The Monk's Tale*. In *The Canterbury Tales*, translated by David Wright, 376–402. Oxford: Oxford University Press, 1985.

Chaucer, Geoffrey. *The Miller's Tale*. In *The Riverside Chaucer*, edited by Larry Benson, 66–77. Boston, MA: Houghton Mifflin, 1987.

Chazan, Robert. *The Jews of Medieval Western Christendom, 1000–1500*. Cambridge: Cambridge University Press, 2006.

Child, Theodore. *Wimples and Crisping Pins*. New York: Harper and Brothers, 1895.

Cifuentes, Lluís. "La promoció intel·lectual i social del barbers-cirurgians a la Barcelona medieval: L'obrador, la biblioteca i els béns de Joan Vicenç (fl. 1421–1464)." *Arxiu de Textos Catalans Antics* 19 (2000): 429–79.

Cifuentes, Lluís. "La medicina en las galeras de la Corona de Aragón a finales de la Edad Media: La caja del barbero y sus libros." *Medicina e Historia* 4, no. 4 (2000): 1–15.

Clark, Laura. "Fashionable Beards and Beards as Fashion: Beard Coats in Thomas Malory's *Morte d'Arthur*." *Parergon* 31, no. 1 (2014): 95–109.

Classen, Albrecht, trans. *The Poems of Oswald von Wolkenstein*. New York: Palgrave Macmillan, 2008.

Clement of Alexandria. *The Instructor*. Translated by William Wilson. In *Ante-Nicene Fathers*, vol. 2, edited by Alexander Roberts, James Donaldson, and A. Cleveland Coxe. Buffalo, NY: Christian Literature Publishing Co, 1885. Revised and edited for New Advent by Kevin Knight. http://www.newadvent.org/fathers/0209.htm. Accessed March 30, 2018.

Coates, Simon. "Scissors or Swords? The Symbolism of the Medieval Haircut." *History Today*, May 1999: 7–13.

Coble-Stevens, Veda. "Speech, Gesture, and Women's Hair in the Gospel of Luke and First Corinthians." In *The Symbolism of Vanitas in the Arts, Literature and Music: Comparative and Historical Studies*, edited by Liana De Girolami, 322–9. Lewiston, NY: Edwin Mellen Press, 1992.

Cohen, Jeffrey Jerome. "On Saracen Enjoyment: Some Fantasies of Race in Late Medieval France and England." *Journal of Medieval and Early Modern Studies* 31, no. 1 (2001): 113–46.

Coletti, Theresa. *Mary Magdalene and the Drama of the Saints: Theater, Gender, and Religion in Late Medieval England*. Philadelphia: University of Pennsylvania Press, 2004.

Collard, Franck. "*Perfidus Physicus* ou *Inexpertus Medicus*. Le cas Jean de Grandville, Médecin du Comte Amédée VII de Savoie." In *Mires, Physiciens, Barbiers et Charlatans. Les Marges de la Médecine de l'Antiquité au XVIe siècle*, edited by Franck Collard and Évelyne Samama, 133–49. Landres: Dominique Guéniot éditeur, 2004.

Collier, Carole. *Dressing Renaissance Florence: Families, Fortunes, and Fine Clothing*. Baltimore: Johns Hopkins University Press, 2005.

Connochie-Bourgne, Chantal, ed. *La Chevalure dans La Littérature et L'Art du Moyen Âge*. Actes du 28e Colloque du CUER MA 20, 21, 22 Février 2003. *Sénéfiance* no. 50 (2004).

Connolly, Philomena, ed. "The Enactments of the 1297 Parliament." In *Law and Disorder in Thirteenth-Century Ireland: The Dublin Parliament of 1297*, edited by James Lydon, 158–61. Dublin: Four Courts, 1997.

Constable, Giles. "'Introduction on Beards in the Middle Ages' in Burchard of Belleveaux's *Apologia de Barbis*." In *Corpus Christianorum, Continuatio Medievalis*, LXII, edited by R.B.C. Huygens, 47–150. Turnholt: Brepols, 1985.

Constable, Giles. *Crusaders and Crusading in the Twelfth Century*. Farnham: Ashgate, 2008.

Cooper, Helen. *The Miller's Tale*. In *The Canterbury Tales, Oxford Guides to Chaucer*, edited by Helen Cooper, 97–107. Oxford: Oxford University Press, 1989.

Cooper, Wendy. *Hair: Sex, Society, Symbolism*. New York: Stein and Day, 1971.

Corson, Richard. *Fashions in Hair: The First Five Thousand Years*. London: Peter Owen Publishers, 2005.

Crouch, Jace. "The Judicial Punishment of *Decalvatio* in the Visigothic Spain: A Proposed Solution Based on Isidore of Seville and the *Lex Visigothorum*." *The Mediterranean Review* 3, no. 1 (June 2010): 59–77.

Culhwch and Olwen: An Edition and Study of the Oldest Arthurian Tale. Edited by Rachel Bromwich and Daniel Simon Evans. Cardiff: University of Wales Press, 1992.

Damweiniau Colan. Edited by Dafydd Jenkins. Aberystwyth: Cymdeithas Lyfrau Ceredigion, 1974.

d'Abano, Pietro. 1565. *Conciliator controversiarum quae inter philosophos et medicos versantur*. Venice. Reprinted in Padua: Antenore, 1985.

D'Angleo, Mary Rose. "Veils, Virgins, and the Tongues of Men and Angels." In *Off With Her Head: The Denial of Women's Identity in Myth, Religion, and Culture*, edited by Howard Eilberg-Schwartz and Wendy Doniger, 131–64. Berkeley: University of California Press, 1995.

Da Foligno, Gentile. *Primus Avi. Canon. Avicenne … cum lucidissima Gentilis Fulgi. expositione*. Venice, 1520.

Da Foligno, Gentile. *Tertius Can. Avic. cum amplissima Gentilis Fulgi. expositione*. Venice 1522.

Da Soller, Claudio. *The Beautiful Woman in Medieval Iberia: Rhetoric, Cosmetics, and Evolution*. PhD Diss., University of Missouri-Columbia, 2005.

De Bourbon, Étienne. *Anecdotes historiques, legends et apologues tires du recueil inedit d'Etienne de Bourbon, Dominicain du XIHe siècle*. Edited by A. Lecoy De La Marche. Paris: Société de l'histoire de France, 1877.

De Courtais, Georgine. *Women's Headdress and Hairstyles in England from AD600 to the Present Day*. London: B.T. Batsford, 1974.

De France, Marie. *Marie de France: Poetry*. Translated by Dorothy Gilbert. New York: W.W. Norton and Company, 2015.

De Gordon, Bernard. *Lilium medicinae*. Paris, 1542.

De La Tour Landry, Geoffrey. *The Book of the Knight of La Tour Landry*. Edited by G.S. Taylor. London: Verona Society, 1930.

De La Tour Landry, Geoffrey. *Le Livre du Chevalier de La Tour Landry, pour l'enseignement de ses filles*. Edited by Anatole de Montaiglon. Nendeln: Kraus Reprint, 1972.

De Lorris, Guillaume, and Jean de Meun. *The Romance of the Rose*. Translated by Charles Dahlberg. Princeton, NJ: Princeton University Press, 1995.

De Miramon, Charles. "Noble Dogs, Noble Blood: The Invention of the Concept of Blood in the Late Middle Ages." In *The Origins of Racism in the West*, edited by Miriam Eliav-Feldon, Benjamin Isaac, and Joseph Ziegler, 200–16. Cambridge: Cambridge University Press, 2009.

De Pisan, Christine. *The Treasure of the City of Ladies or The Book of the Three Virtues*. Translated by Sarah Lawson. London: Penguin, 1985.

De Pizan, Christine. *A Medieval Woman's Mirror of Honor: The Treasury of the City of Ladies*. Translated by Charity Cannon Willard. Tenalfy, NJ: Bard Hall Press, 1989.

De Pizan, Christine. *The Book of the City of Ladies*. Translated by Rosalind Brown-Grant. London: Penguin, 1999.

De Troyes, Chrétien. *The Complete Romances of Chretien de Troyes*. Translated by David Staines. Bloomington: Indiana University Press, 1990.

De Vilanova, Arnau. *Speculum medicinae*. In *Opera Omnia*. Basel, 1585.

De Vilanova, Arnau. *Regimen Sanitatis ad Regem Aragonum*. In *Arnaldi de Villanova Regimen Sanitatis ad Rgem Aragonum*, edited by Luis García Ballester and Michael R. McVaugh, 419–70. Barcelona: Funació Noguera-Universitat de Barcelona, 1996.

De Villermont, Marie. *La Histoire de la Coiffure Féminine*. Paris: Librairie Rénouard, 1892.

De Voragine, Jacobus. *The Golden Legend: Readings on the Saints*, 2 vols. Translated by William Granger Ryan. Princeton, NJ: Princeton University Press, 1993.

Deane, Jennifer Kolpacoff. "Pious Domesticities." In *The Oxford Handbook of Women and Gender in Medieval Europe*, edited by Judith M. Bennett and Ruth Mazo Karras, 262–78. Oxford: Oxford University Press, 2013.

Delis Hill, Daniel. *History of World Costume and Fashion*. Upper Saddle River, NJ: Prentice Hall, 2011.

Demaitre, Luke. *Medieval Medicine: The Art of Healing, from Head to Toe*. Santa Barbara, CA: Praeger, 2013.

Demouy, Patrick. "Le Trésor de la Cathédrale." In *Reims: La Grâce d'une Cathédrale*, edited by Thierry Jordan, 307–19. Strasbourg: Édition La Nuée Bleue, 2010.

Derret, J. Duncan M. "Religious Hair." *Man* 8, no. 1 (March 1973): 100–03.

Devisse, Jean. "A Sanctified Black: Maurice." In *Image of the Black in Western Art*, edited by David Bindman and Henry Louis Gates, II, pt. 1, 139–94. Cambridge, MA: Harvard University Press, 2010.

Diesenberger, Maximilian. "Hair, Sacrality and Symbolic Capital in Frankish Kingdoms." In *The Construction of Communities in the Early Middle Ages: Texts, Resources and Artefacts*, edited by Richard Corradini, Max Diesenberger, and Helmut Reimitz, 173–212. Leiden: Brill 2003.

Dinkova-Brun, Greti. "Biblical Thematics: The Story of Samson in Medieval Literary Discourse." In *The Oxford Handbook of Medieval Latin Literature*, edited by Ralph Hexter and David Townsend, 356–75. Oxford: Oxford University Press, 2012.

Dodwell, C. R. *The Canterbury School of Illumination*, 1066–1200. Cambridge: Cambridge University Press, 1954.

Dodwell, C. R. *Anglo-Saxon Art: A New Perspective*. Ithaca, NY: Cornell University Press, 1985.

Dorin, Rowan. "Mystery of the Marble Man and His Hat: A Reconsideration of the Bari Episcopal Throne." *Florilegium* 25 (2008): 29–52.

Dressler, Rachel. "Gender as Spectacle and Construct: The Gyvernay Effigies at St. Mary's Church, Limington." *Different Visions: A Journal of New Perspectives on Medieval Art*, no. 1 (2008): 1–24.

Duffy, Seán. "The Problem of Degeneracy." In *Law and Disorder in Thirteenth-Century Ireland: The Dublin Parliament of 1297*, edited by James Lydon, 87–106. Dublin: Four Courts, 1997.

Duffy, Seán. *The World of the Galloglass*. Dublin: Four Courts Press, 2007.

Dumas, Geneviève. "Le Soin des Cheveux et des Poils: Quelques Pratiques Cosmétiques, XIII-XVI Siècles." In *La Chevalure dans la Litérature et l'art du Moyen Âge* [Senefiance 50], edited by Chantal Connochie-Bourgne, 129–41. Provence: Publications de l'Université de Provence, 2004.

Guillaume Durand. *The Rationale Divinorum Officiorum: The Foundational Symbolism of the Early Church, Its Structure, Decoration, Sacraments and Vestments*. Louisville: Fons Vitae, 2007.

Dutton, Paul Edward. *Charlemagne's Mustache and Other Cultural Clusters of a Dark Age*. New York: Palgrave Macmillan, 2004.

Easton, Martha. "Was It Good For You Too? Medieval Erotic Art and Its Audiences." *Different Visions: A Journal of New Perspectives on Medieval Art*, no. 1 (2008): 1–30.

Easton, Martha. "'Why Can't a Woman Be More Like a Man?' Transforming and Transcending Gender in the Lives of Female Saints." In *The Four Modes of Seeing: Approaches to Medieval Imagery in Honor of Madeline Harrison Caviness*, edited by Elizabeth Carson Pastan, Ellen M. Shortell, and Evelyn Staudinger Lane, 333–47. London: Ashgate Press, 2009.

Easton, Martha. "Uncovering the Meanings of Nudity in the *Belles Heures* of Jean, Duke of Berry." In *The Meanings of Nudity in Medieval Art*, edited by Sherry Lindquist, 149–81. London, Ashgate Press, 2012.

Edwards, John. "Beginnings of a Scientific Theory of Race? Spain, 1450–1600." In *From Iberia to Diaspora: Studies in Sephardic History and Culture*, edited by Yedida K. Stillman and Norman K. Stillman, 179–96. Leiden: Brill, 1999.

Effros, Bonnie. "Appearance and Ideology." In *Encountering Medieval Dress and Textiles*, edited by Désiré Koslin and Janet Snyder, 7–24. New York: Palgrave, 2002.

Egan, Geoff, and Pritchard, Frances. *Dress Accessories c. 1150–1450*. Woodbridge: Boydell Press, 2008.

Eliav-Feldon, Miriam, Benjamin Isaac, and Joseph Ziegler. "Introduction." In *The Origins of Racism in the West*, edited by Miriam Eliav-Feldon, Benjamin Isaac, and Joseph Ziegler, 1–31. Cambridge: Cambridge University Press, 2009.

Ellington, Donna Spivey. *From Sacred Body to Angelic Soul: Understanding Mary in Late Medieval and Early Modern Europe*. Washington, DC: Catholic University of America Press, 2001.

Entwistle, Joanne. *The Fashioned Body: Fashion, Dress, and Modern Social Theory*. Cambridge: Polity Press, 2015.

Epstein, Marc Michael. "Clothing: Jewish." In *Medieval France: An Encyclopedia*, edited by William Kibler, 449–50. New York: Routledge, 1995.

Evans, Joan. *Dress in Mediaeval France*. Oxford: Clarendon Press, 1952.

Fairhold, Frederick W. *Satirical Songs and Poems on Costume from the 13th to the 19th Century*. London: The Percy Society, 1849.

Fynglwyd, Iorwerth. *Gwaith Iorwerth Fynglwyd*. Edited by Howell L. Jones and E.I. Rowlands. Cardiff: University of Wales Press, 1975.

Fenton, Kirsten A. "Men and Masculinities in William of Malmesbury's Presentation of the Anglo-Norman Court." *Haskins Society Journal* 23 (2014): 115–24.

Ferragud, Carmel. "Barbers in the Process of Medicalization in the Crown of Aragon." In *Medieval Urban Identity: Health, Economy and Regulation*, edited by Flocel Sabaté, 143–65. Cambridge: Cambridge Scholars Publishing, 2015.

Firth, Raymond. *Symbols: Public and Private*. Ithaca, NY: Cornell University Press, 1973.

Fisher, Will. *Materializing Gender in Early Modern English Literature and Culture*. Cambridge: Cambridge University Press, 2006.

Forsyth, Ilene H. *The Throne of Wisdom: Wood Sculptures of the Madonna in Romanesque France*. Princeton, NJ: Princeton University Press, 1972.

Francis and Clare: The Complete Works. Translated by Regis J. Armstrong and Ignatius Brady. New York: Paulist Press, 1982.

Frazer, James George. *The Golden Bough: A Study in Magic and Religion*. New York: MacMillan Company, 1935.

Freitag, Barbara. *Sheela-na-gigs: Unravelling an Enigma*. London: Routledge, 2004.

French, Katherine L. "Genders and Material Cultures." In *The Oxford Handbook of Women and Gender in Medieval Europe*, edited by Judith M. Bennett and Ruth Mazo Karras, 197–212. Oxford: Oxford University Press, 2013.

Freud, Sigmund. "Fetischismus." In *Gesammelte Werke*, edited by Anna Freud et al. London: Imago, 1940–1952.

Frick, Carole Collier. *Dressing Renaissance Florence: Families, Fortunes, and Fine Clothing*. Baltimore: Johns Hopkins University Press, 2005.

Friedman, John Block. "Chaucer's Pardoner, Rutebeuf's 'Dit de l'Herberie,' The 'Dit du Mercier' and Cultural History." *Viator* 38, no. 1 (2007): 289–319.

Friedman, John Block. *Brueghel's Heavy Dancers: TransgressiveClothing, Class, & Culture*. Syracuse, NY: Syracuse University Press, 2010.

Friedman, John Block. "The Iconography of Dagged Clothing and its Reception by Moralist Writers." In *Medieval Clothing and Textiles 9*, edited by Robin Netherton and Gale R. Owen-Crocker, 121–38. Woodbridge, Suffolk: Boydell and Brewer, 2013.

Friedman, John Block. "Coats, Collars, and Capes: Royal Fashions for Animals in the Early Modern Period." *Medieval Clothing and Textiles*, vol. 12, edited by Robin Netherton and Gale R. Owen-Crocker, 61–94. Woodbridge: Boydell and Brewer, 2016.

Friesen, Ilse. "Saints as Helpers in Dying: The Hairy Holy Women Mary Magdalene, Mary of Egypt, and Wilgefortis in the Iconography of the Late Middle Ages." In *Death and Dying in the Middle Ages*, edited by E. DuBruck and B. Gusick, 239–53. New York: Peter Lang, 1999.

Friesen, Ilse E. *The Female Crucifix: Images of St. Wilgefortis Since the Middle Ages*. Ontario: Wilfrid Laurier University Press, 2001.

"From Metz, in the Cool the Other Day." In *The Medieval Pastourelle*, edited and translated by William D. Paden, 256 [Garland Library of Medieval Literature 34–35, ser. A]. New York: Garland, 1987.

"From Saint-Quentin to Cambrai." In *The Medieval Pastourelle*, edited and translated by William D. Paden, 299 [Garland Library of Medieval Literature 34–35, ser. A]. New York: Garland, 1987.

Galen. *1483. Tegni sive ars parva*. In *Articella*. Venice, 1483.

Galen. *De complexionibus*. In *Opera Omnia (II)*. Venice, 1490.

García Ballester, Luis. "The *New Galen*: A Challenge to Latin Galenism in Thirteenth-Century Montpellier." In *Text and Tradition: Studies in Ancient Medicine and its Transmission Presented to Jutta Kollesch*, edited by Klaus-Dietrich Fischer, Diethard Nickel, and Paul Potter, 55–83. Leiden: Brill, 1998. Reprinted in *Galen and Galenism*. Edited by Jon Arrizabalaga, Montserrat Cabré, Lluís Cifuentes, and Fernando Salmón, essay V. Aldershot: Ashgate Variorum Reprints, 2002.

Garver, Valerie L. *Women and Aristocratic Culture in the Carolingian World*. Ithaca, NY: Cornell University Press, 2009.

Geoffrey of Monmouth. *Brut Dingestow*. Edited by Henry Lewis. Cardiff: Cardiff University Press, 1942.

Geary, Patrick. "Ethnic Identity as a Situational Construct in the Early Middle Ages." *Mitteilungen der Anthropologischen Gesellschaft in Wien* 113 (1983): 15–26, reprinted in Medieval Perspectives 3, no. 2 (Fall 1988): 1–17.

Gerald of Wales (Giraldus Cambrensis). *The Topography of Ireland*. Translated by Thomas Forester. In *The Historical Works of Giraldus Cambrensis*, edited by Thomas Wright. London: H.G. Bohn, 1863.

Gerald of Wales. *Journey Through Wales, in The Journey Through Wales and the Description of Wales*. Translated by Lewis Thorpe. Harmondsworth: Penguin, 1978.

Gildas. *The Ruin of Britain and Other Works*. Edited and translated by Michael Winterbottom. Chichester: Phillimore and Co., 1978.

Gerson, Paula, ed. *The Pilgrim's Guide to Santiago de Compostela*, 2 vols. London: Harvey Miller, 1998.

Gessler, Jean. *La Légende de Sainte Wilgeforte ou Ontcommer: La Vierge Miraculeusement Barbue*. Brussels: Éditions Universelle, 1938.

Gil Sotres, Pedro. "Introducción." In *Arnaldi de Villanova Regimen Sanitatis ad Regem Aragonum*, edited by Luis García Ballester and Michael R. McVaugh, 471–886. Barcelona: Fundació Noguera-Universitat de Barcelona, 1996.

Glyn, Guto. "Moliant i wallt du Harri Gruffudd o'r Cwrt Newydd." Edited by Barry J. Lewis, *gutorglyn.net*, Poem 33. http://www.gutorglyn.net/gutorglyn/poem/?poem-selection=033&first-line=%23. Accessed January 10, 2016.

Glyn, Guto. "Molaint i Fathau Goch o Faelor." Edited by Alaw Mai Edwards, *gutorglyn.net*, Poem 3. http://www.gutorglyn.net/gutorglyn/poem/?poem-selection=003&first-line=033. Accessed January 10, 2016.

Goch, Iolo. *Iolo Goch: Poems*. Edited and translated by Dafydd Johnston. Llandysul: Gwasg Gomer, 1993.

Goddard, Eunice Rathbone. *Women's Costume in French Texts of the Eleventh and Twelfth Centuries*. Baltimore: Johns Hopkins University Press, 1927.

Godman, Peter. *Poetry of the Carolingian Renaissance*. Norman: University of Oklahoma Press, 1985.

Goosmann, Erik. "The Long-haired Kings of the Franks: 'Like so Many Samsons?'" *Early Medieval Europe* 20, no. 3 (2012): 233–59.

Green, Monica H. "Documenting Medieval Women's Medical Practice." In *Practical Medicine from Salerno to the Black Death*, edited by Luis García Ballester et al., 321–52. Cambridge: Cambridge University Press, 1994. Reprinted in Monica H. Green, *Women's Healthcare in the Medieval West: Texts and Contexts*, essay II. Aldershot: Ashgate, 2000.

Green, Monica H. "The Possibilities of Literacy and the Limits of Reading: Women and the Gendering of Medical Literacy." In Monica H. Green, *Women's Healthcare in the Medieval West: Texts and Contexts*, essay VII, 1–76. Aldershot: Ashgate, 2000.

Green, Monica H. "Flowers, Poisons and Men: Menstruation in Medieval Western Europe." In *Menstruation: A Cultural History*, edited by Andrew Shail and Gillian Howie, 51–64. Basingstoke: Palgrave MacMillan, 2005.

Green, Monica H. *Making Women's Medicine Masculine. The Rise of Male Authority and Pre-Modern Gynaecology*. Cambridge: Cambridge University Press, 2008.

Green, Monica H., ed. and trans. *The Trotula: An English Translation of the Medieval Compendium of Women's Medicine*. Philadelphia: University of Pennsylvania Press, 2001.

Greco, Gina L., and Christine M. Rose, trans. *The Good Wife's Guide (Le Ménagier de Paris): A Medieval Household Guide*. Ithaca, NY: Cornell University Press, 2009.

Grooms, Chris. *The Giants of Wales: Cewri Cymru*. Lampeter: Mellen, 1993.

Grössinger, Christa. *Picturing Women in Late Medieval and Renaissance Art*. Manchester: Manchester University Press, 1997.

Hallpike, C.R. "Social Hair." *Man* 4, no. 2 (1969): 256–64.

Hanawalt, Barbara. *The Ties that Bound: Peasant Families in Medieval England*. Oxford: Oxford University Press, 1986.

Hanawalt, Barbara. *"Of Good and Ill Repute": Gender and Social Control in Medieval England*. NewYork and Oxford: Oxford University Press, 1998.

Hanska, Jussi. "Sermons on the Tenth Sunday after Holy Trinity: Another Occasion for Anti-Jewish Preaching." In *The Jewish-Christian Encounter in Medieval Preaching* (Routledge Research in Medieval Studies, no. 6), edited by Jonathan Adams and Jussi Hanska. New York: Routledge, 2015.

Harris, Stephen J. "An Overview of Race and Ethnicity in Pre-Norman England." *Literature Compass* 5, no. 4 (2008): 740–54.

Haskins, Susan. *Mary Magdalen: Myth and Metaphor*. New York: Harcourt Brace, 1993.

Heldris de Cornuälle. *Le Roman de Silence*. Translated by Regina Psaki. New York: Garland, 1991.

Helbling, Seigfried. *Der kleine Lucidarius*. In *Peasant Life in Old German Epic*, translated by Clair Hayden Bell. New York: Norton, 1968.

Heng, Geraldine. "The Invention of Race in the European Middle Ages I: Race Studies, Modernity, and the Middle Ages." *Literature Compass* 8, no. 5 (2011): 315–31.

Heng, Geraldine. "The Invention of Race in the European Middle Ages II: Locations of Medieval Race." *Literature Compass* 8, no. 5 (2011): 332–50.

Hershman, P. "Hair, Sex and Dirt." *Man* 9, no. 2 (1974): 274–98.

Hildegard of Bingen. *Hildegard of Bingen: On Natural Philosophy and Medicine*. Translated by Margret Berger. Rochester, NY: D.S. Brewer, 1999.

Hildegard of Bingen. *Hildegard von Bingen's Physica: The Complete English Translation of Her Classic Work on Health and Healing*. Translated by Priscilla Throop. Rochester, VT: Healing Arts Press, 1998.

Historia Peredur vab Efrawc. Edited by Glenys Goetinck. Cardiff: University of Wales Press, 1976.

Holladay, Joan A. "Relics, Reliquaries, and Religious Women: Visualizing the Holy Virgins of Cologne." *Studies in Iconography* 18 (1997): 67–118.

Hollander, Anne. *Seeing Through Clothes*. Berkeley: University of California Press, 1975.

Holloway, Julia Bolton, Joan Bechtold, and Constance S. Wright. *Equally in God's Image: Women in the Middle Ages*. New York: Peter Lang, 1990.

Horden, Peregrine and Elisabeth Hsu, eds. *The Body in Balance. Humoral Medicines in Practice*. New York: Berghahn, 2013.

Hotchkiss, Valerie R. *Clothes Make the Man: Female Cross Dressing in Medieval Europe*. New York: Garland, 1996.

The Hours of Mary of Burgundy. Commentary by Erik Inglis. London: Harvey Miller, 1995.

Hoyoux, Jean. "Reges Crinati: Chevalures, Tonsures et Scalps Chez les Merovingians." *Revue Belge de Philologie et d'Histoire* 26, no. 3 (1948): 479–508.

Hucbald. "Ecloga de Calvis." Translated by Thomas Klein. "In Praise of Bald Men: A Translation of Hucbald's Ecloga de Calvis." *Comitatus: A Journal of Medieval and Renaissance Studies* 26, no. 1 (1995): 1–9.

Husband, Timothy, with the assistance of Gloria Gilmore-House. *The Wild Man: Medieval Myth and Symbolism*. New York: Metropolitan Museum of Art, 1980.

Husband, Timothy B. *The Art of Illumination: The Limbourg Brothers and the Belles Heures of Jean de France, Duc de Berry*. New York: Metropolitan Museum of Art, 2008.

Isidore of Seville. *Etymologies*. Translated by Stephen A. Barney, W. J. Lewis, and J. A. Beach. Cambridge: Cambridge University Press, 2006.

Jacoby, Zehava. "Beard Pullers in Romanesque Art: An Islamic Motif and its Evolution in the West." *Arte Medievale* 1, no. 1–2 (1987): 65–85.

Jacquart, Danielle, and Claude Thomasset. *Sexuality and Medicine in the Middle Ages*. Translated by Matthew Adamson. Princeton, NJ: Princeton University Press, 1988.

James, Edward. "Bede and the Tonsure Question." *Peritia* 3 (1984): 85–98.

Jansen, Katherine Ludwig. *The Making of the Magdalen: Preaching and Popular Devotion in the Later Middle Ages*. Princeton, NJ: Princeton University Press, 2000.

Jansen, Katherine Ludwig. "Mary Magdalen and the Contemplative Life." In *Medieval Religion: New Approaches*, edited by Constance Berman, 249–71. New York: Routledge, 2005.

Jaritz, Gerhard. "The Material Culture of the Peasantry in the Late Middle Ages: 'Image' and 'Reality'." In *Agriculture in the Middle Ages: Technology, Practice, and Representation*, edited by Del Sweeney, 165–88. Philadelphia: University of Pennsylvania Press, 1995.

Jenkins, Dafydd, and Morfydd E. Owen, eds. *The Welsh Law of Women*. Cardiff: University of Wales Press, 1980.

John of Plano Carpini. *History of the Mongols*. In *Mission to Asia*, edited by Christopher Dawson and translated by "a nun of Stanbrook abbey." New York: Harper and Row, 1966.

Johnsson, Peter H. "Locks of Difference: The Integral Role of Hair as a Distinguishing Feature in Early Merovingian Gaul." *Ex Post Facto* 19 (2010): 55–68.

Jolly, Penny Howell. *Hair: Untangling a Social History*. Saratoga Springs, NY: Frances Young Tang Teaching Museum and Art Gallery, Skidmore College, 2004.

Jolly, Penny Howell. "Pubics and Privates: Body Hair in Late Medieval Art." In *The Meanings of Nudity in Medieval Art*, edited by Sherry Lundquist, 183–206. Farnham: Ashgate, 2012.

Jolly, Penny Howell. *Picturing the "Pregnant" Magdalene in Northern Art. 1430–1550*. Aldershot: Ashgate, 2014.

Jones, Malcolm. *The Secret Middle Ages*. Phoenix Mill: Sutton Publishing, 2002.

Jordan, William Chester. "Why Race?" *Journal of Medieval and Early Modern Studies* 31, no. 1 (2001): 165–73.

Kaplan, Paul. *Rise of the Black Magus in Western Art*. Ann Arbor, MI: UMI Research Press, 1985.

Karras, Ruth Mazo. *Common Women: Prostitution and Sexuality in Medieval England*. Oxford: Oxford University Press, 1996.

Karras, Ruth Mazo. *From Boys to Men: Formations of Masculinity in Late Medieval Europe*, Philadelphia: University of Pennsylvania Press, 2002.

Karras, Ruth Mazo. "Holy Harlots: Prostitute Saints in Medieval Legend." *Journal of the History of Sexuality* 1, no. 1 (1990): 3–32.

Kelly, Henry Ansgar. "Metamorphoses of the Eden Serpent during the Middle Ages and Renaissance." *Viator* 2 (1971): 301–27.

Kent, Dale. "Women in Renaissance Florence." In *Virtue and Beauty*, edited by David Brown, 25–47. Washington, DC: National Gallery of Art, 2001.

Kessler, Herbert. *Illustrated Bibles from Tours*. Princeton, NJ: Princeton University Press, 1977.

Kessler, Herbert, and Gerhardt Wolf, eds. *The Holy Face and the Paradox of Representation: Papers from a Colloquium Held at the Bibliotheca Hertziana, Rome, and the Villa Spelman, Florence, 1996.* Bologna: Nuova Alfa Editoriale, 1998.

Killerby, Catherine Kovesi. *Sumptuary Law in Italy, 1200–1500.* Oxford: Clarendon Press, 2002.

King, Helen. "Barbes, Sang et Genre: Afficher la Différence dans le Monde Antique." In *Langages et Métaphores du Corps dans le Monde Antique*, edited by Jérôme Wilgaux and Véronique Dasen, 153–68. Rennes: Presses Universitaire de Rennes, 2008.

Kirkham, Victoria. "Poetic Ideals of Love and Beauty." In *Virtue and Beauty*, edited by David Brown, 49–61. Washington, DC: National Gallery of Art, 2001.

Klein, Karl Kurt and Hans Moser, eds. *Die Lieder von Oswalds von Wolkenstein.* Tübingen: Niemeyer, 1987.

Knapp, Peggy. *Chaucerian Aesthetics.* New York: Palgrave Macmillan, 2008.

Koldeweij, Jos. "Shameless and Naked Images: Obscene Badges as Parodies of Popular Devotion." In *Art and Architecture of Late Medieval Pilgrimage in Northern Europe and the British Isles*, edited by Sarah Blick and Rita Tekippe, 493–510. Leiden: Brill, 2005.

Korhonen, Anu. "Strange Things Out of Hair: Baldness and Masculinity in Early Modern England." *Sixteenth Century Journal* 41, no. 2 (2010): 371–91.

Koslin, Désirée. "Manifest Insignificance: The Consecrated Veil of Medieval Religious Women." In *Sacred and Ceremonial Textiles*. Proceedings of the Fifth Biennial Symposium of the Textile Society of America, 141–7. Chicago: Textile Society of America, Inc., 1996.

Koslin, Désirée. "Robe of Simplicity: Initiation, Robing, and Veiling of Nuns in the Middle Ages." In *Robes and Honor: The Medieval World of Investiture*, edited by Stewart Gordon, 255–74. Lodon: Palgrave Macmillan, 2001.

Koslin, Désirée G. "*He hath couerd my soule inward:* Veiling in Medieval Europe and the Early Church." In *The Veil: Women Writers on Its History, Lore, and Politics*, edited by Jennifer Heath, 160–70. Berkeley: University of California Press, 2008.

Kren, Thomas. "Looking at Louis XII's Bathsheba." In *A Masterpiece Reconstructed: The Hours of Louis XII*, edited by Thomas Kren, 42–61. Los Angeles: Getty Publications, 2005.

Kubiski, Joyce. "Orientalizing Costume in Early Fifteenth-Century French Manuscript Painting (Cité des Dames Master, Limbourg Brothers, Boucicaut Master, and Bedford Master)." *Gesta* 40, no. 2 (2001): 161–80.

Kuhns, Elizabeth. *The Habit: A History of the Clothing of Catholic Nuns.* New York: Doubleday, 2003.

Kutney, Kutney. *Sulphur: History, Technology, Applications, Industry.* Toronto: ChemTec Publishing, 2007.

Lao, Meri. *Sirens: Symbols of Seduction.* Translated by John Oliphant. South Paris, ME: Park Street Press, 1998.

Latini, Brunetto. *The Book of the Treasure (Li Livres dou Tresor).* Translated by Paul Barrette and Spurgeon Baldwin. New York: Garland, 1993.

The Law of Hywel Dda: Law Texts from Medieval Wales Edited and translated by Dafydd Jenkins. Llandysul: Gomer Press, 1986.

The Laws of the Earliest English Kings. Edited and translated by Frederik L. Attenborough. Cambridge: Cambridge University Press, 1922.

Laver, James. *Costume and Fashion.* London: Thames and Hudson, 1995.

Leach, E.R. "Magical Hair." *The Journal of the Royal Anthropological Institute of Great Britain* 88, no. 2 (1958): 147–61.

Leahy, Kevin. "Anglo-Saxon Crafts." In *The Oxford Handbook of Anglo-Saxon Archaeology*, edited by David A. Hinton, Sally Crawford, and Helena Hamerow, 440–59. Oxford: Oxford University Press, 2011.

Le Goff, Jacques. *Must We Divide History Into Periods?* Translated by Malcolm DeBevoise. New York: Columbia University Press, 2015.

L'Engle, Susan. "Addressing the Law: Costume as Signifier in Medieval Legal Miniatures." In *Encountering Medieval Dress and Textiles*, edited by Désiré Koslin and Janet Snyder, 137–53. New York: Palgrave, 2002.

The Letters of Abelard and Heloise. Translated by Betty Radice and edited by M.T. Clanchy. London: Penguin Books, 2003.

Levine, Molly Myerowitz. "The Gendered Grammar of Ancient Mediterranean Hair." In *Off with Her Head! The Denial of Women's Identity in Myth, Religion, and Culture*, edited by Howard Eilberg-Schwartz and Wendy Doniger, 76–130. Berkeley: University of California Press, 1995.

Leyser, Conrad. "Long-haired Kings and Short-haired Nuns: Writing on the Body in Caesarius of Arles." *Studia Patristica* 24 (1993): 143–50.

Lipton, Sara. *Images of Intolerance: The Representation of Jews and Judaism in the Bible Moralisée*. Berkeley: University of California Press, 1999.

Lipton, Sara. *Dark Mirror: The Medieval Origins of Anti-Semitic Iconography*. New York: Metropolitan Books, 2014.

Little, Charles, ed. *Set in Stone: The Face in Medieval Sculpture*. New Haven, CT: Yale University Press, 2006.

Llwyd, Gruffudd. *Gwaith Gruffudd Llwyd a'r Llygliwiaid eraill*. Edited by Rhiannon Ifans. Aberystwyth: Canolfan Uwchefrydiau Cymreig a Cheltaidd, 2000.

Lutz, Cora. "The Letter of Lentulus Describing Christ." *The Yale University Library Gazette* 50, no. 2 (1975): 91–97.

The Mabinogion. Translated by Sioned Davies. Oxford: Oxford University Press, 2008.

Madou, Mireille. "Cornes et Cornettes." In *Flanders in a European Perspective*, edited by M. Smeyers and B. Cardon, 417–26. Leuven: Peeters, 1995.

Magennis, Hugh. "Gender and Heroism in the Old English Judith." In *Writing Gender and Genre in Medieval Literature: Approaches to Old and Middle English Texts*, edited by Elaine M. Treharne, 5–18. Cambridge: D.S. Brewer, 2002.

Mâle, Emile. *Religious Art in France: The Twelfth Century*. Princeton, NJ: Princeton University Press, 1978.

Malborough, Thomas of. *History of the Abbey of Evesham*. Edited and translated by Jane Sayers and Leslie Watkiss. Oxford: Clarendon Press, 2003.

Manca, Joseph. "Blond Hair as a Mark of Nobility in Ferrarese Portraiture of the Quattrocento." *Musei Ferraresi, Bollettino Annuale* 17 (1990/91): 51–60.

Mandeville, Sir John. *The Book of John Mandeville with Related Texts*. Edited by Iain Macleod Higgins. Indianapolis: Hackett, 2011.

Maredudd, Gruffudd ap. *Gwaith Gruffudd ap Maredudd 2: Cerddi Crefyddol*. Edited by Barry J. Lewis. Aberystwyth: Canolfan Uwchefrydiau Cymreig a Cheltaidd Prifysgol Cymru, 2005.

Matthew of Vendôme. *Ars Versificatoria*. In *Matthew of Vendôme: The Art of Versification*, edited and translated by Aubrey E. Galyon. Ames: Iowa State University Press, 1980.

Matthew of Vendôme. *Ars Versificatoria*. Translated by Roger P. Parr. Milwaukee, WI: Marquette University Press, 1981.

Mathews, Thomas. *The Clash of Gods: A Reinterpretation of Early Christian Art*, revised and expanded edition. Princeton, NJ: Princeton University Press, 1993.

McCarthy, Daniel. "On the Shape of the Insular Tonsure." *Celtica* 24 (2003): 140–67.

McCarthy, Daniel. "Illustration and Text on the Book of Kells, Folio 114RV." *Studies in Iconography* 35 (2014): 1–38.

McCracken, Peggy. "'The Boy Who Was a Girl': Reading Gender in the Roman de Silence." *The Romanic Review* 85, no. 4 (1994): 517–36.

McDonald, Andrew. *The Viking Age: A Reader*. Toronto: University of Toronto Press, 2010.

McDonald, Nicola. "Introduction." In *Medieval Obscenities*, edited by Nicola McDonald, 1–16. Rochester, NY: York Medieval Press, 2006.

McNeill, John T., and Helena M. Gamer. *Medieval Handbooks of Penance: A Translation of the Principal "Libri Poenitentiales."* New York: Columbia University Press, Reprinted 1990.

McVaugh, Michael. "The *Experimenta* of Arnald of Villanova." *Journal of Medieval and Renaissance Studies* 1, no. 1 (1971): 107–18.

Mellinkoff, Ruth. *Outcasts: Signs of Otherness in Northern European Art of the Later Middle Ages*, 2 vols. Berkeley: University of California Press, 1993.

"Mentre per una ribiera." In *The Medieval Pastourelle*, edited and translated by William D. Paden, 435 and 437 [Garland Library of Medieval Literature 34–35, ser. A]. New York: Garland, 1987.

Metzler, Irina. "Perceptions of Hot Climate in Medieval Cosmography and Travel Literature." *Reading Medieval Studies* 23 (1997): 69–105.

Mills, Robert. "The Significance of the Tonsure." In *Holiness and Masculinity in the Middle Ages*, edited by P.H. Cullum and Katherine J. Lewis, 109–26. Toronto: University of Toronto Press, 2004.

Monmouth, Geoffrey of. *The History of the Kings of Britain: An Edition and Translation of* De Gestis Britonum. Edited by Michael D. Reeve and translated by Neil Wright. Woodbridge: Boydell Press, 2007.

Montgomery, Scott B. *St. Ursula and the Eleven Thousand Virgins of Cologne: Relics, Reliquaries and the Visual Culture of Group Sanctity in Late Medieval Europe*. Bern: Peter Lang, 2010.

Morey, James H. "The 'Cultour' in the *Miller's Tale*: Alison as Iseult." *The Chaucer Review* 29, no. 4 (1995): 373–81.

Moulinier-Brogi, Laurence. "Esthétique et Soins du Corps dans les Traités Médicaux Latins à la Fin du Moyen Âge." *Médiévales* 46 (2004): 55–72.

Mueller, Joan. *A Companion to Clare of Assisi: Life, Writings, Spirituality*. Leiden: Brill, 2010.

Nanmor, Dafydd. *The Poetical Works of Dafydd Nanmor*. Edited by Thomas Roberts and revised by Ifor Williams. Cardiff: University of Wales Press, 1923.

Neff, Amy. "Wicked Children on Calvary and the Baldness of St. Francis." *Mitteilungen des Kunsthistorischen Institutes in Florenz* 34, no. 3 (1990): 215–44.

Neff, Amy. *A Soul's Journey into God: Franciscan Art, Theology, and Devotion in a Late Duecento Manuscript, the* Supplicationes Variae. Toronto: Pontifical Institute of Medieval Studies, Forthcoming.

Nennius. *The Historia Brittonum*. Edited by David N. Dumville. Cambridge: D.S. Brewer, 1985.

Newton, Stella Mary. *Fashion in the Age of the Black Prince*. Woodbridge: Boydell Press, 1980.

Nightlinger, Elizabeth. "The Female *Imitatio Christi* and Medieval Popular Religion: The Case of St Wilgefortis." In *Representations of the Feminine in the Middle Ages*, edited by Bonnie Wheeler, 291–328. Dallas, TX: Academia Press, 1993.

Nirenberg, David. "Was there Race Before Modernity? The Example of 'Jewish' Blood in Late Medieval Spain." In *The Origins of Racism in the West*, edited by Miriam Eliav-Feldon,

Benjamin Isaac, and Joseph Ziegler, 232–64. Cambridge: Cambridge University Press, 2009.

Nutton, Vivian. "Humoralism." In *Companion Encyclopedia of the History of Medicine*. Edited by William Bynum and Roy Porter, vol. I, 281–91. London: Routledge, 1993.

Ordinacions de la Casa i Cort de Pere el Cerimoniós. Edited by Francisco M. Gimeno, Daniel Gonzalbo, and Josep Trenchs. València: Universitat de València, 2009.

Owein or Chwedyl Iarlles y Ffynnawn. Edited by R.L. Thompson. Dublin: Institute of Advanced Studies, 1968.

Owen-Crocker, Gail. *Dress in Anglo-Saxon England*. Woodbridge: Boydell Press, 2004.

Owen-Crocker, Gail. "Dress and Identity." In *The Oxford Handbook of Anglo-Saxon Archaeology*, edited by David A. Hinton, Sally Crawford, and Helena Hamerow, 92–116. Oxford: Oxford University Press, 2011.

Owen-Crocker, Gail. "Brides, Donors, Traders: Imports into Anglo-Saxon England." In *Textiles and the Medieval Economy: Production Trade, and Consumption of Textiles, 8th–16th Centuries*, edited by Angela Ling-Huang and Carsten Jahnke, 64–77. Oxford: Oxbow Books, 2015.

Paniagua, Juan A. *Studia Arnaldiana. Trabajos en torno a la obra médica de Arnau de Vilanova, c.1240–1311*. Barcelona: Fundación Uriach, 1994.

Parliaments and Councils of Medieval Ireland, 1. Edited by Henry G. Richardson and George O. Sayles. Dublin: Stationary Office, 1947.

Park, Katharine. "Medicine and Natural Philosophy: Naturalistic Traditions." In *The Oxford Handbook of Women and Gender in Medieval Europe*, edited by Judith Bennett and Ruth Karras, 84–100. Oxford: Oxford University Press, 2013.

Pastoureau, Michel. *The Devil's Cloth: A History of Stripes and Striped Fabrics*. Translated by Jody Gladding. New York: Columbia University Press, 2001.

Pearson, Andrea. *Envisioning Gender in Burgundian Devotional Art, 1350–1530: Experience, Authority, Resistance*. Aldershot: Ashgate, 2005.

Pedeir Keinc y Mabinogi. Edited by Ifor Williams. Cardiff: University of Wales Press, 1951.

Pernoud, Régine. *The Retrial of Joan of Arc: The Evidence for Her Vindication*. Translated by J. M. Cohen. San Francisco, CA: Ignatius Press, 1983.

Pernoud, Régine. *Those Terrible Middle Ages! Debunking the Myths*. Translated by Anne Englund Nash. San Fancisco, CA: Ignatius Press, 2000.

Peterkin, Allan. *One Thousand Beards: A Cultural History of Facial Hair*. Vancouver: Arsenal Pulp Press, 2001.

Petrarch. *Sonnets and Shorter Poems*. Translated by David Slavit. Cambridge, MA: Harvard University Press, 2012.

Phelpstead, Carl. "Hair Today, Gone Tomorrow: Hair Loss, the Tonsure, and Masculinity in Medieval Iceland." *Scandinavian Studies* 85, no. 1 (2013): 1–19.

Phillips, Kim M. *Before Orientalism: Asian Peoples and Cultures in European Travel Writing*. Philadelphia: University of Pennsylvania Press, 2014.

Phipps, Elena. *Looking at Textiles: A Guide to Technical Terms*. Los Angeles: J. Paul Getty Trust, 2001.

Platelle, Henri. "Le Problème de Scandale: les Nouvelles Modes Masculines aux XIe et XIIe siècles." *Revue Belge de Philologie et d'Histoire* 53, no. 4 (1975): 1071–96.

Po-Chia Hsia, R. *Trent 1475: Stories of a Ritual Murder Trial*, 2nd ed. New Haven, CT: Yale University Press, 1996.

Pohl, Walter. "Conceptions of Ethnicity in Early Medieval Studies." *Archaeologia Polona* 29 (1991): 39–49.

Pohl, Walter. "Telling the Difference: Signs of Ethnic Identity." In *Strategies of Distinction: The Construction of Ethnic Communities, 300–800*, edited by Walter Pohl and Helmut Reimitz, 17–69. Leiden: Brill, 1998.
Pohl, Walter, and Gerda Heydemann, eds. *Strategies of Identification: Ethnicity and Religion in Early Medieval Europe*. Turnhout: Brepols, 2013.
Pohl, Walter, and Helmut Reimitz, eds. *Strategies of Distinction: The Construction of Ethnic Communities, 300–800*. Leiden: Brill, 1998.
Polo, Marco. *The Description of the World*. Edited by A. C. Moule and P. Pelliot, 2 vols. London: George Routledge and Sons, 1938.
Procès en nulité de la condemnation de Jeanne d'Arc. Edited by Pierre Duparc, 2 vols. Paris: Klincksieck, 1977–1989.
Randolph, Adrian. *Engaging Symbols: Gender, Politics, and Public Art in Fifteenth-Century Florence*. New Haven, CT: Yale University Press, 2002.
Rasmussen, Ann Marie. *Mothers and Daughters in Medieval German Literature*. Syracuse, NY: Syracuse University Press, 1997.
Rawlings, Helen. *Church, Religion and Society in Early Modern Spain*. Basingstoke: Palgrave, 2002.
Raymond of Capua. *The Life of St. Catherine of Siena*. Translated by George Lamb. Charlotte, NC: TAN Books, 2011.
Regimen Sanitatis ad Regem Aragonum. Edited by Luis García Ballester and Michael R. McVaugh, 419–70. Barcelona: Fundació Noguera-Universitat de Barcelona, 1996.
Reynolds, Reginald. *Beards: Their Social Standing, Religious Involvements, Decorative Possibilities and Value in Offence and Defence Through the Middle Ages*. London: Batsford, 1949.
Ribeiro, Aileen. *Dress and Morality*. Oxford: Berg, 2003.
Riccoldo da Montecroce. *The Book of Pilgrimage*. Translated by Rita George- Tvrtković. In *A Christian Pilgrim in Medieval Iraq: Riccoldo da Montecroce's Encounter with Islam*, 175–228. Turnhout: Brepols, 2012.
Ridwan, Haly Ibn. *Commentum in microtegni Galieni*. In *Articella*, Venice, 1483.
Rolland-Perrin, Myriam. *Blonde comme l'Or, La Chevelure Féminine au Moyen Âge*. Aix-en-Provence: Publications de l'Université de Provence, 2010.
Rose, E.M. *The Murder of William of Norwich: The Origins of the Blood Libel in Medieval Europe*. Oxford: Oxford University Press, 2015.
Rose, Patricia. "Bears, Baldness, and the Double Spirit: The Identity of Donatello's *Zuccone*." *Art Bulletin* 63, no. 1 (March 1981): 31–41.
Rossiaud, Jacques. *Medieval Prostitution*. Translated by Lydia G. Cochrane. Oxford: Blackwell, 1998.
Roy, Bruno. "Pilosité et Horripilation dans les *Problèmes d'Aristote*." In *La Chevalure dans la Littérature et l'Art du Moyen Âge* [Senefiance 50], edited by Chantal Connochie-Bourgne, 357–63. Aix en Provence: Publications de l'Université de Provence, 2004.
Rubin, Miri. *Mother of God: A History of the Virgin Mary*. London: Penguin Books, 2010.
Rückert, Claudia. "A Reconsideration of the Woman with a Skull on the Puerta des las Platerías at Santiago de Compostela Cathedral." *Gesta* 51, no. 2 (2012): 129–46.
Ruelle, Pierre. *L'Ornement des Dames (Ornatus mulierum). Texte anglo-normand du XIIIème siècle*. Brussels: Presses Universitaires de Bruxelles, 1967.
Ruiz, Juan. *The Book of Good Love*. Translated by Elizabeth O. Macdonald. London: Dent and Tuttle, 1999.
Sachsenspiegel, Landrecht I. Edited by Karl Eckhardt. Göttingen: Musterschmidt- Verlag, 1956.
Salih, Sarah. "Female Sexualities." *Different Visions: A Journal of New Perspectives on Medieval Art*, no. 5 (2014): 1–22.

Salmón, Fernando. "The Body Inferred: Knowing the Body Through the Dissection of Texts." In *A Cultural History of the Human Body in the Medieval Age*, edited by Linda Kalof, 77–97. Oxford: Bloomsbury, 2014.

Sandler, Lucy Freeman. "A Bawdy Betrothal in the Ormesby Psalter." In *Tribute to Lotte Brand Philip*, edited by William Clark et al., 154–9. New York: Abaris, 1985.

Sawyer, Peter. *The Wealth of Anglo-Saxon England*. Oxford: Oxford University Press, 2013.

Sayers, William. "Early Irish Attitudes toward Hair and Beards, Baldness and Tonsure." *Zeitschrift für Celtische Philologie* 44, no. 1 (1991): 154–89.

Schalick, Walton O. "The Face Behind the Mask: 13th- and 14th-Century European Medical Cosmetology and Physiognomy." In *Medicine and the History of the Body*, edited by Yasuo Otsuka, Shizu Sakai, and Shigehisa Kuriyama, 295–311. Tokyo: Ishiyaku EuroAmerica, 1999.

Schaus, Margaret, ed. *Women and Gender in Medieval Europe: An Encyclopedia*. New York: Routledge, 2006.

Schibanoff, Susan. "True Lies: Transvestism and Idolatry in the Trial of Joan of Arc." In *Fresh Verdicts on Joan of Arc*, edited by Bonnie Wheeler and Charles T. Wood, 31–60. New York: Garland, 1996.

Schulenberg, Jane Tibbetts. *Forgetful of Their Sex: Female Sanctity and Society, Ca. 500–1100*. Chicago: University of Chicago Press, 1998.

Scott, Margaret. *Medieval Dress and Fashion*. London: The British Library, 2009.

Seidel, Linda. "Nudity as Natural Garment: Seeing through Adam and Eve's Skin." In *Meanings of Nudity in Medieval Art*, edited by Sherry Lindquist, 207–30. Farnham: Ashgate, 2012.

Seymour, Michael. "Manuscript Portraits of Chaucer and Hoccleve." *The Burlington Magazine* 124, no. 955 (1982): 618–23.

Shahar, Shulamith. *Growing Old in the Middle Ages*. Translated by Yael Lotan. London: Routledge, 1997.

Shahar, Shulamith. *The Fourth Estate*. Translated by Chaya Galai. London: Routledge, 2003.

Sherrow, Victoria. *Encyclopedia of Hair: A Cultural History*. Westport, CT: Greenwood Press, 2006.

Signori, Gabriela. "Veil, Hat or Hair? Reflections on an Asymmetrical Relationship." *Medieval History Journal* 8, no. 1 (2005): 25–47.

Silverman, Eric. *A Cultural History of Jewish Dress*. London: Bloomsbury, 2013.

Simms, Katharine. "Gaelic Warfare in the Middle Ages." In *A Military History of Ireland*, edited by Thomas Bartlett and Keith Jeffery, 99–115. Cambridge: Cambridge University Press, 1996.

Simpson, Lesley Byrd, trans. *Little Sermons on Sin: The Archpriest of Talavera by Alfonzo Martinez de Toledo*. Berkeley: University of California Press, 1977.

Siraisi, Nancy. *Medieval and Early Renaissance Medicine: An Introduction to Knowledge and Practice*. Chicago: Chicago University Press, 1990.

Sleeman, Margaret. "Medieval Hair Tokens." *Forum for Modern Language Studies* 17, no. 4 (1981): 322–36.

Smith, Virginia. *Clean: A History of Personal Hygiene and Purity*. Oxford: Oxford University Press, 2007.

Snyder, Janet. "From Content to Form: Court Clothing in Mid-Twelfth-Century Northern French Sculpture." In *Encountering Medieval Textiles and Dress: Objects, Texts, Images*, edited by Désirée G. Koslin and Janet E. Snyder, 85–102. New York: Palgrave MacMillan, 2002.

Solomon, Michael R. *The Literature of Misogyny in Medieval Spain: The "Archipreste" de Talavera and the Spill.* New York: Cambridge University Press, 1997.

Song, Cheunsoon, and Lucy Roy Sibley. "The Vertical Headdress of Fifteenth-Century Northern Europe." *Dress* 16, no. 1 (1990): 5–15.

Stafford, Pauline. "The Meanings of Hair in the Anglo-Norman World: Masculinity, Reform, and National Identity." In *Saints, Scholars, and Politicians: Gender as a Tool in Medieval Studies*, edited by Mathilde van Dijk and Renée Nip, 153–71. Turnhout: Brepols, 2005.

Standley, Elisabeth. *Trinkets and Charms: The Use, Meaning, and Significance of Dress Accessories, 1300–1700.* Oxford: Oxford Institute of Archaeology, 2013.

Statutes and Ordinances and Acts of the Parliament of Ireland: King John to Henry V. Edited by Henry F. Berry. Dublin: Her Majesty's Stationery Office, 1907.

Steinberg, Leo. *Sexuality of Christ in Renaissance Art and in Modern Oblivion*, 2nd revised edition. Chicago: University of Chicago Press, 1996.

Stock, Lorraine Kochanske. *The Medieval Wild Man.* New York: Palgrave, 2005.

Strickland, Debra Higgs. *Saracens, Demons, and Jews: Making Monsters in Medieval Art.* Princeton, NJ: Princeton University Press, 2003.

Sütterlin, Christa. "Universals in Apotropaic Symbolism: A Behavioral and Comparative Approach to Some Medieval Sculptures." *Leonardo* 22, no. 1 (1989): 65–74.

Sylvester, Louise, Mark Chambers, and Gale Owen-Crocker, eds. *Medieval Dress and Textiles in Britain: A Multilingual Sourcebook.* Woodbridge: Boydell, 2014.

Synnott, Anthony. "Shame and Glory: A Sociology of Hair." *British Journal of Sociology* 38, no. 3 (1987): 381–413.

Táin bó Cúailnge from the Book of Leinster. Edited by Cecile O'Rahilly. Dublin: Dublin Institute for Advanced Studies, 1967.

Táin bó Cúailnge: Recension I. Edited by Cecile O'Rahilly. Dublin: Dublin Institute for Advanced Studies, 1976.

Tertullian. *On the Veiling of Virgins.* Ante-Nicene Fathers, vol. 4. Translated by S. Thelwall. In *The Ante-Nicene Fathers: Translations of the Fathers down to A.D. 325*, edited by Alexander Roberts and James Donaldson. Grand Rapids, MI: Eerdmans, 1987.

Thomas of Celano. *The First Life of Saint Francis of Assisi.* Translated by Christopher Stace. London: Society for Promoting Christian Knowledge, 2000.

Thrupp, Sylvia. *The Merchant Class of Medieval London 1300–1500.* Ann Arbor: University of Michigan Press, 1962.

Tinagli, Paola. *Women in Italian Renaissance Art: Gender, Representation, and Identity.* Manchester: Manchester University Press, 1997.

Tortora, Phyllis and Keith Eubank. *A Survey of Historical Costume.* New York: Fairchild, 1989.

Trasko, Mary. *Daring Do's: A History of Extraordinary Hair.* Paris: Flammarion, 1994.

Trevisa, John. *On the Properties of Things: John Trevisa's Translation of "Bartholomaeus Anglicus, De Proprietatibus Rerum." A Critical Text*, 3 vols. Edited by M. C. Seymour et al. Oxford: Clarendon Press, 1975–1978.

Trichet, Louis. *La Tonsure: Vie et Mort d'une Pratique Écclésiastique.* Paris: Les Éditions du Cerf, 1990.

Trioedd Ynys Prydein. The Welsh Triads, 3rd ed. Edited and translated by Rachel Bromwich. Cardiff: Cardiff University Press, 2006.

The Trotula: A Medieval Compendium of Women's Medicine. Edited and translated by Monica H. Green. Philadelphia: University of Pennsylvania Press, 2001.

Turisanus (Pietro de' Torrigiani). *Plus quam commentum in parvam Galeni artem.* Venice, 1557.

"Twenty-three Characteristics of Beautiful Women." In *La Parnasse érotique du XVe siècle: Recueil des pièces*, edited by J.M. Angot. Geneva: Slatkine, 1978.

Vassilaki, Maria, ed. *Images of the Mother of God: Perceptions of the Theotokos in Byzantium*. Aldershot: Ashgate, 2005.

Vital, Laurent. "Archduke Ferdinand's Visit to Kinsale in Ireland." Translated by Dorothy Convery, Introduction by Hiram Morgan, 284–8. *CELT: Corpus of Electronic Texts: A Project of University College, Cork*. http://www.ucc.ie/celt/published/T500000-001/index.html. Accessed June 20, 2016.

Vogelsang-Eastwood, Gillian, and William Vogelsang. *Covering the Moon: An Introduction to Middle Eastern Face Veils*. Leuven: Peeters, 2008.

Von Dobschütz, Ernst. *Christusbilder: Untersuchungen zur christlichen Legende*. Leipzig: J.C. Hinrichs, 1899.

Von Hülsen-Esche, Andrea. "À propos de la Porta Romana de Milan: dans quelle Mesure la Sculpture de l'Italie du Nord Reflète-t-elle Certains Aspects de l'Histoire Communale." *Cahiers de Civilisation Médiévale* 38, no. 2 (1992): 147–54.

Von Wolkenstein, Oswald. "Ain Grasserin durck külen tau." In *The Medieval Pastourelle*, edited and translated by William D. Paden, 485 [Garland Library of Medieval Literature 34–35, ser. A]. New York: Garland, 1987.

Wade, Susan. "Gertrude's Tonsure: an Examination of Hair as a Symbol of Gender, Family and Authority in the Seventh-century Vita of Gertrude of Nivelles." *Journal of Medieval History* 39, no. 2 (2013): 129–45.

Walker, Barbara. *The Woman's Dictionary of Symbols and Sacred Objects*. London: Pandora, 1995.

Wallace, Lewis. "Bearded Woman, Female Christ: Gendered Transformations in t he Legends and Cult of Saint Wilgefortis." *Journal of Feminist Studies in Religion* 30, no. 1 (2014): 43–63.

Wallace-Hadrill, J.M. *The Long-haired Kings: and Other Studies in Frankish History*. London: Methuen, 1962.

Wallis, Faith, ed. *Medieval Medicine. A Reader*. Toronto: Toronto University Press, 2010.

Warner, Marina. *From the Beast to the Blonde: On Fairy Tales and Their Tellers*. New York: Farrar, Straus & Giroux, 1995.

Warner, Marina. *Alone of All Her Sex: The Myth and Cult of the Virgin Mary*. London: Vintage, 2000.

Waugh, Christina. "'Well-Cut through the Body': Fitted Clothing in Twelfth-Century Europe." *Dress* 26, no. 1 (1999): 3–16.

Weeda, Claire. "Images of Ethnicity in Later Medieval Europe." PhD thesis, University of Amsterdam, 2012.

Weeda, Claire. "Ethnic Identification and Stereotypes in Western Europe, c. 1100–1300." *History Compass* 12, no. 7 (2014): 586–606.

Weiland, Ludwig, ed. *Monumenta Germaniae Historica: Constitutiones et Acta Publica Imperatorem et Regum* II. Hanover: Impensis Bibliopoli Hahnianai, 1896.

Welch, Evelyn. "Signs of Faith: The Political and Social Identity of Hair in Renaissance Italy." In *La Fiducia Secondo i Linguaggi del Potere*, edited by Paolo Prodi, 379–94. Bologna: Società Editrice il Mulino, 2007.

Welch, Evelyn. "Art on the Edge: Hair and Hands in Renaissance Italy." *Renaissance Studies* 23, no. 3 (2008): 241–68.

Wernher the Gardener. *Meier Helmbrecht*, in *Wernher der Gartenere, Helmbrecht*. Translated by Linda B. Parshall. New York: Garland, 1987.

Wiessner, Edmund, et al., eds. *Die Lieder Neidharts*. Tûbingen: Niemeyer, 1984.

Willard, Pat. *Secrets of Saffron: The Vagabond Life of the World's Most Seductive Spice.* Boston, MA: Beacon Press, 2002.

William of Rubruck. *Journey of William of Rubruck.* In *Mission to Asia*, edited by Christopher Dawson and translated by "a nun of Stanbrook Abbey." New York: Harper and Row, 1966.

Williams, Aled, ed. *The Book of Iorwerth (Llyfr Iorwerth): A Critical and Definitive Text of the Gwynedd (Venedotion) Code of Medieval Welsh Law.* Cardiff: University of Wales Press, 1960.

Williams, Howard. "Transforming Body and Soul: Toilet Implements in Early Anglo-Saxon Graves." In *Anglo Saxon Studies in Archaeology and History* 14, edited by Sarah Semple and Howard Williams, 66–91. Oxford: Oxford University School of Archaeology, 2007.

Winstead, Karen. "St. Katherine's Hair." In *St. Katherine of Alexandria: Texts and Contexts in Western Medieval Europe*, edited by Jacqueline Jenkins and Katherine J. Lewis, 171–99. Turnhout: Brepols, 2003.

Wolfthal, Diane. *Images of Rape: The "Heroic" Tradition and its Alternatives.* Cambridge: Cambridge University Press, 1999.

Wolfthal, Diane. *In and Out of the Marital Bed: Seeing Sex in Renaissance Europe.* New Haven, CT: Yale University Press, 2010.

Wolfthal, Diane. "The Sexuality of the Medieval Comb." In *Thresholds of Medieval Visual Culture: Liminal Spaces*, edited by Elina Gertsman and Jill Stevens, 176–94. Woodbridge and Rochester, NY: Boydell Press, 2012.

Wolfthal, Diane. "Sin or Sexual Pleasure? A Little-known Nude Bather in a Flemish Book of Hours." In *Meanings of Nudity in Medieval Art*, edited by Sherry Lindquist, 279–97. London: Ashgate, 2012.

Wolfram, Herwig. *History of the Goths.* Translated by Thomas J. Dunlap. Berkeley: University of California Press, 1988.

Woods-Marsden, Joanna. "Portrait of the Lady, 1430–1520." In *Virtue and Beauty*, edited by David Brown, 63–87. Washington, DC: National Gallery of Art, 2001.

Ziegler, Joseph. "Médecine et Physiognomonie du XIVe au debut du XVIe siècle." *Médiévales* 46 (2004): 89–108.

CONTRIBUTORS

Montserrat Cabré is Associate Professor of the History of Science at the Universidad de Cantabria, Spain. Her research interests cover the history of medieval women's health care; medical conceptions of the gendered body; and the history of women's knowledge. She has published on the history of cosmetics and hair treatments in the context of medieval and early modern health care, including "Keeping Beauty Secrets in Early Modern Iberia" in Elaine Leong and Alisha Rankin, eds., *Secrets and Knowledge in Medicine and Science, 1500–1800* (2011). She is working on a book on late medieval vernacular women's medicine, and together with Fernando Salmón, she is working on a project on medieval physiology, particularly on the notion of transformation in the humoral body.

Laura Michele Diener is Associate Professor of Medieval History at Marshall University, WV, USA. She graduated from Vassar College and in 2008 completed her doctoral work in history at the Ohio State University, USA. In 2015, she received an MFA in creative writing from the Vermont College of Fine Arts. She has contributed chapters on medieval monastic women to edited volumes and her article "Sealed with a Stitch: Embroidery and Gift-giving among Anglo-Saxon Women" has appeared in the journal *Medieval Prosopography* 29 (2014). She is currently at work on a biography of the Norwegian novelist Sigrid Undset.

Martha Easton is an art historian specializing in the art and architecture of the Middle Ages. She received her PhD from the Institute of Fine Arts, New York University, USA, in 2001, and she has taught at Cooper Union, NY; New York University; Bryn Mawr College, PA; and Seton Hall University, NJ. She also lectured for ten years at the Met Cloisters. She is a founding member of the Material Collective, a collaborative of art historians and others interested in fostering a safe space to think in alternative ways about objects and visual culture in general. In addition to her background in medieval art, she has extensive experience with Japanese art cultivated during the six years she spent living and working in Japan. Her research and publications center on illuminated manuscripts, gender and hagiography, feminist theory, medievalism, and the history of collecting medieval art. She is presently writing a book about medievalism and the collection and display of medieval art in the USA during the early twentieth century, focused on the scientist and art collector John Hays Hammond, Jr., and his spectacular revivalist medieval-style castle, built in the 1920s on the coast of Gloucester, MA.

John Block Friedman is Professor Emeritus of English and Medieval Studies at the University of Illinois, Urbana-Champaign, USA. He is currently a Visiting Scholar at the Center for Medieval and Renaissance Studies at the Ohio State University, USA. He is the author of a number of books and articles. Recent publications include "Dogs in the Identity Formation and Moral Teaching Offered in some Fifteenth-Century Flemish Manuscript Miniatures," in Laura Gelfand, ed., *Our Dogs, Our Selves: Dogs in Medieval* *and Early Modern Art, Literature, and Society* (2016); "Coats, Collars, and Capes: Royal Fashions for Animals in the Early Modern Period," in *Medieval Clothing and Textiles*, vol. 12 (2016); "Dressing the Monstrous Men: *Landsknechte* Clothing in Some Early Modern Danish Church Wall Paintings," in Michael Heyes, ed., *Holy Monsters, Sacred Grotesques* (2018); "Eyebrows, Hairlines, and 'Hairs Less in Sight': Female Depilation in Late Medieval Europe," in *Medieval Clothing and Textiles*, vol. 14 (2018); and edited and translated with Kristen Figg and Kathrin Giogoli, *Book of Wonders of the World Secrets of Natural History MS fr. 22971 Original held in the Bibliothèque nationale de France, Paris. Studies and Translation of the Facsimile Edition Siloé* (2018).

Penny Howell Jolly is Professor of Art History at Skidmore College, USA, where she teaches courses in medieval and Renaissance art. Her research focuses on early Netherlandish painters, such as Jan van Eyck and Rogier van der Weyden; examines depictions of saints, including Jerome and Mary Magdalene; and considers themes relating to pregnancy, gender, and the meaning of dress and hair in art. She has published *Made in God's Image? Eve and Adam in the Genesis Mosaics at San Marco, Venice* (1997); *Hair: Untangling a Social History* (2004); and *Picturing the "Pregnant" Magdalene in Northern Art, 1430–1550: Addressing and Undressing the Sinner-Saint* (2014). Her article "Gender, Dress, and Franciscan Tradition in the Mary Magdalene Chapel at San Francesco, Assisi" is forthcoming in *Gesta* (2019).

Hanna Hopwood Griffiths graduated with a first-class honors degree in Welsh from Cardiff University, UK, and completed an MPhil there. She then spent five years at Jesus College, University of Oxford, where she was awarded a distinction in her MSt degree and worked as a Research Fellow while she completed her DPhil in Medieval and Modern Languages, which was awarded in 2017. During this period, she had opportunities to present television programs for S4C (young people and the news) as well as continuing to work as the Welsh tutor at the Medieval and Modern Languages Faculty and at the University's Language Centre. Since 2016, she has been working as a lecturer for the University of Wales Trinity Saint David's Welsh Language Services Centre and the *Coleg Cymraeg Cenedlaethol*.

Roberta Milliken is Professor of English and Dean of the College of Arts and Sciences at Shawnee State University, OH, USA, where she teaches courses in medieval women's history, medieval literature, Renaissance literature, composition, and women's studies. Her research interests include representations of women in the Middle Ages and the early modern period, Shakespeare, Marlowe, cultural history, women religious, and iconology. She is the author of *Ambiguous Locks: An Iconology of Hair in the Middle Ages* (2012).

Kim M. Phillips is Associate Professor of History at the University of Auckland, New Zealand. In addition to research interests in the histories of gender, the body, and sexualities, she has many publications on medieval travel writing and the global Middle Ages. Her publications on cross-cultural perceptions and encounters include *Before Orientalism: Asian Peoples and Cultures in European Travel Writing, 1245–1510* (2014), (edited with Lisa Bailey and Lindsay Diggelmann) *Old Worlds, New Worlds: European Cultural Encounters c. 1000—c. 1750* (2009), and articles in *History Compass* and *postmedieval*. Her books on women and gender include (as editor) *A Cultural History of Women in the Middle Ages* for the Bloomsbury Cultural History series (2013).

Fernando Salmón is Professor of the History of Science in the medical school at the University of Cantabria, Santander, Spain. His research interests include the history of the modern hospital in the twentieth century and medicine in the Middle Ages. On this last area, he has published on sense perception, pain, madness, the doctor–patient relationship, and the construction of scholastic medical knowledge. His latest publications include "The Pleasures and Joys of the Humoral Body in Medieval Medicine," in Naama Cohen and Piroska Nagy, eds., *Pleasure in the Middle Ages* (2018). He is currently working with Michael R. McVaugh on the analysis and critical edition of the *Arnaldi de Villanova tractatus de parte operativa* to be published as volume VII.2 of the *Arnaldi de Villanova Opera Medica Omnia*.

Alexa Sand is Professor of Art History at Utah State University, USA. Her scholarly work focuses on intersections between gender, piety, and text in later medieval French and francophone art, particularly manuscript illumination and other small-scale works. She is the author of *Vision, Devotion, and Self-Representation in Late Medieval Art* (2014). Recently, she has held short-term fellowships at the Center for Advanced Study in the Visual Arts (CASVA) and the Clark Research Institute, and she is a current board member of the International Center of Medieval Art.

INDEX

Abbas, Haly 125
Abelard, Peter 86
Abraham 30
Absalom 20, 21–3, 24, 128, 138
accessories 10, 50, 53, 54, 62, 79–80
   barbettes 60, 80
   cauls 55, 164, 165
   crespines 62, 80
   fillets 60, 62, 80, 81
   hairpins 12, 56, 57, 60, 66, 74, 79–80, 146
   headbands 57, 58, 147
   ribbons 54, 57, 62, 63, 68, 80
Adam 24, 100, 160–1, 165
adultery 48, 117
Aelred of Rievaulx 33
Africans 131, 132, 133, 170, 171
age 9, 10, 14, 39, 40, 43, 44, 52, 54, 58, 61, 77, 82, 93, 96, 98, 100, 101, 111, 119, 120, 121, 132, 133, 153, 155–6, 160–1, 166, 168
Agius 56
Agnes, St 27, 28
Akbari, Suzanne Conklin 131
Alcuin 23, 56, 58
Alderotti, Taddeo 94, 97, 100
Aldhelm 57
Alessandra Strozzi 67
Alexander the Great 44
Alfonso of Castile 96
alopecia 101, 105, 126. *See also* thinning hair; baldness
Anne of Burgundy 66
Anne, St 66
Anselm of Canterbury 87, 109
Anson, John 33
Apollo 156
Arabs 53, 60, 71, 72, 78, 82, 91, 125
Aristotle 74, 83, 95, 96, 97, 100, 108, 125, 156, 170
Arnold of Villanova 146
Arthur, King 42
Asians 132, 133–4
Augustine, St 22, 169

Averroës 131–2
Avicenna 97

Bacchus 156
baldness 14, 32, 82, 83, 86, 97, 100–1, 105, 121, 126, 138, 139, 142, 149, 157, 168–9
bangs 58, 61, 63, 67
barbers/barbering 30, 53, 58, 71, 87, 88, 91, 103, 106
Bartholomaeus Anglicus 126, 130, 132
Bartlett, Robert 10, 39, 43, 124, 138
Bataille, Nicholas 113
baths 59, 75, 76, 84, 103, 104, 111, 148
Bathsheba 75, 76, 111–12, 117
Bayeux Tapestry 15, 16, 58, 154
beards 5, 10, 12, 14, 15, 20, 21, 23, 28, 29, 31, 38, 39, 40, 45, 52, 54, 63, 67, 72, 83, 86, 95, 96, 108, 119–20, 124, 126, 129, 132, 133, 136, 138, 153, 155, 156, 157, 160, 163, 169
   forked 63, 129, 130
   grabbing/pulling of 40–1, 156
   long 29, 30, 39, 58, 108, 126, 131, 134, 135, 137, 155, 168
   short/trimmed 29, 30, 56, 61, 155
beauty 9, 10, 12, 13, 15, 21, 44–5, 46, 47, 49, 50, 51, 53, 55, 56, 59, 71, 72, 73, 77, 83, 89, 104, 111, 119, 121, 122, 143, 144, 145, 146, 148, 151, 163
Becket, Thomas 35
Bede 73
Belcher, Paul 10
Benedict, St 30
Berg, Charles 6, 7
Biller, Peter 125
Black Death (plague) 3, 140
blood libel 129
Boccaccio, Giovanni 75, 77, 79, 80, 84, 105, 144, 146
Bondel, Jean 113
Boniface 73
Bourdichon, Jean 112

INDEX

braids 11, 19, 21, 26, 45, 53, 55, 56, 59, 62, 63, 67, 74, 75, 79, 80, 128, 133, 143, 158, 164, 165, 166
brides 33, 59, 67, 121, 151, 158, 159, 168
Bridgeman, Jane 158
Burke, Peter 5

Caballero-Navas, Carmen 72, 78
Cabré, Montserrat 72
Caesarius of Arles 10, 32
Cain 170
Calais, St 33
Cameron, Averil 10
Campani, Niccolò 149
Campin, Robert 165
Canute, King 57, 58
Carpini, John of Plano 133
castration 6, 121, 149, 155
Catherine, St 113, 114
Catherine of Siena, St 48–9, 86
Caviness, Madeline 23, 163
Charlemagne 27, 56, 57, 75, 108, 137, 141, 153, 154, 155
Charles the Bald 32, 56, 58, 153
Charles VII 67
chastity 23, 33, 50, 56
Chaucer, Geoffrey 21, 45, 84, 120, 129, 138, 139, 147, 148
Child, Theodore 64
Childeric III 108–9
Christ 21, 22, 28, 29, 30, 111, 114, 117, 120, 121, 129, 139, 141, 156, 157, 166, 168, 169
Christianity/Christians 4, 19, 20, 27, 54, 56, 59, 72, 123, 125, 126, 127, 128, 129, 131, 155, 169, 171
church fathers 4, 5, 19, 54, 109
Clare of Assisi, St, 32, 48, 86, 107–8, 121, 168
Clark, Laura 10
class distinction 3, 5, 9, 14, 15, 32, 38, 39, 40, 43, 50, 52, 53, 54, 56, 62, 65, 67, 69, 71, 76, 78, 80, 81, 103, 104–5, 108, 109, 119, 122, 137–51, 153, 163, 164, 171
Clement of Alexandria 19, 30
Coates, Simon 10
combing hair 11, 46, 47, 77, 103, 105, 112, 113, 117, 166
combs 10, 12, 42, 72–5, 88, 104, 112, 146, 161
    liturgical 35, 73, 103, 166
Comestor, Peter 160

conduct 4, 54, 72, 77, 109
Connochie-Bourgne, Chantal 10
Constable, Giles 10, 29, 155
Constantine the African 126
Cooper, Helen 147
Corson, Richard 88
cross dressing. *See* transvestism
Crucifixion 22, 24, 35, 129, 157, 168
Crusades 3, 9, 14, 29, 30, 54, 59, 78, 83, 88, 119, 131, 155, 162, 171
cultural history 5–6
curled/curling hair 4, 53, 56, 57, 61, 63, 68, 71, 78, 81, 125, 138, 141, 142
curly hair 6, 30, 78, 97, 99–100, 128, 132, 133, 171
Cuthbert, St 35
cutting hair 7, 11, 13, 14, 15, 21, 27, 31, 32, 33, 41, 48, 71, 77, 85–7, 103, 105, 108, 109, 121, 122, 138, 141, 166, 168
Cynwrig ap Rhys 128

D'Angelo, Mary Rose 10
d'Arras, Jean 75
d'Orleans, Gilles 60
da Fabriano, Gentile 168
da Firenze, Andrea 155
da Foligno, Gentile 97, 98
da Soller, Claudio 78
Daniel 156
David 21, 22, 30, 111, 117, 156–7
de Bourbon, Étienne 51
de Bourbon, Jeanne 62
de France, Marie 75, 164
de Gordon, Bernard 96, 138
de la Tour Landry, Geoffrey 46, 48, 64, 65, 77, 84, 147, 162
de Lesse Gozzoli, Benozzo 131
de Liège, Jean 164
de Mondeville, Henry 84, 104
de Neville, Robert 63
de Paris, Ménagier 109, 114
de Pisan, Christine 45, 64–5, 66, 67, 69, 77, 111
de Soissons, Yolande 158
de Toledo, Alfonzo Martinez 138
de Troyes, Chrétien 59, 75, 77
de Vilanova, Arnau 98, 101
de Voragine, Jacobus 26, 113
Delilah 21, 22, 109, 138, 168
della Francesco, Piero 68
della Quercia, Jacopo 156
demons/demonized 23, 24, 129, 131, 133, 134

Derret, J. Duncan 10
devil/devils 22, 46, 48, 83, 84, 133, 148, 162, 165, 166
di Bonaguida, Pacino 155
di Michelino, Domenico 156
Diesenberger, Maximilian 10
disease 50, 91, 92, 93, 96, 98, 101, 102, 148–9
disheveled hair 4, 14, 23, 24, 109, 114–17, 126, 135, 157, 161, 166
Donatello 156–7, 166, 169
Donzio 30
Durandus, William 35
Dürer, Albrecht 128
Dutton, Paul Edward 10, 153
dyeing hair 5, 12, 54, 59, 60, 66, 69, 71, 72, 76, 77–9, 82, 101, 103, 105, 111, 143, 144, 163

Eadmer of Canterbury 60
Easton, Martha 40, 48, 49
Edward I 73
Edward III 80, 129
Edward the Confessor 15, 16, 58, 154
Egan, Geoff 80
Einhard 108
Eleanor of Aquitaine 60
Elijah 168
Elisha 168
Emma, Queen 57
Entwistle, Joanne 53
Erhart, Gregor 26
eroticism 13, 26, 28, 72, 73, 74, 75, 111, 112, 113, 156, 163, 166
ethnicity 10, 14, 39, 42–3, 123–36, 153
Eugenia, St 11, 33
eunuchs 96
Eve 20, 21, 24, 25, 26, 83, 100, 114, 160–1, 166
eyebrows 46, 64, 82, 84, 95, 105, 133, 137, 143, 144, 145, 146, 147, 151, 161, 162
Ezekiel 30

fabliaux 3, 10
fashion 10, 11–12, 19, 52, 53–69, 71, 81, 83, 86, 87, 109, 113, 119, 121, 129–30, 137, 153, 158, 161–2, 164–5
femininity 10, 13, 21, 23, 24, 27, 42, 61, 73, 96, 109, 119, 120–1, 122, 138, 154, 155, 157
feudalism 3, 140

Firth, Raymond 7
fools 109, 139, 140, 141, 153, 168
Fouquet, Jean 145, 146
Fra Angelico 157
Fra Filippo Lippi 66, 162, 164
Francis of Assisi, St 30, 108, 121, 168, 169
Frazier, (Sir) James 6
Friesen, Ilse 10

Galen 83, 91, 92, 93, 97, 99, 108, 125
Galla of Rome 28
Ganymede 156
Geary, Patrick 123, 124
gender 8, 9, 13, 15, 19, 20, 21, 27, 37, 54, 55, 71, 72, 75, 106, 107–22, 124, 153, 156, 160, 171
Gerald of Wales 126, 127, 128
Ghiberti, Lorenzo 156
Ghirlandaio, Domenico 68
Giotto 25, 30, 166, 169
Gisela 56
Gislebertus 160
Glyn, Guto'r 38
Godwinson, Harold 16, 58, 119, 154
Goliath 157
Goosmann, Erik 10, 21
Gottfried of Admont 21
gravoirs 74
grief 10, 44, 98, 99, 166
Gunda 33

hagiography 21, 24, 26, 27, 28, 30, 33, 35, 48, 113, 117
hair color 8, 13, 15, 38, 43, 56, 97, 108, 123, 129, 137, 147
 black/brunette 38, 60, 78, 98, 125, 126, 129, 130, 134, 144–5, 163, 168
 blond/blonde 26, 27, 29, 30, 38, 49, 60, 72, 77–8, 79, 80, 89, 98, 105, 111, 113, 119, 125, 134, 138, 141, 142, 145, 163–4, 168
 as feminine ideal 13, 45, 49, 59, 66, 78, 111, 113, 143, 144, 153, 163–4
 grey/white 38, 39, 77, 97, 98, 101, 124, 125, 126, 130, 132, 137, 156, 168
 red 38, 78, 129, 130, 153, 170
hair length 13, 82, 108, 138, 169
 long 9, 13, 19, 21, 22, 23, 24, 25, 27, 39–40, 43, 46, 47, 49, 54, 59, 60, 63, 71, 77, 86, 96, 108, 111, 113, 124, 126–7, 129, 135, 138, 141, 153, 154, 157, 160, 166

INDEX

short 10, 13, 21, 39–40, 49, 58, 86, 108, 121, 124, 128, 130, 139, 153, 154, 156, 160
hair removal 60, 71, 82–8, 104, 119, 146–7
   depilation 59, 84–5, 86, 104, 143, 145, 146–7, 162
   plucking foreheads 12, 14, 51, 64, 65, 66, 67, 68, 82, 84, 119, 143, 145, 147, 148, 161–2
hairiness 7, 10, 14, 15, 16–17, 29, 72, 82, 117, 121, 126–7, 129, 130, 135, 143, 144–5, 149, 154, 157, 168, 170
hairpieces 12, 60, 63, 66, 72, 80–1, 86, 143, 144, 164
hairstyles 10, 11, 12, 19, 43, 51, 53, 59–61, 80, 123, 124, 129–30, 137, 144
   bowl cut 33, 58, 67, 88
   corne 164–5
   culan 39, 127–8
Hallpike, C.R. 6, 7
Hanawalt, Barbara 75
head coverings 14, 19, 32, 43, 45, 50, 56, 62, 71, 109, 111, 119, 123, 129, 134, 161
   coifs/caps 23, 58, 61, 86, 129, 132, 141, 142, 144, 157
   hats 54, 61, 67, 68, 82, 88, 129
   headcloths 50
   hennins 51, 119
   hoods 30, 45, 58, 61, 63, 67, 82, 109, 141
   turbans 14, 61, 75, 129, 131, 132, 155
headdresses 10, 45, 51, 53, 56, 64, 65, 66, 67, 69, 80, 109, 114, 128, 133, 158, 160, 161, 163, 164
health 91–3, 98, 101, 106
Helbling, Seifried 140
Helen of Troy 143–4
Heng, Geraldine 123
Henry I 109
Henry II 35, 61
Henry V 88
Henry VIII 128
Hercules 156
heretics 4, 5, 131
hermit 16, 17, 27, 30, 33, 48, 117
Hershman, P. 7–8
Hildegard of Bingen 77, 108
Hill, Daniel Delis 54, 62
Hippocrates 91, 96, 125
Hoyou, Jean 10
Hucbald 32

Hugh of Cluny 30
Hugh of Lacerta 30, 31
humoralism/humors 12, 91, 92, 93, 97, 98, 108, 125, 126, 133, 155, 156
hygiene 12, 54, 71, 72, 75–7, 84, 89, 103, 105, 106

Ibn Rushd. *See* Averroës
iconography 11, 20, 21, 23, 24, 27, 28, 29, 35, 37, 50, 129, 130
Idley, Peter 137
Ieuan of the Red 37, 38
Irish 39–40, 58, 61, 125, 126–8, 131, 133
Isabeau of Bavaria 66
Isidore of Seville 21, 124–5, 126
Ivo of Chartres 23

Jacoby, Zehava 10
James, Edward 10
James I of Aragon 96
Jansen, Katherine Ludwig 24
Jean Le Noir 170
Jerome 19, 30, 54
Jesus 24, 29, 38
Joab 22
Joan of Arc, St 33, 121
John, Duke of Berry 67, 75, 87, 113, 114
John, St 24
John of Reading 63
John of Wales 169
Johnsson, Peter H. 10
Jolly, Penny Howell 117
Judaism/Jews 4, 20, 23, 30, 43, 59, 60, 61, 72, 78, 115, 119, 125–6, 128–30, 131, 133, 137, 155, 156, 169
Judas 22, 130, 153, 170
Judith 56
Jupiter 156

Karras, Ruth Mazo 33
Korhonen, Anu 168
Koslin, Désirée 10
Kuhns, Elizabeth 10

Lao, Meri 46
Latini, Bruno 47
Laver, James 54
Lazarus 24, 25
Leach, E. R. 6, 7
Legal codes/laws 11, 24, 32, 33, 37, 40–1, 50, 66, 124, 125, 128, 139. *See also* sumptuary legislation

Levine, Molly Myerowitz 43
Levite's wife 23
Leyser, Conrad 10
lice removal 71, 73, 77, 85, 102, 103
Lipton, Sara 29, 129
long-haired kings. *See* Merovingian kings
Lorenzetti, Ambrogio 134, 158, 159, 166
lust 15, 20, 21, 23, 24, 32, 46, 47, 51, 54, 72, 75, 112, 114, 119, 122, 131, 135, 147, 149, 155, 163, 166
Luttrell, (Sir) Geoffrey 62
Luxuria 24, 25, 115, 166

Mabinogion 38, 40
Magnus, Albertus 82
maidens/maidenhood 43, 45, 52, 54, 59, 63, 72, 75, 109, 110, 114. *See also* virginity
Maitani, Lorenzo 156
Malchus 170
Margaret of Flanders 74
Marina 33
Marshall, William 29
Martel, Charles 109
Martha 24
martyrs 113, 114, 117
Mary Magdalene 20, 21, 24–7, 28, 114, 157, 166, 167, 168
Mary of Bethany 24
Mary of Burgundy 119, 120
Mary of Egypt, St 117, 118, 166
masculinity 13, 21, 23, 28, 30, 31, 32, 37, 40, 42, 61, 96, 108, 109, 117, 120, 121, 122, 127, 128, 130, 138, 154, 155, 156, 157, 168
Matthew of Vendôme 45, 143, 148
Mathews, Thomas 28
Maurice, St 171
Mauro, Giovanni 145
McCarthy, Daniel 10
medical lore 12–13, 32, 82, 87, 91–101, 156
  texts 12, 59, 61, 71, 72, 77, 88, 91, 94, 97, 101, 104, 136, 163
Melchizedek 30
Mellinkoff, Ruth 170
Memling, Hans 75, 76
Mercury 156
mermaids 46–7, 75, 115
Merovingian kings 10, 40, 108, 122, 137, 153
Milliken, Roberta 10, 24, 32, 48, 49, 72, 122, 166
Mills, Robert 10, 32, 34
mirrors 5, 12, 46, 47, 72, 75, 104, 113, 117, 146

misogyny 20, 89, 111, 138, 144, 149
modesty 10, 19, 23, 51, 55, 56, 58, 62, 68, 109, 110, 115, 117, 158, 165
Mongols 133, 134
monks 3, 21, 30, 31–2, 33, 58, 59, 61, 69, 71, 87, 121, 134, 155, 166
Morey, James 147
Moser, Lukas 157, 158
Moses 30, 54
Mueller, Joan 32
Multscher, Hans 171
Muslims 5, 9, 14, 20, 30, 56, 59, 61, 71, 82, 115, 119, 126, 131, 133, 137, 155, 162, 169
mustaches 10, 12, 14, 15, 29, 30, 54, 58, 61, 63, 86, 125, 128, 129, 137, 153, 154

nakedness/nudity 23, 24, 25, 26, 27, 75, 100, 112, 113, 115, 117, 127, 135, 148, 156, 157, 161, 162, 166
Nanmor, Dafydd 45
Neff, Amy 169
Neidhart 140–1, 142
Neptune 156
Nicholas, St 30
nuns 4, 12, 32, 33, 43, 44, 48, 52, 56, 69, 71, 86, 168

old age 15, 39, 40, 44, 77, 81, 83, 84, 98, 100, 133, 147, 154, 155–6, 158, 161, 168
Orderic Vitalis 23, 60–1, 138, 154, 155, 166
other/otherness 4, 14, 15, 17, 30, 61, 72, 115, 123, 124, 126–36, 137, 153, 155, 169–71
Owen-Crocker, Gale 58

pagans 23, 28, 29, 31, 120, 137, 141, 153, 155, 171
Paris, Matthew 30
pastourelle 144–5, 149
Paul, St 19, 20, 23, 30, 31, 32, 54, 56, 108, 109, 111, 137, 138, 163, 168
Paula of Avila 28
peasants 40, 41, 55, 61, 62, 67, 75, 103, 139, 140, 141, 143, 147, 148, 149, 153, 158
penance/penitent 24, 26, 32, 33, 166, 168
Peter of Riga 138
Peter, St 19, 30, 31
Petrarch 153, 163
Phelpstead, Carl 10
Phyllis 74

Pisanello 66
Pisano, Nicola 156
Platelle, H. 10
Pohl, Walter 124
Pollaiuolo, Antonio 166
Polo, Marco 133–4
Potiphar's wife 24
Pritchard, Francis 80
prostitutes 4, 25, 33, 47, 48, 50, 115, 117, 119, 138, 163, 166
Pseudo-Aristotle 125, 138
pubic hair 10, 13, 14, 15, 40, 82–3, 95, 96, 117, 119, 137, 143, 146, 148–9, 156, 157, 161, 162, 163
Pucelle, Jean 27
Pulci, Luigi 145
punishment 13, 15, 32, 33, 39, 41, 46, 48, 52, 77, 83, 109, 115, 117, 121, 122, 127, 128, 141, 142, 147–8, 162, 166, 168

race 9, 123–4, 125, 133–6, 153
Randolph, Adrian 156
rape 23, 24, 27, 111
Raymond of Cupa 48
Raymond of Poitiers 67, 88
razors 12, 34, 58, 72, 87–8, 104, 138, 147
Regino of Prüm 124
relics 27, 29, 33, 35, 111, 115
reliquaries 27, 113, 115
Rhazes 97
Riccold of Monte Croce 133
Ridwan, Haly ibn 94
rituals 6, 52, 71, 75
    coming of age 11, 42, 48, 109
    coronations 159
    marriage 6, 32, 43, 158
    mikveh 76
    religious 6, 20, 31–5, 48, 71, 86, 108, 121, 122, 168 (*see also* tonsure)
    veiling 10, 11, 12, 121, 122, 168
    widowhood 32, 43–4
Roig, Jacme 138
Le Roman de la Rose 72, 75, 77, 81, 83, 164
romances 3, 10, 59, 72, 77, 111, 113, 117, 121, 122, 143
Rose, Patricia 169
Rotrud 57
Ruiz, Juan 78, 83, 144, 148

Sachsenspiegel 15, 40, 48
saints 10, 11, 20, 27, 29, 30, 48, 73, 113, 121, 122, 155

Samson 20, 21, 22, 109, 138, 168
Samuel 30
Sandler, Lucy Freeman 163
Saracens. *See* Muslims
Sayers, William 10, 39
Schedel, Hartmann 129
Schulenburg, Jane Tibbetts 33
scissors/shears 34, 42, 48, 58, 85, 86, 104, 108, 109, 138, 149
Scott, Margaret 10, 59
Scottus, Sedulius 77
Semiramis, Queen 105
sex differences between women and men 4, 8, 9, 13, 14, 95–7, 108, 156
sexual potency 6, 9, 15, 20, 23, 24, 26, 42, 43, 49, 54, 108, 117, 121, 138, 149, 163, 166, 169–70
    loss of 6, 7, 32, 34, 42, 82, 121, 138, 149, 155
Shahar, Shulamith 48
shaving 5, 20, 29, 32, 48, 54, 67, 71, 84, 85, 86
    of beard 20, 30, 33, 42, 128, 155
    customs 11, 30, 31, 34, 58, 59, 61, 87, 104, 128, 133, 155
    of hair 20, 31, 121, 128, 133, 134, 138, 148, 153
    as punishment 31, 32, 33, 42, 48, 52, 121, 168
Sheela-na-gigs 121, 156
Signori, Gabriela 10
Simon of Trent 130
sin 24, 48, 54, 72, 83, 163, 166
Sina, Ibn 94
Siôn Ceri 37
Sleeman, Margaret 10
soap 76–7, 78, 88
Solomon 21
Sorel, Agnès 145, 146
sorrow. *See* grief
Stafford, Pauline 10, 155
status 4, 9, 10, 14, 30, 37, 38, 43, 44, 50, 51, 52, 53, 54, 69, 78, 122, 124, 137, 138, 139, 144, 147, 151, 153, 155, 168
Stephen of Muret, St 30, 31
stereotypes/stereotyping 27, 125, 127, 128, 134, 170
Strickland, Debra Higgs 132
Strozzi, Catarina 67
sumptuary legislation 4, 50, 54, 63, 66, 81, 137, 139, 141, 144, 147. *See also* legal codes/laws
Susanna 156
Synnott, Anthony 7, 8

Tacitus 39, 124
Tertullian 4, 5, 19, 54, 109
Thecla 33
thinning hair 63, 81, 96. *See also* alopecia
tonsure 7, 8, 10, 11, 19, 20, 30, 32–3, 34, 58–9, 86–7, 108, 121, 122, 130, 133, 155, 166, 168, 169
  plates 34–5
Tornabuoni, Giovanna 68
Torrigiani, Pietro 94
transvestism 33, 120, 121
Trotula 59, 66, 71, 76, 77, 78, 79, 82, 84, 85, 111, 144, 146, 148, 161–2, 163
tweezers 58, 65, 72, 82, 84, 105, 146, 147

ugliness 77, 78, 81, 148
Urban II, (Pope) 170, 171
Ursula, St 63, 80, 113–14, 115

van der Goes, Hugo 165
van der Weyden, Rogier 68, 84, 85, 168
van Eyck, Jan 29, 65, 67, 83, 159, 161, 163, 165
vanity 21, 23, 24, 32, 46, 47, 72, 75, 77, 83, 89, 113, 117, 121, 122, 138, 141, 147, 163, 166
veils/veiling 5, 10, 11, 12, 19, 23, 25, 32, 33, 43, 49, 50, 51, 54, 56, 57, 59, 62, 64, 65, 68, 74, 79, 80, 109, 122, 128, 158, 163, 165, 166, 168
Venus 115, 121, 163
Vincent of Beauvais 82
Virgin Mary 26, 27, 30, 49–50, 56, 66, 110–11, 114, 119, 120, 145, 146, 159, 160, 166

virginity 15, 43, 46, 49, 51, 54, 73, 109, 111, 113, 117, 120, 158, 159, 160
virility 6, 13, 40, 42, 72, 82, 96, 108, 117, 130, 138, 155, 156
Vital, Laurent 128
von Hohenzollern, Barbara 165
von Langenstein, Heinrich 163
von Wolkenstein, Oswald 149

Wade, Susan 10
Wallace, Lewis 10
Warner, Marina 37, 50
Weeda, Claire 125
Welch, Evelyn 165
Wernher the Gardener 140, 141–2
Whore of Babylon 112–13, 166
widows 32, 43–4, 52, 75, 80, 104, 158, 166
wild men/wild women 7, 16, 103, 117, 118, 135, 136, 166
Wilgefortis, St 27–9, 120
William of Malmesbury 23, 60, 109
William of Rubruck 133, 134
William the Conqueror 154
wimple 25, 56, 60, 62, 63, 69, 79, 160, 165
Winstead, Karen 10
wisdom 15, 29, 30, 40, 61, 119, 155, 156
witches 3, 115, 163
wives 21, 43, 48, 50, 52, 54, 62, 109, 114, 158, 159, 163
Wolfthal, Diane 10, 23, 75, 112

youth 15, 28, 29, 38, 39, 40, 43, 48, 49, 54, 58, 60–1, 63, 75, 77, 81, 89, 96, 111, 113, 114, 137, 138, 141, 154, 156, 158, 159, 160, 164, 168